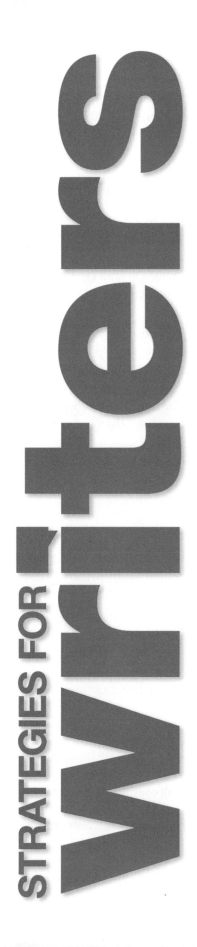

8

Senior Author
Rebecca Bowers Sipe, Ed.D.
Eastern Michigan University

Consulting Authors
Julie Coiro, Ph.D.
University of Rhode Island

Amy Humphreys, Ed.M., NBCT
Educational Consultant

Sara B. Kajder, Ph.D.
University of Pittsburgh

Mark Overmeyer, M.A.
Cherry Creek School District, Colorado

Senior Consultant
James Scott Miller, M.Ed.
National Writing Consultant

ZB **Zaner-Bloser**

Program Reviewers

Zaner-Bloser wishes to thank these educators who reviewed portions of this program and provided comments prior to publication.

Joe Anspaugh
Shelbyville Middle School
Shelbyville, IN

Michele Barto, Ed.D.
Fairleigh Dickinson University
Madison, NJ

Jackie Blosser
Lima City Schools
Lima, OH

Kim Bondy
South Arbor Academy
Ypsilanti, MI

Kelly Caravelli
Meadowbrook Middle School
Poway, CA

Cathy Cassy
St. Louis Public Schools
St. Louis, MO

Penny Clare
Educational Consultant
Lee, NH

Mary Dunton
Literacy Consultant
Sparks, NV

Emily Gleason
Beaverton School District
Beaverton, OR

Denise Gray, Ed.D.
Whiteriver Elementary School
Whiteriver, AZ

Laura Hall
Walton Charter Academy
Pontiac, MI

Donna Jett
Rockwood South Middle
School
Fenton, MO

Christine Johnson, Ed.D.
Boonton Public Schools
Boonton, NJ

Dr. Roma Morris
Columbia School District
Columbia, MS

Rosanne Richards
Southern Nevada Regional
Professional Development
Program
North Las Vegas, NV

Sharlene E. Ricks
Alpine School District
American Fork, UT

Debbie Rutherford
Independent National
Consultant
Omaha, NE

Melinda Springli
Lawton Public Schools
Lawton, OK

Kerry Stephenson
Pendleton County School
District
Butler, KY

Photography: Cover © Liane Carey/age fotostock; Interior models, Tom Dubanowich; Stopwatch image © Royalty-Free/Corbis; p. 3 © Wes Thompson/Corbis; p. 121 © Dennis MacDonald/Alamy; p. 253 © David Muench/Corbis; p. 381 © Cathy Melloan/PhotoEdit.

Art Credits: pp. 4, 26, 48, 122, 146, 180, 254, 308, 382, 408, 436 Illustrated Alaskan Moose Studio; pp. 167, 183, 184, 185, 411, 412, 434 Marilyn Rodgers Bahney Paselsky; pp. 197, 199, 206, 207 Pat Dewitt Grush; pp. 72, 208, 211, 278, 332, 458 Chris Vallo

ISBN 978-0-7367-7283-9

Copyright © 2013 Zaner-Bloser, Inc.

Zaner-Bloser, Inc.
1-800-421-3018
www.zaner-bloser.com
Printed in the United States of America   12   13   14   15   19840   5   4   3   2

SUSTAINABLE FORESTRY INITIATIVE

Certified Chain of Custody
Promoting Sustainable Forestry
www.sfiprogram.org
SFI-00993

Hi, there!

We're your *Strategies for Writers* Writing Partners!

We're here to guide you step-by-step through the stages of the writing process: Prewrite, Draft, Revise, Edit, and Publish.

In each unit, we'll focus on one mode of writing: **narrative, informative/explanatory, argument,** or **descriptive**.

Have you ever wondered what makes a good biography? Or what the elements of a research report are? How about some reasons for writing an editorial or a scientific observation? We'll answer those questions and more.

We'll focus on these six traits of effective writing: **Ideas, Organization, Voice, Word Choice, Sentence Fluency,** and **Conventions**. We'll explain how to apply the traits to each genre of writing, and we'll show you how the traits work together.

In each chapter, we'll first review a model writing sample. Then we'll use a rubric to score the model. Rubrics are a great way to know exactly what is expected as you plan and evaluate your writing. After that, it's your turn to write!

Narrative writing

Table of Contents

Informative/Explanatory writing

Table of Contents

Argument writing

Table of Contents

Descriptive writing

Table of Contents

Appendices

Appendix A: Grammar Practice

Table of Contents

Appendix B: Rubrics

Narrative writing tells a story to the audience.

Hi, I'm Ashley. I'm studying narrative writing in school, and I think it's going to be one of my favorite types of writing. I love telling stories, so I'm looking forward to sharing them in print, too!

IN THIS UNIT

- ☐ **Memoir**
- ☐ **Historical Episode**
- ☐ **Biography**
- **LITERATURE CONNECTION** ▶ **Short Story**
- ☐ **Writing for a Test**

Name: Ashley
Home: Kansas
Interests: history, spending time with family and friends, volunteering for community projects
Favorite Book: *Thief of Hearts* by Laurence Yep

What's a Memoir?

It's a description of an important experience in the author's life. I'll need to figure out which of my experiences will make an interesting memoir.

What's in a Memoir?

Voice
The writer uses voice to express his or her unique style. In other words, my writing should sound like me. To create voice in my writing, I can include phrases and words that I often use.

Narrator
Because the narrator is the person writing the memoir, the story is told in the first-person point of view, using the word *I*.

Reflective Tone
This is how I want my memoir to sound. I'll use a reflective, or thoughtful, tone so the reader will understand how I feel. I can create a reflective tone by asking questions and/or drawing conclusions.

Voice? I totally thought voice was just used for talking.

Sequence
This is the order in which I'll describe my story events. I can include flashbacks that interrupt the chronological order, and I can use transition words to help readers follow the sequence of my story.

Why write a Memoir?

There are many reasons to write a memoir. I jotted some down to help me think about why I want to write my own.

To Entertain
I've had some interesting experiences, and even if I didn't see the humor at the time, things have happened to me that could make readers laugh. Entertaining the reader is one reason to write a memoir.

To Reflect
Writing about an experience can help me reflect on why it was important or what I learned. The reader might be able to connect to my experience and learn from it as well.

To Educate
Some events or experiences can be educational. If I describe what I've learned from my experiences, maybe my readers will learn something too.

To Relay a Message
The experiences I remember best are ones that have affected me in serious ways. They have taught me something about myself or about life in general. Relaying these messages to the reader is another reason to write a memoir.

Linking Narrative Writing Traits to a Memoir

In this chapter, you will reflect on and write about an experience you want to share. This type of narrative writing is called a memoir. Ashley will guide you through the stages of the writing process: Prewrite, Draft, Revise, Edit, and Publish. In each stage, Ashley will show you important writing strategies that are linked to the Narrative Writing Traits below.

Narrative Writing Traits

Ideas
- a clear topic, experience, or series of events
- relevant and descriptive details that support and develop the narrative

Organization
- a beginning that catches the reader's attention and an ending that follows from and reflects on the narrated experience
- a sequence of events that unfolds naturally and logically
- transitions that guide the reader through the story

Voice
- a voice and tone that are appropriate for the purpose and audience
- dialogue that, if used, fits and develops the characters

Word Choice
- precise words and powerful verbs

Sentence Fluency
- a variety of sentences that flow and are a pleasure to read aloud

Conventions
- no or few errors in grammar, usage, mechanics, and spelling

Before you write, read Manny Reyes's memoir on the next page. Then use the memoir rubric on pages 8–9 to decide how well he did. (You might want to look back at What's in a Memoir? on page 4, too!)

Summer Surprise
by Manny Reyes

Narrator

If someone had told me in June that the most surprising event of the summer wouldn't happen until the beginning of September, I would have laughed.

But right before school began, my best friend, Kenny, invited me to spend Labor Day weekend with his family. I thought it was going to be awesome. But when Kenny told me this year's destination, my jaw dropped. "Camping?" I asked. "You're kidding—right?"

Voice

Sequence "Nope," said Kenny. "Mom and Dad want to try something totally new."

I really wasn't sure whether to accept the invitation. Me? Camping? I am a city kid through and through. Then, I thought about how Kenny and I always have a great time no matter what we do. So reluctantly, I said yes.

But when that fateful Friday afternoon arrived, all I wanted to do was hole myself up under my bedcovers and disappear. My heart was filled with dread, and my backpack was stuffed with city comforts. If the bathroom sink had fit, I totally would've crammed it in!

Eventually, the Millers pulled up in their SUV. Gear was tied on top and piled in the seats, along with Kenny and his annoying sister, Grace. Everyone was so chirpy that I really hoped they wouldn't notice my gloomy mood.

We cruised for about two hours, the signs of civilization disappearing as we approached the campsite. Finally, Mr. Miller parked the car, and we unpacked all the stuff. Twilight was descending. "Better start setting up these tents," said Kenny's dad.

Reflective Tone

A question popped into my head: "Could I make it back to the city on foot?" But I was quickly distracted as Mrs. Miller called out directions while we fumbled around with poles and pegs. It was pitch black by the time we finished. Mr. Miller built a campfire, and Kenny and I checked out our tent. It was pretty big inside. I thought, *Maybe this won't be so bad after all!*

As we sat by the fire, we toasted marshmallows and sang campfire songs. It was then that I noticed the knot in my stomach had loosened. I was actually beginning to enjoy this! Bug spray kept away the mosquitoes, and there were bathrooms right down the hill. There was even a lake on the way in, which we were planning on swimming in the next day. "Check it out," said Kenny, pointing up. The sight took my breath away. A sea of stars lit up the sky.

The next day, I woke early. I was excited about eating an outdoor breakfast, and I was a little amazed, too, at how life can surprise you!

Memoir

Rubric

Use this 6-point rubric to plan and score a memoir.

	6	**5**	**4**
Ideas	The writer establishes a context by focusing on a single topic. Narrative techniques (dialogue, description, reflection) enliven the experience.	The writer focuses on one topic. Most narrative techniques, especially dialogue, bring the writer's experience to life.	The writer has one topic. Some narrative techniques, including some dialogue, bring the writer's experience to life.
Organization	The memoir is told in order. A variety of effective transitions moves the reader through the text.	The writing conveys a strong sense of order. Some effective transitions are used.	Most of the memoir is told in order. Transitions are present.
Voice	The narrator's point of view is consistent and appropriate for the purpose and audience.	The narrator's point of view is mostly consistent and appropriate for the purpose and audience.	The narrator's point of view is often consistent and appropriate for the purpose and audience.
Word Choice	Precise words and sensory language accurately convey the meaning and events.	Precise words and sensory language accurately convey the meaning and events most of the time.	Precise words and phrases are mixed with overused and general terms.
Sentence Fluency	Well-written and well-placed questions add suspense.	The memoir includes some questions that are well placed and add suspense.	The memoir includes one or two questions, but they may not build suspense.
Conventions	Verbs are used correctly throughout the memoir. The meaning is clear.	Most verbs are used correctly, and the meaning is clear.	Several verbs are used incorrectly, but the reader can still figure out the meaning.
➕ Presentation	Paragraphs are indented for the dialogue of each speaker.		

Revise

The Rubric Says   The narrator's point of view is consistent and appropriate for the purpose and audience.

Writing Strategy   Use a reflective tone and first-person point of view to convey meaning and insight to the reader.

Writer's Term

Tone

Tone reflects the author's attitude or manner of expression. It's how the writing sounds. Tone can be funny, sarcastic, or even sad, but it should match the writer's purpose. A writer can use a **reflective tone** to express meaning and insight.

The rubric says my point of view should be appropriate for my purpose and audience. Well, my audience is my class, and my purpose is to tell a story about myself. By using a reflective tone, I can help the reader connect with my emotions as I look back on my experience.

[DRAFT]

I supposed Mom was right. ◄──────── [used a reflective tone]

  ʌWith a sigh, I staked out a position on the porch, where I could listen

to the rain. But Steve, who had used up all his patience by lunchtime,
As I tucked myself into bed, I hoped for clear skies the next day. ◄──
would not leave me alone. By dinner, everyone's nerves were fried. ʌ

Reflect

How does Ashley's tone help you connect with her experience?

Apply

Use a reflective tone to let your readers know how you feel.

Revise

Focus on **Word Choice**

The Rubric Says	Precise words and sensory language accurately convey the meaning and events.
Writing Strategy	Use a thesaurus to help find precise words.

The rubric says I should use precise words and sensory language to convey meaning, so I used a thesaurus to help me find synonyms for dull or repeated words that I found in my draft. Take a look at how I replaced some common words with precise words. These words paint a clearer and more meaningful picture of both the characters and the events in my memoir.

[DRAFT]

[used more precise words]

But in the morning, the rain was ~~coming~~ down in sheets. At
                                    pounding

breakfast, Mom passed around French toast as she ~~talked~~ in an
                                                    chirped

upbeat tone that was obviously put on for our benefit. No one was

buying it. "This weekend is officially a bust," I ~~said~~.
                                                   complained

Apply

Use a print or online thesaurus to find precise words to use in your memoir.

Edit

The Rubric Says Verbs are used correctly throughout the memoir. The meaning is clear.

Writing Strategy Make sure that simple and perfect tenses are used correctly.

Writer's Term

Simple Tense/Perfect Tense
The **simple tense** tells what happens in the present, what happened in the past, and what will happen in the future. The **perfect tense** tells what started in the past and is still happening, what began in the past and was completed, and what will begin and end in the future.

Now I'll check for errors in grammar and mechanics. Also, the rubric says I should make sure I use all my verbs correctly. When I reviewed my draft, I found some errors in verb tense, so I'll fix them now.

[DRAFT]

[corrected past perfect tense]

photo
"I see you found the ~~foto~~ album," said Mom. She had seen me take

out a thick, leather-bound book.

[changed past perfect to simple past tense] → fell

As I leafed through the pictures, my eyes ~~had fallen~~ on a

striking girl in a red dress. "Who's this, Mom? She's beautiful."

Reflect

What do you think of Ashley's edits? Do they help you better understand the memoir?

Apply Conventions

Edit for errors in spelling and grammar. Be sure to use verbs correctly.

For more practice with verbs use the exercises on the next two pages.

Simple and Perfect Tense

Know the Rule

- The **simple present tense** tells what happens now.
  Example: Beth and her dog **walk** to the river.

- The **simple past tense** tells what happened in the past. In most cases, add *–ed* to the end of a simple present tense verb.
  Example: Beth **walked** to the river yesterday.

- The **simple future tense** tells what will happen in the future. Add the helping verb *will* to a simple present tense verb.
  Example: Beth **will walk** to the river tomorrow.

- The **present perfect tense** tells what began in the past and may still be happening. Add *has or have* to a simple past tense verb.
  Example: Beth **has walked** to the river many times.

- The **past perfect tense** tells what began in the past and was completed. Add the helping verb *had* to a simple past tense verb.
  Example: Beth **had walked** to the river many times.

- The **future perfect tense** tells what will begin in the future and end in the future. Add the helping verb *will* to a present perfect tense verb.
  Example: Beth **will have walked** many times by the week's end.

Practice the Rule

On a separate sheet of paper, write the verb in parentheses that correctly completes each sentence.

1. Yesterday, Mom (need/needed) almost a dozen eggs to make breakfast.
2. If the rain (stopped/had stopped), we could have gone swimming.
3. Viewing photos (has enlivened/will have enlivened) our family vacation.
4. We (have vacationed/vacation) at the lake house many times.
5. By the week's end, we (have learned/had learned) the value of family.
6. Even Steve (realized/had realized) that spending time with family was OK.
7. I wonder if it (will have rained/will rain) next time.
8. Rain or no rain, we (enjoy/will enjoy) ourselves at the lake house.

Irregular Verbs

Know the Rule

Many verbs are irregular; they do not add *-ed* in the past tense. Let's use the verb *run* as an example.

- Simple present tense
  Example: Amy and her sister **run** five miles.
- Simple past tense
  Example: Amy and her sister **ran** five miles last night.
- Simple future tense
  Example: Amy and her sister **will run** five miles tomorrow.
- Present perfect tense
  Example: They **have run** five miles dozens of times.
- Past perfect tense
  Example: They **had run** five miles last Saturday morning.
- Future perfect tense
  Example: Amy and her sister **will have run** twenty miles by the week's end.

Practice the Rule

On a separate sheet of paper, write each sentence with the correct form of the verb in parentheses.

1. Last Friday, I _____ to my parents about getting a part-time job. (speak)
2. When this batch comes out of the oven, Dad _____ three dozen cookies. (make)
3. Every morning, I _____ a giant glass of fresh-squeezed orange juice. (drink)
4. My parents _____ at that restaurant several times before. (eat)
5. By the end of the game, Charlie _____ four fly balls. (catch)
6. Yesterday, I _____ a new pair of jeans. (buy)
7. Bukala _____ that she might spend the night at Emma's, but she did not. (think)
8. When I got to school, my teacher asked if I _____ my homework. (do)
9. By the time I turn 15, I _____ more than 15,000 meals. (eat)
10. A firm tug on his fishing rod told Uncle Ted that he _____ a large fish! (catch)

Publish

Publishing Strategy   Publish your memoir in a class journal.

Presentation Strategy   Indent a paragraph for each new speaker.

I need to indent, or start a new paragraph, each time a different person speaks. Otherwise dialogue can be very confusing. I'll review my memoir to make sure I've done that. I also need to think about how to publish my memoir. I would really like all of my classmates to read it, so I'll post it in our class journal. But first I need to go over my checklist.

My Final Checklist

Did I—

✔ put all my verbs in the correct tense?

✔ use irregular verbs correctly?

✔ proofread for any errors in spelling and grammar?

✔ indent a new paragraph for each new speaker's dialogue?

Apply

Make a checklist to check your memoir. Then make a final draft to publish.

Rained In

by Ashley

It had been a long, hectic September, so I was thrilled when I heard we would be spending the weekend at our lake house. I couldn't wait to relax on the beach, go canoeing, and eat barbecue. However, when we arrived, it was raining.

This was a big drag. Nevertheless, I tried not to let it get me down. I spent the day writing in my journal and putting together a 300-piece dinosaur puzzle. When I snapped at my little brother, Steve, Mom asked me what was wrong.

"Hello! It's raining!"

"Don't worry, Ashley. There's always tomorrow," said Mom.

I supposed Mom was right. With a sigh, I staked out a position in the comfy chair on the porch, where I could listen to the rain's rhythmic beat. But Steve, who had used up all his patience by lunchtime, would not leave me alone. By dinner (the non-barbecue kind), everyone's nerves were fried. As I tucked myself into bed, I hoped for clear skies the next day.

But in the morning, the rain was pounding down in sheets. At breakfast, Mom passed around French toast as she chirped in an upbeat tone that was obviously put on for our benefit. No one was buying it. "This weekend is officially a bust," I complained. How was I going to get through another soggy day? I plopped on the floor next to the bookcase and looked for something to read.

"I see you found the photo album," said Mom. She had seen me take out a thick, leather-bound book.

As I leafed through the pictures, my eyes fell on a striking girl in a red dress. "Who's this, Mom? She's beautiful."

My mother laughed, "Well thank you, dear. That's me."

"Get out of town!" I said in disbelief. But it was Mom, posing in her prom dress. She told me she had shopped for weeks without finding anything she liked. Then my grandmother brought down the red dress from the attic—and it was perfect.

We settled on the couch, and soon, we were joined by Dad and Steve. Slowly we flipped through the album, savoring each page. Each photograph held a story, a piece of our family's past. Finally peace settled over us, and we were able to enjoy the rest of the day inside, in each other's company.

As we drove home that night, I realized we not only went to the lake house to discover the open space of the outdoors, we also went to discover each other.

Reflect

Does the writing reflect the traits of a good memoir? Check it against the rubric, and don't forget to use the rubric to check your own memoir, too.

What's a Historical Episode?

It's a story that combines historical settings, characters, and events with fictional story elements. I think this will be fun because I can learn about history as I write.

What's in a Historical Episode?

Setting
This is the time and place in which a story happens. When I write my historical episode, I'll choose the setting first because it will give me ideas about characters and plot.

Characters
The characters are the people in the story. They can be fictional or based on real-life people. Either way, my characters will have to act in a way that's true to the setting.

Dialogue
This is the characters' actual words. If I use historical characters, I probably won't know what they really said, but I can imagine the way they spoke at the time. This is one of the ways that I can make my historical episode seem realistic.

Theme
This is the story's message about life. Because I'm setting my episode in the past, I have to be careful to include issues that are still important to people in modern-day times.

Dearest Ellen,
Mother simply does not understand me.

Dear Ellie,
Mom just doesn't get me.

Why write a Historical Episode?

There are many different reasons to write a historical episode. I'll list some here. Maybe this will help me figure out why I want to write.

To Inform
I can gather historical information from a textbook and use it in my historical episode. Then readers can learn from what I write.

To Make Connections
I know that some people don't like to read about history because they think it has nothing to do with current issues. But a good historical episode connects people across the ages because it tells a story that is timeless.

To Entertain
Reading a historical episode can be fun. Entertaining the reader is a good reason to write.

Linking Narrative Writing Traits to a Historical Episode

In this chapter, you will write a story about an event in history. This type of narrative writing is called a historical episode. Ashley will guide you through the stages of the writing process: Prewrite, Draft, Revise, Edit, and Publish. In each stage, Ashley will show you important writing strategies that are linked to the Narrative Writing Traits below.

Narrative Writing Traits

	• a clear topic, experience, or series of events • relevant and descriptive details that support and develop the narrative
	• a beginning that catches the reader's attention and an ending that follows from and reflects on the narrated experience • a sequence of events that unfolds naturally and logically • transitions that guide the reader through the story
	• a voice and tone that are appropriate for the purpose and audience • dialogue that, if used, fits and develops the characters
	• precise words and powerful verbs
	• a variety of sentences that flow and are a pleasure to read aloud
	• no or few errors in grammar, usage, mechanics, and spelling

Before you write, read Carrie Taylor's historical episode on the next page. Then use the historical episode rubric on pages 30–31 to decide how well she did.

Edie's Other Engagement

by Carrie Taylor

Characters   Setting

"Edie, you must be dreaming!" cried Hank. "This is America in 1943! No matter what you want, they'll never let women fly planes in this war. No, Edie, I won't allow it. No fiancée of mine is going to be a World War II Fly Girl."

"Well, Hank," I said, "I agree with you on two things. First, I *am* dreaming. I'm dreaming of the day that I graduate from Women Airforce Service Pilot training and get my pilot's wings. And second, you're right: No fiancée of yours is going to be a pilot in the war. If you're not going to support me in this, I'll just have to do it alone."

Theme   Dialogue

"Then I guess this is it, Edie," Hank said slowly. "I'm very sorry. But I want my wife at home, not on a plane!"

"Then this is good-bye," I sighed. "I leave tomorrow for flight school. I'll always remember you, Hank. I hope you'll understand someday."

It's hard to believe that was almost six months ago. Poor Hank. I miss him sometimes. But I wasn't about to let him tell me that I couldn't follow my dream. And now, can you believe it? I've finished my WASP training, and I'm graduating. Today—December 17, 1943—I will finally get my wings.

I always dreamed I would fly someday. And now I'll have the chance. My mission now is to join other women in ferrying planes to bases across the United States so that our male pilots, who are badly needed at the front, will be released from ferrying duties. Just imagine my excitement!

When I applied to be a Woman Airforce Service Pilot, I thought I didn't stand a chance. Thank goodness my parents didn't feel the same way as Hank. No, Mother and Dad were right there behind me, cheering me on. And now it is graduation day. If only Hank were here to see me now. But wait a minute—there he is!

"Edie, I'm so proud of you," cried Hank. "Now, how about putting this engagement ring back on? It goes perfectly with your new wings."

"No, Hank," I said. "I'm afraid that my only engagement right now is with the U.S. Air Force. It's too bad you couldn't be with me when I really needed your support. I think I'll fly solo for a while."

Rubric

Use this 6-point rubric to plan and score a historical episode.

	6	5	4
Ideas	The topic and theme are clear. Narrative techniques, such as setting and details, establish a historical context.	The topic and theme are clear. Historical details describe the setting and plot.	The topic and theme are somewhat clear. Plot and setting details provide some support.
Organization	Story elements are effectively organized and unfold naturally. The beginning grabs the reader's attention. The conclusion follows from and reflects on the narrated experience.	Story elements are easy to follow. The beginning invites you into the writing. The conclusion reflects on the narrated experience.	Story elements are somewhat easy to follow. The beginning is functional. The conclusion somewhat reflects the narrated experience.
Voice	The writer's voice is engaging and enhances the writing. Dialogue enriches the writing.	The writer's voice has energy and matches the topic. Dialogue is used effectively.	The writer's voice is strong and appropriate at the start, then fades. Some dialogue is used.
Word Choice	Sensory language captures the action and conveys the experience.	Most of the time, sensory language captures the action and conveys the experience.	The language does not consistently capture the action and convey the experience.
Sentence Fluency	Variety in sentence lengths makes the writing flow smoothly.	Many sentences vary in length and are very readable.	Most sentences are easy to read. Sentence variety is evident.
Conventions	Dialogue is punctuated correctly, and proper nouns are capitalized.	Most dialogue is punctuated correctly and most proper nouns are capitalized.	Some errors in punctuation of dialogue and capitalization are evident but don't affect the meaning.

✛ Presentation The historical episode is neat and legible.

3	2	1	
The reader is able to figure out the topic and theme. Most historical details are common knowledge.	The focus of the writing is still coming together. Historical details vaguely depict the setting and plot.	The topic and theme are unclear and lack details. The writer has limited knowledge of the topic.	**Ideas**
The beginning may not grab the reader's attention. The conclusion does not provide the writer's reflection.	Story elements may be out of order. A beginning and/or conclusion are missing.	The writing is not a story. Story elements are not organized.	**Organization**
The writer's voice comes and goes and doesn't always appeal to the audience. Some dialogue is used.	Little of the writer's voice is evident. The voice doesn't work for the topic. Little or no dialogue is used.	The writer's voice is missing. No dialogue is used.	**Voice**
There is very little sensory language. The writer does not convey the experience.	Little or no sensory language is used. The writer does not convey the experience.	Words are incorrectly used and confuse the reader.	**Word Choice**
Sentence beginnings are repetitious. Some sentences may be too long.	Sentences are similar in length and start the same way, making them sound choppy.	It's hard to read the writing. It often needs to be corrected as it is read.	**Sentence Fluency**
Dialogue, punctuation, and capitalization errors are noticed. They may slow down reading.	Dialogue, punctuation, and capitalization errors jump out at the reader. They may hinder reading.	Many errors or lack of punctuation make the writing difficult to read.	**Conventions**

See Appendix B for 4-, 5-, and 6-point narrative rubrics.

Using the Rubric to Study the Model

Historical Episode

Did you notice that the model on page 29 points out some key elements of a historical episode? As she wrote "Edie's Other Engagement," Carrie Taylor used these elements to help her tell the story of a couple in the 1940s. She also used the 6-point rubric on pages 30–31 to plan, draft, revise, and edit the writing. A rubric is a great tool to evaluate writing during the writing process.

Now let's use the same rubric to score the model. To do this, we'll focus on each trait separately, starting with Ideas. We'll use the top descriptor for each trait (column 6), along with examples from the model, to help us understand how the traits work together. How would you score Carrie on each trait?

Ideas

- **The topic and theme are clear.**
- **Narrative techniques, such as setting and details, establish a historical context.**

Carrie focuses on one topic and includes narrative techniques to establish a historical context. This makes me feel like the story really happened. Although it's fiction, the reader learns real-life details along the way, as the writer shares her theme. I learned that World War II was going on in 1943, and women pilots were called Fly Girls, WASPs, or Woman Airforce Service Pilots. Women had never flown planes during a war before.

[from the writing model]

I've finished my WASP training, and I'm graduating. Today—December 17, 1943—I will finally get my wings.

Organization

- Story elements are effectively organized and unfold naturally.
- The beginning grabs the reader's attention.
- The conclusion follows from and reflects on the narrated experience.

Carrie's opening pulled me in right away. I wanted to keep reading to see if Edie would go on to become a pilot. The story's well-organized elements make it easy to read and understand. Carrie's conclusion definitely reflects on the narrated experience.

[from the writing model]

"Edie, you must be dreaming!" cried Hank. "This is America in 1943! No matter what you want, they'll never let women fly planes in this war. No, Edie, I won't allow it. No fiancée of mine is going to be a World War II Fly Girl."

[from the writing model]

"No, Hank," I said. "I'm afraid that my only engagement right now is with the U.S. Air Force. It's too bad you couldn't be with me when I really needed your support. I think I'll fly solo for a while."

Voice

- The writer's voice is engaging and enhances the writing.
- Dialogue enriches the writing.

Carrie was careful to write dialogue that was appropriate for the time period. Her characters' words are realistic and true to their setting and situation. Edie's words below reflect the attitude of a strong and courageous woman of the 1940s.

[from the writing model]

"No, Hank," I said. "I'm afraid that my only engagement right now is with the U.S. Air Force. It's too bad you couldn't be with me when I really needed your support. I think I'll fly solo for a while."

• **Sensory language captures the action and conveys the experience.**

Carrie uses plenty of historical terms to create a strong and convincing image of the time period. However, she first had to do a bit of research to ensure she used the words correctly, like the verb *ferry*.

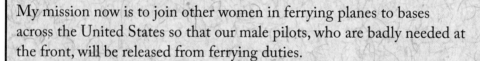

[from the writing model]

My mission now is to join other women in ferrying planes to bases across the United States so that our male pilots, who are badly needed at the front, will be released from ferrying duties.

• **Variety in sentence lengths makes the writing flow smoothly.**

I like how Carrie's sentences aren't all the same length. Check out the paragraph below. It begins with two short sentences and is followed by a longer sentence. Then Carrie ends with another short sentence. This variety makes her writing more interesting to read.

[from the writing model]

I always dreamed I would fly someday. And now I'll have the chance. My mission now is to join other women in ferrying planes to bases across the United States so that our male pilots, who are badly needed at the front, will be released from ferrying duties. Just imagine my excitement!

Conventions
- Dialogue is punctuated correctly, and proper nouns are capitalized.

Carrie includes lots of dialogue between several characters. However, she is careful to keep all dialogue in quotes, so it is easy to follow along.

[from the writing model]

"Then I guess this is it, Edie," Hank said slowly. "I'm very sorry. But I want my wife at home, not on a plane!"

"Then this is good-bye," I sighed. "I leave tomorrow for flight school. I'll always remember you, Hank. I hope you'll understand someday."

✚Presentation The historical episode is neat and legible.

My Turn!

I'm going to write a historical episode set during an interesting time period. I'll use the rubric and good writing strategies. Read on to see how I do it!

Prewrite

Focus on **Ideas**

The Rubric Says   The topic and theme are clear.

Writing Strategy   Choose a historical event and gather information from several different resources.

Last year, my family moved to Kansas from New York. So when I was asked to write a historical episode, I decided to write about a family that settles in Kansas in the late 1870s. To gather information, I read a few articles and a book about sod houses. I also got some information from the Internet, including a primary source: a letter written by a guy who lived in a sod house. Here are some of my notes.

Writer's Term

Primary Source
A **primary source** is the person or book that is closest to the information. For example, a primary source about the Civil War would be the journal, diary, or letter of a person who lived through the war.

My Notes on Sod Houses

✔ hardly any trees, so couldn't build log cabins
✔ used blocks of prairie sod to build "soddies"
✔ cheap to build and didn't burn down in prairie fires
✔ dirt roofs leaked
✔ mice, snakes, and bugs—frequent "guests"

Apply

Choose a historical period in which to set your story. Then think of a story idea. Gather information from a variety of resources.

Prewrite

Focus on **Organization**

The Rubric Says   Story elements are effectively organized and unfold naturally.

Writing Strategy   Make a Story Map to organize story elements.

Writer's Term

Story Map
Use a **Story Map** to organize story elements such as setting, characters, theme, conflict, and resolution.

The rubric says to organize my story elements, so I'll include these on a Story Map. Then I'll use the Story Map to help me stay focused as I write.

Story Map

Setting Post Civil War in Abilene, Kansas, 1876

Major Character(s) The narrator, Jeremy Thompson
Minor Character(s) Jeremy's sister, Lulu

Theme Adjusting to a new place is often difficult.
Conflict Jeremy doesn't like his new home in Kansas.

Plot		
Event 1	Event 2	Event 3
When the Thompsons arrive in Kansas, Jeremy hates it and wants to go back home.	After the neighbors help the Thompsons build a soddie, Jeremy discovers some of its pitfalls.	Jeremy gets a good laugh while teasing Lulu about her method of picking up cow chips.

Resolution Jeremy realizes that teasing Lulu makes him feel more "at home."

Reflect

How do you think a Story Map will help Ashley with her writing?

Apply

Organize story elements by using your notes to make a Story Map.

Draft

Focus on **Organization**

The Rubric Says Story elements are effectively organized and unfold naturally. The beginning grabs the reader's attention.

Writing Strategy Establish the setting and theme right away to engage the reader.

Writer's Term

Setting/Theme
The **setting** is the time and place of the story. Let the audience know the setting as soon as possible to help them understand what's happening. The **theme** is a message about life that the author wants to express in the story.

Now I'll use my Story Map to help me write my draft. According to the rubric, my story elements, such as setting and theme, need to be effectively organized. For example, setting has a huge effect on both plot and theme. If I don't describe these elements right away, my reader may not understand what's going on or why the characters act in certain ways. Look at how I included the setting and theme in my first two paragraphs on the next page.

[DRAFT]

Home, Sod Home

Looks like we made it in time to celebrate the Fourth of July. In a few weeks, our great nation will be 100 years old. But Abilene,

[setting]

Kansas, is a terrible place! Ma says, "Don't worry, Jeremy. It'll grow on you." I doubt it. So far, the only things that have grown on me are the bumps from my bug bites.

This place is nothing like the home we left in Kentucky. There's barely a tree in this place. People on these plains build their homes out of dirt. They call it sod, and they call their houses soddies. I think it's all disgusting. I want to go back to Kentucky.

[theme]

Reflect

Does Ashley's beginning grab your attention? Which techniques capture your interest?

Apply

Write a draft using your Story Map to introduce the setting and theme to your readers.

Revise

Focus on Voice

The Rubric Says	The writer's voice is engaging and enhances the writing. Dialogue enriches the writing.
Writing Strategy	Use dialogue that reflects the time and place in which the characters live.

The rubric says that I should enrich my story with dialogue. That means the dialogue should make my story more interesting and appealing to the reader. When I reread my draft, I realized that I could make the dialogue sound more authentic. In my research, I came across different words that people used during pioneer times, so I replaced some of my original words with more authentic ones that I found.

[DRAFT]

The only good laugh that I have had in the last two months was when my little sister was picking up cow chips. "Girl, What in the ~~world~~ tarnation are you doing?" I asked. "Are you trying to pick up those cow chips or eat ~~them~~ 'em?"

[used dialogue that reflects the setting]

Apply

Add words and speech patterns that fit your chosen historical era to make your dialogue more realistic.

Revise

The Rubric Says   Sensory language captures the action and conveys the experience.

Writing Strategy   Use historically accurate words.

The rubric says my language should reflect the purpose of my writing. In this paper, I want to give the reader a realistic picture of the 1800s in the United States. After reviewing my draft, I realized that several words I used were not true to the time period. So I did some research to find words and phrases commonly used back then. I then used those words in my writing. My characters now sound more real and my story is more convincing.

[DRAFT]

Looks like we made it in time to celebrate the Fourth of

July. In a few weeks, our ~~great~~ fair nation will be 100 years old.

But Abilene, Kansas, is ~~a terrible~~ an abominable place! Ma says, "Don't worry,

Jeremy. It'll grow on you."

[used words from time period]

Reflect

Do Ashley's new word choices make her historical episode sound more convincing?

Apply

Use historically accurate words and phrases to strengthen your writing.

Revise

Focus on  Sentence Fluency

The Rubric Says Variety in sentence lengths makes the writing flow smoothly.

Writing Strategy Use long and short sentences for natural-sounding dialogue.

The rubric says to vary the length of my sentences. After reading my paper aloud, I noticed some dialogue that did not sound natural. I added some shorter and longer sentences to make this part flow more smoothly.

[DRAFT]

[created sentence variety]

> Home! Heck, we don't even have one, nor do we have any logs to build one.

This place is nothing like the home we left in Kentucky. There's

barely a tree in this place. People on these plains build their

Apply

Read your draft aloud. Be sure to vary your sentences for flow and to make the dialogue sound natural.

Edit

The Rubric Says Dialogue is punctuated correctly, and proper nouns are capitalized.

Writing Strategy Punctuate dialogue and use common and proper nouns correctly.

Writer's Term____

Dialogue

Dialogue, a conversation between characters, is always enclosed in quotation marks.

Now it's time to check for errors in spelling, punctuation, and capitalization. I'll make sure I've capitalized proper nouns. The rubric says that I should make sure I've punctuated dialogue correctly, so I'll focus on that, too. Here are some of the edits I made to my draft.

[DRAFT]

I had tears rolling down my cheeks. "So after you're done stabbing them with that fork" I said slowly, "are you planning to use it at Supper?"

[used lowercase letter]

[enclosed a quotation]

[added comma before closing quote]

Reflect

Do you agree with Ashley's edits? Did she overlook anything?

Apply Conventions

Edit your draft for spelling, punctuation, and capitalization.

For more practice with punctuating dialogue and common and proper nouns, use the exercises on the next two pages.

Punctuating Dialogue

Know the Rule

Dialogue, a conversation between characters, is always enclosed in **quotation marks**.

- Use **opening quotes** at the beginning of dialogue.
- Use **closing quotes** at the end of dialogue.
- Begin dialogue with a **capital letter**, unless it has been interrupted by an expression such as *she said*. Add **punctuation** (period, question mark, exclamation point, or comma in place of a period) before the closing quotes. Also, add end punctuation, if necessary, at the end of the sentence containing the dialogue.
- Always begin a new paragraph when the speaker changes.

  Examples:

  "Hey, Jeremy! Why don't you help your sister pick up those cow chips?" asked Pa.

  "Sure thing, Pa," I grinned. "Just let me grab my fork."

Practice the Rule

On a separate sheet of paper, rewrite each sentence, adding quotation marks, commas, and end punctuation in the appropriate places. Use capitalization where needed.

1. Did you know that my great-great-grandfather was a homesteader I asked
2. I didn't Sarah replied tell me about it
3. Well I began his name was Albert, and he moved from Virginia to Nevada in 1861
4. How did he like Nevada Sarah asked
5. They say he liked it quite a bit I said he was, apparently, pretty content.
6. Did he go alone or with his family asked Sarah
7. I think I said that he went with his younger brother
8. Wow exclaimed Sarah he must have been very brave
9. Yes, I believe he was quite adventurous and bold I replied
10. What a trip remarked Sarah it must have been to travel from Virginia to Nevada in 1861

Common and Proper Nouns

Know the Rule

- A **common noun** names any person, place, thing, or idea.
    Example: city, country, river
- A **proper noun** names a particular person, place, thing, or idea. Proper nouns must be capitalized. A proper noun made of several words is considered one proper noun.
    Example: Chicago, Germany, Nile River, United Nations

Practice the Rule

On a separate sheet of paper, write the correct form of each noun in the following sentences.

1. The (sahara/Sahara) Desert is the world's largest hot desert and covers most of northern (Africa/africa).

2. Our last science unit covered (Owls/owls). My favorite by far was the amazing (eurasian eagle owl/Eurasian Eagle Owl).

3. Of all the (Holidays/holidays) throughout the year, Doris is most excited to celebrate the (fourth of july/Fourth of July).

4. During a snow storm, (Main Street/Main street) is always plowed first.

5. The (pacific ocean/Pacific Ocean) is the largest of Earth's five (Oceans/oceans).

6. The largest city in the (state/State) of (California/california) is (Los Angeles/los angeles).

7. (Concord High School/concord high school) has lots of exciting clubs to join, making the first year of (High School/high school) lots of fun.

8. Of all my (Aunts/aunts) and (Uncles/uncles), I am the closest to (Aunt Matilda/aunt Matilda) and (Uncle Sherm/uncle Sherm).

Publish

✚ Presentation

Publishing Strategy	Dramatize your story.
Presentation Strategy	Use a limited number of clear fonts or very neat handwriting.

My historical episode is finished! But how should I publish it? I could add it to a class anthology, or I could submit it to a history-themed magazine that publishes student writing. I love the idea of doing a dramatic reading of my story, maybe even making a recording of it. I will be sure my text is neat and easy to read, and then I'll get a few classmates to help me read it. First though, I want to read through it one last time to make sure it includes all of the items on my checklist.

My Final Checklist

Did I—

✔ punctuate all the dialogue correctly?

✔ capitalize proper nouns?

✔ use lowercase letters for common nouns?

✔ proofread for any errors in spelling and grammar?

✔ use a limited number of clearly readable fonts or my neatest handwriting?

Apply

Make a checklist and check your historical episode. Then make a final copy to publish.

Home, Sod Home

by Ashley

Looks like we made it in time to celebrate the Fourth of July. In a few weeks, our fair nation will be 100 years old. But Abilene, Kansas, is an abominable place! Ma says, "Don't worry, Jeremy. It'll grow on you." I doubt it. So far, the only things that have grown on me are the bumps from my bug bites.

This place is nothing like the home we left in Kentucky. Home! Heck, we don't even have one, nor do we have any logs to build one. There's barely a tree in this place. People on these plains build their homes out of dirt. They call it sod, and they call their houses soddies. I think it's all disgusting. I want to go back to Kentucky.

With help from the neighbors, who are turning out to be a kind and generous bunch, we got our soddy built in pretty good time. Home, sod home. I still don't like this place. When it's dry out, the dust is unbearable. Dirt drifts down from the ceiling of our soddy and adds an unwelcome flavor to our food. It crumbles from the walls and gets stirred up under our feet until there's a coating of dust over everything. When it rains, the roof leaks for days. I swear, I don't know which is worse.

And then there's the matter of fueling the place. Seems we homesteaders must use what we have most of—cow chips. The only good laugh that I have had in the last two months was when my little sister was picking up cow chips. "Girl, what in tarnation are you doing?" I asked. "Are you trying to pick up those cow chips or eat 'em?"

Seems Lulu found the whole chip-picking ordeal distasteful. As she stabbed delicately at each chip with a fork, she said, "I refuse to touch these things. They're foul and dirty and smelly."

I had tears rolling down my cheeks. "So after you're done stabbing them with that fork," I said slowly, "are you planning to use it at supper?"

Lulu glared at me. Then she glared at her fork. A cow chip was poised on the end. "I'm never eating again!" she cried. "And it's all your fault!" She threw down her fork and stomped off. A cloud of dust danced merrily in her wake.

Well, my sister and I were at it again. At least something was starting to feel like home.

Reflect

How did "Home, Sod Home" score when you checked it against the rubric? Don't forget to use the rubric when writing your own historical episode.

What's a Biography?

It's a story about a real person's life. I'm looking forward to writing a biography because there's a world of people I can write about. I can choose someone who really interests me—and become a biographer!

What's in a Biography?

Third-Person Narrator
The writer of a biography narrates the story but is not involved in the action. I'll use the third-person point of view to narrate and objectively present my biography.

Characters
These are the important people in my subject's life. They are often more than story characters. They can also function as great sources of information about the subject of a biography.

Logical Sequence
It makes perfect sense for a writer to start a biography at the beginning of a subject's life and move through it in chronological order. But as long as the sequence is logical, a writer can also flash back and flash forward between key moments in the subject's life.

Direct Quotations
I can include direct quotations from important people in my subject's life. This will help bring my biography to life.

Why write a Biography?

There are many reasons to write a biography. As I made this list, I realized my purpose for writing will probably depend on the subject of my biography.

To Inform
There are many people I've heard of, but don't know much about. The purpose of my biography could be to inform my readers with details about a familiar face or name. Or I could inform my audience about a lesser-known person.

To Teach Lessons
Some people have played important roles in history or have lived their lives as examples for others. If this applies to my subject, my biography can teach valuable lessons to my readers.

To Make Connections
A good biography should tell a story about a real person—someone who is probably like other people in many ways. As I write, I'll remember to think about what my readers might have in common with my subject. That way, my audience can connect with the story.

To Entertain
Reading a biography can be fun. If I make sure I focus on what's most interesting about my subject, I'll be sure to entertain my readers.

Linking Narrative Writing Traits to a Biography

In this chapter, you will write about a person. This type of narrative writing is called a biography. Ashley will guide you through the stages of the writing process: Prewrite, Draft, Revise, Edit, and Publish. In each stage, Ashley will show you important writing strategies that are linked to the Narrative Writing Traits below.

Narrative Writing Traits

**Ideas**
- a clear topic, experience, or series of events
- relevant and descriptive details that support and develop the narrative

**Organization**
- a beginning that catches the reader's attention and an ending that follows from and reflects on the narrated experience
- a sequence of events that unfolds naturally and logically
- transitions that guide the reader through the story

**Voice**
- a voice and tone that are appropriate for the purpose and audience
- dialogue that, if used, fits and develops the characters

**Word Choice**
- precise words and powerful verbs

**Sentence Fluency**
- a variety of sentences that flow and are a pleasure to read aloud

**Conventions**
- no or few errors in grammar, usage, mechanics, and spelling

Before you write, read Stewart Chase's model biography on the next page. Then use the biography rubric on pages 52–53 to decide how well he did. (You might want to look back at What's in a Biography? on page 48, too!)

Biography Model

GILBERT CHASE: A MAN ON THE MOVE
by Stewart Chase

Characters

On the day my Great-Grandpa Gilbert was born, fate was in the mood for practical jokes. You see, Gilbert Chase was born breech on April Fools' Day, 1905. My mother told me that his mother always used to say, "Baby Gil was born breech 'cause he wanted to hit the ground running."

Logical Sequence

Third-Person Narrator

And run he did! It seemed his friends and family could never keep up with him. All through school he was the fastest boy in any race, and his grades were better than everyone else's, too. After he graduated from high school in 1923, he was accepted into the University of Illinois. Four years later, he graduated at the top of his class. In 1928, Gil opened a chain of stores that sold all kinds of electrical appliances. By that time, about two thirds of the country had electricity, and people were buying things on credit. Gil made tons of money.

His first major purchase, a Model T Ford sedan, cost him $295 right off the assembly line. Great-Grandpa Gil loved his new Model T. He drove it all over town. His friends would see him coming, and he'd pick them up for rides. Often he'd stop at the ice cream parlor and treat them to their favorite flavors. "He's generous to a fault, that Gil," his friend Bruce would always say.

And Gil would always reply, "Brucie! What's the fun of having money if you can't share it with your friends?"

Direct Quotation

Those trips to the ice cream parlor paid off because that's where Gil met his future wife. Her name was Alice Smith, and according to Gil, "She was the most beautiful gal I had ever seen." Gil married her, and their wedding took place on July 19, 1929—exactly six months from the day they met.

Gil and Alice lived a very good life, though things got a bit lean during the Great Depression. They had two children—Scott, born in 1931, and Fay, born in 1934—and gave them the best of everything.

On his 40th birthday, Gil's friends and family threw him a huge surprise party at the country club. Gil was so shocked that he sat in a chair and cried.

He said he felt wonderful after the party, but Great-Grandma Alice said he didn't look right. She took him home and put him to bed. When she checked on him just before midnight, Great-Grandpa Gil was dead.

The doctor said that Gil had had a stroke and died in his sleep. My mom says that her Grandpa Gil was just in a hurry to meet his maker.

Rubric

Use this 6-point rubric to plan and score a biography.

	6	5	4
Ideas	Well-chosen descriptive details develop the events and characters. Direct quotations bring the biography to life.	Descriptive details develop the events and characters. Direct quotations support the topic.	Some descriptive details develop the events and characters. Direct quotations may or may not be relevant to the topic.
Organization	The introduction grabs the reader's attention. Transitions effectively and logically sequence the writing.	The introduction somewhat grabs the reader's attention. Transitions sequence the writing.	The introduction is present. Some transitions are used.
Voice	The writer consistently uses a respectful, engaging tone and third-person point of view.	Most of the time, the writer uses a respectful, engaging tone and third-person point of view.	Sometimes the writer uses a respectful or engaging tone. The point of view may be inconsistent.
Word Choice	Precise words capture the action and convey the events.	Precise words capture the action and convey the events most of the time.	The language is functional and makes sense. It makes the meaning clear.
Sentence Fluency	Sentences are clear, including parallel structures that emphasize relationships.	Sentences are clear most of the time, and parallel structures are present.	Sentences are clear some of the time. Parallel structures, if present, are not correct.
Conventions	All sentences are complete and written correctly.	Most sentences are complete and correctly written. The meaning is clear.	Some sentences are incomplete or incorrectly written, but they do not take away from the meaning.

✚Presentation   Visuals are appropriate and well prepared.

3	2	1	
Events and characters are not well-developed. Direct quotations may not be relevant or used at all.	Events and characters are poorly developed. No direct quotations are used.	There is no development of events and characters. No direct quotations are used.	**Ideas**
The introduction is present but weak. Few transitions make the sequence hard to follow.	The introduction is weak or missing. Few or poor transitions are used.	There is no introduction. The sequence loses the reader.	**Organization**
The writer's tone and point of view are inconsistent, creating parts that are unclear or vague.	Limited knowledge of the topic keeps the tone distant. The point of view is unclear.	The writer uses an inappropriate tone. The writer doesn't know the topic.	**Voice**
Some of the language used is unclear. The reader may need to figure out what the writer means.	The language is too vague or general to support the writer's purpose. Words are used incorrectly.	The writing lacks the language to make the message clear.	**Word Choice**
Sentences require careful reading. Often they are incomplete, choppy, or repetitive. Parallel structure is lacking or not correctly used.	Sentences are awkward or incomplete. Parallel structure is missing.	Confusing sentence structure requires editing to make sense of the text.	**Sentence Fluency**
Sentence errors exist that require careful reading, to make sense of the sentences.	Many errors in the sentences make reading difficult.	Word-by-word editing of the sentences is required to make the text readable.	**Conventions**

See Appendix B for 4-, 5-, and 6-point narrative rubrics.

Using the Rubric to Study the Model
Biography

Did you notice that the model on page 51 points out some key elements of a biography? As he wrote "Gilbert Chase: A Man on the Move," Stewart Chase used these elements to help him tell the story of his great-grandfather. He also used the 6-point rubric on pages 52–53 to plan, draft, revise, and edit the writing. A rubric is a great tool to evaluate writing during the writing process.

Now let's use the same rubric to score the model. To do this, we'll focus on each trait separately, starting with Ideas. We'll use the top descriptor for each trait (column 6) along with examples from the model, to help us understand how the traits work together. How would you score Stewart on each trait?

 **Ideas**

- **Well-chosen descriptive details develop the events and characters.**
- **Direct quotations bring the biography to life.**

Stewart focuses his biography on his great-grandfather, Gilbert Chase. He does a good job choosing details and direct quotes to bring Gil to life for the reader.

[from the writing model]

"He's generous to a fault, that Gil," his friend Bruce would always say.

And Gil would always reply, "Brucie! What's the fun of having money if you can't share it with your friends?"

Organization

- **The introduction grabs the reader's attention.**
- **Transitions effectively and logically sequence the writing.**

The reader is immediately drawn in when Stewart opens his biography with the birth of his great-grandfather. Since this event was so unusual and exciting, it is logical for Stewart to start there. In the second excerpt, Stewart makes good use of transition words and phrases to convey the sequence of events in his great-grandfather's life.

[from the writing model]

On the day my Great-Grandpa Gilbert was born, fate was in the mood for practical jokes. You see, Gilbert Chase was born breech on April Fools' Day, 1905. My mother told me that his mother always used to say, "Baby Gil was born breech 'cause he wanted to hit the ground running."

[from the writing model]

After he graduated from high school in 1923, he was accepted into the University of Illinois. Four years later, he graduated at the top of his class. In 1928, Gil opened a chain of stores that sold all kinds of electrical appliances.

Voice

- **The writer consistently uses a respectful, engaging tone and third-person point of view.**

It's important to know why and for whom you are writing. Knowing your purpose and audience dictates the tone you use while writing. Stewart wants to inform the reader about his great-grandfather—a man he admires very much. His tone clearly reflects his purpose.

[from the writing model]

It seemed his friends and family could never keep up with him. All through school he was the fastest boy in any race, and his grades were better than everyone else's, too.

Word Choice

- Precise words capture the action and convey the events.

Stewart's writing is easy to read because he chooses precise words and uses them correctly. In this next passage, Stewart uses the word *lean*. This word has several different meanings (incline, rest against, thin, lacking in fullness), but Stewart uses it to express the idea that Gilbert's family had to do without many things.

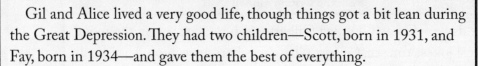

[from the writing model]

Gil and Alice lived a very good life, though things got a bit lean during the Great Depression. They had two children—Scott, born in 1931, and Fay, born in 1934—and gave them the best of everything.

Sentence Fluency

- Sentences are clear, including parallel structures that emphasize relationships.

Stewart uses clear, well-written sentences that flow from one to the next in a way that makes sense. In one place, he words two facts similarly so that the reader knows they are related.

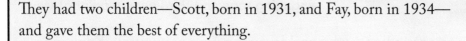

[from the writing model]

They had two children—Scott, born in 1931, and Fay, born in 1934—and gave them the best of everything.

Conventions

- **All sentences are complete and written correctly.**

If Stewart's biography ever contained any sentence fragments, run-ons, or comma splices, he made sure to correct them before publishing his work. It's obvious that Stewart's sentences are complete because each one contains both a subject and a predicate.

[from the writing model]

He said he felt wonderful after the party, but Great-Grandma Alice said he didn't look right. She took him home and put him to bed.

✛Presentation Visuals are appropriate and well prepared.

My Turn!

I'm going to write a biography about someone I'd like to know more about. I'll make sure to use the rubric and good writing strategies. Read on to see how I do it!

Prewrite

Focus on **Ideas**

The Rubric Says   Well-chosen descriptive details develop the events and characters.

Writing Strategy   Choose a person as the focus of the biography. Then write interview questions and conduct an interview.

When my teacher said to write a biography, the first thing I did was choose a subject. I chose my grandmother because everyone says I look and act a lot like her. Then I wanted to do some research about her. Interviewing a person provides accurate and descriptive details. Because my grandmother died before I was born, I decided to interview her children: my father and my aunt. Finally I wrote some interview questions.

My Interview Questions

✔ What do you remember most about my grandma, Mai Chaw?

✔ What would you like other people to know about her?

✔ What memories do you have of Mai Chaw and of leaving Laos?

✔ Do you have any memories of Mai Chaw in the refugee camp?

Apply

Choose a person to be the focus of your biography. Gather information by writing interview questions and conducting an interview.

Prewrite

The Rubric Says   The introduction grabs the reader's attention. Transitions effectively and logically sequence the writing.

Writing Strategy   Plot important events on a Timeline.

Writer's Term

Timeline

A **Timeline** can help you sequence key events in the order in which they happened. Using a Timeline also points out logical transitions that show relationships among the events.

The sequence of events in a biography is key. A Timeline will help me both recall and organize the most important events. If I look at the Timeline when I write my biography, I'll see immediately which events to start out with. As I write, I'll connect the events with transitions, such as *a year after that* or *at the same time as.*

Timeline

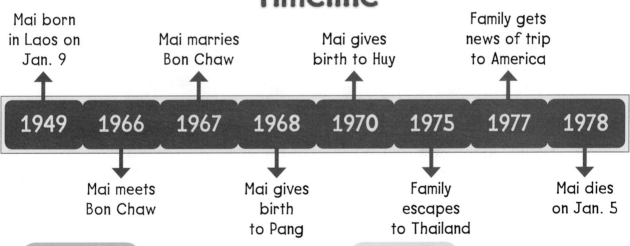

Mai born in Laos on Jan. 9

Mai marries Bon Chaw

Mai gives birth to Huy

Family gets news of trip to America

1949 1966 1967 1968 1970 1975 1977 1978

Mai meets Bon Chaw

Mai gives birth to Pang

Family escapes to Thailand

Mai dies on Jan. 5

Reflect

Do you think Ashley's Timeline will help keep her focused as she writes? Will it help her use transition words to clarify the relationships among the events in her biography?

Apply

Organize your biography by plotting the most important events on a Timeline. Think of how you will use transition words to convey the sequence of events.

Writing a Biography

Draft

The Rubric Says   The writer consistently uses a respectful, engaging tone and third-person point of view.

Writing Strategy   Use words that show respect for the subject and third-person point of view.

Now I'm ready to begin writing. The rubric says I should use a respectful and engaging tone, which makes sense when I consider my purpose. I want my reader to understand my grandmother's life story and what a strong, courageous woman she was. I will be sure to use details, direct quotations, and specific words to convey my feelings about Grandma Mai. I will also use third-person point of view, as that is most appropriate when writing a biography.

After I started writing, I noticed that I used simple and perfect tense verbs correctly. Verb tense has given me trouble in the past, so I'm happy to see my hard work has paid off!

[DRAFT]

The Courage of Mai Chaw

by Ashley

[used third-person point of view]

Mai Chaw and her children were running for their lives, and their lives depended on keeping the raft they were on afloat and unnoticed. As they glided across the Mekong River, away from Laos, Mai wondered if they'd make it to Thailand.

She was num with fear, but she had to go on. Only hours before, she had seen her husband dragged away by communist soldiers. Though it was 1975, and the fighting in Vietnam had ended, Mai's battle was only beginning. She was in for the fight of her life. She had to protect herself and her children from the communist soldiers. They would face certain death if they were found.

My father told us that our mother was very strong.

Reflect

Is the tone engaging and respectful? Does the use of third-person point of view help clarify the biography for the reader?

Apply

Write a draft using a respectful and engaging tone. Be sure to use third-person point of view.

Revise

Focus on **Ideas**

The Rubric Says	Direct quotations bring the biography to life.
Writing Strategy	Use direct quotations from the interview to bring the subject to life.

✏️ Writer's Term

Direct Quotations

Direct quotations are the exact words that someone says. They are enclosed in quotation marks, just like dialogue.

After I drew my audience into Grandma Mai's story, I decided to go back and describe her. Instead of using my own words, I decided to use some direct quotations from my interviews. I guess I was right on track because the rubric says quotations will bring my biography to life. Reading the subject's own words will give the reader more insight into the subject than I could give by merely writing a description.

[DRAFT]

[added a direct quote]

"Our mother survived the journey because she was a very strong person," said my father, Huy Chaw.

~~My father told us that our mother was very strong.~~

"Yes, she was very strong," agreed his sister (my aunt) Pang, "and she was the bravest person I've ever known."

Apply

Add some direct quotations to bring your biography to life.

Revise

The Rubric Says Precise words capture the action and convey the events.

Writing Strategy Use a dictionary to make sure words are used correctly.

I had my teacher look over my draft. He advised me to review what the rubric says about using precise, correct language. I found a few words that were not quite right for my purpose, so I replaced them. Now the story is clearer and easier to understand.

[DRAFT]

— [corrected word usage] —

Mai arrived in the world on January 9, 1949. She was born in

Laos, a small country in Southeast Asia. As soon as she ~~aged~~, she

was old enough

began working in the rice paddy fields with her family. They farmed

their paddies from sunup until sundown. Planting and harvesting rice

backbreaking

was ~~complicated~~ work that left them exhausted. But Mai was strong

and happy.

Reflect

How do the new words help create a clearer picture for the reader?

Apply

Use a print or online dictionary to make sure you used precise words correctly.

Revise

The Rubric Says Sentences are clear, including parallel structures that emphasize relationships.

Writing Strategy Use parallel structure in sentences to make relationships clear.

After revising, I read my paper to a friend. He pointed out two parts of a sentence he found confusing. The two parts were related, but their relationship to one another was unclear. I rewrote the sentence to clarify the relationship. My revision cleared up the confusion.

[DRAFT]

[used parallel structure]

A year after that, Mai had my aunt Pang; ~~my father, Huy, two years later~~ two years after that, she had my father, Huy.

Apply

Revise any sentences that need clarification. Use parallel structure to clarify the relationships within sentences.

The Rubric Says All sentences are complete and written correctly.

Writing Strategy Use commas and conjunctions to fix sentence fragments, run-ons, and comma splices.

Writer's Term

Sentence Fragments/Run-on Sentences/ Comma Splice

A **sentence fragment** is not a complete thought. It is missing either a subject or a predicate. A **run-on sentence** is a compound sentence that is joined incorrectly. A **comma splice** is a compound sentence joined with a comma but no conjunction.

My final step is to check for errors in spelling, punctuation, and capitalization. I also need to fix any sentence fragments, run-ons, or comma splices. Using a comma and a conjunction is an easy way to join a sentence fragment to a related, existing sentence.

[DRAFT]

[fixed fragment with a conjunction]

, but Mai

They were all frightened. Stayed brave through it all.

Reflect

What do you think? Are Ashley's ideas clearer once she edited her writing?

Apply

Conventions

Edit your draft to correct sentence fragments, run-ons, and comma splices.

For more practice in correcting sentence errors, use the exercises on the next two pages.

Write Correct Sentences

Know the Rule

A group of words that is missing a subject or a predicate is a **sentence fragment**.

Fragment: Born in Laos. (subject missing)
Correct: Mai Chaw was born in Laos.
Fragment: The fighting in Vietnam. (predicate missing)
Correct: The fighting in Vietnam had ended.

Run-on sentences and **comma splices** happen when a compound sentence is joined incorrectly. Correct a run-on sentence or a comma splice by adding a semicolon or a comma and a conjunction. You may also break it into two sentences.

Run-on: The United States said they would help they never did.
Comma Splice: The United States said they would help, they never did.
Correct: The United States said they would help; they never did.
Correct: The United States said they would help, **but** they never did.
Correct: The United States said they would help. They never did.

Practice the Rule

Number a sheet of paper 1–8. Write **F** if the item is a fragment, **R** if it is a run-on, or **CS** if it is a comma splice.

1. Some people think that Laos is located in Africa, it is actually in Southeast Asia.
2. China borders Laos to the north The Mekong River forms the western border.
3. Governed by a single party.
4. More than fifty ethnic groups live in Laos they are divided into three broad categories.
5. Rugged mountains in northern Laos.
6. Is home of multi-ethnic and multi-cultural people.
7. Vientiane is the capital, it is the largest city in Laos.
8. Next year I will visit my grandparents who live there, won't it be great to see them?

Conjunctions

Know the Rule

Coordinating conjunctions (*and, but, or, so*) connect words or groups of words (including independent clauses) that are similar.

Subordinating conjunctions (*although, because, since, if,* and *before*) show how one clause is related to another. Subordinating conjunctions are used at the beginning of dependent clauses.

Practice the Rule

Read the sentence pairs below. Decide which coordinating or subordinating conjunction best joins each pair. Rewrite each completed sentence on a separate sheet of paper.

1. For my 13th birthday, my parents gave me a choice: I can take my friends to the movies (and/or) grab a pizza.

2. All of the city's public transportation was shut down (because/although) heavy snow fell for seven hours straight.

3. For extra money, Terese works Wednesdays and Thursdays at the library, (but/and) she babysits on the weekends for the Gilberts.

4. José will soon sign up for driver's ed, (so/since) he is two months away from his 16th birthday.

5. Mr. Lee stayed up past midnight correcting our exams (because/although) he was sick with a fever and cough.

6. Sebastian ran as hard as his legs could take him, (because/but) he still missed the morning bus.

7. I studied really hard for my English test (but/because) I want to get an excellent grade.

8. Oliver was very hungry when he came home for dinner, (although/so) he was excited to see his favorite pasta dish on the stove.

Publish

✚ Presentation

Publishing Strategy   Submit your biography to a website.

Presentation Strategy   Use visuals that enhance the information.

Now that I've finished my biography, I want to publish it. I really want to share my grandmother's story. Submitting my work to a website is perfect! But before I do, I will add a visual—a map of where Mai Chaw is from—to help readers place the action of events. Well-chosen visuals like maps deliver a lot of information to the reader. I will also read through my paper one last time to be sure it includes all of the items on my checklist.

My Final Checklist

Did I—

✔ check my writing for run-ons, sentence fragments, and comma splices?

✔ use conjunctions to join sentences with related ideas?

✔ edit and proofread my paper carefully?

✔ include helpful visuals in the biography?

Apply

Make a checklist and check your biography. Then make a final copy to publish.

The Courage of Mai Chaw

by Ashley

"Still, children, stay very still!" said Mai Chaw. "We must keep the raft nice and steady." Her desperate voice repeated those words until she could no longer speak. She and her children were running for their lives, and their lives depended on keeping that raft afloat and unnoticed. As they glided across the Mekong River, away from Laos, Mai wondered if they'd make it to Thailand.

She was numb with fear, but she had to go on. Only hours before, she had seen her husband dragged away by communist soldiers. Though it was 1975, and the fighting in Vietnam had ended, Mai's battle was only beginning. She was in for the fight of her life. She had to protect herself and her children from the communist soldiers. They would face certain death if they were found.

"Our mother survived the journey because she was a very strong person," said my father, Huy Chaw.

"Yes, she was very strong," agreed his sister (my aunt) Pang, "and she was the bravest person I've ever known." That's how Mai Chaw's children describe her. They say she had been that way from the day she was born.

Mai arrived in the world on January 9, 1949. She was born in Laos, a small country in Southeast Asia. As soon as she was old enough, she began working in the rice paddy fields with her family. They farmed their paddies from sunup until sundown. Planting and harvesting rice was backbreaking work that left them exhausted. But Mai was strong and happy. She was always smiling, and she never complained about hard work.

Mai met Bon Chaw when they were both seventeen. Soon, they fell in love. After a year of preparation, Mai and Bon were married. A year after that, Mai had my Aunt Pang; two years after that, she had my father, Huy.

Things went well for Bon and Mai's family until they got involved in the Vietnam War. Bon fought against communism by guiding American soldiers to safety when their planes were shot down in the jungles of Laos. Bon and several of his countrymen helped save many American soldiers' lives. When the Americans pulled out of Vietnam

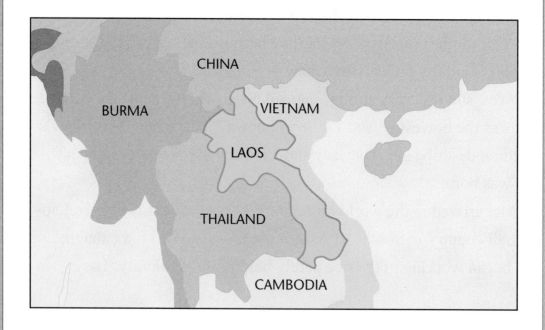

in 1975, the communists killed anyone they thought had helped the Americans. Bon, who had helped American soldiers, was labeled a traitor. The communists tied him up and took him away, leaving Mai to protect their children.

Taking what she could, Mai soon found herself on a raft escaping to Thailand with her children. They were all frightened, but Mai stayed brave through it all. It took weeks, but she finally got herself and the children to a refugee camp.

Mai spent the next two years at the refugee camp, waiting to see if she and her family would be relocated to the United States. On December 29, 1977, word finally came; they would soon be leaving for America. She and her children would be safe! One week later, though, Mai had a heart attack and died.

Mai never saw the United States, but her children and grandchildren definitely benefited from her courageous act.

Reflect

Does the writing reflect the traits of a good biography? Check it against the rubric and remember to use the rubric to score your biography.

What's a Short Story?

It's a complete story that contains a full plot, at least one character, and some sort of conflict that needs to be resolved. I love reading short stories, and now I'm excited that I get to write one.

What's in a Short Story?

Plot
The plot is the sum of all the events that make up a story line. While every plot is different, some key plot parts are found in every good short story: the **introduction** (the main theme is introduced), the **rising action** (events build the tension and interest), the **climax** (tension is the highest), the **falling action** (after the climax, the action slows down), and the **resolution** (the main conflict is resolved).

Characters
Short stories typically contain only a few characters due to the story's limited length. Every short story has a **protagonist** (the main character) and an **antagonist** (a character or story element that opposes the protagonist). Sometimes the antagonist is a side of the protagonist's personality that needs to be overcome, like intense fear or anger.

Conflict
Every good short story contains a conflict, that is, some sort of problem or opposing force the protagonist must overcome. The conflict is what drives the story and keeps the reader wondering "What will happen next? How will the main character overcome this?"

Why write a Short Story?

There are a lot of reasons to write a short story. Here are some of the most common ones.

To Create

Creating a story and characters can be a lot of fun. Once characters exist, it's exciting to see how they'll behave as the story unfolds. Sometimes, in fact, a character can even surprise the writer. I can't wait to "meet" the characters I create for my short story.

To Entertain

I've always loved sharing stories I've written with my family. It's great to read what my friends come up with, too. Whether the story is funny, sad, or thought-provoking, writing short stories is always entertaining.

To Appreciate

Once you've written a short story of your own, you can really learn to appreciate the work of other writers. Understanding *how* a short story is written deepens and broadens your appreciation of authors and their finished work.

Linking Narrative Writing Traits to a Short Story

In this chapter, you will reflect on and write about an experience you want to share. This type of narrative writing is called a short story. Ashley will guide you through the stages of the writing process: Prewrite, Draft, Revise, Edit, and Publish. In each stage, Ashley will show you important writing strategies that are linked to the Narrative Writing Traits below.

Narrative Writing Traits

	• a clear topic, experience, or series of events • relevant and descriptive details that support and develop the narrative
	• a beginning that catches the reader's attention and an ending that follows from and reflects on the narrated experience • a sequence of events that unfolds naturally and logically • transitions that guide the reader through the story
	• a voice that is appropriate for the purpose and audience • dialogue that, if used, fits and develops the characters
	• precise words and powerful verbs
	• a variety of sentences that flow and are a pleasure to read aloud
	• no or few errors in grammar, usage, mechanics, and spelling

Before you write, read Jacinda LeBranch's short story on the next three pages. Then use the short story rubric on pages 78–79 to decide how well she did. (You might want to look back at What's in a Short Story? on page 72, too!)

Crash Course in Babysitting

by Jacinda LeBranch

Introduction

Janie had been waiting for this night for what seemed like years. She had read countless books, watched instructional movies, and even enrolled in her town's babysitting training classes. Her mother was so proud of her dedication and hard work that, as a surprise, she had laminated Janie's CPR Certification card. Now the big night had arrived. Tonight she was babysitting the Driscoll children, Nicholas and Maddy, and she just couldn't wait.

Characters

Plot

"Janie, let's go!" her father called. "You don't want to be late for your first job!"

"I'm just grabbing my bag, Dad!" Janie replied. She had loaded her special babysitting bag with supplies: crayons and coloring books, a first-aid kit, and several special bedtime books. Janie grabbed the emergency contact list from her desk and placed it in her front pocket. She ran downstairs and got into the car with Dad. "I'm finally on my way!" she thought.

The Driscolls lived a few miles away, down a long and winding road. Gnarled trees lined both sides of the road and hundred-foot pine trees lined one side, creating areas of deep shadow even the brightest sun could not penetrate. Janie fought the spooky feeling the surroundings gave her and tried focusing on her job.

"We're here, Janie," her father said. "Have a great night and remember—call us if you need anything."

"No problem," Janie said, a bit too quickly. "I can do this, remember?"

The Driscolls lived in a 200-year old colonial home. Janie loved its shuttered windows, enormous chimney, and vine-covered walls. The house had an old, friendly look that made Janie feel safe. Mrs. Driscoll opened the door before Janie could even ring the bell.

"Come in, Janie. We're running a little late, so just follow me while I finish up, and I'll tell you everything you need to know."

Janie put her bag down and followed Mrs. Driscoll around listening to her instructions. "Above all else, remember to turn on Maddy's nightlight. She's scared of the dark, and this special nightlight works wonders."

Five minutes later, the Driscolls were driving away, and little Nicholas and Maddy were quizzing Janie, asking what they could play first. "How about a game of Candyland?" suggested Janie.

Game after game was played. Janie found herself having just as much fun as the kids, but she was getting hungry. "Let's have a snack," she suggested. Janie went into the kitchen while the kids sat at the table. She noted the restaurant's phone number on the refrigerator door, just where Mrs. Driscoll had said it would be. It wasn't until they were all dipping their cookies into their milk that Janie noticed how heavily it was raining and how the wind was howling outside. The lights flickered here and there, and Janie started to feel her heart beat faster. "That's strange," she thought. "I don't remember anyone saying anything about a storm tonight." But she told herself it was all fine and took the kids upstairs to get into their pajamas.

Protagonist

Antagonist

Rising action

Upstairs the noise from the storm was even worse. Janie could hear the rain pouring over the roof, and the walls seemed to creak with every blast of wind. She felt a little frightened but reminded herself, "I've got to stay calm for the children." While the kids brushed their teeth, Janie went downstairs and quietly gathered three flashlights, just in case the power went out.

Just as she was returning upstairs, a furious howl of wind battered the house and the lights went out. Maddy immediately began to wail, but Janie jumped into action. She soothingly called up the stairs, "Don't worry, Maddy! I'm coming! Be brave!" Janie carefully made her way back to the flashlights in the kitchen and then returned upstairs, where

Rising action

she found both children crumpled and crying on the floor. "Look, the power's out, but we're OK. I have flashlights for everyone and we can make this fun. Don't be scared. Come on, let's go downstairs."

Climax

The sound of the storm was somewhat dulled in the family room, but the dark windows were like two blank eyes silently watching them, and Janie didn't like it. She had just drawn the heavy velvet curtains when it happened. A boom shook the entire house, and it seemed to come from the front door! The children went into hysterics! Even Janie let out a scream, but she quickly recovered and embraced the children. Janie knew a tree had hit the house, but she didn't know how bad the damage was. To distract Nicholas and Maddy she said, "Let's play a camping game." She grabbed the blanket from the sofa and made a "tent" using some of the furniture. She gave each child a flashlight. "OK, you camp out for a few minutes while I go use the phone."

Janie called the restaurant and reached Mr. Driscoll. "You did the right thing, Janie. We'll be there as soon as we can!"

Falling action

The Driscolls arrived after a while. "Sorry we couldn't get back sooner. Trees are down. Power is out. What a storm! Were you afraid, Maddy?" Mrs. Driscoll said.

"It was fun!" exclaimed Maddy. "We went camping, and Janie told us stories. Then we made silly faces with the flashlights." Seeing Maddy so happy, Janie's fear was replaced with pride. She knew her first job had been a success!

Resolution

Mr. Driscoll drove Janie home, carefully maneuvering the car around branches and debris in the road. Her parents had a hundred questions. "Mrs. Driscoll called about the tree. . . we were so worried," her mother explained.

"I was fine. Really, we all were fine. All my studying helped," she laughed, "but I wish I had taken the 'What to Do When a Tree Hits the House' class, too!"

Rubric

Use this 6-point rubric to plan and score a short story.

	6	5	4
Ideas	The plot and the conflict are clear. The resolution satisfies and solves the character's central problem.	The plot and the conflict are clear. The resolution may leave questions unanswered.	The plot and the conflict are clear. The resolution may not solve the central problem.
Organization	The story is well organized. Events unfold naturally and logically and are well paced to build tension.	The story is organized. Events appear to be in order, but action is needed to build tension.	The story is organized. Most events are in order, but action is needed to build tension.
Voice	The narration and dialogue are distinct and unique. The characters sound realistic.	Most of the dialogue sounds natural. The voice of one character needs to be stronger.	Most of the dialogue sounds natural. Several characters' voices need to be stronger.
Word Choice	The writer uses specific nouns and strong verbs. The words capture the action and bring the story to life.	The writer uses specific nouns most of the time. One or two verbs could be stronger.	The writer uses specific nouns most of the time. Several verbs need to be stronger.
Sentence Fluency	The sentences vary in length. Fragments are used creatively and effectively.	Most of the sentences vary in length. Some sentences could be shortened for dramatic effect.	Most of the sentences vary in length. Fragments may be confusing or misplaced.
Conventions	The writing has been carefully edited. Pronouns are clear and used correctly.	Minor errors are present but do not interfere with meaning. Pronouns are used correctly.	A few errors cause confusion. One or two pronouns are used incorrectly.

✛ Presentation   The use of white space allows the reader to focus on the text.

3	2	1	
The plot is clear. The conflict is not developed enough. The resolution may not solve the character's problem.	The plot and conflict are not clear. The resolution introduces new or unrelated details.	The plot and conflict are not clear. Conflict and resolution are not developed or are unrelated.	**Ideas**
The story is somewhat organized. Many events appear out of order. Action may be weak.	Events may be misplaced or missing. The events do not flow well or build tension.	The events are not organized. The story is very difficult to follow or incomplete.	**Organization**
Some of the dialogue sounds awkward or flat. All characters' voices need to be stronger.	The narrator speaks for the characters too often. The dialogue is weak or flat.	The writer does not connect with the reader. Dialogue is not present.	**Voice**
The writer uses ordinary or non-specific language. Nouns and verbs need to be stronger.	The writer repeats many words. In places, the language dulls the story.	The writer uses ordinary words that do not tell a story.	**Word Choice**
Few of the sentences vary in length. Fragments are not used effectively.	Many sentences are similar in length. The writing is predictable in places.	Many sentences are incomplete. The ideas are not connected or clear.	**Sentence Fluency**
Many errors are repeated and cause confusion. Some pronouns are used incorrectly.	Serious errors interfere with meaning. Most pronouns are used incorrectly.	The writing has not been edited.	**Conventions**

See Appendix B for 4-, 5-, and 6-point narrative rubrics.

Short Story
Using the Rubric to Study the Model

Did you notice that the model on pages 75–77 points out some key elements of a short story? As she wrote "Crash Course in Babysitting," Jacinda LeBranch used these elements to help her write a short story. She also used the 6-point rubric on pages 78–79 to plan, draft, revise, and edit the writing. A rubric is a great tool to evaluate writing during the writing process.

Now let's use the same rubric to score the model. To do this, we'll focus on each trait separately, starting with Ideas. We'll use the top descriptor for each trait (column 6), along with examples from the model, to help us understand how the traits work together. How would you score Jacinda on each trait?

- **The plot and the conflict are clear.**
- **The resolution satisfies and solves the character's central problem.**

I like how Jacinda sets up the plot in the very first paragraph. There's no question—Janie has worked hard to become an official babysitter, and the night has finally arrived. As the story continues, both the conflict (How will Janie deal with the storm and the children's fear?) and the resolution (she remembers her training) are also clear.

[from the writing model]

She had read countless books, watched instructional movies, and even enrolled in her town's babysitting training classes. Her mother was so proud of her dedication and hard work that, as a surprise, she had laminated Janie's CPR Certification card. Now the big night had arrived. Tonight she was babysitting the Driscoll children, Nicholas and Maddy, and she just couldn't wait.

Organization

- The story is well organized.
- Events unfold naturally and logically and are well paced to build tension.

Jacinda tells each event in the order in wihch it happened, and this chronological organization really helped me follow the story. She does a great job showing how Janie's fear developed throughout the night. I really felt the tension building as the storm progressed.

[from the writing model]

It wasn't until they were all dipping their cookies into their milk that Janie noticed how heavily it was raining and how the wind was howling outside. The lights flickered here and there, and Janie started to feel her heart beating faster. "That's strange," she thought. "I don't remember anyone saying anything about a storm tonight."

Voice

- The narration and dialogue are distinct and unique.
- The characters sound realistic.

I was impressed with how realistic the characters sounded in Jacinda's story. I could easily envision her father's gentle concern and Janie's slight irritation with his offer to help. Janie's dialogue, both internal and out loud, helped me understand and connect with her personality.

[from the writing model]

"We're here, Janie," her father said. "Have a great night and remember—call us if you need anything."
"No problem," Janie said, a bit too quickly. "I can do this, remember?"

Word Choice

- The writer uses specific nouns and strong verbs.
- The words capture the action and bring the story to life.

Jacinda's creative choice of words really brought her story to life for me. Words like *furious howl*, *battered*, and *wail* painted such a vivid picture I could almost hear the storm raging outside my own window!

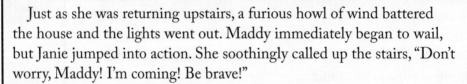

[from the writing model]

Just as she was returning upstairs, a furious howl of wind battered the house and the lights went out. Maddy immediately began to wail, but Janie jumped into action. She soothingly called up the stairs, "Don't worry, Maddy! I'm coming! Be brave!"

Sentence Fluency

- The sentences vary in length.
- Fragments are used creatively and effectively.

To help her writing move smoothly along, Jacinda uses a variety of sentence lengths. Shorter sentences add drama or emphasis to an event, while fragments express her own creative writing style. This variety kept the writing lively and, just as important, it kept me interested.

[from the writing model]

The Driscolls arrived after a while. "Sorry we couldn't get back sooner. Trees are down. Power is out. What a storm! Were you afraid, Maddy?" Mrs. Driscoll said.

**Conventions**

- **The writing has been carefully edited.**
- **Pronouns are clear and used correctly.**

I couldn't find a single spelling, grammar, or punctuation mistake anywhere in Jancinda's story. She worked really hard and it shows! She also did a great job using pronouns accurately. I'll be sure to do the same when I write my own short story.

[from the writing model]

Janie called the restaurant and reached Mr. Driscoll. "You did the right thing, Janie. We'll be there as soon as we can!"

✛Presentation The use of white space allows the reader to focus on the text.

My Turn!

Now it's my turn to write a short story. I'll use the rubric and good writing strategies to help me. Read on to see how I do it!

Prewrite

Focus on **Ideas**

The Rubric Says   The plot and the conflict are clear.

Writing Strategy   Brainstorm characters and conflict.

The rubric says that both the plot and conflict should be clear. It does make sense to figure these things out before I start writing. After all, the entire short story revolves around the protagonist and the conflict he or she faces. My notes about possible characters and conflicts are below. Now that I've studied them, I think the story about Sage has some possibilities.

Brainstorming Notes for My Short Story

Possible characters

✔ Lightning Jack, an older, champion runner who wishes to be young again

✔ Carmen, a teenage girl who awoke to find she was 100 years in the past

✔ Sage, a teenage girl who doesn't have a lot of money

Possible conflicts

✔ Jack wishes to be young again so much that his anger keeps him from enjoying the present, especially at a family reunion

✔ Carmen needs to solve the mystery of how she went back in time and reverse it—before it's too late

✔ Sage desperately wants to go on her class trip, but how can a 13-year-old make that much money on her own?

Apply

Brainstorm possible characters and conflicts. Create a list and then choose the ones that feel right for your short story.

Focus on Organization

The Rubric Says The story is well organized.

Writing Strategy Use a Story Frame to sequence events.

✎ **Writer's Term**

Story Frame
A **Story Frame** is an excellent tool to help map out and pace each of the elements in a story. It helps to organize the sequence of events from the introduction to the resolution.

Now that I've chosen my protagonist and conflict, I'll create a Story Frame to help me place each element of my short story. The rubric says my story should be well organized, and using a Story Frame is a great way to start.

Story Frame	
Setting	The story mostly takes place in Sage's apartment.
Introduction	Sage is crying because she can't afford to go with her 8th grade class to Washington, D.C.
Rising Action (Event 1)	Sage wishes she had a job.
Rising Action (Event 2)	Sage's mother needs Sage to bring her money at work.
Rising Action (Event 3)	A nurse notices Sage's hand-made duct tape purse.
Climax	Sage has many orders for her unique purses.
Falling Action (Event 1)	Sage works all weekend with Lee making purses.
Resolution	Sage raises enough money to go on the school trip!

Reflect

Look at the events of Ashley's Story Frame. Are they arranged in time order?

Apply

Use a Story Frame to plan and sequence the events in your short story.

Draft

The Rubric Says   The writer uses specific nouns and strong verbs. The words capture the action and bring the story to life.

Writing Strategy   Use specific nouns and strong verbs.

Now it's time to begin writing! Before I start, though, I'll review the rubric again. It says that my story will come to life if I use specific nouns and strong verbs. It's true. I know from reading other people's short stories that one or two specific and carefully selected words are much more powerful than a series of weak words. I'll be sure to "show" my readers what I mean, rather than simply tell them. For example, the phrase *she sucked in great gulps of air* is much more powerful and descriptive than *she was feeling very tired and out of breath.*

I'll open by showing how crushed Sage feels. That will grab my reader's attention. I won't worry too much about grammar, spelling, and punctuation because I'll go back and fix any errors later. Time to get started!

[DRAFT]

A Sticky Situation Solved
By Ashley

"I can't believe I won't be going on my own eight-grade school trip," sighed Sage. "I've waited all year to go to Washington, d.c., and now...well, now everyones going without me!"

[used strong verbs]

Sage quietly hung up the phone and silently sobbed into her pillow. She had been talking with her best friend, Lee, but hated to let anyone hear her cry. Plus, her mom had no idea how sad she was over having to miss the end-of-the-year trip, and Sage wanted to keep it that way. After all, it wasn't her mom's that Grandma got sick and needed them to stay near her in Ohio until she got better. This had caused Sage to miss a lot of school, along with all the fund raising for the trip. Now she didn't have enough money to pay her way to Washington.

Reflect

What do you think? How well did Ashley use specific language to "show" rather than just tell her readers what she means?

Apply

Write a draft using your Story Frame as a guide. Don't worry about spelling or grammar just yet.

Revise

Focus on **Ideas**

The Rubric Says The plot and the conflict are clear. The resolution satisfies and solves the character's central problem.

Writing Strategy Include details that develop and resolve the plot.

After reviewing the rubric, I started thinking my resolution needed some work—something more. The rubric says the resolution should satisfy the reader and solve the character's central problem. The way I ended my draft just doesn't seem satisfying. There are loose ends that need to be tied up and a few questions that need to be answered. But I don't want to just give the answers; that would be boring. So I wrote a few paragraphs, adding details and dialogue to fully resolve the plot. What do you think?

[DRAFT]

Sage had earned more than enough money to pay for the class

trip. She had so much extra, in fact, that she asked her teacher,

Mr. Barnaby, if he could donate the surpluss to another student

who might also be missing the trip due to lack of funds.

"Sage, that's really kind of you! I do know of someone who needs money to go on the trip. Can I tell him who donated the money, so he can thank you?" Mr. Barnaby asked.

"Please don't. I'm just so happy I'll get to see Washington after all. One thing I never want to see again, though, is a roll of duct tape. Anything but that!"

[added details to develop and resolve the plot]

Apply

Include details or use dialogue to clearly define the plot and conflict as well as to create a satisfying resolution.

Revise

The Rubric Says | The story is well organized. Events unfold naturally and logically and are well paced to build tension.

Writing Strategy | Follow the Story Frame to organize events.

I want my readers to be able to follow the events in my story. If I follow the Story Frame, the story elements will fall into place and unfold naturally. In a well-written story, the tension builds all the way to the climax and decreases in the resolution.

> ### Writer's Term
>
> **Story Elements**
> **Rising Action:** Events occur to build tension and bring the protagonist and conflict together.
> **Climax:** The protagonist is face to face with the conflict. Tension is the highest.
> **Resolution:** The protagonist has overcome the conflict or challenge.

[DRAFT]

[used logical sequence of events to help build tension]

"There's one thing, though. I need you to bring me a little money so I can grab some dinner between shifts, OK?"

"No problem! I'll be right there"

Sage grabbed her key and her purse, locked the door behind her, and jogged the three blocks to the nursing home. She made her way to the nurses station and waited for her mother. As Sage stood at the counter, another nurse looked down at Sage's purse and widened her eyes. "Where'd you get that purse, Sage?" she asked. "I absolutely *love* it! Is that made of duct tape?"

Reflect

How would Ashley's story have been affected if she hadn't followed her Story Frame?

Apply

Follow your Story Frame to keep your story's events in a logical order.

Revise

Focus on **Sentence Fluency**

The Rubric Says   The sentences vary in length. Fragments are used creatively and effectively.

Writing Strategy   Experiment with sentence fragments.

I was a little surprised to read in the rubric that using fragments creatively was encouraged. Normally, fragments are incomplete sentences that need to be fixed! But real life dialogue *does* include fragments, so I'll use some to really bring my characters to life. I'll just be sure the fragments make sense so my reader isn't confused.

[DRAFT]

"I wish, but she can't," Sage replied. "I wish I could get a job! Then I could earn the money myself and still make the trip. Sometimes, I hate being 13!"

[used fragment effectively]
Well...homework...

"Yeah, me too." Lee paused. "I'd better hang up. But if I think of anything, I'll let you know. Sage—this trip won't be as fun without you."

Apply

Use a variety of sentence lengths for flow. Include a few fragments to creatively enhance a scene or dialogue.

Edit

The Rubric Says   The writing has been carefully edited. Pronouns are clear and used correctly.

Writing Strategy   Check the use of subject, object, and indefinite pronouns.

Writer's Term

Pronouns

A **subject pronoun** acts as the subject of a sentence.

An **object pronoun** replaces a direct or indirect object.

Indefinite pronouns (**someone, everybody**) do not take the place of nouns; they are used as nouns.

Time to edit! I'll carefully review my short story and fix any spelling, punctuation, and capitalization errors I find. I'll check my pronouns, too. Pronouns help create variety, but if used incorrectly, they only confuse the reader.

[DRAFT]

[used correct subject pronoun]

"Sage, I've been asked to work a double shift. Normally, you know I'd never do this...it's too long to leave you alone, but ~~us~~ we really could use the money. How do you feel about it? You know you can call Mrs. Mills downstairs if you need anything, right?"

Reflect

Were you able to find any spelling, grammar, or capitalization mistakes that Ashley missed?

Apply Conventions

Check your draft for spelling, punctuation, and capitalization. Be sure you've used all subject, object, and indefinite pronouns correctly.

For more practice using subject, object, and indefinite pronouns, use the exercises on the next two pages.

Subject and Object Pronouns

Know the Rule

Subject pronouns (*I, you, he, she, it, we, they*) can be used before an action verb. They act as the subject of a sentence.

> **Examples: I** am going to see the new dance movie with Nick and Kavitha.
> **They** have already seen the movie, but **they** liked it a lot.

Object pronouns (*me, you, it, him, her, us, them*) can be used after an action verb or a preposition. They are the object of the verb or preposition.

> **Examples:** Meet **me** at the theater at 7 P.M.
> Look for **us** near the concession stand.

Practice the Rule

Copy the following sentences on a separate sheet of paper. Fill in the blanks with the correct subject or object pronoun.

1. My best friend, Erika, and I are leaving for the movies now. _____ have waited for months for opening night.

2. I think Stephen is coming with _____ to see the movie.

3. I know _____ has been looking forward to seeing it as much as _____ have.

4. This will probably be the most popular movie of the summer; everyone has been talking about _____.

5. My mother will drive _____ to the theater.

6. After the movie, we'll meet Marie and Ben for ice cream. Do _____ want to join us?

7. I haven't seen those two in a while; I'm looking forward to getting together with _____.

8. After we've had ice cream, Erika will call her mother so that _____ can drive us home.

9. Of course, I'll thank _____ for the ride.

10. I'm really excited; this is going to be a fun evening for _____.

Indefinite Pronouns

Know the Rule

> **Indefinite pronouns** name individuals or groups that are not named by specific nouns. Unlike other pronouns, an indefinite pronoun does not take the place of or refer to a noun. Instead, it functions as a noun itself. Some indefinite pronouns always take a singular verb. Common indefinite pronouns are *anyone, anybody, everyone, everybody, someone, somebody, no one, nothing, either, neither.*
>
> **Examples:** Has **anyone** seen my blue sweatshirt?
>
> Some pronouns (*all, any, some, none*) are singular or plural, depending on how they are used in the sentence.
>
> **Examples: All** is quiet tonight.
> I have nine cousins. **All** live in Florida.

Practice the Rule

Copy the following sentences onto a separate sheet of paper. Choose the correct indefinite pronoun from above to complete each sentence.

1. _____ heard the cat crying, so it spent the night outside in the rain.

2. I don't want a single friend to miss out on the fun, so _____ is invited.

3. Mr. Baxter told the class that making lollipops was so easy, _____could do it.

4. _____ can fill in for Misha, as both have already memorized the lines.

5. So many wish for fame and money, but _____ can bring a person true happiness.

6. Hundreds of runners begin the marathon; however, only _____ will cross the finish line.

7. Because I forgot to put stamps on my postcards, _____ were delivered.

8. The Millers needed so much help after the flood, _____ came and helped clean up.

9. Father doesn't care who does it, but _____ better clean up the dishes after dinner!

10. _____ has the power to make another person smile; a kind word costs nothing and is such an easy thing to give.

Publish

✚ Presentation

Publishing Strategy   Send your short story to a magazine.

Presentation Strategy   Don't crowd the text.

I did it—I wrote a short story! I'm so proud of my work that I've decided to submit my story to a literary magazine. The school librarian can help me find magazines that publish students' fiction, and my teacher offered to help me write a cover letter to the magazine's editor. I'll be sure to neatly type my story using a legible font. I'll also use plenty of white space around and between the lines of text to keep things easy to read. But first, I'll read the story one last time to make sure I've done everything on my final checklist.

My Final Checklist

Did I—

✔ correctly use subject and object pronouns?

✔ use the correct indefinite pronouns?

✔ neatly type my story and number each page?

✔ use white space effectively?

✔ check my spelling, grammar, punctuation, and capitalization?

Apply

Make a checklist to check your short story. Then make a final copy to publish.

A Sticky Situation Solved

By Ashley

"I can't believe I won't be going on my own eighth-grade school trip," sighed Sage. "I've waited all year to see the cherry trees of Washington, D.C. in bloom, and now…well, now everyone's going without me!"

Sage quietly hung up the phone and silently sobbed into her pillow. She had been talking with her best friend, Lee, but hated to let anyone hear her cry. Plus, her mother had no idea how sad she was over having to miss the end-of-the-year trip, and Sage wanted to keep it that way. After all, it wasn't her mom's fault that Grandma got sick and needed them to stay near her in Ohio until she got better. This had caused Sage to miss a lot of school, along with all the fund raising for the trip. Now she didn't have enough money to pay her way to Washington.

"Sage, honey…I'm leaving in ten minutes," her mother called. "Come to the kitchen and let me walk you through dinner."

Sage got up and tried to dry her eyes. She smoothed her hair, took a deep breath, and walked to the kitchen.

"Dinner is chicken soup," her mother began. "I made it this morning, so you just need to heat it up. Hey! What's the matter, honey?"

"Nothing," said Sage. "Nothing's wrong...honest. I think I might have allergies or something. I just heat up the soup, right?"

"Yes, reheat what you want; I'll fix mine when I get home." Sage nodded and tried to force a smile.

"OK. Have a great night, Mom." And her mother left the apartment to head for the nursing home three blocks away.

A bit later, Lee called again. "Sage, are you sure you can't find $300 for the trip? Maybe your grandmother can lend you the money?"

"I wish, but she can't," Sage replied. "I wish I could get a job! Then I could earn the money myself and still make the trip. Sometimes, I hate being 13!"

"Yeah, me too." Lee paused. "Well…homework…I'd better hang up. But if I think of anything, I'll let you know. Sage—this trip won't be as fun without you."

Sage fought back the tears. She stood a few moments by the phone before turning her attention to the stack of books on the table.

Just as she was getting settled in with her American history chapter, the phone rang again. This time, it was her mother.

"Sage, I've been asked to work a double shift. Normally, you know I'd never do this…it's too long to leave you alone, but we really could use the money. How do you feel about it? You know you can call on Mrs. Mills downstairs if you needed anything, right?"

"It's fine, Mom. I'm just about to settle in with a book."

"There's one thing, though. I need you to bring me a little money so I can grab some dinner in between shifts, OK?"

"No problem! I'll be right there."

Sage grabbed her key and her purse, locked the door behind her, and jogged the three blocks to the nursing home. She made her way to the nurses' station and waited for her mother. As Sage stood at the counter, another nurse looked down at Sage's purse and widened her eyes. "Where'd you get that purse, Sage?" she asked. "I absolutely *love* it! Is that made of duct tape?"

"Yeah, thanks. I made it myself."

"Wow! Hey—if I paid you, say $15, could you make me one, too?"

"Sure! That'd be great! I could have one ready for you tomorrow."

Soon other nurses heard about Sage's unique purse, and by the time she left the building, Sage had twenty orders. "I can't believe it! I might actually be able to earn enough money for the school trip!" She ran home to share her good news with Lee.

The girls worked all weekend. They made clutch purses, over-the-shoulder bags, and larger purses. Roll after roll of tape was used, and after two and a half days of hard work, they had a pile of almost 40 purses to sell!

"Well, my hands ache and I'm exhausted, but you're coming on the trip! That makes it all worthwhile," exclaimed a jubilant Lee. "You did it, Sage! You raised the money on your own!"

"*We* did it, Lee," reminded Sage. "I never, *ever* could have done all this in a weekend without you. You're such a great friend. Thanks."

Sage had earned more than enough money to pay for the class trip. She had so much extra, in fact, that she asked her teacher, Mr. Barnaby, if he could quietly donate the surplus to another student who might also be missing the trip due to lack of funds.

"Sage, that's really kind of you! I do know of someone who needs money to go on the trip. Can I tell him who donated the money, so he can thank you?" Mr. Barnaby asked.

"Please don't. I'm just so happy I'll get to see Washington after all. One thing I never want to see again, though, is a roll of duct tape. Anything but that!"

Reflect

How did Ashley do? Did she use all the traits of a good short story in her writing? Check it against the rubric. Don't forget to use the rubric to check your own short story!

Narrative test writing

Read the Writing Prompt

I know that every writing test starts with a writing prompt. Most writing prompts have three parts:

Setup This part of the writing prompt gives you the background information you need to get ready to write.

Task This part of the writing prompt tells you exactly what you are supposed to write: a personal memoir.

Scoring Guide This section tells how your writing will be scored. To do well on the test, you should include everything on the list.

R emember the rubrics you've been using? When you take a writing test, you don't always have all of the information that's on a rubric. But the scoring guide is a lot like a rubric. It lists everything you need to think about to write a good paper. Like the rubrics you've used, many scoring guides are based on the six important traits of writing:

Think about a time when you helped another person or people in some way.

Write a personal memoir about that experience.

Be sure your writing

- has a clear topic and uses narrative techniques, such as dialogue and description, to develop the events.

- is well organized and uses transitions to make the sequence of events clear.

- uses a voice that reflects the purpose.

- has precise, concrete words.

- includes prepositional phrases for sentence variety.

- contains correct grammar, punctuation, capitalization, and spelling.

Writing Traits
in the Scoring Guide

Look at the scoring guide in the writing prompt on page 99. Not every writing prompt will include all six writing traits, but this one does. The chart below can help you better understand the connection between the scoring guide and the writing traits in the rubrics you've been using.

 **Ideas**
- Be sure your writing has a clear topic and uses narrative techniques, such as dialogue and description, to develop the events.

 **Organization**
- Be sure your writing is well organized and uses transitions to make the sequence of events clear.

 **Voice**
- Be sure your voice reflects the purpose of your writing.

 **Word Choice**
- Be sure your writing has precise, concrete words.

 **Sentence Fluency**
- Be sure your writing includes prepositional phrases for sentence variety.

 **Conventions**
- Be sure your writing contains correct grammar, punctuation, capitalization, and spelling.

Look at Eric Weismann's story on the next page. Did he follow the scoring guide?

A New Face

by Eric Weismann

"Students, I'd like to introduce you to Andrew Mancini," said our teacher, Ms. Kennedy, one morning as we began class.

It was midway through my eighth grade year at South Lincoln, and it seemed weird to me that we were getting a new student at this time of year. I wondered how Andrew felt. He was a tall, gangly kid, with a thick mop of brown hair that fell across his eyes. He wore clothes that were too small, showing his sharp wrists and bony ankles. His sneakers looked like they came straight from a garage sale. When Ms. Kennedy introduced him, he half smiled and looked down at his desk.

That first day at school, I noticed that Andrew was really quiet and wasn't very happy. He kept chewing on his pencil and looking out the window. At lunchtime, he sat all by himself. I felt really bad for him. Did he want to be by himself, or did he think that no one wanted to hang out with him? I wanted to say something, but I wasn't sure how to approach him.

That night, I told my parents about Andrew. "It has to be hard to start all over again in a new school, making friends and finding your way around," my mom said, "especially when everyone around you already knows one another."

My dad suggested that I introduce Andrew to some of my friends. "Just start out by saying hello to him," he said. "Ask him if he likes to play basketball."

The next day, I made a point of saying hello to Andrew first thing in the morning. "Did you and your family just move to the area?" I asked him.

Andrew perked up a bit. "Yeah, my dad got transferred here from California."

"Well, I think you'll like it here," I told him. "You want to meet my friends?"

"Yeah!" he said.

At lunch, he sat with my friends and me. We all found out that we had a lot in common.

"Hey," he said, "do you guys like to play basketball?"

"Of course," I said.

He laughed. "You know, maybe this new school isn't so bad after all."

Using the Scoring Guide to Study the Model

Let's use the scoring guide to check Eric's writing test, "A New Face." How well does his essay meet each of the six writing traits?

- **The writing has a clear topic and uses narrative techniques, such as dialogue and description, to develop the events.**

Eric gets me interested with details about Andrew. I can visualize what Andrew looked like and imagine how he must have felt.

> He was a tall, gangly kid, with a thick mop of brown hair that fell across his eyes. He wore clothes that were too small, showing his sharp wrists and bony ankles. His sneakers looked like they came straight from a garage sale. When Ms. Kennedy introduced him, he half smiled and looked down at his desk.

- **The story is well organized and establishes a sequence of events that is clear and easy to follow.**
- **The writer uses a variety of transitions to clarify the sequence of events.**

Eric tells the story in a logical order. He uses transitional phrases (underlined below) to tell the reader how much time passes between one event and the next. Here is an example.

> <u>That first day at school</u>, I noticed that Andrew was really quiet and wasn't very happy. He kept chewing on his pencil and looking out the window. <u>At lunchtime</u>, he sat all by himself. I felt really bad for him. Did he want to be by himself, or did he think that no one wanted to hang out with him? I wanted to say something, but I wasn't sure how to approach him.

Voice

- **The voice reflects the purpose of the writing.**

Eric uses first-person point of view and a serious yet friendly tone in his writing. His voice is appropriate for the purpose, which is to write a memoir about the time he helped someone.

My dad suggested that I introduce Andrew to some of my friends. "Just start out by saying hello to him," he said. "Ask him if he likes to play basketball."

The next day, I made a point of saying hello to Andrew first thing in the morning. "Did you and your family just move to the area?" I asked him.

Word Choice

- **The writing has precise, concrete words.**

Eric uses well-chosen language to tell his story. Words such as *gangly, sharp, bony,* and *garage sale* are precise and concrete. They make Eric's description vivid and interesting to read.

He was a tall, gangly kid, with a thick mop of brown hair that fell across his eyes. He wore clothes that were too small, showing his sharp wrists and bony ankles. His sneakers looked like they came straight from a garage sale. When Ms. Kennedy introduced him, he half smiled and looked down at his desk.

Using the Scoring Guide to Study the Model

Sentence Fluency

- **The writing includes prepositional phrases for sentence variety.**

Eric uses a variety of sentence patterns. He avoids repetition by starting some of his sentences with a prepositional phrase. He also includes complex sentences. Here's an example.

At lunch, he sat with my friends and me. We all found out that we had a lot in common.

Conventions

- **The writing contains correct grammar, punctuation, capitalization, and spelling.**

It looks like Eric spelled all words correctly and used the right punctuation. Don't forget to check for mistakes in your own work. For example, if you know you often forget to capitalize proper nouns, you should pay close attention to capitalization. Editing for grammar and mechanics at every step of the writing process will help you avoid errors on your final test.

Planning My Time

Before giving us a writing prompt, my teacher always tells us how much time we'll have to complete the test. Since I know the steps of the writing process, I can think about how much time I'll need for each step. Then I'll be sure to have enough time to do everything I need. If the test takes an hour, here's how I can organize my time. Planning your time will help you, too!

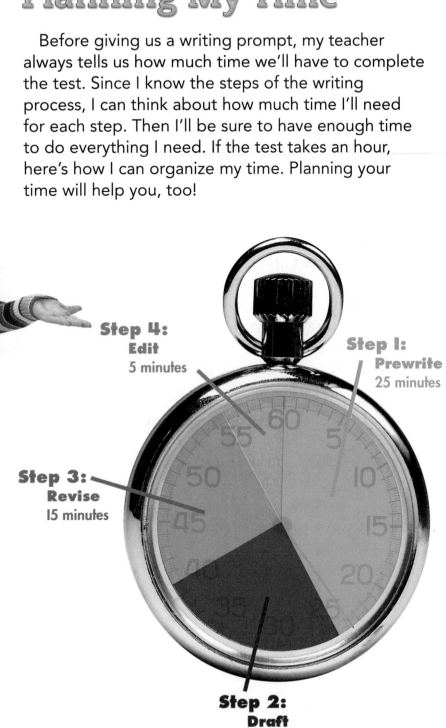

Step 4:
Edit
5 minutes

Step 1:
Prewrite
25 minutes

Step 3:
Revise
15 minutes

Step 2:
Draft
15 minutes

Prewrite

Focus on **Ideas**

Writing Strategy **Study the writing prompt to find out what to do.**

The first thing I do is study my writing prompt, so I'll know exactly what I'm supposed to do. Usually, a writing prompt has three parts, but the parts aren't always labeled. Look for the setup, task, and scoring guide in your writing prompt, just like I did on mine below. Then label each part and circle key words in the setup and the task that tell what kind of writing you need to do and who your audience will be. I circled my topic in purple, and what kind of writing I'll be doing (a memoir) in red. The writing prompt doesn't say who the audience is, so I'll write for my teacher.

My Writing Test Prompt

Setup — Have you ever had an experience where the outcome was not what you expected it to be?

Task — Write a memoir about an experience that turned out differently than what you expected.

Scoring Guide — Be sure your writing

- has a clear topic and uses narrative techniques, such as dialogue and description, to develop the events.

- is well organized and establishes a sequence of events that is clear and easy to follow.

- uses a variety of transition words to clarify the sequence of events.

- uses a voice that reflects the purpose.

- has precise, concrete words.

- includes prepositional phrases for sentence variety.

- contains correct grammar, punctuation, capitalization, and spelling.

Think about how the scoring guide relates to the six writing traits in the rubrics you've studied. Not all of the traits will be included in every scoring guide, but you need to remember all of them to write a good essay.

- **Be sure your writing has a clear topic and uses narrative techniques, such as dialogue and description, to develop the events.**

I want to grab the reader's interest right away, so I'll be sure to include plenty of descriptive details.

- **Be sure your writing is well organized and uses transitions to make the sequence of events clear.**

I want my reader to be able to follow the story, so I'll make sure the way I organize my memoir makes sense.

- **Be sure your voice reflects the purpose of your writing.**

I will be sure to write with a voice that appropriately reflects the purpose and subject matter of my writing.

- **Be sure your writing has precise, concrete words.**

I need to be sure that my words are precise and easy to understand. They should clearly describe my topic.

- **Be sure your writing includes prepositional phrases for sentence variety.**

I can add life to my writing by using different kinds of sentences. Prepositional phrases will help make my sentences flow.

- **Be sure your writing contains correct grammar, punctuation, capitalization, and spelling.**

I should always remember to check my grammar and mechanics anytime I write.

Prewrite

Focus on **Ideas**

Writing Strategy   Respond to the task.

Writers always gather information before they begin writing. When you write to take a test, you can find a lot of information in the writing prompt. Let's take another look at the task, since this is the part of the writing prompt that explains what I'm supposed to write. Remember there's not much time! That's why it's really important to think about how you'll respond before you begin to write.

I see that first I have to come up with a time when an experience turned out differently than I expected. I recently took a surprising visit to a nursing home, so I'll jot down some notes about it.

Task — Write a memoir about an experience that turned out differently than what you expected.

Notes

✔ I went to Green Oaks Retirement Home.

✔ I did crafts with the residents.

Apply

Think about how you'll respond to the task part of your writing prompt before you begin to write. Then jot down some notes to help you gather information.

Prewrite

Writing Strategy Choose a graphic organizer.

I don't have a lot of time, so I'll begin organizing my ideas right away. I'll start by choosing a graphic organizer. I'm writing my memoir in chronological order, so I'll use a Story Frame to help me record story events.

Setting	Green Oaks Retirement Home, a local nursing home
Introduction	supposed to do a community service project at Green Oaks and wasn't happy about it
Rising Action (Event 1)	director took me to room; people waiting seemed bored
Rising Action (Event 2)	director introduced me
Rising Action (Event 3)	residents started making necklaces
Climax	residents started having a good time
Falling Action (Event 1)	helped Mrs. Fields find pretty beads
Falling Action (Event 2)	Rose did a great job
Falling Action (Event 3)	residents were pleased; probably lonely and enjoyed the company
Falling Action (Event 4)	residents thanked me and invited me back
Resolution	visit Green Oaks once a month

Reflect

How can including details in your graphic organizer help you when you begin to write?

Apply

Choose a graphic organizer that's appropriate for the type of essay you are writing.

Prewrite

Focus on **Organization**

Writing Strategy Check the graphic organizer against the scoring guide.

In a test, there's usually not much time to revise, so that makes prewriting more important than ever! Before I get started, I'll check my Story Frame against the scoring guide in the writing prompt.

Setting	Green Oaks Retirement Home, a local nursing home
Introduction	supposed to do a community service project at Green Oaks and wasn't happy about it
Rising Action (Event 1)	director took me to room; people waiting seemed bored
Rising Action (Event 2)	director introduced me
Rising Action (Event 3)	residents started making necklaces
Climax	residents started having a good time
Falling Action (Event 1)	helped Mrs. Fields find pretty beads
Falling Action (Event 2)	Rose did a great job
Falling Action (Event 3)	residents were pleased; probably lonely and enjoyed the company
Falling Action (Event 4)	residents thanked me and invited me back
Resolution	visit Green Oaks once a month

- Be sure your writing has a clear topic and uses narrative techniques, such as dialogue and description, to develop the events.

In my Story Frame, I made clear statements about my topic and included details.

- Be sure your writing is well organized and uses transitions to make the sequence of events clear.

I'll use the introduction from my Story Frame. Then, I'll use the details from the other boxes as they are already in chronological order.

- Be sure your voice reflects the purpose of your writing.

I will use first-person point of view.

- Be sure your writing has precise, concrete words.

I'll use clear and accurate words to describe the events listed in my Story Frame.

- Be sure your writing includes prepositional phrases for sentence variety.

I'll need to remember to do this as I write.

- Be sure your writing contains correct grammar, punctuation, capitalization, and spelling.

I'll edit for proper grammar and mechanics after I write my memoir.

Reflect

Check your graphic organizer against the scoring guide. How did you do? If you forgot a point, go back and include it now.

Apply

Before you start to write, reread the scoring guide in the writing prompt to be sure you know what to do.

Draft

Focus on **Ideas**

Writing Strategy Engage the reader with relevant, descriptive details.

My Story Frame already includes some interesting details that will help make my memoir exciting. But I checked it one more time to see if there were any more details that I wanted to add to my draft. I thought of some things I'd like to include while writing. Take a look at my draft.

Getting Crafty
by Ashley   [added relevant details]

Doing crafts at a nursery home was not how I wanted to spend my Saturday but I had made a committment to visit the Green Oaks Retirement Home as part of my school community service project. And I wasn't too happy about it!

The director, Ms. Hill, led me into a room where some of the ederly residents were sitting. Almost all of them were women in wheelchairs, and they seemed pretty bored, too!

Ms. Hill introduced me.

One lady told me I had a pretty name and I thanked her.

Ms. Hill said the lady, Rose, could no longer see. I wondered how

Proofreading Marks

⌐ Indent   ℓ Take out something
≡ Make uppercase ⊙ Add a period
/ Make lowercase ⊬ New paragraph
∧ Add something   ⓢⓟ Spelling error

she'd be able to do a craft. I thought I was wasting my time!

I told the ladies we were going to be making beaded necklaces. I tied the ends for them and set them out in front of them. I told them it was easy and showed them how to get started. I could tell they started to have a good time.

One woman, Mrs. Fields, asked, "Ashley, which do you think would look prettiest? I showed her a few beads that I thought would look good on her necklace.   **[added descriptive details]**

I noticed that even Rose was doing a great job using her hands to feel for beads and string them on.

When we finished, some of the residents were pretty pleased with their necklaces. Everyone seemed to be in a better mood. They were probably lonely there. Liked to have people come and visit.

They told me thanks and asked if I'd come again. I was happy to have brightened their day, and I promised I'd be back soon.

Now, I visit the green oaks retirement home once a month, and I always look forward to going!

Reflect

What do you think about Ashley's details? Will they keep her readers interested?

Apply

Read your draft. Make sure all your details are relevant and descriptive.

Revise

 **Focus on Organization**

Writing Strategy   Use transition words to show the sequence of events.

Now that I have written my draft, I'll read it over to see how I did. The scoring guide says to make sure the sequence of events is clear and easy to follow. I can use transitions, such as *first, next, before breakfast,* and *later on,* to do this. Looking at my draft, I found a few places where adding transitions could make the sequence clearer.

[DRAFT] ⟶ **[added transitions]**

When I arrived,

The director, Ms. Hill, led me into a room where some of the ederly residents were sitting. Almost all of them were women in wheelchairs, and they seemed pretty bored, too!

Apply

Use transition words, phrases, and clauses in your memoir to guide your readers through the action.

Revise

Focus on **Voice**

Writing Strategy Use first-person point of view.

I'll read my draft again to see if there are any places that need to be stronger. The scoring guide says my voice should reflect the purpose of my writing. Using first-person allows me to share my personal thoughts and feelings with the reader.

As I read, I noticed a place where I could be clearer about my personal thoughts. I'll add some words to make it better.

[DRAFT]

———[used first-person]———

than when I had first arrived—even me! I realized that Everyone seemed to be in a much better mood. They were

probably lonely there.

Reflect

How does using first-person point of view help Ashley connect with her readers?

Apply

Use first-person point of view in your memoir.

Revise

Writing Strategy   Use precise, concrete words.

I'll read my paper again to see if any parts could be more precise. The scoring guide says that I should use precise, concrete words to explain my story, and I see some places where I can do this.

The paragraph about beading the necklaces seems a little confusing. I'll change some words to make them more concrete.

[DRAFT]

—————————————————[used precise, concrete words]———————————————

▼ I told the ladies we were going to be making beaded necklaces.

of each of the residents' strings   out beads ◄

I tied the ends ~~for them~~ and set ~~them out~~ in front of them. I told

them it was easy and showed them how to get started. I could tell

they started to have a good time.

Apply

Replace vague words with precise, concrete vocabulary.

Edit

Writing Strategy   Check grammar, punctuation, capitalization, and spelling.

There's just one last step! The scoring guide says to use correct grammar and mechanics. I always leave plenty of time to check for errors in these important areas!

Getting Crafty

by Ashley

Doing crafts at a ~~nursery~~ _{nursing} home was not how I wanted to spend my Saturday, but I had made a ~~committment~~ commitment to visit the Green Oaks Retirement Home as part of my school community service project. And I wasn't too happy about it!

When I arrived, The director, Ms. Hill, led me into a room where some of the ~~ederly~~ elderly residents were sitting. Almost all of them were women in wheelchairs, and they seemed pretty bored, too!

Ms. Hill introduced me. "Ashley," said one lady. "What a pretty name." "Thanks," I mumbled.

~~One lady told me I had a pretty name and I thanked her.~~

Ms. Hill said the lady, Rose, could no longer see. I wondered how she'd be able to do a craft. I thought I was wasting my time!

Apply

Check your grammar, punctuation, capitalization, and spelling every time you write for a test.

[FINAL DRAFT]

I told the ladies we were going to be making beaded necklaces. I tied the ends of each of the residents' strings and set out beads in front of them. I told them it was easy and showed them how to get started. I could tell they started to have a good time.

One woman, Mrs. Fields, asked, "Ashley, which do you think would look prettiest?" I showed her a few beads that I thought would look good on her necklace.

I noticed that even Rose was doing a great job using her hands to feel for beads and string them on.

When we finished, some of the residents were pretty pleased with their necklaces. Everyone seemed to be in a much better mood than when I had first arrived—even me! I realized that they were probably lonely there, *and* Liked to have people come and visit. *Before I left,* They told me thanks and asked if I'd come again. I was happy to have brightened their day, and I promised I'd be back soon.

Now, I visit the green oaks retirement home once a month, and I always look forward to going!

Reflect

Is Ashley's writing missing anything? Use the writing prompt's scoring guide to check her writing. Remember to check your writing against the scoring guide, too!

I'm finished! You just have to remember to use the writing process when you take a writing test. The process is a little different for a test, but you'll do fine as long as you remember these important tips.

TEST TIPS

1. **Study the writing prompt before you start to write.** Most writing prompts have three parts: the setup, the task, and the scoring guide. The parts probably won't be labeled. You'll have to figure them out for yourself!

2. **Make sure you understand the task before you start to write.**

   - Read all three parts of the writing prompt carefully.

   - Circle key words in the task part of the writing prompt that tell what kind of writing you need to do. The task might also identify your audience.

   - Make sure you know how you'll be graded.

   - Say the assignment in your own words to yourself.

3. **Keep an eye on the clock.** Decide how much time you will spend on each part of the writing process and try to stick to your schedule. Don't spend so much time prewriting that you don't have enough time left to write.

4. **Reread your writing. Check it against the scoring guide at least twice.** Remember the rubrics you've used? A scoring guide on a writing test is just like a rubric. It can help you keep what's important in mind.

5. **Plan, plan, plan!** You don't get much time to revise during a test, so planning is more important than ever.

6. **Write neatly.** Remember: If the people who score your test can't read your writing, it doesn't matter how good your essay is!

Informative/ Explanatory

writing explains something to the reader.

H i, I'm Briana. In school, I'm studying informative/explanatory writing. I think this will really help me because sometimes when I try to explain something, the information just doesn't come out right. I often skip over important details because I'm so excited about what I have to say. But I think studying informative/ explanatory writing will teach me to organize my ideas.

IN THIS UNIT

- ☐ **Response to Literature**
- ☐ **Research Report**
- ☐ **How-To Guide: Instructional Text**
- **MATH CONNECTION** ▶ **Explanatory Essay**
- ☐ **Writing for a Test**

Name: Briana
Home: Michigan
Interests: ballet dancing,
caring for animals,
horseback riding,
astronomy
Favorite Book: *The Star Fisher*
by Laurence Yep
Favorite Food: sushi

What's a **Response to Literature?**

It's an opportunity to respond to a book that I have read. I will be writing a book report because I can say what I really think about the book—just like a real book reviewer.

What's in a **Response to Literature?**

Summary
To understand my report, readers will need to know something about the book. I'll include a short summary that contains just the right amount of background information.

Details
Details are facts, examples, and quotations from the source. I'll share concrete details from my book so my reader will understand my response.

Response
The purpose of my book report is to let readers know what I think about a book. My response will include details that support my recommendation.

Quotations
I'll include short quotations from the book. I can paraphrase (use my own words) for longer ones.

Why write a Response to Literature?

There are many different reasons to respond to literature. I wrote several of them here. Take a look!

To Entertain

A response to literature doesn't have to be boring! If I really like a book, then I want to share my feelings with the audience. I can do this by writing in an entertaining—yet informative—style.

To Inform

The main reason for writing a response to literature is to inform the audience about a book. A response to literature must include a summary of the book and details to support the writer's statements about the book.

To Influence

A writer might feel strongly about a particular book. If so, he or she can influence people to either read the book or avoid it.

To Compare and Contrast

A particular book might be similar to other books in style, plot, characters, and/or theme. Or one book might be totally different from others that are written by the same author. Comparing and contrasting books is one purpose for writing a response to literature.

Linking Informative/Explanatory Writing Traits to a **Response to Literature**

In this chapter, you will summarize and tell about a book you have read. This type of informative/explanatory writing is called a response to literature. Briana will guide you through the stages of the writing process: Prewrite, Draft, Revise, Edit, and Publish. In each stage, Briana will show you important writing strategies that are linked to the Informative/Explanatory writing traits below.

Informative/Explanatory Writing Traits

Ideas
- a clear, focused topic
- concrete, relevant facts, definitions, and details that support and develop the topic

Organization
- information that is organized into an attention-grabbing introduction, an informative body, and a conclusion that supports the information or explanation presented
- transitions that connect ideas and clarify relationships

Voice
- a voice and tone that are appropriate for the purpose and audience

Word Choice
- language that is precise and concise
- domain-specific vocabulary that is explained as necessary

Sentence Fluency
- clear sentences that vary in length and structure

Conventions
- no or few errors in grammar, usage, mechanics, and spelling

Before you write, read Lizzie Webber's book report on the next page. Then use the response to literature rubric on pages 126–127 to decide how well she did. (You might want to look back at What's in a Response to Literature? on page 122, too!)

King of Shadows

A book report by Lizzie Webber

Summary

I would like to tell you about a really interesting book. *King of Shadows* was written by Newbery winner Susan Cooper. The book is about a group of young American actors called the Company of Boys. They travel to London's new Globe Theatre to put on Shakespeare's play *A Midsummer Night's Dream*. One of the actors, Nathan Field, gets seriously ill. He falls asleep one night and awakens the next morning to find that he's still in London, only now the year is 1599. No longer acting in the Company of Boys, Nat is now in the Lord Chamberlain's Men, performing alongside William Shakespeare.

Several things appeal to me about this book. I like the way that Cooper seamlessly weaves fact and fiction together. Using the same play as the backdrop for both time periods, she moves Nat, as well as her readers, back and forth between the present and the past. For example, Nat is rehearsing to play Puck in the present, so he fits Puck's role in the past.

Examples

Cooper also changes the characters' speech from modern American English (in the present) to Elizabethan English (in the past). This clarifies when and where the action takes place.

But I have to admit that there were also times when I was frustrated by *King of Shadows*. For example, I didn't know until the very end why Nat had to go back to 1599. Once I knew, the whole story made perfect sense. I also didn't know why the author spent so much time on details that, at the time, seemed unimportant. For example, near the beginning of the book, Cooper takes a whole paragraph to describe a muscle twitch under Richard Burbage's left eye. When I got to the end of the book, however, I realized why that twitch was so important. That's when I realized that all of Cooper's details are intentional, right down to the names of the directors: Richard Burbage in the past, and Arby (RB), which stands for Richard Babbage, in the present.

Recommendation

Overall, I highly recommend *King of Shadows,* as I'm sure everyone will be delighted when the secret of the book is revealed.

Details

Response

Response

Rubric

Use the rubric to plan and score a response to literature.

	6	5	4
Ideas	A clear purpose and viewpoint are supported by relevant and well-chosen examples and concrete details.	A clear purpose and viewpoint are supported by several relevant examples.	The writing has a purpose and viewpoint, which are supported by some examples.
Organization	Responses are organized into broad categories. Varied transition words guide the reader through ideas and concepts.	Responses are organized into categories. Some transitions are used.	Responses are somewhat organized. An occasional transition word is used effectively.
Voice	Active voice enlivens the style and brings energy to the writing throughout the piece.	The writer's active voice often enlivens the style and brings energy to the writing.	The writer's voice is active in the beginning, but fades.
Word Choice	Precise language avoids wordiness or redundancy throughout.	The language is mostly clear and precise. Few unnecessary words are included.	The language is somewhat clear and precise. Some words could be deleted for clarity.
Sentence Fluency	A variety of sentence types works together to deliver information.	The writing has a variety of sentence types.	The writing has some variety of sentence types. Some spots need attention.
Conventions	Verbal phrases are clear and titles are written correctly.	There are a few errors with verbal phrases and titles, but they do not affect meaning.	There are some noticeable errors with verbal phrases and titles, which affect the meaning.

✚ Presentation Page numbers and footers help organize the response to literature.

3	2	1	
The purpose and viewpoint are vague, and examples are few or irrelevant.	The purpose and viewpoint are unclear, and there are few or no examples.	The purpose, viewpoint, and examples are missing from the writing.	**Ideas**
Responses are not well organized. Transition words do not move the text along smoothly.	Responses require work to read. The text order is confusing. Transition words do not move the text along smoothly.	Responses are missing. The writer has limited knowledge about the book. Transition words are missing.	**Organization**
Active voice comes and goes throughout the report.	The writing lacks active voice and energy.	The writing has no voice and is dull throughout the piece.	**Voice**
The language is mostly precise. Some wordiness or vague words could be problematic.	Some of the writing is unclear or too general. Too much redundancy affects the meaning.	Vague or wrong word choices take away from the writing. The writing doesn't make sense.	**Word Choice**
Sentences need to be read carefully. There is a lot of repetition.	The sentences are either too long or too short. There is little variety in sentence beginnings.	The writing is hard to read. Sentences are alike, incomplete, or incorrect.	**Sentence Fluency**
Several errors with verbal phrases and titles distract the reader from the meaning.	Errors with verbal phrases and titles jump out and affect the meaning. The reader must reread to make sense of the text.	Verbal phrases and titles contain many errors. The report is very difficult to read.	**Conventions**

See Appendix B for 4-, 5-, and 6-point informative/explanatory rubrics.

Using the Rubric to Study the Model

Response to Literature

Did you notice that the model on page 125 points out some key elements of a response to literature? As she wrote "King of Shadows," Lizzie Webber used these elements to help her explain what she thought of the book, *King of Shadows*. She also used the 6-point rubric on pages 126–127 to plan, draft, revise, and edit the writing. A rubric is a great tool to evaluate writing during the writing process.

Now let's use the same rubric to score the model. To do this, we'll focus on each trait separately, starting with Ideas. We'll use the top descriptor for each trait (column 6), along with examples from the model, to help us understand how the traits work together. How would you score Lizzie on each trait?

Ideas

- **A clear purpose and viewpoint are supported by relevant and well-chosen examples and concrete details.**

Lizzie clearly states her purpose in the first sentence of the lead paragraph. After a brief summary of the book, she then gives her viewpoint and uses several examples to support it.

[from the writing model]

Several things appeal to me about this book. I like the way that Cooper seamlessly weaves fact and fiction together. Using the same play as the backdrop for both time periods, she moves Nat, as well as her readers, back and forth between the present and the past. For example, Nat is rehearsing to play Puck in the present, so he fits Puck's role in the past.

Organization

- Responses are organized into broad categories.
- Varied transition words guide the reader through ideas and concepts.

Lizzie begins with important, broader points and works through to the lesser important points. She uses transition words, such as *for example*, to connect her ideas.

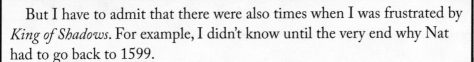

[from the writing model]

But I have to admit that there were also times when I was frustrated by *King of Shadows*. For example, I didn't know until the very end why Nat had to go back to 1599.

Voice

- Active voice enlivens the style and brings energy to the writing throughout the piece.

Lizzie uses active voice to state her opinions with strength and clarity. She avoids weaker passive sentences such as *A whole paragraph was used to describe . . . .*

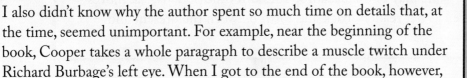

[from the writing model]

I also didn't know why the author spent so much time on details that, at the time, seemed unimportant. For example, near the beginning of the book, Cooper takes a whole paragraph to describe a muscle twitch under Richard Burbage's left eye. When I got to the end of the book, however, I realized why that twitch was so important.

Word Choice

- **Precise language avoids wordiness or redundancy throughout the piece.**

Lizzie uses precise, direct language to come right to the point. She does not clutter up her sentences with unnecessary or repetitive words.

[from the writing model]

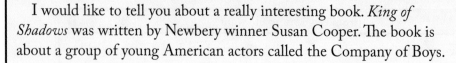

I would like to tell you about a really interesting book. *King of Shadows* was written by Newbery winner Susan Cooper. The book is about a group of young American actors called the Company of Boys.

Sentence Fluency

- **A variety of sentence types works together to deliver information.**

Lizzie mixes simple, declarative sentences with longer, more complex sentences. In this way, she keeps her writing lively and conveys important information to the reader.

[from the writing model]

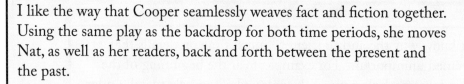

I like the way that Cooper seamlessly weaves fact and fiction together. Using the same play as the backdrop for both time periods, she moves Nat, as well as her readers, back and forth between the present and the past.

Conventions

- Verbal phrases are clear and titles are written correctly.

I know that a verbal is a verb form that acts like a noun, adjective, or adverb, and I appreciate how Lizzie uses verbal phrases to begin some of her sentences. Sometimes verbal phrases cause confusion in sentences, but Lizzie uses them clearly. Look at the following example in which the introductory verbal phrase, *No longer acting in the Company of Boys*, clearly describes the subject, Nat.

[from the writing model]

No longer acting in the Company of Boys, Nat is now in the Lord Chamberlain's Men, performing alongside William Shakespeare.

⁺Presentation Page numbers and footers help organize the response to literature.

My Turn!

I'm going to write a response to literature about a book I read recently. I'll follow the rubric and use good writing strategies. Read along to find out how I do it!

Prewrite

Focus on **Ideas**

The Rubric Says A clear purpose and viewpoint are supported by relevant and well-chosen examples and concrete details.

Writing Strategy Read a book on a topic of interest. Then list responses about the book.

When my teacher said to write a book report, the first thing I did was choose a book. I take ballet, and I absolutely love to dance. So I chose *Another Way to Dance* by Martha Southgate. After I finished reading, I looked back through the book and jotted down some things that I liked and disliked about it. I want to share what I think about the book, and putting my thoughts on paper is the first step. I put smiley faces next to the details I did like and frowns next to the details I did not like.

Another Way to Dance

☺ interesting and well-developed main characters

☹ the same things said too many times

☹ too much obsessing on Vicki's part

☺ very good/accurate descriptions of Vicki's ballet classes

☺ realistic feelings and actions toward Vicki's family members

☹ corny and overused ending

Apply

Choose a book to read. Then jot down notes about the things you liked and disliked.

Prewrite

The Rubric Says   Responses are organized into broad categories.

Writing Strategy   Make a Two-Column Chart to organize important details into categories.

Writer's Term

Two-Column Chart

A **Two-Column Chart** can help you organize details from the book under general or broad categories. List details under the categories in each column to support your response.

The rubric says my responses should be organized into broad categories, so I'll use a Two-Column Chart to list the details I liked and disliked by category. I'll put the most important category at the top of each column and work down from there.

Two-Column Chart

Like	Dislike
Topic	**Repetition**
very good/accurate descriptions of Vicki's ballet classes	the same things said too many times
Realistic Portrayal	**Weak Characterization**
realistic feelings and actions toward Vicki's family members	too much obsessing on Vicki's part
Main Characters	**Weak Ending**
interesting and well-developed main characters	corny and overused ending

Reflect

Is the Two-Column Chart clearly organized? How will it help Briana stay focused as she writes?

Apply

Organize your book report by making a Two-Column Chart that identifies categories and lists details by order of importance.

Draft

The Rubric Says   A clear purpose and viewpoint are supported by relevant and well-chosen examples and concrete details.

Writing Strategy   State the purpose so the reader will understand why the author is writing.

✎ Writer's Term

Purpose

Sometimes an author has more than one **purpose**. An author's purpose can include one or more of the following:
- to inform or explain
- to entertain or amuse
- to influence
- to compare and contrast

The reason I'm writing my book report is to tell the reader something about the book and to share my reactions. My purpose is to inform and explain my ideas about the book. I'll use my Two-Column Chart to help me organize the details I'll use in my draft.

According to the rubric, I need to have a clear purpose supported by relevant examples and concrete details. I'll choose details right out of the book to support my viewpoint. Of course, the reader needs to know which book I've read, so I'll begin by naming it.

I'll do my best to avoid grammar and spelling errors. But mainly, I just want to concentrate on getting my ideas down on paper. I can always go back later to proofread.

Proofreading Marks

⊐ Indent
≡ Make uppercase
／ Make lowercase
∧ Add something

ℓ Take out something
⊙ Add a period
⌗ New paragraph
ⓈⓅ Spelling error

[DRAFT]

Another Way to Dance

[title of book]

A book report by Briana

[purpose]

After reading <u>Another Way to Dance</u> by Martha Southgate, I had mixed feelings. I'd like to share some of them with you now. Having studied ballet myself, I found the premise of the book particularly interesting. A fourteen-year-old African American girl named Vicki is accepted into the summer dance program at the School of American Ballet in New York City. The book chronicles everything that happens to Vicki that summer. She experiences several things that help her mature, including an exciting first date and a devastating encounter with a racist schoolmate.

[summary]

In many ways, I think the author does a good job of describing Vicki and her experiences. As I read I could almost smell the dance studio, hear the music and activity, and feel my muscles straining to move along with Vicki's.

[details in book]

Reflect

How did Briana use the Two-Column Chart to write her draft?

Apply

Use your Two-Column Chart to help write your draft.

Revise

Focus on Organization

The Rubric Says   Varied transition words guide the reader through ideas and concepts.

Writing Strategy   Add transition words to illustrate or contrast ideas.

Writer's Term

Transitions

Transition words connect ideas and sentences in writing. Some transition words, such as **for example, specifically,** and **for instance,** indicate that the writer is going to offer further information. Other transition words, such as **however, nevertheless,** and **on one hand,** help contrast ideas.

The rubric says that I should use a variety of transition words to guide the reader through my ideas and concepts. I know that transition words help connect the ideas in my writing and clarify the relationships. I reread my draft and found a place where I could add a transition word to connect contrasting ideas.

[DRAFT]

Nevertheless

If you love ballet—and you really love Baryshinikov—*Another Way to Dance* is worth the read. But if you tend to get impatient with reading about the struggles of a confused and insecure adolescent, you might want to pass on this one. [added a transition word to connect contrasting ideas]

Apply

Use transition words to connect and clarify ideas in your book report.

Revise

Focus on Voice

The Rubric Says	Active voice enlivens the style and brings energy to the writing throughout the piece.
Writing Strategy	Change passive voice to active voice to make the report clearer.

Writer's Term

Active Voice/Passive Voice

If the subject of a sentence performs the action, the verb is in the **active voice**. If the subject is acted upon by something else, the verb is in the **passive voice**. Active voice adds strength and energy to writing.

Active Voice: Janice **sang** a lively song.
Passive Voice: A lively song **was sung** by Janice.

The rubric says that active voice will enliven the style and energize my writing. So I reread part of my draft where I had used passive voice. Then I changed it to active voice.

[DRAFT]

[changed passive voice to active]

I especially liked Vicki's "Aunt" Hanna, her girlfriend Stacey, her

boyfriend Michael, and Michael's mother. ~~Vicki is shown by~~ Michael and

show Vicki ◄——
Stacey that there's another way to view the world around her. ~~And she~~

show Vicki ◄——
~~is shown by~~ Stacey and Michael's mother that there's another way to

dance.

Reflect

How does Briana's change enliven and energize her writing?

Apply

Review your draft to see where you can change passive voice to active voice to energize your writing.

Revise

Focus on Word Choice

The Rubric Says — Precise language avoids wordiness or redundancy throughout the piece.

Writing Strategy — Take out unnecessary words.

The rubric says my writing should be clear and precise, not wordy. It says to avoid redundancy, too. Sometimes, repeating a word or phrase can be effective. Other times, though, repetition can be distracting.

As I reread my draft, I will look for words I use too often. Repeating a word tends to weaken its effect. I will also look for places where I used more words than are necessary and take out the extra words.

[DRAFT]

[avoided redundancy]

[took out extra words]

I mean, every ballet dancer loves Misha. But please, give me a break!

After a while,
~~I mean,~~ I was bored with all that fantasizing. I was ~~so very~~ much more interested in Vicki's real relationship with Michael than the one that went on in her head.

Apply

Read your draft. Take out unnecessary repetitions and words.

Edit

Focus on Conventions

The Rubric Says	Verbal phrases are clear and titles are written correctly.
Writing Strategy	Make sure introductory verbal phrases describe the subject, and be sure titles are correct.

Writer's Term

Introductory Verbal Phrases

A **verbal** is a verb form that acts like a noun, an adjective, or an adverb. An **introductory verbal phrase** comes at the beginning of a sentence and describes the subject.

Introductory verbal phrases can make my writing more interesting, but I need to be sure my spelling is correct. As I wrote my draft, I circled words I didn't know how to spell. I also made a note on my draft to remind me to use italics for the title when I type my final copy.

[DRAFT]

[corrected spelling error]

maintenance

I also got tired of the fact that Vicki was such a high-maintnence

she made me wish

character. Constantly crying over one thing or another, I wished she

would just stop! [corrected subject of introductory verbal phrase]

Reflect

How do the corrections clarify the writing? What do they say about Briana as a writer?

Apply

Conventions

Edit your draft to be sure that each introductory verbal phrase describes the subject. Also check to see that titles are in the proper format.

For more practice with introductory verbal phrases and titles, use the exercises on the next two pages.

Introductory Verbal Phrases

Know the Rule

A **verbal** is a verb form that acts as a noun, an adjective, or an adverb. An **introductory verbal phrase** comes at the beginning of a sentence and describes the subject.

> **Correct:**
> **Laughing loudly,** Andrew enjoyed the show.
> (The introductory verbal phrase is *Laughing loudly,* and the verbal is *Laughing.* The verbal phrase describes the subject, *Andrew.*)

When the introductory verbal phrase doesn't describe the subject, it causes confusion for the reader. Here is an example of a verbal phrase that does not describe the subject.

> **Incorrect:**
> **Laughing loudly,** the show was enjoyable for Andrew.
> (Here again, the phrase is *Laughing loudly,* but it incorrectly describes *the show.*)

Practice the Rule

Number a sheet of paper 1–8. Read each sentence and decide whether the modifying word or phrase clearly describes the subject. If it does, write **yes**. If it does not, write **no**. Rewrite two of the unclear sentences correctly.

1. Sitting on the couch like a friend, my favorite book awaits me.
2. Filled with humorous stories, I can hear its pages call to me.
3. Salvaged by several tapings, I see its cover wink at me.
4. Smiling in anticipation, I pick up the book.
5. Slowly spinning on my heel, I turn and sit down.
6. Turning to the first page, I eagerly start to read.
7. Laughing out loud, each story is funnier than the last.
8. Written by my aunt, I cherish the book.

Titles

Know the Rule

Use **correct style and capitalization for titles.** Underline the titles of books, magazines, newspapers, movies, CDs, and DVDs. If you are using a computer to write your paper, these titles should be in italics. Use quotation marks around the titles of songs, stories, and poems. Capitalize the first word and the last word in titles. Capitalize all other words except articles, short prepositions, and coordinating conjunctions. Remember to capitalize short verbs, such as *is* and *are*.

Practice the Rule

Number a sheet of paper 1–10. Copy the sentences below and either underline or put quotation marks around each title. Make sure the correct words are capitalized.

1. One of my little sister's favorite things to do is sit under a tree with the latest issue of American Girl magazine.
2. For years my uncle was a reporter for the travel section in The New York Times.
3. My favorite song off of Coldplay's Parachutes CD is Yellow.
4. I can't think of anything funnier than Shel Silverstein's poem Sick, in the book Where the sidewalk Ends.
5. Out of all of the Harry Potter books, The goblet of Fire was surely my family's favorite.
6. Aesop's fable, The Tortoise and the hare, has inspired so many other stories, songs, cartoons, and even movies.
7. The movie Holes was based on Louis Sachar's book of the same name.
8. Katherine Paterson has won two Newbery Awards, one for Bridge To Terabitihia and one for Jacob have I loved.
9. Hasan won the school poetry contest by reciting the Road not taken.
10. Katie sang America the beautiful at the school assembly.

Publish

+Presentation

Publishing Strategy	Display your book report in the library.
Presentation Strategy	Use page numbers and footers to organize the report.

Now that I've finished my book report, how should I publish it? I think I would reach the largest audience if I posted it in the school library. First I'll get permission from the school librarian. Then I'll make a clean copy that's easy to read. Rather than writing my report by hand, I'll use a computer. I should remember to print each page on one side only, in case I have to pin my report to the bulletin board. I also need to include a footer on pages two and three. A footer, which consists of my name, the book title, and page number, ensures that no pages are lost or in the wrong order. Before I post it, though, I'll read through it one last time.

My Final Checklist

Did I—

✔ use introductory verbal phrases correctly?

✔ use underlines, italics, and quotation marks correctly with titles?

✔ carefully check my report for correct spelling, capitalization, and punctuation?

✔ write my report neatly and clearly, or use readable fonts?

✔ use footers on the pages in my report?

Apply

Make a checklist to check over your book report. Then make a final copy to publish.

Another Way to Dance

A Book Report by Briana

After reading *Another Way to Dance* by Martha Southgate, I had mixed feelings. I'd like to share some of them with you now. Having studied ballet myself, I found the premise of the book particularly interesting. A fourteen-year-old African American girl named Vicki is accepted into the summer dance program at the School of American Ballet in New York City. The book chronicles everything that happens to Vicki that summer. She experiences several things that help her mature, including an exciting first date and a devastating encounter with a racist schoolmate.

In many ways, I think the author does a good job of describing Vicki and her experiences. For example, the passages describing Vicki's ballet classes are very accurate and detailed. As I read them, I could almost smell the dance studio, hear the music and activity, and feel my muscles straining to move along with Vicki's.

I also think that the author does a good job of capturing Vicki's complicated feelings toward her family. Since her parents are newly divorced, Vicki feels a mixture of sympathy and resentment toward them. She also feels that she can't be entirely honest with her mother, so she bottles up her emotions. I think all of this is quite realistic.

One more thing I think the author does well is reveal the personalities of some of the characters. I especially liked Vicki's "Aunt" Hannah, her girlfriend Stacey, her boyfriend Michael, and Michael's mother. Michael and Stacey show Vicki that there's another way to view the world around her. Stacey and Michael's mother show Vicki that there's another way to dance.

There were, however, some things that I didn't like about the book. The author kept talking about the same things over and over. Vicki's constant fantasizing about Baryshnikov is one example. I mean, every ballet dancer loves Misha. But please, give me a break! After a while, I was bored with all that fantasizing. I was much more interested in Vicki's real relationship with Michael than the one that went on in her head.

I also got tired of the fact that Vicki was such a high-maintenance character. Constantly crying over one thing or another, she made me wish she would just stop! It's not that some of her problems weren't completely valid. It's just that

Briana   *Another Way to Dance*   2

after a while, they got really old. Many times, I just wanted to tell her, "Calm down, girl! Just get over yourself and relax! And join the real world while you're at it."

After all that reading, the thing that disappointed me the most was the ending. It sounded like such a cliché. I was really hoping that the author would include a juicy morsel to chew on for a while after I finished the book—some theme or life lesson that Vicki learned after all that obsessing. Instead, I got a corny and overused ending.

Nevertheless, if you love ballet—and you really love Baryshnikov—*Another Way to Dance* is worth the read. But if you tend to get impatient with reading about the struggles of a confused and insecure adolescent, you might want to pass on this one.

Reflect

What do you think? Did Briana use all the traits of a good response to literature in her writing? Check it against the rubric. Don't forget to use the rubric to check your own response to literature, too.

Briana   *Another Way to Dance*   3

What's a **Research Report?**

A research report contains information that a writer discovers about a topic after asking questions and researching the answers. I'd like to learn more about research assignments so that they won't seem so overwhelming.

What's in a **Research Report?**

Narrow Topic
I need to make sure my topic is specific enough to be covered in my report. For example, Ancient Egypt is too broad; Becoming a Scribe is more specific.

Attention-Grabbing Introduction
I want to make sure that I grab the reader's attention in my introduction. I can do this by starting with an interesting fact or quote about my topic.

Quotes and Paraphrases
When I need information that supports a main point in my report, I'll use an exact quote from an expert, or I'll use my own words to paraphrase someone else's ideas.

Works Consulted
It's important to list all the sources that I used while writing. I'll do this in my list of Works Consulted. This way, readers will know where I found my information.

Why write a **Research Report?**

I'm not yet sure of my purpose in writing a new research report, but here are some reasons I've used in the past.

To Explain

Whether it's background on a general topic or in-depth knowledge about something more specific, discovering information and sharing it with the reader is one good reason to write a research report.

To Compare and Contrast

Sometimes people best understand a topic when they compare it to something else. For instance, you might understand soccer better if you compare it to rugby. Examining similarities and differences is one purpose for writing a research report.

To Understand Issues

Writing a research report can help a person understand important issues. If a writer decides to research a current event, he or she will probably find out what caused the event.

To Inform

People often read about a topic before they make an important decision such as getting a dog, becoming a vegetarian, or studying abroad. Researching a topic in order to make an informed decision is a good reason to write a research report.

Linking Informative/Explanatory Writing Traits to a Research Report

In this chapter, you will research a topic and write about it. This type of informative/explanatory writing is called a research report. Briana will guide you through the stages of the writing process: Prewrite, Draft, Revise, Edit, and Publish. In each stage, Briana will show you important writing strategies that are linked to the Informative/Explanatory Writing Traits below.

Informative/Explanatory Writing Traits

- a clear focused topic
- concrete, relevant facts, definitions, and details that support and develop the topic

- information that is organized into an attention-grabbing introduction, an informative body, and a conclusion that supports the information or explanation presented
- transitions that connect ideas and clarify relationships

- a voice and tone that are appropriate for the purpose and audience

- language that is precise and concise
- domain-specific vocabulary that is explained as necessary

- clear sentences that vary in length and structure

- no or few errors in grammar, usage, mechanics, and spelling

Before you write, read Julie Fleming's research report on the next three pages. Then use the research report rubric on pages 152–153 to decide how well she did. (You might want to look back at What's in a Research Report? on page 146, too!)

UNDERSTANDING PHOBIAS

by Julie Fleming

Narrow Topic

Attention-Grabbing Introduction

Fears—we all have them. Walking alone at night, crossing dangerous intersections, and speaking in front of a crowd are all common fears. However, fears become abnormal when they become so irrational or exaggerated that a person never leaves the house. That's when fears turn into phobias.

Fear is a normal response to a scary situation. A phobia is an unreasonable response and is not normal. A phobia keeps people from doing the things that they want or need to do, such as going to work, school, or social functions. Judy Monroe, author of *Phobias: Everything You Wanted to Know, But Were Afraid to Ask*, quotes Anne Marie Albana at the Center of Stress and Anxiety Disorders at the State University of New York at Albany: "A phobia is an unrealistic fear that is all out of proportion to the actual threat. The fear of spiders, for instance, would be present even when there were no spiders around" (15–16). There are more than 500 phobias currently listed on the Internet. They fall into three common types: **Quote** specific phobia, social phobia, and agoraphobia. Let's look at them one at a time.

The most common type is a specific phobia, or a simple phobia. As the name suggests, a specific phobia is an unreasonable fear of a specific thing, animal, or situation. Most specific phobias are related to the fear of animals, environments, or bodily harm or injury. Fear of animals is the most common. Which animal is feared most? The results of a 2001 Gallup poll put snakes at the top of the list.

Specific environmental phobias include fear of storms, lightning, thunder, and earthquakes. Others include the fear of school, elevators, cars, airplanes, open spaces, closed spaces, and heights. Specific body phobias include the fear of pain, germs, blood, and terminal illnesses.

The second type of phobia is related to social fear. People with social phobias have intense fear of social situations. An example of an especially difficult social phobia is a situation in which a person thinks that he or she will be watched and judged by others. People with social phobias spend great amounts of time trying to avoid public situations. For some, drinking a cup of coffee or writing a check in public is enough to cause immense fear.

← Paraphrase

According to the American Psychological Association (APA), the most common social phobia is giving a speech in public. However, others include eating in restaurants, attending parties, dating, playing sports, and dancing.

The third kind of phobia, and the most disabling one, is agoraphobia. Of the people with agoraphobia, women outnumber men two to one. The most common fears suffered by these people are the fear of leaving home and the fear of being in a public place that would be difficult to leave quickly.

Agoraphobia sounds quite similar to social phobia, but they differ in one major way. Although people with social phobias fear looking foolish in public, people with agoraphobia fear having anxiety attacks and losing control. Symptoms of an anxiety attack could include chest pains and a racing heart, shortness of breath, hot or cold flashes, nausea, sweating, and fainting. These symptoms can last from several minutes to several hours. Fearing these symptoms, many people with this phobia do not ever leave home.

What are the causes of all of these phobias? Several theories exist. Among them is the belief that phobias are psychological. Judy Monroe states: Quote ↵

> Some researchers say that phobias arise when people ignore unresolved problems and conflicts. If someone has a stressful home life, for example, and never gets any help, then that person's anxiety will grow. Over time, that anxiety can change into a phobia. The phobia is the way that person manages the fearful situation. It symbolizes the real fear and allows the person to focus all fear onto one situation or thing. (70–71)

Other researchers believe that people's body chemistry makes them more prone to phobias. Still other researchers say that phobias are hereditary. A person with agoraphobia, for example, often has a parent or other relative who also has the condition.

Another theory states that phobias can be learned, either by watching a family member or by having an unpleasant personal experience. If a person were to become frightened while trapped in an elevator, he or she might develop claustrophobia, an irrational fear of closed spaces.

Yet another theory, offered by Dr. Harold Levinson, states that 90 percent of all phobias are caused by physical problems with the inner ear. Levinson reports that he has helped many patients with a combination of therapy and medicines for inner-ear disorders.

The good news about phobias is that there are many effective ways to treat and to cure them. One of the newest is virtual-reality therapy. The virtual-reality simulator, which works like an arcade game, gradually and safely exposes a person to the situation they most fear. In this way, patients can be exposed to airplanes, elevators, balconies, footbridges, different kinds of audiences, and even a jungle in Vietnam, all without leaving the room.

Well before virtual-reality therapy was invented, therapists were taking their patients on trips to real places. Through the USAir (currently US Airways) Fearful Flyer Program, people with aerophobia actually worked on their fear of flying by taking a short flight with their instructor and classmates.

Doctors prescribe antidepressants and anti-anxiety drugs to some people with phobias. Other treatments include individual therapy, group therapy, and self-help books. Also effective are programs that combine breathing and meditation exercises with vitamins, herbs, and foods that fight stress.

Many researchers feel that the most important way for people to overcome their phobias is to seek help in confronting them. According to an article in *Time International,* "The harder phobics work to avoid the things they fear, the more the brain grows convinced that the threat is real" (60).

Confronting fears helps people with phobias get rid of them. This works in much the same way that turning on the light helps children see that the "monster" in the corner is really a chair piled with clothes. Of course, facing fears isn't easy for patients with phobias. But if done gradually and gently, many can greatly decrease their fears, if not overcome them completely.

Sources

Works Consulted

Dolliver, Mark. "These Are a Few of Our Least-Favorite Things." *AdWeek* 26 Mar. 2001, eastern ed.: 15.

"Fear Not! PHOBIAS: For Millions of Sufferers, Science Is Offering New Treatments—and New Hope." *Time International* 14 May 2001: 60.

Heller, Sharon, Ph.D. *The Complete Idiot's Guide to Conquering Fear and Anxiety.* New York: Alpha Books, 1999.

Monroe, Judy. *Phobias: Everything You Wanted to Know, But Were Afraid to Ask.* Springfield: Enslow, 1996.

Stern, Richard. *Mastering Phobias: Cases, Causes, and Cures.* New York: Penguin, 1996.

Research Report

Rubric

Use this 6-point rubric to plan and score a research report.

	6	5	4
Ideas	The topic is appropriate in scope. Interesting, concrete details and well-chosen facts hold the reader's attention.	The topic is appropriate in scope. Interesting details and facts are included.	The writer has a general grasp of the scope of the topic. Some interesting details are present.
Organization	The report is well organized. It has a strong introduction, body, and conclusion.	The writer seldom wanders from the main point. Introduction, body, and conclusion are interesting.	The organizational pattern usually works. Introduction and conclusion are present.
Voice	The writer's voice maintains a formal tone and style. The writer demonstrates extensive knowledge of the topic.	The voice reflects the writer's knowledge and maintains a formal tone and style.	The voice reflects some formality and knowledge on the part of the writer.
Word Choice	Domain-specific vocabulary is used appropriately and explained clearly.	Domain-specific vocabulary is used appropriately but not always explained.	Some domain-specific vocabulary is used incorrectly or not explained.
Sentence Fluency	There is striking variety in sentence beginnings and length. The writing flows exceptionally well.	There is strong variety in sentence structures. The writing is smooth and easy to read.	There is some variety in sentence beginnings and length. A few choppy areas are present.
Conventions	Commas are used correctly and effectively. Compound and complex sentences are punctuated correctly.	There are a few errors with commas and compound and complex sentences, but they do not affect the meaning.	There are some notice-able errors with commas and compound and complex sentences. They affect the meaning.

✚ Presentation   The report is legible and uses appropriate multimedia and visuals.

3	2	1	
The topic is too big or too small. Details and facts rely on common knowledge.	The topic needs to be narrowed. Details are general and underdeveloped.	Much of the writing exists only to fill the space. The reader is left with many questions.	**Ideas**
Introduction and conclusion are present but need work. Some of the writing needs to be reordered.	Introduction or conclusion is either missing or needs work. The writing lacks order.	There is no real introduction or conclusion. No organizational structure is present.	**Organization**
The voice comes and goes. It is not always clear that the writer is knowledgeable or interested.	The writing has a hint of formality. The writing is not ready to be shared.	The voice does not reflect knowledge or interest in the topic.	**Voice**
Words are often general or vague. Little or no domain-specific vocabulary is used.	Sometimes words and phrases are misused. Domain-specific words are absent or misused.	Words and phrases are consistently vague or misused. No domain-specific words are used.	**Word Choice**
Too many sentences are similar in length and beginnings. The reader may have to reread for understanding.	Choppy, run-on, or incomplete sentences may slow down the reader.	Many sentence problems make reading the writing difficult.	**Sentence Fluency**
Several errors with commas and compound and complex sentences distract the reader from the meaning.	Errors with commas and compound and complex sentences affect the meaning. The reader must reread to make sense of the text.	There are many errors with commas and compound and complex sentences. The report is very difficult to read.	**Conventions**

See Appendix B for 4-, 5-, and 6-point informative/explanatory rubrics.

Research Report
Using the Rubric to Study the Model

Did you notice that the model on pages 149–151 points out some key elements of a research report? As she wrote "Understanding Phobias," Julie Fleming used these elements to help her explain what she learned about people's fears. She also used the 6-point rubric on pages 152–153 to plan, draft, revise, and edit the writing. A rubric is a great tool to evaluate writing during the writing process.

Now let's use the same rubric to score the model. To do this, we'll focus on each trait separately, starting with Ideas. We'll use the top descriptor for each trait (column 6), along with examples from the model, to help us understand how the traits work together. How would you score Julie on each trait?

- **The topic is appropriate in scope.**
- **Interesting, concrete details and well-chosen facts hold the reader's attention.**

The topic of phobias is not too narrow or too broad to cover in a three-page report. Julie clearly defines the different types of phobias and provides interesting facts and examples that hold the reader's attention.

[from the writing model]

Agoraphobia sounds quite similar to social phobia, but they differ in one major way. Although people with social phobias fear looking foolish in public, people with agoraphobia fear having anxiety attacks and losing control. Symptoms of an anxiety attack could include chest pains and a racing heart, shortness of breath, hot or cold flashes, nausea, sweating, and fainting.

Organization

- The report is well organized.
- It has a strong introduction, body, and conclusion.

Julie's report is well-organized and immediately captures the audience's interest. She describes something everyone can relate to—fears. The last line of the introduction leads smoothly into the rest of the report—the body and the conclusion.

[from the writing model]

Fears—we all have them. Walking alone at night, crossing dangerous intersections, and speaking in front of a crowd are all common fears. However, fears become abnormal when they become so irrational or exaggerated that a person never leaves the house. That's when fears turn into phobias.

Voice

- The writer's voice maintains a formal tone and style.
- The writer demonstrates extensive knowledge of the topic.

Julie has clearly done her research. She quotes experts and paraphrases ideas to explain different definitions and theories about phobias. This added information keeps Julie's voice serious and formal, yet holds the reader's attention.

[from the writing model]

Other researchers believe that people's body chemistry makes them more prone to phobias. Still other researchers say that phobias are hereditary. A person with agoraphobia, for example, often has a parent or other relative who also has the condition.

• Domain-specific vocabulary is used appropriately and explained clearly.

When Julie introduces vocabulary specific to the topic of phobias, she never assumes her reader is familiar with the new word. She makes sure to clearly define the new domain-specific vocabulary. This allows the reader to keep up with the discussion and reflects Julie's thorough research.

[from the writing model]

Another theory states that phobias can be learned, either by watching a family member or by having an unpleasant personal experience. If a person were to become frightened while trapped in an elevator, he or she might develop claustrophobia, an irrational fear of closed spaces.

• There is striking variety in sentence beginnings and length.
• The writing flows exceptionally well.

Julie uses introductory verbal phrases to introduce variety to her writing and keep it interesting. This example shows how she uses an introductory verbal phrase to avoid an otherwise wordy sentence.

[from the writing model]

Fearing these symptoms, many people with this phobia do not ever leave home.

Conventions

- Commas are used correctly and effectively.
- Compound and complex sentences are punctuated correctly.

Julie uses the proper conjunctions and punctuation to join compound and complex sentences. Notice how she uses a comma and the conjunction *but* to join these two independent clauses into one compound sentence.

[from the writing model]

Agoraphobia sounds quite similar to social phobia, but they differ in one major way.

This next sentence is a complex sentence with both a dependent and an independent clause. Julie uses a comma to separate the two clauses.

[from the writing model]

As the name suggests, a specific phobia is an unreasonable fear of a specific thing, animal, or situation.

⁺Presentation The report is legible and uses appropriate multimedia and visuals.

My Turn!

I'm going to write a research report about an interesting topic. I'll use the rubric and good writing strategies. Read along to see how I do it.

Writing a Research Report

Prewrite

Focus on Ideas

The Rubric Says The topic is appropriate in scope.

Writing Strategy Choose a topic, survey some sources, and make a 3 W's Chart. Then make note cards.

My teacher told us that we'd be writing research reports. I really like watching the night sky with my telescope, so I decided to choose a topic related to astronomy. Astronomy, as a whole, is too much to cover in my report. Instead, I chose to write about deadly asteroid threats. Narrowing the topic to a manageable size will help me write a clear and informative paper. My first step was to gather information at the library. Here are some sources I chose for my report.

Source	Why I Chose It
"Deadly Space Threats Get More Attention." <u>The Columbus Dispatch</u>	Newspaper article about asteroids and comets that could hit Earth
"Danger from the Sky." <u>Cricket</u>	Magazine article about asteroids and meteors
Vogt, Gregory L. <u>The Search for the Killer Asteroid</u>	Book about the times that asteroids have hit Earth

Apply

Choose a narrow topic and gather information from at least three credible sources.

3 W's Chart

A **3 W's Chart** organizes your ideas about a topic. It lists **what** your questions are, **what** information you already know, and **where** you might find answers to your questions.

After I chose my topic and began my research, I decided to make a 3 W's Chart to organize the information that I found. Notice on my chart how some of the information can be found in more than one place. This is good because if I find the same information in different sources, it's probably correct.

3W's Chart

What are some of my questions?	What do I already know?	Where can I find answers/ explanations?
What are asteroids, and where are they found?	They're pieces of rock that move through space.	The Search for the Killer Asteroid
What are the differences among asteroids, meteoroids, meteors, and meteorites?	I'm not sure—will need to find out.	article in Cricket magazine, The Search for the Killer Asteroid
What important meteorites have hit Earth? What were their effects?	One hit Arizona around 50,000 years ago. It left a huge crater.	Website on Barringer Meteorite Crater, Cricket article
Why are scientists so concerned about asteroids, and why do they study them so closely?	They're afraid one could slam into Earth and cause mass destruction—and possible extinction.	Internet article from Space.com, newspaper article on space threats, MIT website, Cricket article
Is there any way to stop asteroids from slamming into Earth?	I don't know—will need to find out.	The Search for the Killer Asteroid, newspaper article on space threats, Cricket article

Apply

Make a 3 W's Chart about your topic to decide what you want to know, what you already know, and where you can find the answers.

Writer's Term

Note Cards

A **note card** is a place, usually an index card, to put information about a topic. It should contain the following:

- a label identifying the topic
- a number so the cards don't get mixed up
- the question(s) from your 3 W's Chart that you would like to get answered
- information relating to the topic (either paraphrased or directly quoted), followed by an *F* for *Fact* or an *O* for *Opinion*
- the source of the information

Use one note card for each source.

After I made my 3 W's Chart, I made note cards. Near the top of each card, I wrote one or more questions from my 3 W's Chart. Then I used each card to focus on information that would answer the question(s) at the top.

Asteroids 1

3 W's Question: What are asteroids, and where are they found?
- They're lumps of rock and/or metal; also called minor planets. **F**
- Most are found between Mars and Jupiter, in the asteroid belt. **F**
- Some come dangerously close to Earth. **O**
- Some scientists believe that an asteroid may someday cause mass destruction and the extinction of our species. **O**

From: "Danger from the Sky." <u>Cricket</u> Oct. 1998: 22–26.

Reflect

How is a 3 W's Chart helpful in planning a report? How will Briana's note cards help her focus on subtopics?

Apply

Use your 3 W's Chart to make note cards.

Focus on Organization

The Rubric Says	The report is well organized.
Writing Strategy	Make an Outline to organize the information.

Writer's Term

Outline

An **Outline** shows the main points and the supporting details of the paragraphs in an essay. A **Topic Outline** contains words and phrases to help a writer organize information. A **Sentence Outline** contains complete sentences. Use the same form for both outlines:

- Use Roman numerals (I, II, III) for major sections or topics.
- Use capital letters (A, B, C) for major paragraphs.
- Use Arabic numerals (1, 2, 3) for the supporting details within each paragraph.
- Use lowercase letters (a, b, c) for less important details within each paragraph.
- Use a period after each symbol.

I created a Topic Outline to organize the body of my report. I gave the outline the same title as my report. Then I listed the main ideas and supporting details in the order that I plan to discuss them. Making an outline helps me ensure that I will organize my report well.

Outline

Asteroid Alert!

I. Asteroids ◄——— **first main idea**
   A. What they are ◄— **paragraph topic**
      1. Space rock and/or metal
      2. Leftover debris from formation of universe ◄— **supporting details**
   B. Where they are
      1. Between Mars and Jupiter, in asteroid belt
      2. Kept there by Jupiter's gravity

II. Differences among asteroids, meteoroids, meteors, meteorites
- A. Meteoroids: pieces of asteroids that have collided
- B. Meteors: meteoroids that fall into Earth's atmosphere
  1. Meteors that pass near/over Earth: near-Earth objects (NEOs)
  2. Meteors that make bright streaks across sky: shooting, or falling, stars
- C. Meteorites: meteors that fall to Earth

III. Important meteorites that have damaged Earth
- A. Barringer Meteorite Crater, Arizona (a.k.a. Meteor Crater)
  1. Hit Earth 50,000 years ago
  2. Was traveling 45,000 mph
  3. Made a crater 4,150 feet wide and 570 feet deep
  4. Meteorite estimated at 100 feet in diameter and 60,000 tons
- B. Tunguska Valley, Siberia
  1. Exploded above Earth in 1908
  2. Could be seen 466 miles away in daylight
  3. Could be felt 50 miles away
  4. Started a 30-mile area on fire
- C. Yucatán Peninsula, Mexico
  1. Hit Earth 65 million years ago
  2. Was 5 miles wide
  3. Was traveling 150,000 mph
  4. Changed Earth's climate
  5. Believed to have caused extinction of dinosaurs
- D. The moon
  1. Hit Earth 4.5 billion years ago
  2. Was the size of Mars
  3. Was traveling 25,000 mph
  4. Sent rubble into orbit
  5. Orbiting rubble formed the moon

IV. Why scientists are concerned about asteroid activity
- A. Two NEOs passed less than 500,000 miles (6 hours) away
  1. March 1989
  2. October 2001

B. One NEO passed within 280,000 miles
  1. June 1996
  2. Would have been as destructive as all nuclear weapons at once
C. Earth will be threatened by asteroids again
  1. Asteroids 1 kilometer (0.62 miles) across
    a. Hit every 100,000 to 300,000 years
    b. Would disrupt global climate
    c. Could cause extinction of some species
  2. Asteroids 100 meters (328 feet) across or larger
    a. Hit every 1,000 to 3,000 years
    b. Could eliminate a city
    c. Could create a tsunami
V. Actions scientists are taking to avoid disaster
  A. Researchers are locating, recording, and rating new asteroids
  B. Scientists are proposing ways of destroying or averting asteroids
    1. Attach rocket engine to asteroid and alter its orbit
    2. Destroy asteroid with an atomic bomb

Reflect

How will the Outline help Briana write her paper?

Apply

Use your note cards to organize ideas into an Outline.

Draft

Focus on Organization

The Rubric Says	The report has a strong introduction, body, and conclusion.
Writing Strategy	Write an attention-grabbing introduction.

Now I'm ready to write my research report. It's going to be pretty long, so for now, I'll just focus on getting my ideas down on paper. I'll do my best with spelling and grammar, but I can fine-tune everything later.

The rubric says my report needs a strong introduction. But I can't stop there. My report also needs a body full of interesting facts to keep the reader engaged, as well as a conclusion that wraps everything up. I want to open my report with a bang. I know this is a fact-based research paper, but that doesn't mean my opening paragraph can't be fun!

I've got an idea! I've always thought it would be fun to be a TV news announcer, so I think I'll open with a news scene.

[DRAFT]

Asteroid Alert!

by Briana

[attention-grabbing introduction]

"We interupt this program to bring you a special report. Scientists at the University of Arizona's Spacewatch center have downgraded their previous Torino Scale rating of Asteroid 2003CB from 1 to 0. This means that the likelihood of the asteroid's collision with Earth is less likely than something the same size hitting Earth within the next few decades. Citizens all over the globe can now breathe easier as they look into friendlier skies. . . . And now we return you to your regularly scheduled program."

Is the paragraph fact or fiction? It's hard to tell. That's because it's filled with facts. For one, there really is a Spacewatch center in Arizona where scientists study the skies for asteroid "attacks" and near misses. For another, the Torino scale exists.

Apply

Draft an introduction using interesting details or a unique approach to capture your reader's attention.

[DRAFT]

Just what are asteroids, and why are they important? Also called planetoids or minor planets, asteroids range in size from just a few yards across to several hundred miles across.

Many scientists believe that asteroids are leftover "space debris" from some heavenly bodies that collided when the universe formed. Most asteroids are located between the orbits of Mars and Jupiter in an area known as the asteroid belt. They are located there because Jupiter's gravitational pull on the asteroids is stronger than any other planet's. When Jupiter's orbit changes, an asteroid's orbit also will change, and it will be pulled into another planet's orbit. When an asteroid gets pulled into Earth's orbit, it will begin to travel toward Earth. This is why an asteroid sometimes gets close to, or even crashes into, Earth.

What are meteoroids, meteors, and meteorites? When asteroids collide with each other they shatter into smaller pieces called meteoroids. These meteoroids sometimes fall into Earth's atmosphere. When they do they are called meteors. Meteors that pass near Earth are called near Earth objects, or NEOs. The ones that burn up as they streak brightly across the sky are called shooting stars. The ones that hit Earth before they burn up are called meteorites.

[DRAFT]

Some meteorites have been large enough to form craters when they hit Earth. The best example of a crater is the Barringer Meteorite Crater in Arizona. (It is also known as the Meteor Crater.) About 50,000 years ago, a meteorite traveling almost 45,000 miles per hour struck Arizona in the area between what are now the towns of Winslow and Flagstaff. It created a crater about 4,150 feet wide and 570 feet deep. Scientists estimate that the meteorite was 100 feet in diameter and 60,000 tons in weight.

Another meteorite exploded several miles above the Tunguska Valley in Siberia in 1908. This explosion was so bright that it could be seen 466 miles away in broad daylight. The explosion was so powerful that it could be felt as far as 50 miles away. It also started a forest fire 30 miles wide.

Reflect

Did the Outline help Briana draft an organized research report? How well did her introduction grab your attention?

Apply

Use the information in your Outline to draft your research report.

Revise

Focus on **Voice**

The Rubric Says	The writer demonstrates extensive knowledge of the topic.
Writing Strategy	To sound like an expert, use examples and quotes from credible sources.

Writer's Term

Paraphrasing vs. Plagiarizing

To **paraphrase** is to restate the meaning of a particular passage in your own words.

Don't **plagiarize**! To plagiarize means to present another person's writing as your own work.

The rubric tells me to express my knowledge of the topic. I should keep the voice of my research paper formal, yet compelling. Adding quotes or paraphrased information can really help. But just any old quotes won't work, so I reviewed my note cards and found specific quotes to support my main points. I carefully inserted these quotes to flow naturally with what I had already written. I sound like an expert now, and my paper is even more interesting to read.

I know I can't use an author's words without giving proper credit. I will be sure to introduce the quotes properly and list my sources in the Works Consulted section.

Citing Sources: Works Consulted

When **citing sources,** use the **Works Consulted** page at the end of your paper to list where you found your information. The examples below show how to present this information. Be sure to include each source used, regardless of whether direct quotes were pulled from it. Pay special attention to the order of the information and the use of punctuation. List your sources alphabetically according to authors' last names. When there is no author, use the first word in the title.

To cite a book:

Author's last name, author's first name. *Book title*. City of publication: Publisher, date of publication.

To cite a magazine or a newspaper article:

Author's last name, author's first name. "Article title." *Magazine/newspaper title* Date of publication: page number(s).

To cite an article in an online periodical:

Author's last name, author's first name. "Article title." *Online periodical title* Date of publication. Date of access, Web address.

To cite a website:

Author's last name, author's first name. *Website title*. Date of last update. Sponsor of website. Date of access, Web address.

[DRAFT]

Although scientists often disagree on how much money and time should be spent tracking NEOs, most agree that Earth could someday be threatened by a devastating asteroid.

[added quotes]

According to an article written by Robert Roy Britt, a collision with a large asteroid "would rock the planet, disrupt the global climate for years, and could render some species extinct." Britt also says, "Such an event could eliminate a city or create a tsunami that might inundate shore communities and even large cities along multiple coastlines."

Reflect

How do quotes from the source strengthen the writer's voice?

Apply

Read your draft. Be sure to use quotes so that you sound like an expert on your topic.

Revise

Focus on Word Choice

The Rubric Says	Domain-specific content vocabulary is used appropriately and explained clearly.
Writing Strategy	Explain terms related to the topic.

After I finished my rough draft, it was time to go back and search for any areas that needed work. I had already inserted several quotes and paraphrased quite a lot of facts. It is clear I have done my research. However, I know it is important to explain some of the terms. Sharing my research won't help if my readers can't understand my words!

I found a place where I had not explained the meaning of an asteroid-related term. I went back and added an explanation. How do you think I did?

[DRAFT]

Is the paragraph fact or fiction? It's hard to tell. That's because it's filled with facts. For one, there really is a Spacewatch center in Arizona where scientists study the skies for asteroid "attacks" and near misses. For another, the Torino scale exists.

[explained term] → Adopted in 1999, the scale is used to measure and categorize the risk that steroids and other near-Earth objects (NEOs) pose to Earth.

I felt so much better about my writing after I had taken the time to add a few words of explanation that I decided to check other content words and terms I used in my report. Looking at my definition of the word *asteroids*, I thought I could do a better job of explaining the word. After all, my report is all about asteroids! The reader should have a clear, detailed picture of what I mean.

[DRAFT]

[explained another term] → Simply put, asteroids are pieces of space rock, or metal, or both.

Just what are asteroids, and why are they important? Also

they

called planetoids or minor planets, ~~asteroids~~ range in size from just

a few yards to several hundred miles across.

Reflect

How do Briana's explanations help engage the reader's interest?

Apply

Make sure you've explained all your domain-specific content vocabulary, so you don't confuse your readers.

Revise

Focus on Sentence Fluency

The Rubric Says   There is striking variety in sentence beginnings and length.

Writing Strategy   Use introductory verbal phrases to vary the sentences.

When I revise my sentences, I should be sure that they vary in how they begin and how long they are. Using verbals is one way to vary them. Look at my revisions below. After adding the first verbal, *Creating*, it sounded as if a scientist had created the crater! I then went back and made more edits so that it all made sense again. Be careful! Using verbals takes practice.

[DRAFT]

About 50,000 years ago, a meteorite traveling almost 45,000 miles

per hour struck Arizona in the area between what are now the

                                           Creating

towns of Winslow and Flagstaff. ~~It created~~ a crater about 4,150

feet wide and 570 feet deep. ~~Scientists estimate that~~ the meteorite

estimated by scientists to be

was 100 feet in diameter and 60,000 tons in weight.

[used introductory verbal phrase to add variety]

Apply

Add variety to your writing by using introductory verbal phrases.

Edit

The Rubric Says Commas are used correctly and effectively. Compound and complex sentences are punctuated correctly.

Writing Strategy Check the commas in compound and complex sentences and other places.

Writer's Term.

Compound Sentences/Complex Sentences
A **compound sentence** consists of two closely related independent clauses joined by a comma and a coordinating conjunction (**and, but, or**) or by a semicolon. A **complex sentence** consists of an independent clause and a dependent clause that begins with a subordinating conjunction (**although, because, if, as,** or **when**).

Now I need to check for errors in spelling and grammar. The rubric also says that I should pay special attention to how I use commas. Here's how I edited two complex sentences.

[DRAFT]

[formed complex sentences correctly]

What are meteoroids, meteors, and meteorites? When asteroids collide with each other, they shatter into smaller pieces called meteoroids. These meteoroids sometimes fall into Earth's atmosphere. When they do, they are called meteors. Meteors that

Reflect

Used correctly, how do commas guide the reader?

Apply  Conventions

Edit your draft for spelling, punctuation, and capitalization. Also make sure you've formed compound and complex sentences correctly.

For more practice using commas, use the exercises on the next two pages.

Compound and Complex Sentences

Know the Rule

A **compound sentence** consists of two closely related independent clauses. An independent clause can stand alone as a sentence, but two independent clauses should be joined by a comma and a coordinating conjunction (*and, but, or*) or by a semicolon.

> **Example:** An NEO passes Earth, **but** a meteorite hits it.
> **Example:** An NEO passes Earth; a meteorite hits it.

A **complex sentence** consists of an independent clause and a dependent clause. A dependent clause cannot stand alone as a sentence because it begins with a subordinating conjunction such as *although, because,* or *when.*

> **Example: Because** some asteroids are potentially harmful, scientists keep watching the skies.
> **Example: When** an asteroid poses no threat to Earth, it gets a Torino rating of 0.

Practice the Rule

Read the sentences below. Write **CX** if the sentence is complex. Write **CD** if the sentence is compound. Then copy each dependent clause onto the paper.

1. The Torino Impact Hazard Scale is relatively new; it was adopted in 1999.

2. It was developed by Richard Binzel; he worked on it for several years.

3. Because so many new asteroids were being discovered, Binzel felt the need to help the public understand them.

4. When a new asteroid is discovered, scientists gather information about it.

5. They calculate the asteroid's future position, and they assign a rating to it.

6. While he was a student at the Massachusetts Institute of Technology, my brother had the opportunity to meet Richard Binzel.

7. He learned about the Torino Impact Hazard Scale, and he even got to observe some of the research.

8. Because he knew Richard Binzel, he learned firsthand about the color codes for asteroids.

Commas

Know the Rule

Knowing how to use **commas** properly is a powerful tool in writing. Commas help clarify and strengthen sentences. Commas tell a reader where to pause. A comma is used to separate an **introductory word,** such as *yes* or *well*, from the rest of a sentence. It is also used with a conjunction to join independent clauses in a compound sentence and to separate a **noun of direct address** from the rest of a sentence. A noun of direct address names a person who is being spoken to.

Practice the Rule

Number a sheet of paper 1–10. Copy the sentences below. Insert commas where you think they belong. Remember, reading a sentence aloud can help you decide where a comma, or pause, is needed.

1. Please make my sub with turkey cheese tomatoes lettuce and mayonnaise.
2. No Katherine did not call back yet about the basketball game tickets.
3. I have completed all of my homework but I still have to stay in because I have chores to do.
4. For my birthday I was hoping to grab a pizza watch a movie and come back home for cake and ice cream with some friends.
5. Stephen could you please remember to take off your muddy shoes when you enter the house?
6. Yes Stewart you may have Isaac Rion and Matthew over next Sunday.
7. I'd like to study astronomy in college or maybe I'll study meteorology.
8. Some people still consider Pluto a planet but other people disagree.
9. The moon will be full tonight but we won't see it because of the clouds.
10. Sam you forgot your backpack!

Publish + Presentation

Publishing Strategy	Publish your research report as a slide presentation.
Presentation Strategy	Prepare legible, attractive slides with appropriate graphics.

I finished my research report, and now I want to publish it. I think it would be fun to present my report to my class the way a reporter would deliver a special news report. A slide show would work perfectly. I will make easy-to-see slides that feature interesting graphics that enhance each point, but I'll include very few words because I will be doing the talking. But first, I'll review my draft to make sure it includes all the items on my checklist.

My Final Checklist

Did I—

✔ include compound and complex sentences in my report?

✔ correctly punctuate the compound and complex sentences?

✔ use commas correctly throughout my report?

✔ create slides that are legible and appealing to look at?

✔ use helpful graphics and not too many words on my slides?

Apply

Make a checklist to check your research report. Then make a final copy to publish.

Asteroid Alert!

by Briana

"We interrupt this program to bring you a special report. Scientists at the University of Arizona's Spacewatch center have downgraded their previous Torino Scale rating of Asteroid 2003CB from 1 to 0. This means that the likelihood of the asteroid's collision with Earth is less likely than something the same size hitting Earth within the next few decades. Citizens all over the globe can now breathe easier as they look into friendlier skies. . . . And now we return you to your regularly scheduled program."

Is the paragraph fact or fiction? It's hard to tell. That's because it's filled with facts. For one, there really is a Spacewatch center in Arizona where scientists study the skies for asteroid "attacks" and near-misses. For another, the Torino Scale exists. Adopted in 1999, the scale is used to measure and categorize the risk that asteroids and other near-Earth objects (NEOs) pose to Earth.

Just what are asteroids, and why are they important? Simply put, asteroids are pieces of space rock, or metal, or both. Also called planetoids or minor planets, they range in size from just a few yards across to several hundred miles across.

Many scientists believe that asteroids are leftover "space debris" from some heavenly bodies that collided when the universe formed. Most asteroids are located between the orbits of Mars and Jupiter in an area known as the asteroid belt. They are located there because Jupiter's gravitational pull on the asteroids is stronger than any other planet's. When Jupiter's orbit changes, an asteroid's orbit will also change, and it will be pulled into another planet's orbit. When an asteroid gets pulled into Earth's orbit, it will begin to travel toward Earth. This is why an asteroid sometimes gets close to, or even crashes into, Earth.

What are meteoroids, meteors, and meteorites? When asteroids collide with each other, they shatter into smaller pieces called meteoroids. These meteoroids sometimes fall into Earth's atmosphere. When they do, they are called meteors. Meteors that pass near Earth are called near-Earth objects, or NEOs. The ones that burn up as they streak brightly across the sky are called shooting stars. The ones that hit Earth before they burn up are called meteorites.

Some meteorites have been large enough to form craters when they hit Earth. The best example of a crater is the Barringer Meteorite Crater in Arizona. (It is also known as the Meteor Crater.) About 50,000 years ago, a meteorite traveling almost 45,000 miles per hour struck Arizona in the area between what are now the towns of Winslow and Flagstaff. Creating a crater about 4,150 feet wide and 570 feet deep, the meteorite was estimated by scientists to be 100 feet in diameter and 60,000 tons in weight.

Another meteorite exploded several miles above the Tunguska Valley in Siberia in 1908. This explosion was so bright that it could be seen 466 miles away in broad daylight. The explosion was so powerful that it could be felt as far as 50 miles away. It also started a forest fire 30 miles wide.

An even more important impact happened 65 million years ago. Scientists believe that an asteroid at least five miles wide crashed into Mexico's Yucatán Peninsula at about 150,000 miles per hour. This crash sent dust and other debris high into Earth's atmosphere. The debris blocked so much of the sunlight for so long that Earth's climate changed entirely. Much of the plant life died. This caused the plant-eating dinosaurs to die off. This, in turn, caused the meat-eating dinosaurs to die off because their food supply had disappeared.

Many astronomers believe that the most violent asteroid impact of all might have occurred 4.5 billion years ago. At that time, an asteroid the size of Mars traveled more than 25,000 miles per hour before smashing into Earth. This sent a huge amount of rubble into orbit. For a while, the rubble just continued to orbit Earth. Over time, however, due in part to Earth's gravitational pull, the rubble came together and formed the moon.

Because of many NEOs' potential for destruction, scientists all over the world have become concerned about asteroids. Two particularly frightening NEOs, sighted in March 1989 and October 2001, sped past Earth at a distance of less than 500,000 miles—twice the distance to the moon—and missed a collision with Earth by a mere six hours.

In June 1996, an even scarier near-miss occurred when Asteroid 1996 JA1 passed within only 280,000 miles of Earth. Scientists estimate that if that asteroid had crashed into Earth, it would have had as much destructive power as all the nuclear weapons on Earth exploding at the same time.

Although scientists often disagree on how much money and time should be spent tracking NEOs, most agree that Earth could someday be threatened by a devastating asteroid. According to an article written by Robert Roy Britt, a collision with a large asteroid "would rock the planet, disrupt the global climate for years, and could render some species extinct." Britt also says, "Such an event could eliminate a city or create a tsunami that might inundate shore communities and even large cities along multiple coastlines."

What actions are being taken to avoid NEO crashes? Researchers all over the world are continuing to locate new asteroids. Once located, each asteroid's size and orbit is measured and recorded. Then the asteroid is assigned a rating on the Torino Scale, which, according to Carl Pilcher, Science Director for solar system exploration in the NASA Office of Space Science in Washington, D.C., "is a major advance in our ability to explain the hazard posed by a particular NEO." Carl further explains, "If we ever find an object with a greater value than one, the scale will be an effective way to communicate the resulting risk" ("MIT").

Scientists are also proposing ways to destroy or avert devastating NEOs that might be on their way to Earth. One proposal is to attach rocket engines to the asteroids to alter their orbit and move them out of Earth's path. Another proposal is to destroy the asteroids with spacecraft loaded with atomic bombs.

Scientists remain alert, but fortunately, Earth has not had to take on an NEO yet. Thankfully "the attack of the killer asteroid" is still only fiction.

Works Consulted

Bridges, Andrew. "Deadly Space Threats Get More Attention." *The Columbus Dispatch* 13 May 2001: C4.

Britt, Robert Roy. "Asteroid Discoveries May Outpace Ability to Assess Threat to Earth." *Space.com* 19 Oct. 2001.

"Danger from the Sky." *Cricket* Oct. 1998: 22–26.

"MIT Researcher Creates Scale to Assess Earth-Asteroid Close Encounters." *MIT News* 22 July 1999. 20 Oct. 2006, http://web.mit.edu/newsoffice/nr/1999/asteroid.html.

Vogt, Gregory L. *The Search for the Killer Asteroid.* Brookfield: Millbrook, 1994.

What is the Barringer Meteorite Crater? 1998. 20 Oct. 2006, http://www.barringercrater.com/science/main/htm.

Reflect

Did Briana earn a high score for each writing trait on the research report rubric? Don't forget to use the rubric to evaluate your own report.

What's a **How-To Guide?**

Instructional text like a how-to guide explains how to do or make something. I've used product booklets to assemble or build things. However, I found that many of them were incomplete or not very helpful. I'm looking forward to learning about this kind of writing because I want to do a better job of writing my own how-to guide!

What's in a **How-To Guide?**

Explanation
This is the point of a how-to guide: to explain clearly, and in great detail, how to do something or put something together.

Sequence
A how-to guide should be structured so that it presents the sequential steps of a process. I'll keep this in mind when I organize my ideas.

Friendly Tone
This is how I want my guide to sound. The best instructions "speak" to readers in a helpful way, taking them by the hand and guiding them through the steps of a process. I'll try to use a friendly tone when I write my guide.

Visuals
Sometimes words alone can't explain a particular part or step in a process. That's why it's important to include pictures, drawings, or diagrams in a how-to guide.

Why write a **How-To Guide?**

There are many reasons to write a how-to guide. I'll list some here.

To Explain How Something Works

A how-to guide can explain how something—a computer, an engine, a radio—works. Educating readers about what goes on behind the scenes is one good reason to write a guide.

To Explain How to Assemble Something

Writing a how-to guide is probably the best way to tell others how to put something together—whether it's a bicycle, a bookcase, or a barn.

To Explain a Process

You don't have to build something to need instructions. Writing a how-to guide is also a good way to explain a process such as drawing scenery or conducting a successful Internet search.

To Give Directions

Sometimes, a writer needs to give directions. In this case, writing a how-to guide can be a good way to tell the reader what actions to take. For instance, parents might need to leave a list of instructions for a babysitter or leave a note on the refrigerator telling their kids which chores to do.

Linking Informative/Explanatory Writing Traits to a **How-To Guide**

In this chapter, you will explain how to do something. This type of informative/explanatory writing is called a how-to guide. Briana will guide you through the stages of the writing process: Prewrite, Draft, Revise, Edit, and Publish. In each stage, Briana will show you important writing strategies that are linked to the Informative/Explanatory Writing Traits below.

Informative/Explanatory Writing Traits

Ideas
- a clear, focused topic
- concrete, relevant facts, definitions, and details that support and develop the topic

Organization
- information that is organized into an attention-grabbing introduction, an informative body, and a conclusion that supports the information or explanation presented.
- transitions that connect ideas and clarify relationships

Voice
- a voice and tone that are appropriate for the purpose and audience

Word Choice
- language that is precise and concise
- domain-specific vocabulary that is explained as necessary

Sentence Fluency
- clear sentences that vary in length and structure

Conventions
- no or few errors in grammar, usage, mechanics, and spelling

Before you write, read Adrian Desmond's how-to guide on the next three pages. Then use the how-to guide rubric on pages 186–187 to decide how well he did. (You might want to look back at What's in a How-To Guide? on page 180, too!)

"Building" a Sailboat Cake

by Adrian Desmond

For years, my brother has dreamed of owning a sailboat. For his birthday this year, I decided to build him one—well, sort of. I made him a sailboat cake. It was pretty easy once I got started. And if I could do it, so could you! Here are the steps to follow to make a sailboat cake.

<u>First,</u> decide on the kind of cake you want to make. <u>Next,</u> buy a boxed cake mix that will work in a pan that is 13 × 9 × 2 inches, and buy one package, 7.2 ounces, of white frosting mix. Bake the cake according to the directions on the box. <u>When it's done,</u> set the cake pan on a rack until the cake is cool enough to cut. <u>Then,</u> cut the cake diagonally into three pieces, as shown in Diagram 1. (You may want to leave the cake in the pan, which makes the pieces easier to handle.) <u>Finally,</u> place the uncovered pan of cut cake pieces in the freezer, and set a timer for one hour. Freezing the pieces will make them easier to frost.

Sequence

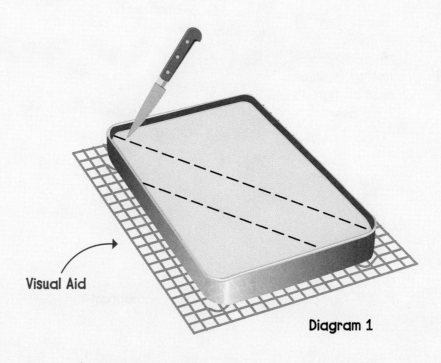

Visual Aid

Diagram 1

Friendly Tone

While the cake is in the freezer, you'll need to do two things. First, prepare the frosting according to the directions on the package. When it is nice and fluffy, put one cup of it into a medium-sized bowl. Take a few tablespoons of frosting from there, and put it into a small-sized bowl. Then, set all three bowls aside. Next, make an ocean on which to set your sailboat. You can do this by covering a 20 × 18-inch tray or piece of heavy cardboard with aluminum foil.

When the timer sounds, take the pieces of cake out of the freezer and arrange them into a sailboat, as shown in Diagram 2. As you arrange the sails, leave plenty of space between them for the mast, the pole from which the sails are hung.

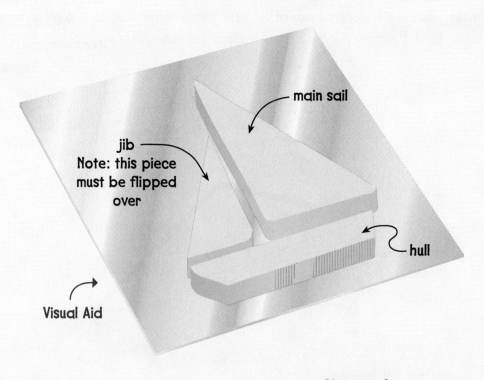

main sail

jib
Note: this piece
must be flipped
over

hull

Visual Aid

Diagram 2

Before you add the mast, frost the sails. Use the frosting from the largest bowl to carefully frost the sails. You may want to make a few waves in the frosting to suggest an ocean breeze. If you want, you can put some of the frosting from this bowl into a square plastic bag with one corner cut off. Then, you can squeeze the frosting out to make a cloud and sea gulls. (See Diagram 3.) Next, take the medium-sized bowl of frosting and gently fold one tablespoon of cocoa into it. When the frosting is well blended, spread it over the hull, the long body of the sailboat. Finish off the hull by adding some portholes, or windows: Take five white, ring-shaped candies, and place them as you see them in Diagram 3. Finally, make water by mixing blue food coloring into the small bowl of frosting. Use another square plastic bag with a corner cut off to draw some waves.

Now it's time for the mast. Roll up a 14 × 4-inch sheet of aluminum foil and place it between the sails. If you wish to add a bit of color, attach a red paper flag at the top.

Now your cake is ready to set sail. Wish your "passengers" *bon voyage,* as well as *bon appétit*!

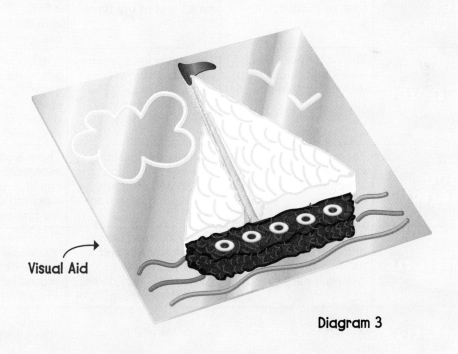

Visual Aid

Diagram 3

Rubric

Use this 6-point rubric to plan and score a how-to guide.

	6	5	4
Ideas	The topic is well-developed. Steps are clear, focused, and easy to follow. Concrete details and pictures support the instructions.	The topic is developed. Steps are clear and focused. Details and pictures share information that is helpful.	The topic is somewhat developed. Some of the steps are clear and focused. Details and pictures are adequate but don't share new information.
Organization	Appropriate and varied transitions clarify the relationships among the steps.	Appropriate transitions support the writing and clarify the relationships among the steps most of the time.	Some transitions are used to clarify the relationships among the steps.
Voice	The writer uses an informative and friendly tone to connect with the audience.	The writer uses an informative and friendly tone most of the time.	The writer begins with an appropriate tone, but it fades. The connection with the audience is not maintained.
Word Choice	The writer uses precise words and clearly defines domain-specific vocabulary.	The writer uses precise words but doesn't define every one. The language works very well for the topic.	The language is adequate and used correctly. Some domain-specific vocabulary is used, but it is not explained clearly.
Sentence Fluency	There is striking variety in sentence length and structure. Reading is a pleasure.	There is significant variety in sentence length and structure. The writing is easy to read.	There is some variety in sentence length and structure. A few awkward sentences are present.
Conventions	Appositives and direct and indirect objects are used correctly. The writing is easy to read.	There are a few errors with appositives and direct and indirect objects, but they do not affect the meaning.	There are some noticeable errors with appositives and direct and indirect objects that affect the meaning.

+Presentation Posters and other visual aids are informative and easy to read.

3	2	1	
The topic is not developed. Some of the steps are unclear and leave the reader with questions. Details and pictures need more attention.	The writer needs more information. Steps are missing and details are lacking.	The writing is not organized into steps. Details are vague and incomplete. The reader may feel confused.	**Ideas**
Transitions are present but need work to make the relationships among the steps clear.	The writing is confusing and difficult to follow. Transitions are rarely used.	The writing is hard to follow. The reader may feel confused. Transitions are missing.	**Organization**
The writer's tone may be too formal or distant. It may be inappropriate.	The writer sounds uninterested in either the topic or the audience.	The voice is extremely weak or absent. The writer's purpose is unknown.	**Voice**
The language is general and often vague. Domain-specific vocabulary is not explained.	The writing lacks precise words, so the message is not clear. More information would help.	The writing is filled with vague, unclear language. The words simply fill the spaces.	**Word Choice**
Little variety in sentence length and beginnings may cause the need to reread.	There are many choppy or incomplete sentences and repeated beginnings. Sentences are too long or too short.	The writing is a struggle to read. There are many poorly constructed or incomplete sentences.	**Sentence Fluency**
Several errors with appositives and direct and indirect objects distract the reader from the meaning.	Errors with appositives and direct and indirect objects force the reader to reread to make sense of the text.	There are many errors with appositives and direct and indirect objects. The text is very difficult to read.	**Conventions**

See Appendix B for 4-, 5-, and 6-point informative/explanatory rubrics.

How-To Guide

Using the Rubric to Study the Model

Did you notice that the model on pages 183–185 points out some key elements of a how-to guide? As he wrote "'Building' a Sailboat Cake," Adrian Desmond used these elements to help him explain how to make a cake shaped like a sailboat. He also used the 6-point rubric on pages 186–187 to plan, draft, revise, and edit the writing. A rubric is a great tool to evaluate writing during the writing process.

Now let's use the same rubric to score the model. To do this, we'll focus on each trait separately, starting with Ideas. We'll use the top descriptor for each trait (column 6), along with examples from the model, to help us understand how the traits work together. How would you score Adrian on each trait?

Ideas

- **The topic is well-developed.**
- **Steps are clear, focused, and easy to follow.**
- **Concrete details and pictures support the instructions.**

Adrian does a great job explaining all of the steps and substeps in his guide. The details and diagrams really help the reader understand and "see" each step.

[from the writing model]

When the timer sounds, take the pieces of cake out of the freezer and arrange them into a sailboat, as shown in Diagram 2. As you arrange the sails, leave plenty of space between them for the mast, the pole from which the sails are hung.

Organization

- **Appropriate and varied transitions clarify the relationships among the steps.**

Adrian uses several transitions to organize his guide into sequential steps. The following passage is a good example. Notice how each main step flows smoothly to the next.

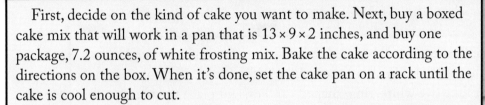

[from the writing model]

First, decide on the kind of cake you want to make. Next, buy a boxed cake mix that will work in a pan that is $13 \times 9 \times 2$ inches, and buy one package, 7.2 ounces, of white frosting mix. Bake the cake according to the directions on the box. When it's done, set the cake pan on a rack until the cake is cool enough to cut.

Voice

- **The writer uses an informative and friendly tone to connect with the audience.**

I like the way Adrian's writing sounds helpful and friendly, as if he's right there talking the reader through the process of making the cake. This friendly tone helps make the instructions easier to follow. I feel like I know Adrian as a friend!

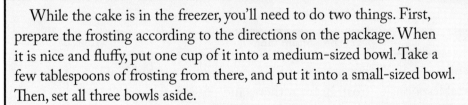

[from the writing model]

While the cake is in the freezer, you'll need to do two things. First, prepare the frosting according to the directions on the package. When it is nice and fluffy, put one cup of it into a medium-sized bowl. Take a few tablespoons of frosting from there, and put it into a small-sized bowl. Then, set all three bowls aside.

- **The writer uses precise words and clearly defines domain-specific vocabulary.**

Adrian's instructions are clear and easy to follow because he uses precise words and defines all domain-specific vocabulary, or jargon. In the following example, I underlined the two words that might be unfamiliar terms to the reader. You can see how Adrian defines each one, right after using it.

[from the writing model]

When the frosting is well blended, spread it over the <u>hull</u>, the long body of the sailboat. Finish off the hull by adding some <u>portholes</u>, or windows: Take five white, ring-shaped candies, and place them as you see them in Diagram 3.

- **There is striking variety in sentence length and structure. Reading is a pleasure.**

Adrian doesn't stick with just one sentence pattern; instead, he uses different kinds of sentences to add variety. Take a look at the passage below. Notice how Adrian uses a complex sentence followed by a compound statement. This makes his writing flow from one point to the next.

[from the writing model]

When it is nice and fluffy, put one cup of it into a medium-sized bowl. Take a few tablespoons of frosting from there, and put it into a small-sized bowl.

**Conventions**

- **Appositives and direct and indirect objects are used correctly. The writing is easy to read.**

I can tell that Adrian proofread his writing because I didn't find any mistakes. He also uses appositives correctly. I know that an appositive is a phrase that defines a noun and that it needs to be set off from the rest of the sentence by commas. In this passage, notice how Adrian correctly inserts a comma to separate the definition of a mast from the rest of the sentence.

[from the writing model]

As you arrange the sails, leave plenty of space between them for the mast, the pole from which the sails are hung.

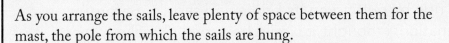**Presentation** Posters and other visual aids are informative and easy to read.

My Turn!

I'm going to write a how-to guide about something I can do well. I'll follow the rubric and use good writing strategies. Read on to see how I do it!

Prewrite

Focus on **Ideas**

The Rubric Says	Steps are clear, focused, and easy to follow.
Writing Strategy	Choose a process to explain. List the main steps in the process.

I'm really crazy about horses, and I love to go riding every chance I get. A lot goes into preparing for a safe and enjoyable ride—for both the rider and the horse. Since my assignment was to write a how-to guide, it seemed only natural to write about tacking up. Tacking up involves getting a horse ready to ride by putting on its bridle and saddle. Before I start writing my explanation, I thought it would be useful to make a checklist of the main steps involved in the process. Here's what I came up with.

Tacking Up—Main Steps

✔ Position the bridle, and put the bit in the horse's mouth.

✔ Pull the bridle over the horse's ears.

✔ Buckle the noseband and the throatlatch, making sure they are not too tight.

✔ Position the blanket or saddle pad over the horse's withers.

✔ Place the saddle on top of the blanket.

✔ Fasten and adjust the girth, making sure it is not too tight.

✔ Check the fit one last time to make sure the horse is comfortable.

Apply

Choose a process to explain. Then jot down the major steps involved in completing the task.

Prewrite

The Rubric Says   Appropriate and varied transitions clarify the relationships among the steps.

Writing Strategy   Make a Sequence Chain to arrange steps in a sequential order.

Writer's Term

Sequence Chain

A **Sequence Chain** shows the chronological steps of a complex process. Substeps should be placed, in order, below each step.

I will use a Sequence Chain to order the steps and substeps in the process. It will be easy to add transition words when I write my draft.

Sequence Chain

Topic: Tacking Up

Step 1: Position bridle; put bit in mouth.
   a. Use thumb to guide bit in.
   b. Make sure it clears horse's teeth.

Step 2: Pull bridle over ears.
   a. Pull ears through headstall and browband.
   b. Pull forelock out from under browband.

Step 3: Buckle noseband and throatlatch comfortably.
   a. Fit two fingers under noseband.
   b. Fit width of hand between throatlatch and cheek.

Step 4: Position blanket or pad over withers.

Step 5: Place saddle on top of blanket.
   a. Unfold girth and let it hang down.
   b. Reach carefully under belly and grab girth strap.

Step 6: Fasten and adjust girth by slipping fingers between girth and horse's body.

Step 7: Make one last check for fit by checking for pinched skin.

Result: The horse is tacked up and ready to ride.

Reflect

How will the Sequence Chain help keep Briana's writing organized?

Apply

Use a Sequence Chain to organize the steps and substeps in your process.

Draft

Focus on **Voice**

The Rubric Says   The writer uses an informative and friendly tone to connect with the audience.

Writing Strategy   Use a friendly tone and second-person point of view to connect with the audience.

Now I'll use my Sequence Chain to help me write my draft. According to the rubric, I should make a strong connection with my readers. I plan to address the audience directly, using casual phrases and expressions that I use when speaking to my friends.

I also know how impersonal directions can be, especially when it sounds like they were written with no particular person in mind. So I'll also use the second person pronoun *you* to address my readers.

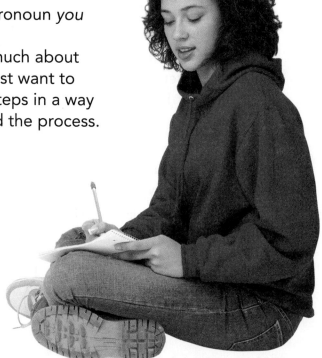

Right now, I won't worry too much about grammar and spelling errors. I just want to concentrate on presenting the steps in a way that will help readers understand the process.

[DRAFT]

Tacking Up a Horse

by Briana   [used a friendly tone]

Have you ever watched someone fit a horse with a bridle and a saddle? If you have, you've seen the process of "tacking up." Tacking up properly is very important. Below are the steps involved in the process of tacking up. If you follow these steps carefully, you're sure to make the ride enjoyable, for both horse and rider alike.

First, you will need to put on the horse's bridle. Begin by unfastening all of the buckles. You should put the bit into the horse's mouth. To insert the bit without hurting the horse, slide your thumb into its mouth. Gently guide the bit into place, making sure it clears the teeth and rests comfterbly on the tongue.

Once the bit is positioned, slide the bridle over the horse's head. Then, pull the forelock out from under the browband.

[used second-person point of view]

Reflect

Read the beginning of Briana's draft. Is her tone helpful, and does it address the audience directly?

Apply

As you write your draft, use an informative, friendly tone. Use second-person pronouns to address your audience.

Revise

Focus on **Ideas**

The Rubric Says Concrete details and pictures support the instructions.

Writing Strategy Add explanatory details and pictures.

I just reread my draft, and it feels like something is missing. The rubric says to use pictures and concrete details, so I'll reread my draft, looking for places to further my explanation with helpful diagrams and specific details.

[DRAFT]

Have you ever watched someone fit a horse with a bridle and a saddle? If you have, you've seen the process of "tacking up." Tacking up properly is very important. Below are the steps involved in the process of tacking up. If you follow these steps carefully, you're sure to make the ride enjoyable, for both horse and rider alike.

If the process is not followed correctly, a person could cause a horse discomfort or injury. **[added concrete details]**

[DRAFT]

[added concrete details]

(Always remember to stand to the left of the horse.)

First, you will need to put on the horse's bridle. Begin by unfastening all of the buckles. You should put the bit into the horse's mouth. To , behind its teeth insert the bit without hurting the horse, slide your thumb into its mouth.

Gently guide the bit into place, making sure it clears the teeth and

rests comfterbly on the tongue.
Be careful not to hurt its ears as you pull them through the headstall and browband.
Once the bit is positioned, slide the bridle over the horse's head.

Then pull the forelock out from under the browband.

Next, position the noseband and throatlatch and buckle them by slipping two fingers between it and the horse's nose securely. Check that the noseband is not too tight. Check the

throatlatch by putting a hand's width between it and the horse's (See Diagram 1.) cheek.

[added a picture]

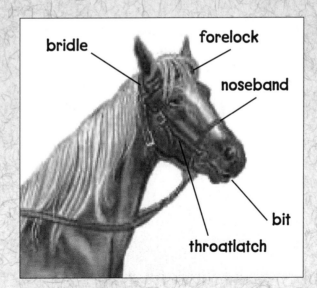

Diagram 1

bridle

forelock

noseband

throatlatch

bit

Apply

Add concrete details and pictures to make your how-to guide easier to understand.

Revise

Focus on Word Choice

The Rubric Says The writer uses precise words and clearly defines domain-specific vocabulary.

Writing Strategy Make sure all topic-related language is used correctly and explained.

I read my how-to guide to a classmate who told me that he'd never tacked up a horse before. He was confused by some of the terms I used. The rubric also reminds me to explain special terms in my writing. I'll read my draft again to define words that are specific to my topic so my audience will understand my instructions.

Writer's Term

Domain-Specific Vocabulary
Domain-specific vocabulary is language that pertains to the topic. For example, an equestrian would use words like **headgear, bridle,** and **bit** to describe horseback riding equipment. To show knowledge and courtesy to readers who are not familiar with a topic, a writer should explain special terms in informational text.

[DRAFT]

[explained special terms] (Always remember to stand to the left of the horse.)
First, you will need to put on the horse's bridle. Begin by unfastening
, or headgear
all of the buckles. You should put the bit into the horse's mouth.
(The bit helps the rider control the horse.)   , behind its teeth
To insert the bit without hurting the horse, slide your thumb into its mouth

Gently guide the bit into place, making sure it clears the teeth and

rests comfterbly on the tongue.

[DRAFT]

Be careful not to hurt its ears as you pull them through the headstall and browband.

Once the bit is positioned, slide the bridle over the horse's head.

, the long hair between the horse's ears,

Then pull the forelock out from under the browband.

, the straps across the horse's nose and face,

Next, position the noseband and throatlatch and buckle

by slipping two fingers between it and the horse's nose

them securely. Check that the noseband is not too tight. Check the

throatlatch by putting a hand's width between it and the horse's
(See Diagram 1.)
cheek.

[explained special terms]

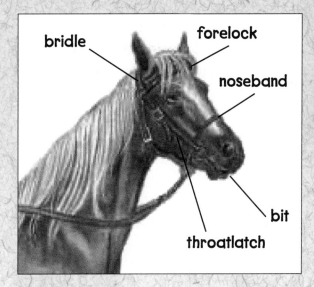

Diagram 1

bridle
forelock
noseband
bit
throatlatch

Reflect

Briana added explanations for words related to her topic. How do her changes help the reader understand the topic?

Apply

Read your draft. If you have used vocabulary related to your topic, be sure to include explanations.

Revise

Focus on Sentence Fluency

The Rubric Says	There is striking variety in sentence length and structure.
Writing Strategy	Use compound and complex sentences for variety.

The rubric says that my sentences should be varied. One way to create a variety of sentences is to use compound and complex sentences. I remember learning about these kinds of sentences not too long ago. Since I already know how to use them correctly, I'll focus on using them to add variety to my writing, just like the rubric says. Take a look at my changes below to see how I created variety by forming a complex sentence out of two closely related statements.

[DRAFT]

[added variety by forming a complex sentence]

Before you
~~Now it's time~~ to put on the saddle. To begin, position a blanket or saddle pad over the horse's withers, or shoulders.

Apply

Use compound and complex sentences to add variety to your writing.

The Rubric Says	Appositives and direct and indirect objects are used correctly.
Writing Strategy	Check to see that appositives have been set off with commas.

Writer's Term

Appositives

An **appositive** is a word or a phrase that identifies a noun or a pronoun. An appositive usually follows the noun it identifies, and it is usually separated from the rest of the sentence by one or more commas.

Now I need to check for errors. I always check spelling, punctuation, and capitalization, but the rubric says I should also check to see if appositives have been set off with commas. I used appositives to explain terms related to my topic, and I remembered to use correct punctuation when I added them to my draft.

[DRAFT]

Be careful not to hurt its ears as you pull them through the headstall and browband. Once the bit is positioned, slide the bridle over the horse's head.

Then pull the forelock out from under the browband. , the long hair between the horse's ears, ◄—— [used appositive correctly]

[used appositive correctly] ——►, the straps across the horse's nose and face,
Next, position the noseband and throatlatch and buckle them securely.

Reflect

Why does punctuating appositives correctly improve the flow of writing?

Apply

Conventions

Edit your draft for spelling, punctuation, and capitalization. Make sure that appositives have been set off with commas.

For more practice, use the exercises on the next two pages.

Appositives

Know the Rule

An **appositive** is a word or a phrase that identifies a noun or a pronoun.
An appositive usually follows the noun it identifies, and it is usually separated
from the rest of the sentence by one or more commas.

• If the appositive appears at the end of a sentence, put a comma right after the
noun being identified.

Example: I usually ride Daisy, **my favorite horse**.

• If the appositive appears mid-sentence, put one comma before it and one
comma after it.

Example: Daisy, **my favorite horse,** has brown and white spots.

Practice the Rule

Number a sheet of paper 1–10. Read each sentence. Copy the appositive and
write the noun it identifies.

1. My family, the Mirabelli family, loves to have lots of parties.
2. Whenever there's a party at my house, I like to make my favorite appetizer,
The Ball.
3. The Ball, a cheese ball made with cream cheese, was named by my cousin Patty.
4. Patty, the daughter of Uncle Wes and Aunt Mary, says that The Ball is her
favorite food.
5. The recipe, a six-step process, is really quite easy to follow.
6. First you mix the main ingredients, cream cheese and pineapple.
7. The spice, cayenne pepper, is added next.
8. John, my younger brother, loves lots of pepper!
9. The sixth step, the final one, is to roll the ball in chopped nuts.
10. You can use either walnuts or, my favorite, almonds.

Direct and Indirect Objects

Know the Rule

A **direct object** is a noun or pronoun that receives the action of the verb. Only action verbs take a direct object.

> **Example:** Carl tossed Jackie the **ball**.

To find the direct object, say the verb *tossed* and then ask *What did Carl toss?* The direct object is **ball**.

An **indirect object** is a person or thing to whom something is given, told, or taught. The indirect object is a noun or pronoun; it comes before the direct object.

> **Example:** Carl tossed **Jackie** the ball.

To test whether a word is an indirect object, move it after the direct object and put the word *to* or *for* in front of it. The indirect object is **Jackie**.

Practice the Rule

Copy the sentences on a separate sheet of paper. Circle the direct objects. Underline any indirect objects.

1. Grandpa, please pass Lindsey the peas.
2. The judge walked around the room three times and then handed Matthew the blue ribbon for best dog in the Junior Division.
3. Mr. Plimpton pushed his car down the street to the nearest gas station when he ran out of gas last Saturday.
4. My mother hands me money every time we hear the ice cream truck in the summer at the lake.
5. Pepper, that naughty little dog from down the road, chewed our garden hose and then chased Charlie up a tree!
6. I love picking blueberries at Emerson Farm every summer.
7. Aunt Viola gave me a beautiful handmade quilt.
8. Oliver gave his mom a nice surprise for her birthday!

Publish

+Presentation

Publishing Strategy	Present the how-to guide as a speech to the class.
Presentation Strategy	Use the illustrations to make posters and other visual aids.

Now that I've finished my how-to guide, I need to decide how to publish it. I could post it online or on a class bulletin board. But my classmates know I love to go horseback riding, so I think it would be fun to read my guide as a speech. I can enlarge the diagrams and make them into posters, and I can use a model of a tacked-up horse while I talk. I'll make sure my posters have all the information from my diagrams and that the labels are easy to read from a distance. To prepare, I'm going to practice in front of a mirror until I feel comfortable. But before I present, I'll read through my guide one last time to make sure it includes all of the items on my checklist.

My Final Checklist

Did I—

- ✔ correctly use and punctuate appositives in my guide?
- ✔ correctly use direct and indirect objects?
- ✔ edit and proofread carefully?
- ✔ make sure my posters contained all the information found in the diagrams in my how-to guide?
- ✔ create easy-to-read labels for my posters?

Apply

Make a checklist to check your how-to guide. Then make a final copy to publish.

Tacking Up a Horse
by Briana

Have you ever watched someone fit a horse with a bridle and a saddle? If you have, you've seen the process of "tacking up." Tacking up properly is very important. If the process is not followed correctly, a person could cause a horse discomfort or injury. Below are the steps involved in the process of tacking up. If you follow these steps carefully, you're sure to make the ride enjoyable, for both horse and rider alike.

First, you will need to put on the horse's bridle, or headgear. (Always remember to stand to the left of the horse.) Begin by unfastening all of the buckles. When finished, you should put the bit into the horse's mouth. (The bit helps the rider control the horse.) To insert the bit without hurting the horse, first slide your thumb into its mouth, behind its teeth. Then gently guide the bit into place, making sure it clears the teeth and rests comfortably on the tongue.

Once the bit is positioned, slide the bridle over the horse's head. Be careful not to hurt its ears as you pull them through the headstall and browband. Then pull the forelock, the long hair between the horse's ears, out from under the browband.

Next, position the noseband and throatlatch, the straps across the horse's nose and face, and buckle them securely. Check that the noseband is not too tight by slipping two fingers between it and the horse's nose. Check the throatlatch by putting a hand's width between it and the horse's cheek. (See Diagram 1.)

Diagram 1

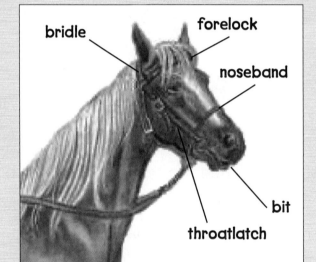

Before you put on the saddle, position a blanket or saddle pad over the horse's withers, or shoulders. Slide the blanket or pad back so that the horse's hair lies flat and doesn't get pulled the wrong way. Place the saddle on top of it. Unfold the girth, the strap that goes underneath the horse, and let it hang down. Then reach under the horse's belly and grab the girth strap. Fasten the girth and then adjust it. Again make sure it's not too tight by running your hand between it and the horse's body.

Before you finish tacking up, you should check one last time to make sure everything fits the horse comfortably. Then gently pull the horse's forelegs forward to release any skin that might be pinched or wrinkled. And there you have it—your horse is tacked up! Now you're ready for a wonderful ride.

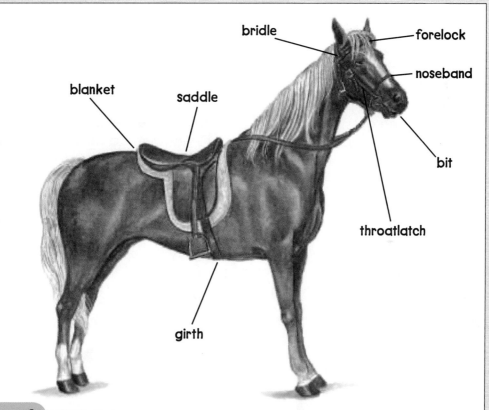

Diagram 2

Reflect

What do you think? How did Briana use the traits to write her how-to guide? Check it against the rubric. Don't forget to use the rubric to check your own guide, too.

What's an **Explanatory Essay?**

It's an essay that explains how something came to be or why something is the way it is. It presents detailed information and analyzes a subject.

What's in an **Explanatory Essay?**

Body
This is the central part of the essay, where I give the actual explanation. I'll use carefully sequenced paragraphs and include supporting facts, specific details, and examples.

Introduction
The introduction includes a thesis statement that clearly tells what is being explained. A strong introduction gets the reader interested in and prepared for the information to come.

Conclusion
I will close, or conclude, my essay in a way that will help readers remember what I explained. I want them to be able to apply what they read to other situations or subject areas.

Style
As I write, I'll make sure the words I use are appropriate for the purpose of the assignment. In explanatory writing, I will be sure to use a formal style.

Why write an **Explanatory Essay?**

There are many reasons to write an explanatory essay. Here are just a few.

To Inform

Sometimes a writer may write to inform readers about a topic that is current, intriguing, or applicable to everyday life. Often, when you write to inform, you find that you learn more about the topic yourself!

To Explain

An explanatory essay may explain facts about a topic and then show how that topic relates to the larger world. You may explain why readers should engage in a specific behavior and how it positively impacts the world around them.

To Understand

You can write an explanatory essay to demonstrate or expand your own understanding of the topic.

Linking Informative/Explanatory Writing Traits to an **Explanatory Essay**

In this chapter, you will explain a topic. This type of informative/explanatory writing is called an explanatory essay. Briana will guide you through the stages of the writing process: Prewrite, Draft, Revise, Edit, and Publish. In each stage, Briana will show you important writing strategies that are linked to the Informative/Explanatory Writing Traits below.

Informative/Explanatory Writing Traits

- a clear, focused topic
- concrete, relevant facts, definitions, and details that support and develop the topic

- information that is organized into an attention-grabbing introduction, an informative body, and a conclusion that supports the information or explanation presented
- transitions that connect ideas and clarify relationships

- a voice and tone that are appropriate for the purpose and audience

- language that is precise and concise
- domain-specific vocabulary that is explained as necessary

- clear sentences that vary in length and structure

- no or few errors in grammar, usage, mechanics, and spelling

Before you write, read Edwin Cruz's model explanatory essay on the next page. Then use the explanatory essay rubric on pages 212–213 to decide how well he did. (You might want to look back at What's in an Explanatory Essay? on page 208, too!)

The Fascination with Fractals
by Edwin Cruz

Introduction

You might have not liked math all that much in the past, but that is about to change! If you've ever stared intently at clouds in the sky, a fern, tree, or a snowflake, you are looking at patterns of fractals, a type of geometric shape. Just look around and you'll see math taking an endless variety of beautiful shapes!

The New Oxford American Dictionary states that a *fractal* is "a curve or geometric figure, each part of which has the same statistical character as the whole. Fractals are useful in modeling structures (such as eroded coastlines or snowflakes) in which similar patterns recur at progressively smaller scales."

As you look at a fractal, you will see a pattern that becomes more complex as it is enlarged in size. Fractals can be generated by computers or occur as natural processes in nature. For example, landscape designers use fractals when they are designing parks or recreation centers.

Formal style

Fractals have certain properties. Two of them are self-similarity and iterative formation. Fractals are self-similar when the sides of their figure are proportionate. One triangle may be three times as wide and three times as long as a smaller one. The ratio is 3:1. When the length of the smaller figure can be multiplied by the ratio and it is the same size as the bigger figure, the fractal has self-similarity.

Body

The second property, iterative formation, refers to repetition within the shape. Fractals are most often created by iteration, or repetition. When making a fractal, take a figure and change it so the new figure is more complex. Keep making this same change over and over and you have a fractal.

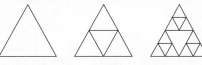

The Sierpinski Triangle

One famous fractal is the Sierpinski Triangle. It is self-similar because each new triangle in this sequence is drawn in the same way. It is iterative because each new triangle is drawn in terms of the previous one.

Conclusion

If you're interested in fractals, you can easily find computer programs that produce these fascinating shapes. Or you can take a look at your dinner plate—broccoli is a fractal! For those who are looking for an area of math that's both intriguing and beautiful, fractals will not disappoint.

Explanatory Essay

Rubric

Use this 6-point rubric to plan and score an explanatory essay.

	6	5	4
Ideas	A thesis statement clearly states the topic. Concrete details inform and explain the thesis statement.	A thesis statement clearly states the topic. One or two details could be clarified or expanded.	A thesis statement is present. Several details could be developed or clarified.
Organization	The essay has an introduction, body, and conclusion. Appropriate transitions connect the ideas effectively.	The essay has an introduction, body, and conclusion. One or two transitions could be added or improved.	The essay has an introduction, body, and conclusion. More or better transitions are needed to connect ideas.
Voice	The writer's voice establishes and maintains a formal style.	The writer's voice establishes and maintains a formal style most of the time.	The writer's voice is somewhat formal.
Word Choice	Domain-specific vocabulary is used and defined correctly.	Most domain-specific words are used and defined correctly.	A few domain-specific words are used correctly but not defined.
Sentence Fluency	Sentence beginnings are varied. Helpful introductory phrases make the writing smooth.	Most sentence beginnings are varied. Some introductory phrases make the writing smooth.	Several sentences begin the same way, interrupting the flow.
Conventions	Prepositional phrases and modifiers are used and placed correctly.	Prepositional phrases are used correctly. One modifier may be misplaced.	Prepositional phrases are used correctly. Several modifiers may be misplaced.

✚Presentation   The format helps readers access the information through a slide show and visuals.

3	2	1	
A thesis statement is present. Too few details inform and explain.	The thesis statement is not clear. Details do not inform or explain.	A topic is not stated. Details may be unrelated or incomplete.	**Ideas**
The body of the essay is not developed. Transitions may be confusing or missing.	The essay lacks an introduction or conclusion. Transitions are not used.	The writing is not organized into paragraphs. Transitions are not used.	**Organization**
The voice does not maintain a formal style.	The voice is not appropriate for the purpose.	The voice is very weak or absent.	**Voice**
Several domain-specific words are used incorrectly.	Many words are overused. Repetition dulls meaning.	Words are very basic and limited. Many are used incorrectly.	**Word Choice**
Too many sentences in a row begin the same way, causing the reader to stop and reread.	All sentences begin the same way. The essay does not use introductory phrases.	Sentences are incomplete or written incorrectly.	**Sentence Fluency**
Prepositional phrases are used correctly. Modifiers are used incorrectly.	Prepositional phrases and modifiers are used incorrectly.	The writing has not been edited.	**Conventions**

See Appendix B for 4-, 5-, and 6-point informative/explanatory rubrics.

Explanatory Essay
Using the Rubric to Study the Model

Did you notice that the model on page 211 points out some key elements of an explanatory essay? As he wrote "The Fascination with Fractals," Edwin Cruz used these elements to help explain his topic. He also used the 6-point rubric on pages 212–213 to plan, draft, revise, and edit the writing. A rubric is a great tool for evaluating writing during the writing process.

Now let's use the same rubric to score the model. To do this, we'll focus on each trait separately, starting with Ideas. We'll use the top descriptor for each trait (column 6), along with examples from the model, to help us understand how the traits work together. How would you score Edwin on each trait?

- **A thesis statement clearly states the topic.**
- **Concrete details inform and explain the thesis statement.**

I didn't know much about fractals before I read Edwin's essay. I appreciated the way he clearly states the topic of his essay and includes informative details. Look how he uses concrete details and examples to explain what fractals are and where they occur.

[from the writing model]

As you look at a fractal, you will see a pattern that becomes more complex as it is enlarged in size. Fractals can be generated by computers or occur as natural processes in nature. For example, landscape designers use fractals when they are designing parks or recreation centers.

Organization

- The essay has an introduction, body, and conclusion.
- Appropriate transitions connect the ideas effectively.

Edwin's essay includes a strong introduction that draws readers in and gets them excited about the topic and a body that includes many important and specific details about the topic. Transitions like *The second property* and *When making a fractal* helped me keep track of where I was in the essay and anticipate the information I was about to read.

[from the writing model]

The second property, iterative formation, refers to repetition within the shape. Fractals are most often created by iteration, or repetition. When making a fractal, take a figure and change it so the new figure is more complex.

Voice

- The writer's voice establishes and maintains a formal style.

Edwin uses a formal style to inform readers by defining fractals, describing their attributes, and providing examples. He avoids using casual words that he might use in a conversation with a friend, because his essay is written to inform and be taken seriously.

[from the writing model]

Fractals can be generated by computers or occur as natural processes in nature. For example, landscape designers use fractals when they are designing parks or recreation centers.

- Domain-specific vocabulary is used and defined correctly.

When Edwin introduces a new word or property of fractals, he provides a definition and explanation. That was really helpful to me, since I didn't know much about fractals.

[from the writing model]

Fractals are self-similar when the sides of their figure are proportionate. One triangle may be three times as wide and three times as long as a smaller one. The ratio is 3:1.

- Sentence beginnings are varied.
- Helpful introductory phrases make the writing smooth.

Edwin begins his sentences in a variety of different ways. He starts some of his sentences with introductory phrases (*For example, If*). The phrases make the text flow and also serve the purpose of linking ideas together.

[from the writing model]

If you're interested in fractals, you can easily find computer programs that produce these fascinating shapes. Or you can take a look at your dinner plate—broccoli is a fractal!

Conventions

• Prepositional phrases and modifiers are used and placed correctly.

Edwin uses prepositional phrases and modifiers to add information and to make his ideas flow smoothly. In each case, he places the phrase or modifier correctly so that there's no confusion about what it refers to. Look at these examples.

[from the writing model]

As you look at a fractal, you will see a pattern that becomes more complex as it is enlarged in size.

[from the writing model]

When the length of the smaller figure can be multiplied by the ratio and it is the same size as the bigger figure, the fractal has self-similarity.

⁺Presentation The format helps readers access the information through a slide show and visuals.

My Turn!

Now it's my turn to write an explanatory essay. I'll use the rubric and good writing strategies to help me. Read on to see how I do it.

Prewrite

Focus on **Ideas**

The Rubric Says	A thesis statement clearly states the topic. Concrete details inform and explain the thesis statement.
Writing Strategy	Choose and narrow a topic that can be explained in an essay. Take notes.

My math teacher asked the class to write about a math concept in the real world. She wanted us to show our understanding of the topic and be able to explain it to others in a way that is accurate and easy to understand, especially if they don't have prior knowledge of the topic.

I chose to write about geodesic domes, structures like the Biosphere II. My essay will need accurate information that explains what a geodesic dome is and why it is useful. I went to the library to find information on the Internet. Here are some of the notes I took about what I learned online. I'll use these notes to help me write a thesis statement and supporting details.

My Notes About Geodesic Domes

✔ Geodesic domes are made of triangles that are connected together in a pattern. Each fractional part of the dome is a geodesic sphere.

✔ The first dome to be recorded was constructed by Walter Bauersfeld in Germany in 1923. The Spaceship Earth Pavillion at Disney's Epcot is an example of a full sphere.

✔ *Frequency* is a word that describes how many smaller triangles make up a dome.

Apply

Choose a math topic to research online. Make notes on your findings. Be sure to keep track of your sources.

Prewrite

The Rubric Says   The essay has an introduction, body, and conclusion.

Writing Strategy   Use an Outline to organize your notes.

The rubric reminds me to organize my ideas into an introduction, body, and conclusion. I took many notes on geodesic domes, so I'll use an Outline to organize them. Using the Outline, I can shape my essay. I've decided on a few questions my essay needs to answer to explain the topic to readers. See part of my Outline below.

Writer's Term

Outline

An **Outline** shows the main points or reasons and supporting details or facts in a piece of writing. Each main point or reason should have a Roman numeral. Each supporting detail or fact should have a capital letter.

Outline

I. What is a geodesic dome?
  A. A dome made of connecting polygons called icosahedrons.
  B. An icosahedron is made up of 12 vertices, 20 faces, and 30 sides divided into smaller triangles.
II. What makes it special?
  A. It is a very stable structure and resistant to weathering and natural disasters.
  B. It can be constructed quickly and easily with minimal materials.
  C. It doesn't need internal columns or load-bearing walls.
III. Where can you see them?
  A. Spaceship Earth at Epcot in Orlando, Florida
  B. Mitchell Park Conservatory in Milwaukee, Wisconsin

Reflect

How does making an Outline help Briana write her explanatory essay?

Apply

Create an Outline using your notes. Think about information you want to include in the introduction, body, and conclusion.

Draft

Focus on Word Choice

The Rubric Says	Domain-specific vocabulary is used and defined correctly.
Writing Strategy	Make sure unfamiliar words are defined.

Now that my Outline is complete, I'm ready to begin writing a draft of my essay. Since I'm explaining what a geodesic dome is, I'll need to use words that are specific to that topic. I'm pretty sure some of these words will be unfamiliar to my readers. If I don't want to lose my readers, I'll have to make sure I give clear definitions. I may have to use a dictionary or other reference materials to make sure my definitions are accurate, but I will use my own words in my essay.

I'm not going to focus on punctuation and spelling as I draft my essay. I'm more concerned about getting my ideas down on paper. I'll go back and correct my writing later.

Geodesic Domes

by Briana

[defined unfamiliar word]

Have you ever heard of or seen a geodesic dome? They aren't found in outer space, but right here on Earth! A geodesic dome is a structure created by an intricate design of polygons connected together.

Geodesic domes are constructed of icosahedrons. An icosahedron is a polyhedron—a three-dimensional geometric solid with faces and edges. An icosahedron has 12 vertices, 20 faces, and 30 sides. An icosahedron looks like many triangles put together to make a sphere-like polygon.

The edges of the triangles that make up the icosahedron are split into more triangles. For example, if you take a triangle ans split its edges into 2 triangles, you will have total of 4 triangles. if you take a triangle and split its edges into 3 triangles, you will have a total of 9 triangles. If you split its edges into 4 triangles, you will have 16 tirangles. The result of an icosahedron being split over and over again is a geodesic dome. A geodesic dome is an icosahedron that is split over and over again.

Reflect

Did Briana use vocabulary that makes the topic easy to understand? Did she define domain-specific words?

Apply

Use your Outline to draft an explanatory essay. Use domain-specific words and terms that relate to the topic. Define them as necessary.

Writing an Explanatory Essay

The Rubric Says Concrete details inform and explain the thesis statement.

Writing Strategy Take out details that are not necessary.

After rereading my draft, I noticed that I included details that don't have much to do with the thesis or repeat what has already been said. I should delete details that don't support the topic of my essay or that make it difficult to understand the topic. Look at how I revised my writing to make it clearer.

> **Writer's Term___**
>
> **Thesis Statement**
> A **thesis statement** is one or two sentences that tell the essay's main idea. It often answers a question. Readers often look for a thesis statement, so it is a courtesy to include one.

[DRAFT]

For example, if you take a triangle ans split its edges into 2 triangles, you will have a total of 4 triangles. If you take a triangle and split its edges into 3 triangles, you will have a total of 9 triangles. If you split its edges into 4 triangles, you will have 16 triangles. The result of an icosahedron being split over and over again is a geodesic dome. ~~A geodesic dome is an icosahedron that is split over and over again.~~

[deleted repetitive detail]

Apply

Read your draft. Make sure the details you include support your thesis statement. Revise your writing so all details help the reader understand your topic.

Revise

The Rubric Says	Appropriate transitions connect the ideas effectively.
Writing Strategy	Use transition words or phrases to connect sentences and paragraphs.

The rubric says to use transitions to connect ideas. Transitions guide the reader from one idea to the next and from one paragraph to the next. Using transitions effectively helps ensure that the reader understands the topic. I'll review my draft for transitions. In this part, I'll repeat ideas in order to transition, or link, them.

[DRAFT]

An icosahedron has 12 vertices, 20 faces, and 30 sides. An

icosahedron looks like many triangles put together to make a

sphere-like polygon.

To make the sphere,

The edges of the triangles that make up the icosahedron are

split into more triangles.

[used repetition to link ideas]

Reflect

How does Briana use repetition to guide the reader?

Apply

Read your draft. Use helpful transitions and repetition to link ideas.

Writing an Explanatory Essay

Revise

Focus on Sentence Fluency

The Rubric Says	Sentence beginnings are varied. Helpful introductory phrases make the writing smooth.
Writing Strategy	Begin sentences with introductory phrases (*for example, as a result*).

The rubric reminds me that sentences should flow smoothly when the essay is read. When a few sentences in a row start the same way, the writing may sound stiff or choppy. If I remember to use introductory phrases, my sentences will flow nicely and the ideas in my sentences will be logically connected. Look at how I've revised my writing to vary the way I begin sentences.

[DRAFT]

An icosahedron is a polyhedron—a three-dimensional geometric

solid with faces and edges. An icosahedron has 12 vertices, 20

faces, and 30 sides. ~~An icosahedron~~ <ins>As a result, it</ins> looks like many triangles put

together to make a sphere-like polygon.

[added introductory phrase]

Apply

Read your draft. Make revisions to ensure sentences begin differently and flow smoothly.

The Rubric Says   Prepositional phrases and modifiers are used and placed correctly.

Writing Strategy   Check the use and placement of prepositional phrases and modifiers.

The rubric says I need to remember to use prepositional phrases and modifiers correctly. Prepositional phrases give readers more information. However, if they are placed incorrectly in the sentence, they become a type of misplaced modifier that can confuse the reader. I found one sentence where I had misplaced a modifier. Here's how I fixed it.

Writer's Term_____

Prepositional Phrase
A **prepositional phrase** begins with a preposition (such as **about, around, from,** or **on**) and ends with the object of the preposition. It is placed near the noun or verb it describes. Use prepositional phrases to add information to a sentence.

[DRAFT]

[corrected misplaced modifier]

With smaller surface areas,
    ^Geodesic domes are way more energy efficient than traditional

structures~~with smaller surfaces.~~

Reflect

How does using prepositional phrases and modifiers correctly help the reader understand the ideas in Briana's essay?

Apply   Conventions

Edit your draft to correctly place prepositional phrases and modifiers. For more practice, use the exercises on the next two pages.

Prepositional Phrases

Know the Rule

A **prepositional phrase** can tell how, what kind, when, how much, or where. A prepositional phrase begins with a **preposition** such as *about, around, at, by, from, in, into, of, on, over, to,* or *with*. It ends with a noun or pronoun that is the **object of the preposition**. The words between the preposition and its object are part of the prepositional phrase. A prepositional phrase can appear at the beginning, middle, or end of a sentence.

> **Example:** The equations **on the first page** are our homework tonight.

Practice the Rule

Number a sheet of paper 1–10. Write the prepositional phrase or phrases from each sentence. Circle the preposition.

1. To measure the sides of each polygon, use the tape measure.
2. Subtract the smaller number from the larger number to find the difference.
3. Before class, Ashley remembered to get her calculator from her locker.
4. We could practice drawing fractals using software in the computer lab.
5. Does either of these patterns include fractals?
6. In a fraction, the denominator tells how many total parts.
7. Because I finished my algebraic equations early, I looked back at my answers one more time.
8. Which structure in the museum is a geodesic dome?
9. Along which path should I go to find the shortest distance between point A and point B?
10. What facts do you want to share about the uniqueness of the geodesic dome?

Placement of Modifiers

Know the Rule

Dangling modifiers are phrases that do not clearly refer to any particular word in a sentence. Frequently the dangling modifier appears at the beginning of a sentence. The problem often has to be fixed by rewriting the sentence.

> Example: **Looking** down the road, a **car** came closer.
> Correct: Looking down the road, I saw a car come closer.

A **misplaced modifier** is a word, phrase, or clause that is separated from the word it modifies. Usually the problem can be fixed by moving the word or words to a different place in the sentence.

> Example: The **dog** dug a hole in the yard **with droopy ears**.
> Correct: The dog with droopy ears dug a hole in the yard.

Practice the Rule

Number a sheet of paper 1–10. Write **dangling** or **misplaced** to describe the problem with each sentence.

1. We completed the math problems on the board slowly.
2. Listening intently, my head began to ache.
3. Manny rushed into math class, who was running late.
4. Beautifully drawn, the girl admired the pictures.
5. The girl ran across the street in the blue shirt.
6. After redoing the problems again, the equation is wrong.
7. In the cafeteria, everyone was almost sitting.
8. The coach announced on Monday the roster would be posted.
9. The party was a success, having planned everything accordingly.
10. Who is the man tallest in the group?

Writing an Explanatory Essay

Publish

+Presentation

Publishing Strategy	Present the explanatory essay as a slide show.
Presentation Strategy	Display information clearly.

I think a slide show would be a great way to present my explanatory essay. This way I can share the interesting information I found on geodesic domes with the whole class! Each slide should include one main point from my essay, along with just a few details. If I include too much information on a single slide, it will be hard for my audience to read. I want to make sure I use a font that is easy to read from a distance. The visuals I insert on the slides should go along with the information on the screen. I'll use a checklist to prepare my slide show.

My Final Checklist

Did I—

✔ check the grammar, usage, mechanics, and spelling?

✔ make sure prepositional phrases and modifiers are placed correctly?

✔ use a clear, readable font?

✔ create visuals that complement the text?

Apply

Make a checklist to check your own explanatory essay. Then publish your final copy to share with your audience.

Geodesic Domes
by Briana

Have you ever heard of or seen a geodesic dome? They aren't found in outer space, but right here on Earth! A geodesic dome is a structure created by an intricate design of polygons connected together.

Geodesic domes are constructed of icosahedrons. An icosahedron is a polyhedron—a three-dimensional geometric solid with faces and edges. An icosahedron has 12 vertices, 20 faces, and 30 sides. As a result, it looks like many triangles put together to make a sphere-like polygon.

To make the sphere, the edges of the triangles that make up the icosahedron are split into more triangles. For example, if you take a triangle and split its edges into 2 triangles, you will have a total of 4 triangles. If you take a triangle and split its edges into 3 triangles, you will have a total of 9 triangles. If you split its edges into 4 triangles, you will have 16 triangles. The result of an icosahedron being split over and over again is a geodesic dome.

You can find geodesic domes in many different frequencies. The frequency of a dome describes the number of smaller triangles into which a larger triangle is divided. The higher the frequency, the more sphere-like the geodesic dome.

Because geodesic domes are structurally sound, they are able to withstand weathering and natural disasters better than a more box-like structure. With smaller surface areas, geodesic domes are more energy efficient than traditional structures. They are also easy to construct and require fewer materials. A geodesic dome supports itself and doesn't require internal columns or load-bearing walls.

You may be wondering where on Earth you can find a geodesic dome. Do you think you've seen one? You have if you've ever visited Epcot at Disney World in Florida or the Mitchell Park Conservatory in Milwaukee, Wisconsin!

Reflect

Did Briana use the traits of a good explanatory essay? Check it against the rubric. Be sure to use the rubric to check your own work, too.

- Icosahedrons make up geodesic domes.
- The frequency of the dome describes the number of smaller triangles into which a larger triangle is divided.

Informative/ Explanatory test writing

Read the Writing Prompt

When you take a writing test, you will be given a writing prompt. Most writing prompts have three parts:

Setup This part of the writing prompt gives you the background information you need to get ready to write.

Task This part of the writing prompt tells you exactly what you are supposed to write: a how-to guide.

Scoring Guide This section tells how your writing will be scored. To do well on the test, you should include everything on the list.

Remember the rubrics you've used? When you take a writing test, you don't always have all of the information that's on a rubric, but the scoring guide is a lot like a rubric. It lists everything you should think about as you write. Like the rubrics you've previously used, most scoring guides are based on the six traits of writing:

Ideas   Organization   Voice

Word Choice   Sentence Fluency   Conventions

Think of a chore that you enjoy. This should be something that others normally find dull or routine. For example, do you like to tinker around, cleaning, washing, and/or organizing things? Do you enjoy cooking, baking, or washing the family car?

Write a how-to guide explaining how to accomplish a chore that you actually enjoy.

Be sure your writing

- supports the topic with well-chosen facts and concrete details.

- introduces the topic clearly and is organized logically.

- sounds serious yet engaging.

- uses words correctly.

- flows smoothly.

- contains correct grammar, punctuation, capitalization, and spelling.

Writing Traits
in the Scoring Guide

Reread the scoring guide in the writing prompt on page 231. Not every test prompt will include each of the six writing traits, but this one does. You can use the following chart to help you better understand the connection between the scoring guide and the writing traits in the rubrics you've used.

- Be sure your writing supports the topic with well-chosen facts and concrete details.

- Be sure your writing introduces the topic clearly and is organized logically.

- Be sure your writing sounds serious yet engaging.

- Be sure you use words correctly.

- Be sure your writing flows smoothly.

- Be sure your writing contains correct grammar, punctuation, capitalization, and spelling.

Look at Kyle Greer's how-to guide on the next page. Did he follow the scoring guide?

HOW TO MOW A LAWN

by Kyle Greer

Are you looking for a great way to earn extra money? If so, I have the perfect job for you: mowing other people's lawns. Here are the steps to take to mow a great lawn.

First, you'll need to get your equipment ready. You can use a gas mower, an electric mower, or a push mower. I think the gas and electric mowers are better because they are easier to handle. If you use a gas mower, be sure that it has enough gas and oil. An electric mower, like the one that I use, needs to be charged, so be sure to charge yours. Also, most mowers have settings for grass length, so make sure your mower is set properly.

Then you'll need to walk through the yard that you're going to mow, picking up items that will get in your way, such as rocks and sticks or toys. It's important to do this because otherwise it can wreak havoc on your mower's blades, ruin the items that you mow over, and/or cause things to fly up toward you as you mow.

Before you start your mower, you'll want to put on safety glasses or goggles, as well as sneakers or work boots to protect your feet. Now you're ready to start the power. You do this by either pushing a button or using the pull cord. Once the mower is started, mow along the outside of the lawn. Go in one direction across the lawn and then back in the other direction right beside where you first mowed. Repeat this again and again until you reach the edge of the lawn opposite to where you first began.

I use a mulching mower that cuts up the grass clippings and puts them back into the grass as I mow. But if you use a mower that has a grass collector, you will periodically need to check the bag on the mower to see how full it is getting. When it gets full, you will need to empty the clippings into a bag that you can leave for the homeowner to either use as compost or properly dispose of. Be sure to turn the mower off or make sure that the blade is stopped before emptying the bag.

Now the lawn is mowed. Turn off the mower and check your work one last time to be sure you didn't miss anything. Good job!

Using the Scoring Guide to Study the Model

Now we'll use the scoring guide to check Kyle's writing test, "How to Mow a Lawn." Let's see how well his essay meets each of the six writing traits.

- **The writing supports the topic with well-chosen facts and concrete details.**

Kyle does a thorough job of explaining how to mow a lawn. He points out the facts, such as what is needed to prepare equipment.

> If you use a gas mower, be sure that it has enough gas and oil. An electric mower, like the one that I use, needs to be charged, so be sure to charge yours. Also most mowers have settings for grass length, so make sure your mower is set properly.

- **The writing introduces the topic clearly and is organized logically.**

Kyle wrote the steps in his guide in the order that they are to be followed. He begins with a short explanation of equipment preparation. Then he explains the importance of removing items from the grass and putting on safety gear before mowing the lawn. I like the way Kyle organized his guide, and the way he stresses safety, too.

> Before you start your mower, you'll want to put on safety glasses or goggles, as well as sneakers or work boots to protect your feet. Now you're ready to start the power.

Voice

- **The writing sounds serious yet engaging.**

Kyle keeps his voice serious throughout his writing, but he includes some personal experiences to make the subject more interesting.

If you use a gas mower, be sure that it has enough gas and oil. An electric mower, like the one that I use, needs to be charged, so be sure to charge yours. Also, most mowers have settings for grass length, so make sure your mower is set properly.

Word Choice

- **Words are used correctly.**

Kyle uses homophones correctly. He uses *It's* instead of *Its*, and he uses the word *wreak* instead of *reek*, which has a totally different meaning!

It's important to do this because otherwise it can wreak havoc on your mower's blades, ruin the items that you mow over, and/or cause things to fly up toward you as you mow.

Using the Scoring Guide to Study the Model

• **The writing flows smoothly.**

Kyle's guide flows smoothly. Even though it's step-by-step, the writing still contains enough sentence variety to make it interesting and easy to read.

I use a mulching mower that cuts up the grass clippings and puts them back into the grass as I mow. But if you use a mower that has a grass collector, you will periodically need to check the bag on the mower to see how full it is getting. When it gets full, you will need to empty the clippings into a bag that you can leave for the homeowner to either use as compost or properly dispose of.

• **The writer correctly uses grammar, punctuation, capitalization, and spelling.**

I think Kyle's how-to guide is error-free. But I know it's important to check for mistakes in my own work, so I'll be sure to do this as I write. And remember, you should check the conventions at every step of the writing process so that you can avoid having errors on your final test, too!

Focus on Organization

Writing Strategy Choose a graphic organizer.

Since I don't have much time, I'll start organizing my ideas. The scoring guide says my writing should be organized logically, so I'll use a Sequence Chain to organize the steps in my how-to guide.

Topic: How to be a good pet sitter

Step 1: Ask the pet owners for details.
   a. Visit the pet owner's home.
   b. Write down a list of important instructions.
   c. Find out when they'll leave and when they'll return.
   d. Ask how often you need to stop by and what you need to do.
   e. Get the keys so you can get in the house.
   f. Get emergency numbers.

Step 2: When it's time for your visit, call the pet by name.
   a. Give the pet some love and attention while you're there.

Step 3: Give the pet its food and water.

Step 4: If the owners requested it, take the pet for a walk.
   a. Make sure to take waste bags with you.
   b. Remember to put the pet on a leash.

Step 5: Repeat the above steps for as many times as the owners requested.
   a. Leave the owners a note to tell them how things went.

Result: The pet is well cared for, and the owners appreciate it!

Reflect

Does Briana's Sequence Chain contain enough steps?

Apply

Use a Sequence Chain to arrange steps in the order that they should be followed.

Prewrite

Focus on Organization

Writing Strategy	Check the graphic organizer against the scoring guide.

I won't have much time to revise during a writing test, so prewriting is more important than ever. Before I start writing, I'll check my Sequence Chain against the scoring guide in the writing prompt.

Topic: How to be a good pet sitter

Step 1: Ask the pet owners for details.
   a. Visit the pet owner's home.
   b. Write down a list of important instructions.
   c. Find out when they'll leave and when they'll return.
   d. Ask how often you need to stop by and what you need to do.
   e. Get the keys so you can get in the house.
   f. Get emergency numbers.

Step 2: When it's time for your visit, call the pet by name.
   a. Give the pet some love and attention while you're there.

Step 3: Give the pet its food and water.

Step 4: If the owners requested it, take the pet for a walk.
   a. Make sure to take waste bags with you.
   b. Remember to put the pet on a leash.

Step 5: Repeat the above steps for as many times as the owners requested.
   a. Leave the owners a note to tell them how things went.

Result: The pet is well cared for, and the owners appreciate it!

Ideas
- Be sure your writing supports the topic with well-chosen facts and concrete details.

I'll be sure to use lots of concrete details to make my ideas clear. I've already written some facts on my Sequence Chain, but I'll be sure to include even more in my guide.

Organization
- Be sure your writing introduces the topic clearly and is organized logically.

I'll mention my topic in my introduction, and I'll use my Sequence Chain to help me write the body. This will help me keep things well-organized.

Voice
- Be sure your writing sounds serious yet engaging.

I'll keep the tone serious and include some of my own experiences to keep the reader interested.

Word Choice
- Be sure you use words correctly.

As I write, I'll make sure to use the correct words.

Sentence Fluency
- Be sure your writing flows smoothly.

I'll use different kinds of sentences to make one step flow to the next.

Conventions
- Be sure your writing contains correct grammar, punctuation, capitalization, and spelling.

I'll pay close attention to this as I write. Then I'll go back and edit my draft before turning it in.

Reflect

The Sequence Chain is a good start. Do you think anything is missing?

Check your graphic organizer against the scoring guide before you start to write. This will help you remember what to do once you begin the writing process.

Draft

Focus on **Ideas**

Writing Strategy   Provide plenty of explanatory details for the reader.

I used my Sequence Chain to outline the steps of my how-to guide, but the scoring guide says I also need to provide plenty of explanatory details for the reader. As I write, I'll include the steps from my Sequence Chain, and I'll also include details that explain why each step is important. After all, the reader may not have taken care of a pet before!

[DRAFT]

How to Be a Good Pet Sitter

by Briana

Being a pet sitter is an important responsbility. I've done a lot of pet sitting and have learned some important tips for taking care of other people's animals.

The first step is to get details and instructions from the pet owner. The pet sitter should do this in person so that they can meet the pet and get a better idea of how things are done. They might also want to make a list of instructions such that they don't forget anything.

They might also want to make a list of instructions such that they don't forget anything.

[explanatory details]

First, you need to ask the pet owner when you'll be pet sitting. Make sure you are free. Ask how often you need to come over. Find out what you need to do. Find out what the pet eats. Ask where the

[DRAFT]

food is kept. Ask about any special needs the pet has, such as going outside after it eats or going on a walk. You'll also need to know where the leash is kept if you are going to take a dog for a walk, and you'll want to get the keys to the house so that you can get in. Its also important to get the vet's number, along with the phone number where the owner can be reached.

When you first go to the house to pet-sit, call out the pet's name so that it won't be scared. Pet or play with it and give it some food and water.

[explanatory details]

If you're supposed to let the animal out, now is a good time to do it. Be sure that you take waste bags with you if you have a dog to walk, and make sure the dog is on a leash.

Before you leave, give the animal one last bit of attention, and make sure that you haven't forgotten anything. Then repeat the steps above as often as necessary, four as many times a day as needed.

On your last visit, leave the owners a note, summarizing what their pet did. Most pet owners really seem to appreshiate this!

Reflect

Does Briana's how-to guide include enough details? Will the reader understand the process?

Apply

Provide explanations and details to help your readers understand the steps in your how-to guide.

Revise

Focus on Organization

Writing Strategy   Use appropriate transition words.

After I completed my draft, I realized that some of the steps in my guide were bunched together. I know that using transition words, such as *first*, *next*, and *then*, can help clarify my writing. Transition words send a signal to the reader that a new step has begun.

[DRAFT]

[added transition words]

When you first go to the house to pet-sit, call out the pet's name

Then,

. Next,

so that it won't be scared. Pet or play with it and give it some food

and water.

Apply

Use helpful and well-placed transition words to guide the reader through your writing.

Writing Strategy Address the reader directly.

The scoring guide says my voice should be serious yet engaging. My report is full of information, so keeping my voice serious was easy. I am always more engaged with writing that speaks directly to me. If I use second-person point of view, and address my audience as *you*, keeping my reader engaged will be easy.

[DRAFT]

[used second-person point of view]

The first step is to get details and instructions from the pet owner.
~~The pet sitter~~ You should do this in person so that ~~they~~ you can meet the pet
and get a better idea of how things are done. ~~They~~ You might also want
to make a list of instructions such that ~~they~~ you don't forget anything.

Reflect

How does using the second-person point of view engage the reader?

Apply

It's easy to keep your audience engaged when you use second-person point of view to address your reader directly.

Revise

Focus on **Word Choice**

Writing Strategy   Choose the right word.

The scoring guide says to check my writing to be sure I have used words properly. Homophones can be tricky. I keep a list of troublesome ones, like *accept/except* and *two/too*, so I was surprised to see that I had written *four* instead of *for*. I think it happened because I used *many times* in the same sentence. This would definitely confuse the reader. It's time to revise it!

[DRAFT]

make sure that you haven't forgotten anything. Then repeat the steps

above as often as necessary, ~~four~~ ^{for} as many times a day as needed.

[choose the right word]

Apply

Use a dictionary or homophone resource to check words that sound alike. Then read your draft to make sure you use the right word every time.

Edit

Focus on Conventions

Writing Strategy Check the grammar, punctuation, capitalization, and spelling.

There's one last step! The scoring guide says that I should check for correct grammar, punctuation, capitalization, and spelling. I'll reread my how-to guide to be sure my test is error-free. I always make sure I have enough time to check my grammar and mechanics, since it's a really important step!

How to Be a Good Pet Sitter

by Briana

Being a pet sitter is an important ~~responsbility~~ responsibility. I've done a lot of pet sitting and have learned some important tips for taking care of other people's animals.

The first step is to get details and instructions from the pet owner. ~~The pet sitter~~ You should do this in person so that ~~they~~ you can meet the pet and get a better idea of how things are done. ~~They~~ You might also want to make a list of instructions such that ~~they~~ you don't forget anything.

First, you need to ask the pet owner when you'll be pet sitting, and then ~~Make~~ make sure you are free. Ask how often you need to come over, and find out what you need to do. Find out what the pet eats, and ask where the

Apply

Don't forget to check grammar, punctuation, capitalization, and spelling every time you write for a test.

[FINAL DRAFT]

food is kept. Ask about any special needs the pet has, such as going

outside after it eats or going on a walk. You'll also need to know

where the leash is kept if you are going to take a dog for a walk,

and you'll want to get the keys to the house so that you can get in. It's

also important to get the vet's number, along with the phone number

where the owner can be reached.   Pets can get lonely when their owners
are away, so it's nice to give them
some attention when you are there.

When you first go to the house to pet sit, call out the pet's name

so that it won't be scared. Then, Pet or play with it, Next, and give it some food

and water. It's really important for animals to have water to
drink; otherwise, they can get sick and dehydrated.

If you're supposed to let the animal out, now is a good time to do

it. Be sure that you take waste bags with you if you have a dog to

walk, and make sure the dog is on a leash.

Before you leave, give the animal one last bit of attention, and

make sure that you haven't forgotten anything. Then repeat the steps

above as often as necessary, ~~four~~ for as many times a day as needed.

On your last visit, leave the owners a note, summarizing what their

pet did. Most pet owners really seem

to ~~appreshiate~~ appreciate this!

Reflect

What do you think? Is this test ready to turn in? Why or why not? Before you turn in your writing, always remember to check it one last time against your writing prompt's scoring guide.

Well now, that wasn't so bad! Just remember to use the writing process when you take a writing test. The process is just a little different for a test, but if you keep in mind these important tips, I'm sure you'll do just fine!

TEST TIPS

1. **Study the writing prompt before you start to write.** Most writing prompts have three parts: the setup, the task, and the scoring guide. The parts probably won't be labeled. You'll have to figure them out for yourself!

2. **Make sure you understand the task before you start to write.**

   - Read all three parts of the writing prompt carefully.
   - Circle key words in the task part of the writing prompt that tell what kind of writing you need to do. The task might also identify your audience.
   - Make sure you know how you'll be graded.
   - Say the assignment in your own words to yourself.

3. **Keep an eye on the clock.** Decide how much time you will spend on each part of the writing process and try to stick to your schedule. Don't spend so much time prewriting that you don't have enough time left to write!

4. **Reread your writing. Compare it to the scoring guide at least twice.** Remember the rubrics you've used? A scoring guide on a writing test is like a rubric. It can help you keep what's important in mind.

5. **Plan, plan, plan!** You don't get much time to revise during a test, so planning is more important than ever.

6. **Write neatly.** Remember: If the people who score your test can't read your writing, it doesn't matter how good your essay is!

Argument
writing convinces the reader of something.

Hi, my name is Luis. We're studying argument writing in school. I'm excited about trying to convince readers of my opinions. I can't wait to try it!

IN THIS UNIT

- [ ] **Editorial**
- [ ] **Argument Essay**
- [ ] **Speech**
- SCIENCE CONNECTION ▶ **Formal Proposal**
- [ ] **Writing for a Test**

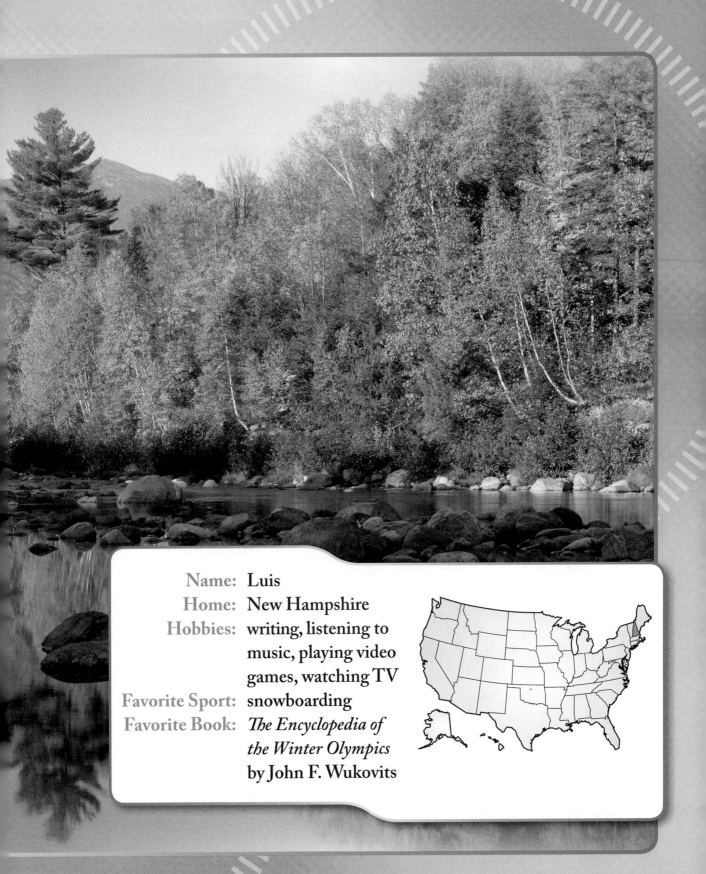

Name: Luis
Home: New Hampshire
Hobbies: writing, listening to music, playing video games, watching TV
Favorite Sport: snowboarding
Favorite Book: *The Encyclopedia of the Winter Olympics* by John F. Wukovits

What's an Editorial?

It's a type of argument writing that is published in newspapers or magazines. I have strong opinions, so I'm looking forward to writing about an issue that affects me.

What's in an Editorial?

Opinion
In an editorial, a writer expresses his or her opinion about an important problem. Then, it's up to the reader to decide if he or she agrees.

Problem and Solutions
This is the focus of an editorial. The writer states a problem and offers some possible solutions. Thinking about an issue that affects me is going to help me come up with possible solutions.

Counterclaims
It's important to remember that there are usually two sides to every issue. I will include valid opposing claims in my editorial to fairly address every side or viewpoint of my argument.

Evidence
An editorial is opinion-based, which means it's really important for the writer to include details, facts, and examples that back up his or her beliefs. Without this kind of information, the reader might not trust the writer's credibility.

Why write an Editorial?

There are all kinds of reasons to write an editorial. I've listed some here, and I'll use these ideas to help me decide on a purpose for my own writing.

To Inform

The writer of an editorial can educate the reader with facts and details. In turn, the reader can decide what to do with the information.

To State a Position

Convincing readers to agree with an opinion or position is the focus of most editorials and, in my opinion, is the strongest reason to write them.

To Call to Action

Sometimes, an editorial writer wants readers to do more than just agree with his or her opinions. Here, the writer's purpose is to urge readers to take action.

To Lead

People sometimes look to folks in leadership positions for guidance on relevant issues. When a politician or a class council member writes an editorial, the reader receives that person's advice on an important issue or problem.

Linking Argument Writing Traits to an Editorial

In this chapter, you will send your opinion about an important issue to a newspaper or magazine. This type of argument writing is called an editorial. Luis will guide you through the stages of the writing process: Prewrite, Draft, Revise, Edit, and Publish. In each stage, Luis will show you important writing strategies that are linked to the Argument Writing Traits below.

Argument Writing Traits

**Ideas**
- a clearly stated position or claim
- relevant supporting evidence that comes from reliable, credible sources
- alternate or opposing claims that are acknowledged and addressed with logical evidence

**Organization**
- a strong introduction that presents the writer's position, a body that supports the position, and a conclusion that sums up the argument and/or offers a call to action
- transitions that clarify the relationships among ideas

**Voice**
- a voice and tone that are appropriate for the purpose and audience

**Word Choice**
- language that is compelling

**Sentence Fluency**
- sentences that vary in length and structure

**Conventions**
- no or few errors in grammar, usage, mechanics, and spelling

Before you write, read Julia Powell's editorial on the next page. Then use the editorial rubric on pages 258–259 to decide how well she did. (You might want to look back at What's in an Editorial? on page 254, too!)

The Fate of the Main Street Theater

by Julia Powell

Problem

In three weeks, the city of Springside is planning to tear down its oldest landmark, the Main Street Theater. First opened in 1927, this historical building has deteriorated to such a degree that it is too expensive to save. The theater, which stood empty for years, is situated in a prime location in the center of downtown. Two groups have their eyes on that location and are fighting to gain support for their plans. One group wants a multilevel parking garage. The other wants a park with an amphitheater. Both groups want support from the people of Springside in the upcoming election. Therefore, we must educate ourselves about the pros and cons of both proposals.

Solutions

Evidence

First, let's look at the park proposal. The best thing about it is that it would give people some much-needed green space downtown. During the day, downtown workers would have a place to relax and eat lunch. Plays and concerts in the amphitheater would draw people downtown in the evening. This would provide business and income for the stores and restaurants in the area. The park itself would not make money for the city, but its existence would benefit the entire downtown area in other ways, both financially and ecologically.

Counterclaim

On the negative side, however, the costs of designing and building the park would come from our pockets, possibly from a tax levy. The additional cost to maintain the park would be covered by various garden clubs in Springside.

Now, let's look at the garage. What would be good about it? If people know they have a convenient place to park, they're much more likely to come downtown and frequent the businesses there. This would attract new businesses, which might consider Springside a good place to call home.

Counterclaim

What's the downside? Some people say a garage would be an eyesore, especially if it's not well maintained. Others say it would be a "crime magnet" that would invite trouble if not well guarded. Yes, hiring people to maintain and guard the garage would create a few jobs. However, I doubt that the hourly fees charged for parking would be enough to pay these workers and maintain the facility.

Personally, I'm in favor of using the site for a downtown park. How about you? Which side will you take when you vote? Choose carefully now! The vote you cast in the upcoming election will affect Springside for years.

Writer's opinion

Rubric

Use this 6-point rubric to plan and score an editorial.

	6	5	4
Ideas	The problem is clearly stated. The editorial offers logical solutions supported by relevant evidence.	The problem is stated. The editorial offers some logical solutions supported by relevant evidence.	The problem is stated. The editorial offers some solutions. Most evidence is relevant.
Organization	The editorial has strong introduction, body, and concluding sections.	The editorial has a strong introduction and body. The concluding section could be stronger.	The editorial has a strong introduction. The body and concluding sections could be stronger.
Voice	The writer maintains a formal tone and first-person point of view.	The writer maintains a formal tone most of the time and first-person point of view.	The writer's tone may be informal in parts. First-person point of view is maintained.
Word Choice	Precise, powerful words clarify the relationships within the argument. Neutral words avoid bias.	Most words are precise and clarify relationships within the argument. Neutral words avoid bias.	Some words are precise. Neutral words avoid bias.
Sentence Fluency	Sentence structures and lengths are exceptionally varied and flow smoothly. The writer's ideas are easy to follow.	Most sentences are varied and flow smoothly. Most of the writer's ideas are easy to follow.	Some sentences share the same beginnings and do not flow smoothly. Most of the writer's ideas are easy to follow.
Conventions	Compound personal pronouns are correct. All subjects and predicates are complete. This piece is thoroughly edited.	Most compound personal pronouns are correct. Most subjects and predicates are complete.	Several errors in the use of compound personal pronouns, subjects, and predicates distract the reader but don't affect the meaning.

✚ Presentation The editorial is neat, accurately typed, and in the appropriate format.

3	2	1	
The problem may not be stated clearly. The editorial offers one solution. The evidence may be relevant.	The problem is not stated clearly. The editorial offers one solution. The evidence is not relevant.	The writer is still searching for the problem and solutions. The writing is incomplete.	**Ideas**
The editorial has an introduction and body. The concluding section is weak or incomplete.	The editorial has an introduction and body. The concluding section is incomplete or absent.	The writing is not organized. It lacks introduction, body, and concluding sections.	**Organization**
The writer's tone may be harsh or strident. Second-person point of view is used.	The writer's tone may be inappropriate. Second-person point of view is used.	The writer's tone is inappropriate or very weak. Point of view is inconsistent.	**Voice**
Words are often unclear or vague. Some biased words are used.	Words are often misused. Biased words may offend the reader.	Words and phrases are consistently vague. Biased and offensive words may be present.	**Word Choice**
Sentence beginnings are often alike, and sentences are often similar in length.	The writing is filled with choppy or run-on sentences. There is little or no variety in sentence structure or length.	Many sentences are incorrect or incomplete. Ideas are hard to follow.	**Sentence Fluency**
Noticeable errors in the use of compound personal pronouns, subjects, and predicates slow down the reader.	Many errors in the use of compound personal pronouns, subjects, and predicates make reading difficult.	Serious, frequent errors in the use of personal pronouns, subjects, and predicates make the writing difficult to read.	**Conventions**

See Appendix B for 4-, 5-, and 6-point argument rubrics.

Using the Editorial Rubric to Study the Model

Did you notice that the model on page 257 points out some key elements of an editorial? As she wrote "The Fate of the Main Street Theater," Julia Powell used these elements to help her offer her opinion about a local issue. She also used the 6-point rubric on pages 258–259 to plan, draft, revise, and edit the writing. A rubric is a great tool to evaluate writing during the writing process.

Now let's use the same rubric to score the model. To do this, we'll focus on each trait separately, starting with Ideas. We'll use the top descriptor for each trait (column 6), along with examples from the model, to help us understand how the traits work together. How would you score Julia on each trait?

Ideas

- **The problem is clearly stated.**
- **The editorial offers logical solutions supported by relevant evidence.**

Julia draws readers into her editorial by stating the problem in the first sentence. Then, she explains how two different groups have proposed to solve the problem. Later in the editorial, she presents relevant evidence to support her position. Although she's in favor of a park, she also points out the fact that it will require funding.

[from the writing model]

Two groups have their eyes on that location and are fighting to gain support for their plans. One group wants a multilevel parking garage. The other wants a park with an amphitheater.

- **The editorial has strong introduction, body, and concluding sections.**

Julia follows up on her introduction with a body that clearly sets out the facts about both sides of the issue. In her conclusion, she states her opinion and calls on readers to voice their own preferences. This is a strong and engaging way to wrap up the editorial.

[from the writing model]

Personally, I'm in favor of using the site for a downtown park. How about you? Which side will you take when you vote? Choose carefully now! The vote you cast in the upcoming election will affect Springside for years.

- **The writer maintains a formal tone and first-person point of view.**

Julia helps me connect with her editorial by using first-person point of view but keeps her tone serious at the same time. If her voice was too casual, it might be hard to take her arguments seriously. Her use of the pronouns *I* and *we* really help me identify with her opinion.

[from the writing model]

Yes, hiring people to maintain and guard the garage would create a few jobs. However, I doubt that the hourly fees charged for parking would be enough to pay these workers and maintain the facility.

Word Choice

- Precise, powerful words clarify the relationships within the argument.
- Neutral words avoid bias.

Precise words add strength and clarity to Julia's writing. Words like *convenient* and *frequent* are more effective than words like *easy* and *visit*. Julia also uses neutral words that do not judge either side of the issue. She presents the arguments and opposing claims without judgment or bias.

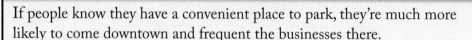

[from the writing model]

If people know they have a convenient place to park, they're much more likely to come downtown and frequent the businesses there.

Sentence Fluency

- Sentence structures and lengths are exceptionally varied and flow smoothly.
- The writer's ideas are easy to follow.

Julia writes interesting sentences. Did you notice how they vary in structure and length? I especially like the way she asks the reader questions in the conclusion. The writing held my interest, and it was easy to follow her ideas.

[from the writing model]

Personally, I'm in favor of using the site for a downtown park. How about you? Which side will you take when you vote? Choose carefully now! The vote you cast in the upcoming election will affect Springside for years.

**Conventions**

- Compound personal pronouns are correct.
- All subjects and predicates are complete.
- This piece is thoroughly edited.

I know that a compound personal pronoun like *herself, themselves,* or *yourself* must refer to its antecedent. Julia makes sure each compound personal pronoun refers back to the subject of its sentence. Coordinating conjunctions are used correctly, and all her subjects and predicates are complete.

[from the writing model]

The park itself would not make money for the city, but its existence would benefit the entire downtown area in other ways, both financially and ecologically.

✛Presentation The editorial is neat, accurately typed, and in the appropriate format.

My Turn!

I'm going to write an editorial about something I feel strongly about. I'll follow the rubric and use good writing strategies. Read on to see how I do it!

Prewrite

Focus on **Ideas**

The Rubric Says	The problem is clearly stated. The editorial offers logical solutions supported by relevant evidence.
Writing Strategy	State the problem clearly and offer logical solutions.

I'm on the staff of our school newspaper. I contribute poems, articles, and editorials. So when my teacher said we were going to write an editorial about an important school or community problem, I knew exactly what to write about: Our administration is upset about the clothes some kids are wearing to school. They want us to start wearing uniforms.

First, I jotted down the issue. Next, I wrote down possible ways to solve it. Then, I listed pros and cons to figure out how readers might disagree with my solutions. Fairly addressing possible counterclaims will only help strengthen my editorial. To develop strong arguments, I then interviewed a friend who has to wear a uniform to school every day.

Problem: Our administration is upset about the clothes that some students wear to school.

Why it's a problem: They feel that the students' clothing causes discipline problems.

Possible solutions:

1. School uniforms for all students

Pros
It's the "great equalizer."
You never have to wonder/worry about what to wear to school.
It saves parents money on kids' wardrobes and accessories.

Cons
Everyone looks the same every day.
Students can't express individuality through clothing.
You get singled out in public—and ridiculed!

2. Dress code that restricts certain clothing

Pros
It allows for individual expression, within limits.
Students can wear different outfits every day.
Parents don't waste money on new uniforms for their kids.

Cons
Dress code guidelines would be set per administration's personal opinions.
Some kids will try to test/abuse the rules.
Student rebellion could end up proving the administration's point.

Think about a problem, along with several possible solutions. Gather information by jotting down the pros and cons of each solution.

Prewrite

Focus on **Organization**

The Rubric Says   The editorial has strong introduction, body, and concluding sections.

Writing Strategy   Make a Problem-Solution Frame to organize the pros and cons of several solutions.

The rubric says my editorial should consist of an introduction, body, and conclusion. I think I will use a Problem-Solution Frame to organize the information I want to use. The organizer will help me state the problem I want to discuss in the introduction and list the facts I'll need for the body. Problem-Solution Frames also help all sides of the problem.

My introduction needs to explain the problem clearly and in an interesting way. The body should thoroughly explain all of the arguments and counterarguments. The conclusion needs to summarize the problem and call the reader to action.

Writer's Term

Problem-Solution Frame
You can use a **Problem-Solution Frame** to analyze a problem and its possible solutions. Then after comparing and contrasting solutions, you can choose the best way to solve the problem.

Problem-Solution Frame

Problem Box

What is the problem?	Our administration is upset about the clothes that some students wear to school.
Why is it a problem?	They feel that the students' clothing causes discipline problems.

Solution Box

Solution 1	Solution 2
School uniforms for all students	Dress code that restricts certain clothing

Pros	Cons	Pros	Cons
It's the "great equalizer."	Everyone looks the same every day.	It allows for individual expression, within limits.	Dress code guidelines would be set per the administration's personal opinions.
You never have to wonder/worry about what to wear to school.	Students can't express individuality through clothing.	Students can wear different outfits every day.	Some kids will try to test/abuse the rules.
It saves parents money on kids' wardrobes and accessories.	You get singled out in public—and ridiculed!	Parents don't waste money on new uniforms for their kids.	Student rebellion could end up proving the administration's point.

Reflect

What do you think? How will Luis's Problem-Solution Frame help him write a well-organized editorial?

Apply

Make a Problem-Solution Frame to organize your ideas for your editorial.

Draft

Focus on *Ideas*

The Rubric Says The editorial offers logical solutions supported by relevant evidence.

Writing Strategy State a problem and offer some helpful solutions for the reader.

Now I'll use my Problem-Solution Frame to help me write my editorial. The rubric says I should support all my reasons with relevant evidence. This will make my argument stronger because it means I will provide evidence to support my reasons and address the counterclaims.

Using the cons I have already listed, I can add counterclaims to my editorial. For now, I'm just going to get my ideas down on paper. I know I can go back and fix any spelling, grammar, and punctuation mistakes later, when I edit. Read the beginning of my editorial on the next page.

Writer's Term

Counterclaim

A **counterclaim,** or con, is an argument or viewpoint that goes against the writer's argument. A counterclaim is also called an opposing claim.

[DRAFT]

To Uniform or Not to Uniform?   [problem]

There's a debate raging at Oakbrook School. The administration is concerned about our clothing. They claim it is disrespectful and causing us to become rebellious. As a result, they are trying to impose school uniforms as soon as next semester. Needless to say, this has caused some students to speak out. Certainly, uniforms are one solution. But there are [solution 1]
others. How about a restricted dress code, for instance? [solution 2]

First, let's look at uniforms. My strongest argument against them is that they impose upon students' right to express individuality. Fashion is a big part of a teenager's life. If you and me look the same everyday, how will we be allowed to express ourself? If us students have to conform to the "fashion" of a uniform, the only way to express ourself will be through your hairstyles.

Another problem with uniforms is that although we will look the same in school, we'll stand out in public. Can you imagine? We'll feel like we're wearing costumes all the time!   [counterclaim]

There are a few advantages to wearing uniforms, however. The most important one is that uniforms are the "great equalizer."

Reflect

How will stating counterarguments make Luis's editorial stronger?

Apply

Write a draft that states a problem and some possible solutions.

Revise

Focus on Organization

The Rubric Says	The editorial has strong introduction, body, and concluding sections.
Writing Strategy	Summarize the problem and call the reader to action in the conclusion.

Writer's Term

Call to Action

The **call to action** asks the audience to agree with the writer and to participate in solving the problem. The call to action is sometimes stated in the conclusion.

At this point, I am happy with my introduction and body paragraphs. But the conclusion should bring my message to a close. I don't think it does yet.

The conclusion is the last thing to be read. It should not only summarize the problem and include a call to action, but it should also leave an impression on the reader. I think I will revise and strengthen my last sentence to reflect my main arguments.

[DRAFT]

Nonetheless, I'd like to ask for your support in fighting for a dress code. Let us prove ourself to the administration. Let us show that we can be responsable and mature. We can "dress for success"
~~win—and keep—our right to choose our own clothes!~~ ←
in this effort. We can ~~do it~~!

[strengthened conclusion]

Apply

Restate your position clearly and include a strong call to action in the conclusion.

The Rubric Says	The writer maintains a formal tone and first-person point of view.
Writing Strategy	Use a formal tone and the pronouns *I, me, we,* and *us.*

I read my editorial again and then reviewed the rubric. It says that I should use a formal tone and first-person point of view. I consistently use first-person pronouns. However, there are a few areas where my tone could be a bit more serious. I need to match my voice to my audience and purpose. My audience consists of other students, but if I sound too casual, my argument may not be taken seriously.

[DRAFT]

[revised for a formal tone]

cost-effective

They take the guesswork out of what to wear. They are also also ~~cheap~~

eliminate   elaborate wardrobes   accessories

since they ~~wipe out~~ the need for ~~fancy clothes~~ and ~~stuff~~.

Reflect

How can establishing a too-casual tone in an editorial work against the writer's purpose?

Apply

Read your draft aloud. Make sure to use first-person pronouns and a formal tone.

Revise

Focus on Word Choice

The Rubric Says Precise, powerful words clarify the relationships within the argument. Neutral words avoid bias.

Writing Strategy Choose precise, neutral words.

The rubric says my words should be both precise and neutral. I want my reader to agree with my opinion, so it's important that I don't use any words that might offend or drive my reader away. Word choice is so important when discussing opinions. I can see how words like *weak* and *complain* might offend some people, so I will replace them with neutral words now.

[DRAFT]

[used neutral words]

has a downside

Of course, this solution ~~is kind of weak~~. Some students might abuse

argue

the dress code and try to test its limits. They might ~~complain~~ that

violate

what they're wearing does not ~~go against~~ the rules. [used precise words]

Apply

Choose precise and neutral words to voice your opinion.

Edit

Focus on Conventions

The Rubric Says

Compound personal pronouns are correct. All subjects and predicates are complete. This piece is thoroughly edited.

Writing Strategy

Make sure pronouns are used correctly. Compound personal pronouns should refer to the subject.

Writer's Term

Compound Personal Pronouns

A **compound personal pronoun** is a pronoun that ends in **-self** or **-selves**. This type of pronoun always refers to the subject in a sentence, and it must agree with the subject in number and gender.

Now it's time to proofread my editorial. The rubric reminds me to make sure all my personal pronouns are correct and that all subjects and predicates are complete. I will also make sure that all compound subjects and predicates are joined by a coordinating conjunction.

[DRAFT]

[used pronouns correctly]

                                                I
a big part of a teenager's life. If you and ~~me~~ look the same
                                        ourselves   we
every day, how will we be allowed to express ~~ourself?~~ If ~~us~~ have

to conform to the "fashion" of a uniform, the only way to express
 ourselves   our
~~ourself~~ will be through ~~your~~ hairstyles.

Reflect

How does editing carefully show respect for the reader?

Apply

Conventions

Edit your draft. Make sure you use pronouns correctly.

For additional practice on using compound personal pronouns and compound subjects and predicates, see the exercises on the next two pages.

Compound Personal Pronouns

Know the Rule

A **compound personal pronoun** is a pronoun that ends in -*self* or -*selves*. It usually shows that the subject of a sentence is doing something to or for itself. A compound personal pronoun used in this way is called a reflexive pronoun.

> **Example:** I made **myself** a cup of tea.

Sometimes, a compound personal pronoun is used for emphasis. A compound personal pronoun used in this way is called an intensive pronoun.

> **Examples:** Mrs. Jenkins built the table **herself**.
> Carson changed the tire **himself**.

A compound personal pronoun usually refers back to the subject of the sentence; therefore, it must match its subject in number and gender.

Practice the Rule

Number a sheet of paper 1–10. Write the compound personal pronoun that correctly completes each sentence and the subject to which it refers.

1. I sat _____ down last night to write an editorial for our school newspaper.

2. We have been talking among _____ about the cafeteria food.

3. The cafeteria employees _____ are unhappy with it.

4. In an editorial, you can really express _____.

5. The students _____ have written many editorials.

6. Coach Decker can get _____ a lot of attention by writing an editorial.

7. The menu _____ needs to be changed first.

8. We students can help _____ by suggesting healthy foods we already like to eat.

9. Our principal, Ms. Martino, made _____ a note to address the menu at the next school board meeting.

10. The students should all be proud of _____ for making a difference at school!

Compound Subjects and Predicates

Know the Rule

A **compound subject** is two or more subjects joined by a coordinating conjunction (*and, or, nor*).

> **Example:** Tori's **grandmother and grandfather** invited the entire family over for a giant barbecue.

A **compound predicate** is two or more verbs joined by a coordinating conjunction (*and, or, nor*).

> **Example:** Tomorrow, you **can walk or ride** your bike to school.

Practice the Rule

Number a sheet of paper 1–10. Write the compound subject or compound predicate in each sentence. Circle the coordinating conjunction.

1. Ana, Katherine, and Lee piled into the soccer team's bus.
2. By Sunday, I must finish *A Tale of Two Cities*, write a three-page response, and study for a history exam.
3. Buddy, Sparky, or Doc will win first prize in the dog show next month.
4. James will not play his trumpet in the concert but will sing with the choir.
5. Due to the power outage, Mr. Templeton will arrive late or cancel my piano lesson.
6. James and Jackie take dance lessons from the same instructor.
7. Next year they will tour with the high-school band and play in concerts all over the Midwest.
8. Five years ago, my brother and twin sister played in the high-school marching band.
9. They still practice and play their tubas every day!
10. Would Ana, Katherine, and Lee have room on the bus for a couple of zany tuba players?

Publish

+Presentation

Publishing Strategy Publish the editorial in the school newspaper.

Presentation Strategy Make sure the editorial is neat, accurately typed, and in the appropriate format.

Now that I'm done, I need to publish my editorial. I feel strongly about this issue, so I want to submit it for publication in our school newspaper. Before my editorial can be published, though, I need to be sure that it's in the proper format required by the newspaper and that it's neatly and accurately typed. If there are misspelled words and typos, no one will take my argument seriously. I'll also read it through one last time to make sure it includes all the items on my checklist.

My Final Checklist

Did I—

✔ use compound personal pronouns correctly?

✔ join compound subjects and predicates with a coordinating conjunction?

✔ neatly type my editorial in the proper format?

✔ check for spelling, grammar, and punctuation errors?

✔ put my name on each page of my editorial?

Apply

Use the checklist to prepare a neat, final copy, and publish it.

To Uniform or Not to Uniform?

by Luis

There's a debate raging at Oakbrook School. The administration is concerned about our clothing. They claim it is disrespectful and causing us to become rebellious. As a result, they are trying to impose school uniforms as soon as next semester. Needless to say, this has caused some students to speak out. Certainly, uniforms are one solution. But there are others. How about a restricted dress code, for instance?

First let's look at uniforms. My strongest argument against them is that they impose upon students' right to express individuality. Fashion is a big part of a teenager's life. If you and I look the same every day, how will we be allowed to express ourselves? If we have to conform to the "fashion" of a uniform, the only way to express ourselves will be through our hairstyles.

Another problem with uniforms is that although we will look the same in school, we'll stand out in public. Can you imagine? We'll feel like we're wearing costumes all the time!

There are a few advantages to wearing uniforms, however. The most important one is that uniforms are the "great equalizer." The amount of money a family has is all but indistinguishable when everyone's clothing looks the same. Uniforms are also time-savers. They take the guesswork out of what to wear. They are also cost-effective since they eliminate the need for elaborate wardrobes and accessories. I know of a girl who said her parents saved at least $300 in clothing costs because she wears a uniform to school!

Before I sound like I'm in favor of school uniforms, let me propose another solution: a dress code that prohibits certain clothing. This would let students know exactly which items are no-nos. This solution still allows students to express their individuality, but it sets certain limitations. For example, T-shirts endorsing tobacco or alcohol products would be forbidden, as would shirts with "suggestive" slogans.

Of course, this solution has a downside. Some students might abuse the dress code and try to test its limits. They might argue that what they're wearing does not violate the rules. This would be problematic. Because of their behavior, these teens just might prove the administration correct in saying that clothing causes disruptive behavior!

Nonetheless, I'd like to ask for your support in fighting for a dress code. Let us prove ourselves to the administration. Let us show that we can be responsible and mature. We can "dress for success" in this effort. We can win—and keep—our right to choose our own clothes!

Reflect

How well do you think Luis did using all of the traits of a good editorial in his writing? Check it against the rubric, and don't forget to use the rubric to check your own editorial.

What's an Argument Essay?

It's a type of writing that builds a convincing argument. To argue convincingly, a writer needs to support a claim with clear reasons and evidence.

What's in an Argument Essay?

Claim
The claim is the opinion or position taken by the writer regarding an idea or topic. The claim should be clearly stated in the introduction.

Opposing Claim
A good writer will always include opposing or alternate claims, just to show readers they have considered the subject from all sides. An argument is actually strengthened when counterclaims are logically addressed.

Reasons and Evidence
A good writer will support a claim with solid reasons and factual evidence. Reasons explain why the writer holds the opinion, while evidence—concrete facts and solid examples—support those reasons.

Logical Reasoning
The way a writer builds an argument is called reasoning. Effective reasoning is well-organized and logical. Reasons and supporting evidence need to be presented in a clear, easy-to-follow way.

PROS

CONS

Why write an Argument Essay?

There are many reasons to write an argument essay. I'll list a few of them here. Can you think of any more?

To Convince
We all have opinions we feel strongly about—so strongly that we try to convince others to hold the same positions. An argument essay is a powerful tool to use when trying to change the opinions of readers.

To Inform
Learning is a lifelong process. An argument essay can help readers make positive changes in their lives and reap the benefits that come from understanding a topic in a new way.

To State a Position
People make decisions every day. But it's very important to make an informed decision. A good argument essay can help clarify an issue and get readers to act. Understanding all sides of an issue is the best way to form an opinion that is based on fact.

Linking Argument Writing Traits to an Argument Essay

In this chapter, you will build an argument to support your position on a topic. This type of argument writing is called an argument essay. Luis will guide you through the stages of the writing process: Prewrite, Draft, Revise, Edit, and Publish. In each stage, Luis will show you important writing strategies that are linked to the Argument Writing Traits below.

Argument Writing Traits

- a clearly stated position or claim
- relevant supporting evidence that comes from reliable, credible sources
- alternate or opposing claims that are acknowledged and addressed with logical evidence

- a strong introduction that presents the writer's position, a body that presents the argument, and a conclusion that sums up the argument and/or offers a call to action
- transitions that clarify the relationships among ideas

- a voice and tone that are appropriate for the purpose and audience

- language that is compelling

- sentences that vary in length and structure

- no or few errors in grammar, usage, mechanics, and spelling

Before you write, read Lori Kaspar's argument essay on the next three pages. Then use the argument essay rubric on pages 284–285 to decide how well she did. (You might want to look back at What's in an Argument Essay? on page 278, too!)

Give a Student a Laptop, Give a Student the World

by Lori Kaspar

The world is a *big* place, and we eighth-grade students at Greenleaf Middle School deserve to explore it. Having technology in the classroom will open the door to discovery and opportunity. Laptops will help us build essential computer skills, improve our study time, and raise our grades.

Claim

Evidence

Many studies show the benefits of having technology in the classroom. But did you know that laptops help raise students' grades? Consider this important data from the article, "Learning with Technology—The Impact of Laptop Use on Student Achievement" by James Cengiz Gulek and Hakan Demirtas. It shows that students' grades are higher with laptops.

Factual evidence

Program Enrollment (2003-04 Cumulative Grade Point Averages by Grade)

Grade	Laptop	Non-Laptop
6	3.50	3.13
7	3.28	2.94
8	3.23	3.07

Cons

Some believe that providing a laptop for each student in eighth grade will be too expensive. They do not want to spend the money on middle-school students. Others want to begin a laptop program in the middle school on a limited basis. They want students to share laptops and save money. Still others oppose them because they believe that the Internet is distracting and unreliable. These are valid concerns, but they can be easily addressed and proved false.

Opposing claims

Pros

Let me begin by asking, "What is the real cost of a student body that is behind in technological understanding?" There are students at Greenleaf who cannot afford their own computers or Internet access at home. This economic barrier is one our school district can and should overcome. In today's world, knowing how to use a computer for word-processing, communicating, and conducting research is essential.

Reasons

Additionally, limiting the number of laptops would shut out many more students. Who would be responsible for keeping track of shared laptops? Would they be available whenever students need to use them? It seems to me that repair and replacement costs can be reduced by teaching students how to care for their own laptops. Once students learn the basics and take responsibility for maintenance, replacement costs would be reduced.

Having access to one's own laptop makes better use of study time, too. Every student knows how time-consuming it can be to handwrite long papers and reports. It also consumes irreplaceable resources like paper.

Finally, with planning, most Internet distractions can be averted. Schools can set Internet policies, and teachers can review and recommend credible sites. With supervision, students will learn responsible computer and Internet habits. In the long run, I believe that *not* providing every student with a laptop will cost more in lost education opportunities.

Reasons

Solutions

If you oppose a laptop program at Greenleaf Middle School, could it be because you would rather spend the money on other activities? It's true that the district may need to reduce other programs to fund a laptop program in the middle school. But shouldn't academics come first? After all, access to a good education will keep students in school.

Conclusions

After answering the opposing claims, it seems clear that providing laptops for all students is a positive investment in our future. When you review all the evidence, I believe you will agree that the benefits far outweigh the initial cost. Laptops will help us perform better in school and help us succeed in a very big world!

Works Cited

Chen, Grace. "How Your Child Can Benefit from New Public School Laptop Programs." September 3, 2009. Public School Review. November 10, 2010. http://www.publicschoolreview.com/articles/142.

Gulek, James Cengiz, and Hakan Demirtas. "Learning With Technology: The Impact of Laptop Use on Student Achievement." January 2005. November 10, 2010. http://pdfcast.org/pdf/learning-with-technology-the-impact-of-laptop-use-on-student-achievement.

"The Pros and Cons of Laptop Use in the Classroom," Associated Content from Yahoo 2011, accessed March 19, 2012, http://www.associatedcontent.com/article/915119/the_pros_and_cons_of_laptop_use_in.html.

Zucker, Andrew. "Starting School Laptop Programs: Lessons Learned." November 2005. November 10, 2010. http://www.ubiqcomputing.org/Lessons_Learned_Brief.pdf.

Reflect

What do you think? How well has Lori used the Argument Writing Traits to convince her readers to agree with her opinion?

Rubric

Use this 6-point rubric to plan and score an argument essay.

	6	5	4
Ideas	The argument supports the claim with clear reasons and relevant evidence. The argument is balanced: Evidence supports the claim and refutes opposing claims.	The argument supports the claim with reasons and evidence. The argument is mostly balanced.	Some reasons and evidence may be too general to support the claim. The argument is somewhat balanced.
Organization	Reasons and evidence are organized logically and effectively. A variety of effective transitions creates cohesion and clarifies ideas.	Reasons and evidence are organized logically. Transitions create cohesion and clarify ideas.	Reasons and evidence are not always organized logically. More or better transitions would help organize the ideas.
Voice	The voice and tone are perfect for the purpose and audience and are consistent throughout the essay.	The voice and tone are appropriate for the purpose and audience and are consistent in most of the essay.	The voice and tone are appropriate for the purpose and audience, but they are not consistent.
Word Choice	Precise words convey the writer's message. There are no unnecessary words.	Precise words convey the writer's message most of the time. There are few unnecessary words.	Precise words convey the writer's message in places. There is a noticeable number of unnecessary words.
Sentence Fluency	Sentence types are varied successfully for flow and effect.	Sentence types are varied for flow and effect.	Varying the types of several sentences would improve the flow and effect of the writing.
Conventions	Pronouns are used correctly. The meaning of the text is clear.	There are a few errors with pronouns but they do not affect clarity.	Noticeable errors with pronouns do not impair meaning or readability.

+Presentation Text features, such as headings, paragraph indentations, and charts, enhance the argument.

3	2	1	
Some reasons and evidence do not support the claim. The argument clearly favors one position.	Reasons and evidence are weak or missing. The argument presents two opposing claims for balance.	The argument is not clear. It is hard to tell what the writer believes.	**Ideas**
Reasons and evidence are not well organized. Some transitions mislead the reader.	The organization of reasons and evidence is not clear. Transitions are missing or used incorrectly.	The reader cannot make sense of the reasons and evidence. Transitions are not used.	**Organization**
The voice and tone may be inconsistent or inappropriate in parts of the essay.	The voice and tone are not appropriate for the purpose and audience.	The voice and tone are very weak or absent.	**Voice**
Some words are too general. Wordy sentences cause the reader some confusion.	Many words are too general or vague. Overly wordy sentences mislead the reader.	Many words are too vague or are incorrect. The reader cannot make sense of the writing.	**Word Choice**
Too many similar sentences make the writing choppy and limit the effectiveness on the reader.	Most of the sentences are very basic and similar. Some are incorrect.	Sentences are constructed awkwardly or incorrectly. It is hard for the reader to understand the meaning.	**Sentence Fluency**
Noticeable, distracting errors with pronouns cause the reader to slow down.	Many errors with pronouns confuse the reader.	Frequent errors with pronouns make the script hard to read.	**Conventions**

See Appendix B for 4-, 5-, and 6-point argument rubrics.

Argument Essay

Using the Rubric to Study the Model

Did you notice that the model on pages 281–283 points out some key elements of an argument essay? As she wrote "Give a Student a Laptop, Give a Student the World," Lori Kaspar used these elements to help her present her argument. She also used the 6-point rubric on pages 284–285 to plan, draft, revise, and edit the writing. A rubric is a great tool to evaluate writing during the writing process.

Now let's use the same rubric to score the model. To do this, we'll focus on each trait separately, starting with Ideas. We'll use the top descriptor for each trait (column 6), along with examples from the model, to help us understand how the traits work together. How would you score Lori on each trait?

Ideas

- **The argument supports the claim with clear reasons and relevant evidence.**
- **The argument is balanced: Evidence supports the claim and refutes opposing claims.**

Lori jumps right in and clearly states her claim. I like that. She then provides factual evidence to back up her stance. I admire how she tackles several opposing claims directly. It's easy to agree with her point of view when counterclaims are addressed so logically.

[from the writing model]

There are students at Greenleaf who cannot afford their own computers or Internet access at home. This economic barrier is one our school district can and should overcome. In today's world, knowing how to use a computer for word-processing, communicating, and conducting research is essential.

Organization

- Reasons and evidence are organized logically and effectively.
- A variety of effective transitions creates cohesion and clarifies ideas.

It is easy to understand Lori's position because she has carefully and logically organized all of her supporting reasons and evidence. Her ideas flow naturally from one to the next, and I never feel lost or confused. She uses transitions, such as *Finally* and *In the long run*, to show how several ideas are linked or related.

[from the writing model]

Finally, with planning, most Internet distractions can be averted. Schools can set Internet policies, and teachers can review and recommend credible sites. With supervision, students will learn responsible computer and Internet habits. In the long run, I believe that *not* providing every student with a laptop will cost more in lost education opportunities.

Voice

- The voice and tone are perfect for the purpose and audience and are consistent throughout the essay.

Lori clearly knows who her audience is—adults who hold the power to make important financial decisions. Wanting to be taken seriously, she uses a respectful and formal voice throughout the essay. Even though her voice is firm and passionate about the subject, she always maintains a friendly and polite tone.

[from the writing model]

The world is a *big* place, and we eighth-grade students at Greenleaf Middle School deserve to explore it. Having technology in the classroom will open the door to discovery and opportunity. Laptops will help us build essential computer skills, improve our study time, and raise our grades.

Word Choice

- Precise words convey the writer's message.
- There are no unnecessary words.

Lori carefully chose each and every word for her essay. Her writing is full of well-chosen words that deliver her message. There are no unnecessary words to weigh down and weaken her writing either. The result—her message is clear, energetic, and powerful.

[from the writing model]

Additionally, limiting the number of laptops would shut out many more students. Who would be responsible for keeping track of shared laptops? Would they be available whenever students need to use them? It seems to me that repair and replacement costs can be reduced by teaching students how to care for their own laptops.

Sentence Fluency

- Sentence types are varied successfully for flow and effect.

Lori uses a variety of sentence types and structures, which allows her writing to flow smoothly. She even included a few questions to get the reader actively involved with her essay. With so much variety, it was easy to stay interested in what she had to say.

[from the writing model]

If you oppose a laptop program at Greenleaf Middle School, could it be because you would rather spend the money on other activities? It's true that the district may need to reduce other programs to fund a laptop program in the middle school. But shouldn't academics come first?

 **Conventions**

• Pronouns are used correctly.
  The meaning of the text is clear.

Lori obviously took her time editing her essay; I couldn't find a single error! She even uses pronouns correctly, as you can see in the sentences below. Without any mistakes to confuse me or slow my reading down, I understood Lori's message loud and clear.

[from the writing model]

After answering the opposing claims, it seems clear that providing laptops for all students is a positive investment in our future. When you review all the evidence, I believe you will agree that the benefits far outweigh the initial cost. Laptops will help us perform better in school and help us succeed in a very big world!

✚Presentation Text features, such as headings, paragraph indentations, and charts, enhance the argument.

My Turn!

I'm going to write an argument essay to support my position on a topic. I'll follow the rubric and use good writing strategies. Follow along to see how I do it!

Prewrite

Focus on **Ideas**

The Rubric Says	The argument supports the claim with clear reasons and relevant evidence.
Writing Strategy	Decide on a position. Find credible evidence to support the position.

I may not be an adult yet, but I still have strong opinions about issues in the world. When I found out we were writing an argument essay, I was so excited. This is my chance to express my stance on a topic that's important to me. But which topic will I choose? I feel strongly about so many things—recycling, reducing our carbon footprint, and even starting school later in the morning.

After a little thought, I decided to write about the fact that I think school should start a little later in the morning. A little more sleep could really help students' performances. But my opinion is not enough. I'll need to gather supporting evidence to back up my position. I'll research on the Internet and at the library to find the evidence I need.

As I began my research, I remembered what my teacher said about using credible and reliable sources for fact gathering. A reliable source is any source—website, book, or other—that provides accurate, trustworthy information. Not everything on the Internet is true, so it's important to choose websites carefully. I'll ask myself: Does the website look professional? Is information up-to-date? What links, if any, are on the site? If the links are all sales related, perhaps the website is geared more toward making money than providing facts.

Writer's Term

Credible Website

A **credible website** is an online source that contains accurate, trustworthy, up-to-date information. An example of a credible website is www.britannica.com. Information on this site comes from the same people who write the *Encyclopedia Britannica*, a current and respected source.

As I take notes, I'll be sure to paraphrase the information, or use my own words to explain the point. I don't want to plagiarize, or take the credit for another person's hard work!

Writer's Term

Paraphrase/Plagiarize

To **paraphrase** is to restate the meaning of a particular passage in your own words.

Don't **plagiarize**! To plagiarize means to present another person's ideas as your own.

Reflect

Is Luis right about researching websites? What experience do you have in checking the reliability of websites?

Apply

Choose reliable, credible sources for your research. Be sure to use your own words as you take notes and keep track of your sources.

Prewrite

Focus on Organization

The Rubric Says   Reasons and evidence are organized logically and effectively.

Writing Strategy   Use a Sentence Outline to organize the argument.

Writer's Term

Sentence Outline
A **Sentence Outline** organizes notes by writing complete sentences for the main points and supporting details. Each main point has a Roman numeral. The supporting details under each main point have capital letters (A, B, C). The Introduction and Conclusion are not included in this type of outline.

Now that I've collected reasons and evidence to support my argument, I need to organize all of the information. The better the organization, the easier it will be to write my draft. I've used lots of different graphic organizers before, but a Sentence Outline will work best for this assignment.

A Sentence Outline uses a format that helps me write out my main points and the supporting details for each main point. Writing paragraphs and staying on-topic will be easy once the outline is complete. Check out my Sentence Outline on the following page. It really helped me organize all my notes.

Sentence Outline

I. Chemical changes occur during puberty that require more sleep.
   A. Sleep patterns (circadian rhythms) change.
   B. According to the National Sleep Foundation, teens need 9¼ hours of sleep per night.
   C. Most teens don't get enough sleep and may be sleep deprived.
   D. Symptoms of sleep deprivation include impaired memory, difficulty focusing and meeting deadlines, lower grades, an increase in moodiness, and even depression.

II. Cons: Not everyone agrees that a later start time would be beneficial.
   A. Starting school one hour later means school ends one hour later.
   B. Students in after-school activities, such as sports, might run into scheduling conflicts.
   C. Bus schedules would have to change.
   D. Some bus companies might be reluctant to change hours.

III. Pros: Several states with later high-school start times report positive results.
   A. Students missed fewer days.
   B. Drop-out rates went down.
   C. Grades went up.
   D. Students reported fewer mood swings.
   E. Teachers noted that students seemed calmer, and there were fewer fights.
   F. There were fewer car accidents involving teen drivers on school days.

IV. Solutions
   A. Reschedule events and routes.
   B. Shorter routes could service the elementary schools first.
   C. Longer routes may encounter less traffic.

Reflect

Look over Luis's Sentence Outline. Has he included enough supporting evidence? How will it help him write his essay?

Apply

Use your notes to complete a Sentence Outline. Organize your information in a clear and logical way.

Draft

Focus on **Organization**

The Rubric Says	Reasons and evidence are organized logically and effectively. A variety of effective transitions creates cohesion and clarifies ideas.
Writing Strategy	Organize the reasons and evidence in a logical order.

Now that my Sentence Outline is complete, it's time to start writing! I'm feeling confident about the amount of supporting reasons and evidence I've collected. Now I'll use my outline to write my draft. I will follow it to put all my paragraphs in order. I'll also remember to explain any terms, such as *sleep deprivation*, for my readers. My teacher says that when information is clear and logically organized, the whole argument is stronger. I'll also be sure to use plenty of transitions to connect and clarify my ideas. That way, readers can easily follow my argument, point by point.

As I write, I'll focus on getting all my ideas down on paper. After my draft is complete, I can go back and correct any spelling, grammar, or punctuation mistakes. Here I go!

[DRAFT]

A Little More Sleep Goes a Long Way

by Luis

Everyone agrees that being a teenager can be challenging. So many changes take place over a few years that it's no wonder teens often feel overwhelmed and just plain tired. Our bodies and our ideas are changing. Yikes! Sometimes, life seems unfair! One change that would lead to positive results in school would be to allow us teens to sleep later on school mornings. By delaying the start of school by just an hour, many of the challenges us teens face every day in school could be overcome.

Claim

Evidence

It is a proven fact that our need for sleep increases as we enter puberty. Sleep patterns, also known as circadian rhythms, make it almost impossible to fall asleep before 11:00 p.m. Most high school days begin at 7:30 a.m., which means that most of us are functioning on too little sleep. According to the National Sleep Foundation, teenagers require 9¼ hours of sleep per night. I'm sure most of us are not getting that amount.

Factual evidence

Most teens don't get enough sleep and may be sleep deprived. Sleep deprivation is a serious condition. Symptoms include impaired memory, difficulties in focusing and meeting deadlines, lower

Opposing claim

[DRAFT]

grades, and an increase in moodiness, even depression. The following chart shows the results for a group of sophomores who were asked how many hours they sleep on weeknights.

Number of Sleep Hours During Weeknights for Sophomores

Number of Students (y-axis): 0, 5, 10, 15, 20, 25, 30

Hours of Sleep (x-axis): less than 5; 5 to less than 6; 6 to less than 7; 7 to less than 8; 8 and plus

■ Number of Students

Cons

So why hasn't a delay in start time been made in all high schools? Although this poll is convincing, not everyone agree that a later start time would be beneficial. Starting school one hour later means school *ends* one hour later. This fact can create several challenges. Students in after-school activities, such as sports, might run into scheduling conflicts. Bus schedules would have to be revised. Some bus companies might be reluctant to change its hours of operation, the hours of the day when it's open for business. And everyone knows that buses can be noisy and uncomfortable, as well. These things may seem difficult to overcome, but with cooperation they can be solved.

Opposing claim

Pros

Convincing data indicate positive results from starting high school later. The results were really amazing!

[DRAFT]

Factual evidence

Students missed fewer days, drop-out rates went down, and grades went up. There were fewer car accidents involving teen drivers on school days. As little as one extra hour of sleep has many benefits.

Solutions

If you oppose a later start time due to after-school activites and bus shedules, I say just reshedule the events and routes. Buses could service the elementary schools first and then the high schools. Older students often live far from their schools. Buses with longer routes may encounter less traffic. It may take time to get used to new hours, but they should be changed for the health of teens.

Conclusions

Overall, the "pros" far out-weigh the "cons." Each challenge can be overcome with a little planning. The goal of attending school is to get a good education. Sleepy teens like my friends and I find it difficult to learn in class. Why not set up all students for sucess? It's time to make our lives more managable by setting the school clocks ahead by 60 minutes.

Reflect

What do you think? Is Luis's argument clearly defined? Does he include his supporting reasons and evidence? Are his details organized logically?

Apply

Use your Sentence Outline to write a draft of an argument essay. Make sure you clearly state your claim in the introduction, and organize your supporting details logically.

Revise

Focus on **Voice**

The Rubric Says	The voice and tone are perfect for the purpose and audience and are consistent throughout the essay.
Writing Strategy	Maintain a consistent, appropriate voice and tone.

Now to start revising. As I check the rubric, I see that both my voice and tone should be perfect for the purpose and audience. My purpose is to convince my reader to agree with me that school should start later for teens, and my audience includes adults who can actually make this change. This essay needs a formal tone, and it should carry through the entire essay. Using a serious voice signals to the reader that I know what I am talking about and that my claim should be taken seriously. Informal or too-casual expressions might weaken my argument. As I read my introduction, I realized that I needed to revise my last two sentences. I think my revisions will strengthen this part.

[DRAFT]

Everyone agrees that being a teenager can be challenging. So many changes take place over a few years that it's no wonder teens often feel overwhelmed and just plain tired. Our bodies and our ideas are changing. ~~Yikes! Sometimes, life seems unfair!~~ One change that would bring about positive results in school would be to allow us teens to sleep later on school mornings.

[deleted to maintain a formal tone]

Reflect

How has Luis's revision strengthened his argument?

Apply

Read your draft. Be sure to use an appropriate voice and maintain a formal tone throughout the essay.

Revise

The Rubric Says	Precise words convey the writer's message. There are no unnecessary words.
Writing Strategy	Replace vague words and take out unnecessary words.

The rubric says I need to use precise words and avoid unnecessary ones. This is good advice! The more precise my language, the stronger and clearer my argument will be for the reader. I'll use a thesaurus to replace vague words that weaken my argument and remove unnecessary words that distract the reader.

[DRAFT]

[deleted unnecessary words]

Bus schedules would have to be revised. Some bus companies might be reluctant to change its hours of operation; ~~the hours of the day when it's open for business~~. These ~~things~~ obstacles may seem difficult to overcome, but with cooperation they can be solved.

[replaced vague word]

 **Reflect**

How have Luis's revisions strengthened his writing and clarified his argument?

 Apply

Read your draft. Replace vague or weak words with precise, strong language. Take out unnecessary words.

Revise

Focus on Sentence Fluency

The Rubric Says	Sentence types are varied successfully for flow and effect.
Writing Strategy	Write a variety of sentences.

Writer's Term

Verb Moods

There are five **verb moods: indicative, imperative, interrogative, conditional,** and **subjunctive**. The mood of a verb indicates the writer's attitude, whether it is to convey a fact, give a command, ask a question, express a possibility, or convey information contrary to fact.

I know varying sentences helps the flow of my writing. Using various verb moods can keep readers interested, too. Although the most common mood is indicative, switching things up can be very effective. I want my reader to think and respond to those who oppose my position. Here's a perfect place to ask a question. I can combine two sentences in the same paragraph. I think my changes make it easier for my readers to follow my main point.

[DRAFT]

[changed to interrogative mood]

If you oppose a later start time due to after-school activites and bus shedules, ~~I say just~~ why not reshedule the events and routes? Buses could service the elementary schools first and then the high schools. Because Older students often live far from their schools. Buses with longer routes may encounter less traffic.

[combined sentences]

Apply

Strengthen your argument essay by using a variety of sentences.

Edit

The Rubric Says   Pronouns are used correctly. The meaning of the text is clear.

Writing Strategy   Make sure that pronouns have been used correctly.

Writer's Term___

Pronouns and Antecedents

A **pronoun** is a word that takes the place of a noun. Pronouns must have clear antecedents. An **antecedent** is the word that a pronoun refers to or replaces. A pronoun must agree with its antecedent in number (singular or plural), gender (male or female), and case (subject or object).

Now it's time to proofread my essay. I'll check for errors in spelling and punctuation, but the rubric also says to make sure that I've used pronouns correctly. I'll do all of this now.

[DRAFT]

[used correct pronoun]

me

Sleepy teens like my friends and I find it difficult to learn in class.

success

Why not set up all students for ~~sucess~~? It's time to make our lives

manageable

more ~~managable~~ by setting the school clocks ahead by 60 minutes.

[corrected spelling errors]

Reflect

How did Luis do? Did he use a variety of verb moods for effect? Has he fixed any mistakes in mechanics? Has he used pronouns correctly?

Apply

Conventions

Edit your draft for spelling, punctuation, and capitalization. Make sure that all pronouns are used correctly.

For more practice with pronouns, use the exercises on the next two pages.

Pronouns and Antecedents

Know the Rule

A **pronoun** is a word that can take the place of a noun. It must have a clear **antecedent**. An antecedent is the word that a pronoun refers to or replaces. A pronoun must agree with its antecedent in number (singular or plural), gender (male or female), and case (subject or object).

Subject pronouns include *I, he, she, we,* and *they.* Use a subject pronoun as the subject of a clause or sentence.
> **Example:** My aunt uses that shampoo. **She** says **it** works well.

Object pronouns include *me, him, her, us,* and *them.* Use an object pronoun after an action verb or preposition.
> **Example:** Mom paid Tim and Todd. She paid **them** $10.

The pronouns *it* and *you* can be either subjects or objects.
> **Example:** **You** bought **it**. **It** belongs to **you**.

Practice the Rule

Rewrite each sentence on a separate sheet of paper. Fill in the missing pronoun and circle the antecedent.

1. My friends and I were in a restaurant, and _____ were eating lunch.
2. We heard this man behind us, and _____ had the greatest voice.
3. The man was telling a story, and _____ sounded like an announcer.
4. Christa and Peter thought _____ might know him.
5. His voice sounded familiar because _____ was rich and deep.
6. When _____ took a closer look, Christa and Peter recognized the man.
7. The three of us were stunned: _____ was our science teacher, Mr. Edmunds!
8. Mr. Edmunds was just as surprised to see us at the table behind _____ .
9. He admitted that he was too full for his dessert and offered _____ to all of us.
10. Christa was the only one still hungry, so Peter and I gave it all to _____ .

Pronouns in Compound Subjects and Objects

Know the Rule

Use a **subject pronoun** in a compound subject.
> **Example:** My family and **I** enjoy watching soccer games together.

Use an **object pronoun** in a compound direct object, a compound indirect object, or a compound object of a preposition.
> **Example:** Sometimes, Aunt Christine and Uncle Roland watch with **us**.
> We usually serve **them** pizza and ice cream.

Practice the Rule

Rewrite each of the following sentences. Then underline the correct subject pronoun or object pronoun. At the end of the sentence, write **S** if the pronoun is a subject pronoun, or **O** if the pronoun is an object pronoun.

1. Calahan is late! When did (him/he) leave his house?
2. Josephine is at the door. Who will let (her/she) in?
3. Aunt Rose has been up since dawn. (Her/She) has been cooking all morning.
4. I am such a nervous wreck! Could someone please get (I/me) a box of tissues?
5. Mae and Peter's wedding is going to be beautiful. (They/Them) were so kind to invite us.
6. Aria and Dennis are going hiking. (I/Me) am going with them.
7. (Us/We) won't leave for hiking until after the wedding, of course!
8. This entire weekend has been so special for (I/me).
9. It's been years since I've seen my cousins, and I've missed (they/them) so much.
10. After the hiking trip, though, (we/I) all are going to need a good, long nap.

Publish ✛ Presentation

Publishing Strategy   Send my essay to the School Board.

Presentation Strategy   Use text features, such as headings, paragraph indents, and visuals.

My essay is complete! I feel so strongly about this issue that I'll send a copy to the School Board. Maybe my essay will convince the Board to act. I'll type my essay on my computer, using only a few simple fonts. I'll make sure my headings are neat and indent my paragraphs. Then I'll print one black and white copy for me so I can check it one last time. Finally I'll use a color printer to make the copies I need so the graph in the essay will stand out. Here's the checklist I'll use to finalize my essay.

My Final Checklist

Did I—

✔ correct any spelling, capitalization, and punctuation errors?

✔ use subject pronouns and object pronouns correctly?

✔ make sure all pronouns and their antecedents agree?

✔ use clear headings, indent the paragraphs, and include helpful visuals?

✔ put my name on the title page?

Apply

Make a checklist to check your argument essay. Then make a final copy to publish.

A Little More Sleep Goes a Long Way

by Luis

Everyone agrees that being a teenager can be challenging. So many changes take place over a few years that it's no wonder teens often feel overwhelmed and just plain tired. Our bodies and our ideas are changing. One change that would bring about positive results in school would be to allow us teens to sleep later on school mornings. By delaying the start of school by just an hour, many of the challenges we teens face every day in school could be overcome.

Evidence

It is a proven fact that our need for sleep increases as we enter puberty. Sleep patterns, also known as circadian rhythms, make it almost impossible to fall asleep before 11:00 p.m. Most high school days begin at 7:30 a.m., which means that most of us are functioning on too little sleep. According to the National Sleep Foundation, teenagers require 9¼ hours of sleep per night. I'm sure most of us are not getting that amount.

Most teens don't get enough sleep and may be sleep deprived. Sleep deprivation is a serious condition. Symptoms include impaired memory, difficulties in focusing and meeting deadlines, lower grades, and an increase in moodiness, even depression. The following chart shows the results for a group of sophomores who were asked how many hours they sleep on weeknights.

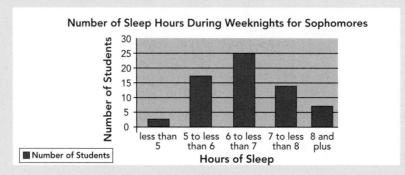

Number of Sleep Hours During Weeknights for Sophomores

Cons

So why hasn't a delay in start time been made in all high schools? Although this poll is convincing, not everyone agrees that a later start time would be beneficial. For one thing, starting school one hour later means school *ends* one hour later. This fact can create several challenges. For example, students in after-school activities, such as sports, might run into scheduling conflicts. In addition, bus schedules would have to be revised. Furthermore some bus companies might be reluctant to change their hours of operation. These obstacles may seem difficult to overcome, but with cooperation they can be solved.

Pros

Convincing data indicates positive results from starting high school later. Students missed fewer days, drop-out rates went down, and grades went up. But the positive effects do not stop there.

there. Students reported feeling less depressed, and teachers noted that students seemed calmer and there were fewer fights. In addition, there were fewer car accidents involving teen drivers on school days. As little as one extra hour of sleep has many benefits.

Solutions

If you oppose a later start time due to after-school activities and bus schedules, why not reschedule the events and routes? Buses could service the elementary schools first and then the high schools. Because older students often live far from their schools, buses with longer routes may encounter less traffic. It may take time to adjust to new hours, but they should be changed for the health of teens.

Conclusions

Overall, the "pros" far outweigh the "cons." Every challenge can be overcome with a little planning. After all, the goal of attending school is to get a good education. Sleepy teens like my friends and me find it difficult to learn in class. Why not set up all students for success? It's time to make our lives more manageable by setting the school clocks ahead by 60 minutes. Who can say "no" to a healthy idea?

Reflect

What do you think? Did Luis use all the traits of a good argument essay? Check his writing against the rubric. Don't forget to use the rubric to check your own essay, too.

What's a Speech?

It's a type of argument writing that tries to convince listeners to take a specific action. I'm not afraid to take a stand, so writing this speech should be interesting—as long as I pick an important topic!

What's in a Speech?

Call to Action
This is the purpose of my speech—to get people to do something about the problem I describe in my writing. Getting people to act is going to take some convincing!

Evidence
I'll use evidence to back up the opinions and arguments in my speech. I know it's the evidence that wins people over, so I'll include facts, examples, and details in my speech.

Convincing Tone
This is how I want my speech to sound. I want my audience to agree with me, but also to feel strongly enough to take action. To create a convincing tone, I'll make strong, calm statements that rely on evidence rather than hype or loaded words.

Questions and Answers
Often, speakers can convince people by answering their questions. As I write, I'll think about the questions my audience might have. Then, I'll provide the answers in my speech.

Why write a Speech?

There are a bunch of reasons to write a speech. I'll list some reasons here, and I'll keep them in mind as I decide why I want to write a speech.

To Inform
A speech focuses on a problem and calls on listeners to act. But the audience might not have enough information to take a stand, so it's important to provide it for them.

To Express an Opinion
In a speech, it's not enough to share your views. The speaker needs to convince the audience to agree with his or her ideas. Keeping this purpose in mind can help a person make decisions while writing.

To Call to Action
Often, a speaker wants an immediate response from listeners—a response that involves taking action to solve the problem described in the speech. Having this specific purpose can help a speechwriter maintain focus.

To Present Solutions
Sometimes a writer can be clear about a problem but unsure about the best course of action. Writing a speech can be a good way to analyze the situation, come up with solutions, and decide on the best course of action.

Linking Argument Writing Traits to a Speech

In this chapter, you will write a speech to convince your listeners to agree with you. Luis will guide you through the stages of the writing process: Prewrite, Draft, Revise, Edit, and Publish. In each stage, Luis will show you important writing strategies that are linked to the Argument Writing Traits below.

Argument Writing Traits

	• a clearly stated position or claim • relevant supporting evidence that comes from reliable, credible sources • alternate or opposing claims that are acknowledged and addressed with logical evidence
	• a strong introduction that presents the writer's position, a body that supports the position, and a conclusion that sums up the argument and/or offers a call to action • transitions that clarify the relationships among ideas
	• a voice and tone that are appropriate for the purpose and audience
	• language that is compelling
	• sentences that vary in length and structure
	• no or few errors in grammar, usage, mechanics, and spelling

Before you write, read Nola Fabian's speech on the next page. Then use the speech rubric on pages 312–313 to decide how well she did. (You might want to look back at What's in a Speech? on page 308, too!)

Save Our Books

by Nola Fabian

Imagine an ordinary bookcase filled with your favorite books. Smell the worn pages? Are the titles beckoning you? See the crinkled jacket covers and ragged spines? Well, savor that thought because publishing companies are starting to post books online, which means that hand-held books might become obsolete. That's why I'm asking you to take action by demanding that publishers continue to develop and support "real" books. **Call to action**

Am I sounding a false alarm? I don't think so. Recently, publishers have made a startling number of titles available online, and growing numbers of authors are also allowing some form of online publication. **Questions and answers**

Soon, publishers may even find ways to post books on the Internet after they go out of print. Just think of the devastating effect this will have on book collectors (and traders) worldwide. Many of these people have spent the better part of their lives collecting out-of-print titles and valuable old books.

So you may ask, what has led to this recent trend in publishing? In a word: technology. Word processing software makes it easy to manage massive amounts of text. The Internet has become a literate community, and advances in computer systems include a variety of portable gadgets.

OK, so it is possible to move the world of literature onto the Web. But is it probable? In some areas, it is becoming more profitable to publish solely on the Web. This summer, a handful of magazine publishers announced that they will be posting some issues exclusively online. **Evidence**

So if publishing online is cheaper and easier, why fight it? Well, a book is more than a collection of words. Many readers enjoy the weight of the book, the texture of the cover, the smell of the ink, and the sound of the pages rustling. Hand-held books are often associated with meaningful memories of a person's journey into the literate world. Not to mention, some people cannot afford to access books online. While computers are readily available in most schools and libraries, not everyone owns a home PC. **Formal tone**

Have I convinced you that we must act now and demand "real" books? If you agree, then sign my petition today and don't forget to stop by your local bookstore on your way home and buy a hand-held book. You never know—it could be the last "real" book you ever buy! **Call to action**

Rubric

Use this 6-point rubric to plan and score a speech.

	6	5	4
Ideas	The writer distinguishes clearly between fact and opinion. The evidence is factual, relevant, and credible.	The writer distinguishes between fact and opinion. Evidence is factual, credible, and mostly relevant.	The writer often distinguishes between fact and opinion. Some of the evidence is irrelevant or not credible.
Organization	The speech is organized around a call to action. The question-and-answer pattern helps the audience understand the claim and the reasons that support it. The conclusion is effective and memorable.	The speech is organized around a call to action. The question-and-answer pattern helps the audience understand the claim and most reasons that support it. The conclusion is effective.	The speech is organized around a call to action. The question-and-answer pattern helps the audience understand the claim and some reasons that support it. The conclusion may be weak.
Voice	The writer maintains a formal tone and first-person point of view to create an effective argument.	The writer maintains a formal tone most of the time and first-person point of view.	The writer's tone may be informal in parts. First-person point of view is maintained.
Word Choice	Neutral words avoid bias and emphasize the evidence throughout. The writing is precise and coherent.	Neutral words avoid bias and emphasize the evidence throughout. The writing is precise and coherent most of the time.	Most words avoid bias and emphasize the evidence throughout. Some vague or general words are used.
Sentence Fluency	A variety of sentence patterns makes the writing interesting to read and smooth flowing.	Most of the writing contains sentences of varying patterns.	Some sentence patterns vary. Variety would improve the flow.
Conventions	Progressive tense and auxiliary verbs are always used correctly to convey meaning to the reader.	The meaning is clear even with a few minor errors in the use of progressive tense and auxiliary verbs.	Some noticeable errors in the use of progressive tense and auxiliary verbs occasionally distract the reader.

✛Presentation Appropriate line breaks and margins make the speech easy to read.

3	2	1	
Some of the facts may not be relevant or accurate. Some of the reasons are not supported by evidence.	The writer does not distinguish between fact and opinion. There is little relevant evidence.	Fact and opinion are not distinguishable. Evidence is incomplete or not included.	**Ideas**
The speech is somewhat organized around a call to action. Question-and-answer pattern is somewhat effective. The conclusion is very weak.	There is no call to action. Question-and-answer pattern is not effective. The conclusion is incomplete or missing.	The writing is not organized. Question-and-answer pattern is not used. A conclusion is missing.	**Organization**
The writer's tone may be harsh or strident. Second-person point of view is used.	The writer's tone may be inappropriate. Second-person point of view is used.	The writer's tone is inappropriate or very weak. Point of view is inconsistent.	**Voice**
Neutral words are used. The writing is not precise enough to be consistently coherent.	Some biased or loaded words are used and may offend readers. Most words are vague or overused.	Biased and imprecise words throughout the speech fail to convey a coherent message.	**Word Choice**
Many sentences in a row share the same pattern. The writing becomes dull or predictable.	All the sentences share the same pattern. The writing does not flow smoothly.	Sentences are incorrect or incomplete. The writing is very difficult to read.	**Sentence Fluency**
Noticeable, distracting errors in the use of progressive tense and auxiliary verbs confuse the reader.	Many errors in the use of progressive tense and auxiliary verbs make the writing hard to understand.	The writing is very hard to understand. Few or no progressive tense or auxiliary verbs are used correctly.	**Conventions**

See Appendix B for 4-, 5-, and 6-point argument rubrics.

Using the Rubric to Study the Model
Speech

Did you notice that the model on page 311 points out some key elements of a persuasive speech? As she wrote "Save Our Books," Nola Fabian used these elements to help her persuade her audience to support printed books. She also used the 6-point rubric on pages 312–313 to plan, draft, revise, and edit the writing. A rubric is a great tool to evaluate writing during the writing process.

Now let's use the same rubric to score the model. To do this, we'll focus on each trait separately, starting with Ideas. We'll use the top descriptor for each trait (column 6), along with examples from the model, to help us understand how the traits work together. How would you score Nola on each trait?

- **The writer distinguishes clearly between fact and opinion.**
- **The evidence is factual, relevant, and credible.**

Nola's speech is effective because she explains each reason with facts, examples, and other evidence to convince her audience. In this example, she supports her reason with good examples to explain why the audience should fight against online books.

[from the writing model]

Many readers enjoy the weight of the book, the texture of the cover, the smell of the ink, and the sound of the pages rustling. Hand-held books are often associated with meaningful memories of a person's journey into the literate world.

**Organization**

- The speech is organized around a call to action.
- The question-and-answer pattern helps the audience understand the claim and the reasons that support it.
- The conclusion is effective and memorable.

I noticed that Nola gives a call to action in the beginning and, again, at the end of her speech. She also uses a question-and-answer pattern in her speech that helped me follow all her reasons and held my interest. Her conclusion is very effective. It sure got me thinking about how much I value my own "real" books.

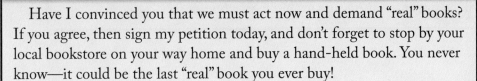
[from the writing model]

Have I convinced you that we must act now and demand "real" books? If you agree, then sign my petition today, and don't forget to stop by your local bookstore on your way home and buy a hand-held book. You never know—it could be the last "real" book you ever buy!

**Voice**

- The writer maintains a formal tone and first-person point of view to create an effective argument.

Nola uses a formal, knowledgeable tone to express her opinion. It's also clear that Nola wants her audience to know how much she cares about her topic. Her words "I don't think so" made me stop and think. I bet everyone at the bookstore who heard her speech did, too.

[from the writing model]

... I don't think so ... Soon, publishers may even find ways to post books on the Internet after they go out of print. Just think of the devastating effect this will have on book collectors (and traders) worldwide. Many of these people have spent the better part of their lives collecting out-of-print titles and valuable old books.

 **Word Choice**

- Neutral words avoid bias and emphasize the evidence throughout.
- The writing is precise and coherent.

I appreciate how Nola uses logical reasoning without resorting to biased or loaded words. For example, in the lines below, she uses *profitable* instead of *lucrative,* which can sometimes imply greed. And she uses the neutral word *publishers* rather than *big corporations,* which can have a negative meaning.

[from the writing model]

In some areas, it is becoming more profitable to publish solely on the Web. This summer, a handful of magazine publishers announced that they will be posting some issues exclusively online.

 **Sentence Fluency**

- A variety of sentence patterns makes the writing interesting to read and smooth flowing.

Nola's speech is easy and enjoyable to read because many of her sentences are put together differently. Too many subject-predicate sentences become monotonous and hard to read. Nola's sentence variety helped keep me interested.

[from the writing model]

Not to mention, some people cannot afford to access books online. While computers are readily available in most schools and libraries, not everyone owns a home PC.

Conventions

• Progressive tense and auxiliary verbs are always used correctly to convey meaning to the reader.

Nola's speech flows smoothly because there aren't any mistakes. When she shifts from one verb tense to another, she always gets it right. In the passage below, notice how she switches from the present tense *is* to the present progressive tense *is becoming* in one smooth transition.

[from the writing model]

OK, so it is possible to move the world of literature onto the Web. But is it probable? In some areas, it is becoming more profitable to publish solely on the Web.

✚Presentation Appropriate line breaks and margins make the speech easy to read.

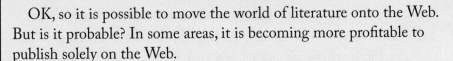

I'm going to write a speech about something I feel strongly about. I'll follow the rubric and use good writing strategies. Read on to see how I do it!

Prewrite

Focus on **Ideas**

The Rubric Says   The writer distinguishes clearly between fact and opinion. The evidence is factual, relevant, and credible.

Writing Strategy   State a position on an issue and list facts that support it.

I'm excited to write my speech because I have a strong opinion on a particular issue. The rubric says I must distinguish between fact and opinion, and that makes sense. I want my position to be solid and credible. My dad is a musician, and we talk a lot about how people download copyrighted music from the Internet. I think this practice is wrong, but many of my friends do not agree! Backing up my opinion with some strong facts might help to change their minds. I'll begin by stating my position and listing the facts I've learned.

My Notes

My Position: Stop illegal downloads.

Reason 1: It violates copyright laws.

Reason 2: It teaches disrespect for the law.

Reason 3: It harms musicians.

Apply

Choose an issue you feel strongly about. Then list facts and examples from credible sources.

The Rubric Says   The speech is organized around a call to action.

Writing Strategy   Make an Argument Map to organize a speech.

According to the rubric, my speech should be organized around a call to action. I can use my notes to make an Argument Map, which will help me plan my speech.

Writer's Term

Argument Map
An **Argument Map,** like a Story Map, organizes the "action," or reasons, around the "high point," or call to action.

ARGUMENT MAP

Call to Action: Stop illegal downloads.

Reason 1: It violates copyright laws.
- **Evidence:** Songs composed after 1922 are protected by law.
- **Evidence:** Royalty fees must be paid for songs.
- **Evidence:** People have been punished for violating the United States Copyright Act.

Reason 2: It teaches disrespect for the law.
- **Evidence:** Disrespect for the law is distressing.
- **Evidence:** Disrespect is taught to younger siblings.
- **Evidence:** Illegal downloads can be a "gateway" to breaking other laws.

Reason 3: It harms musicians.
- **Evidence:** Royalties are musicians' livelihood.
- **Evidence:** Musicians' wages are lost.
- **Evidence:** Dad compares illegal downloading with stealing from an art gallery.

Reflect

How will the Argument Map help Luis write his speech?

Apply

Make an Argument Map to organize your speech.

Draft

Focus on Voice

The Rubric Says   The writer maintains a formal tone and first-person point of view to create an effective argument.

Writing Strategy   Use a formal tone and first-person point of view to convince the audience.

Now I'll use my Argument Map to help me write my speech. The rubric says I should use a formal tone to convince my audience. I already know that many of my readers (my classmates) are opposed to my view, so I will have to do a lot of convincing! I thought long and hard about what it takes for someone to convince me of something, and I decided that I will present my reasons, using a confident, knowledgeable voice. I have to be careful, though, that I don't sound like I'm judging or scolding people who might not agree with my position. I'll also remember to use the first-person point of view to express my opinion and connect with my audience.

I'll do my best with spelling, grammar, and punctuation, but I know that I can fix mistakes at any point in the writing process. For now, though, I'll pay close attention to my use of compound personal pronouns, since I know they sometimes give me trouble.

[DRAFT]

Stop Stealing Songs

by Luis

Last week, my friend and I is working on a history project together, and I borrowed his laptop for a minute to do some research. I work best with a little "study music," so he reccomended one of the songs in his music folder. When I opened the folder, however, I was shocked. It contained almost 3,000 songs. He told me that he himself had downloaded them for free.

Here's the problem: These songs aren't really free—they are copyrighted material that has been shared illegally. I know that my views on this issue are unpopular, and that downloading music has been such a wide spread practice that it has become a part of our modern culture. However, I think that if more people understand why this practice is wrong, they will stop. That's why I'm here today, asking each and every one of you to stop these illegal downloads.
[formal tone]

Reflect

Does Luis use a respectful tone? How can you tell? What point of view does he use?

Apply

Use your Argument Map to draft your speech. Use a formal tone and first-person point of view.

Revise

Focus on Ideas

The Rubric Says The evidence is factual, relevant, and credible.

Writing Strategy Include details that are factually correct and from reliable sources.

After I finished my draft, I checked the rubric. It reminded me to use factual and credible evidence. Books are very reliable, but I got a lot of my facts online. I know there's misleading or incomplete information on the Internet. I'll make sure I verify any facts I find online in at least two other places.

[DRAFT]

Because my dad is a musician, I know that any song composed by an American before 1922 is in the public domain. That means that it belongs to everyone and can be shared or performed freely. So when you download songs on the Internet, you are violating the United States Copyright Act.

[added factual evidence]

Yet music composed after 1922 cannot be used without permission. And even with permission, royalties must be paid.

Apply

Add evidence from credible sources to your speech to convince the audience.

Revise

The Rubric Says	Neutral words avoid bias and emphasize the evidence throughout.
Writing Strategy	Replace biased or emotional words with neutral ones.

Writer's Term

Biased Words/Loaded Words
Loaded words and **biased words** express unfair judgment. For example, **shack** might be used as a biased or negatively loaded word for the more neutral term **house**.

I checked the rubric again and was reminded how important it is to avoid biased and loaded words. I want to convince my audience with facts and examples, not with tricky language. But when I reread my draft, I was surprised to see that I had included some biased words. I guess it's because I feel so strongly about this issue! I'll use neutral words throughout my speech so I won't sound overly emotional or judgmental.

[DRAFT]

[replaced biased words]

Many of these ~~criminals~~ (defendants), some of whom are teenagers just like us, are currently on trial. If convicted, they will have to pay hundreds of thousands of dollars in fines. Now you're probably thinking there's no way that the government can prosecute all ~~thieves~~ (file-sharers). But are you really willing to take that chance?

Reflect

How do biased words diminish or undermine a writer's position? How do Luis's changes improve his speech?

Apply

Review your draft to see if you used any biased or loaded words. If so, replace them with neutral words.

Revise

Focus on Sentence Fluency

The Rubric Says   A variety of sentence patterns makes the writing interesting to read and smooth flowing.

Writing Strategy   Avoid using the subject-verb pattern for every sentence.

After rereading my speech, I was happy to see that I used different kinds of sentences to keep things interesting. The rubric says to use a variety of sentence patterns to make the writing smooth. I get so bored when I read something almost entirely written in the subject-verb pattern. Just starting a sentence with a clause or phrase is very effective. I will revise any sentences that could use some variety.

[DRAFT]

[changed sentence pattern]

As I mentioned before,

~~I already told you~~ my dad is a musician. Maybe that's why I feel so strongly about this issue. He knows that people find it hard to understand how anyone can actually "own" a piece of music.

Apply

Be sure to use a variety of sentence structures throughout your speech.

The Rubric Says	Progressive tense and auxiliary verbs are always used correctly to convey meaning to the reader.
Writing Strategy	Make sure that progressive tense verbs and auxiliary verbs are used correctly.

Writer's Term

Progressive Tense Verbs

Progressive tense verbs are verbs that show continuing action. To form the progressive tense, use the correct form of the verb **to be** before another verb ending in **-ing**.

Now I'm ready to proofread my writing. I always check for errors, especially the kind I tend to repeat. The rubric reminds me to use verbs correctly. It turns out that I did use some progressive tense verbs incorrectly. Here are some of my edits.

[DRAFT]

When a record label produces and sells an artist's music, the artist
is
paid royalty fees for each copy sold. This is how artists make

money—its they're job. When you download an artist's music without
are
paying for it, you is stealing that person's livelihood.

[used correct auxiliary verb]   [corrected a progressive tense verb error]

Reflect

What does proofreading carefully "say" about a writer?

Apply   Conventions

Edit your draft for grammar and mechanics, making sure that progressive tense and auxiliary verbs are also used correctly.

For more practice with progressive tense and auxiliary verbs, use the exercises on the next two pages.

Progressive Tense Verbs

Know the Rule

The **progressive tense** shows continuing action.
To form the **present progressive tense,** add *am, is,* or *are* in front of a present participle verb (a verb ending in *-ing*).
> **Example:** Joe **is walking** home.

- To form the **past progressive tense,** add *was* or *were* in front of a present participle verb.
> **Example:** Joe **was walking** home.

- To form the **future progressive tense,** add *will be* in front of a present participle verb.
> **Example:** Joe **will be walking** home tomorrow.

Practice the Rule

Number a sheet of paper 1–10. Read each sentence carefully. If the sentence contains a progressive tense verb error, write the verb correctly. If it contains no error, write **Correct**.

1. My friend Nicole is taking voice lessons after school.
2. Currently her music class were holding auditions for new members.
3. I were thinking about signing up for an audition.
4. Nicole said that if I am accepted, I will be attending her class.
5. But last night, I am feeling nervous about it.
6. What I am proposing is a different plan, one I was hoping she will accept.
7. I was thinking of writing a speech that convinces more students to audition.
8. Talented students who were singing in choirs around the city could compete.
9. Both Nicole and I are volunteering our time to promote worthwhile events.
10. I guess I'll be writing a speech rather than singing for my supper!

Auxiliary Verbs

Know the Rule

An **auxiliary verb,** or helping verb, works with a main verb. Auxiliary verbs have a variety of purposes. Some auxiliary verbs, such as *can, could, should, might, may,* and *must* show how likely it is that something will happen. Some auxiliary verbs, such as *did, had, is, will,* and *would,* indicate the tense of the main verb.

> **Example:** Ms. McGonagle said we **might leave** class early to collect leaf samples from the school yard.

> **Example:** Next week, we all **will arrange** the collected leaves for a class display.

Practice the Rule

Number a sheet of paper 1–10. Use auxiliary verbs to complete the sentences.

1. In three days, my Aunt Claire _____ returning from her trip to Seattle, Washington.
2. Ever since I was a baby, she _____ gone to Seattle every year to visit my grandparents.
3. This year, she said she _____ bring me a souvenir from Seattle's famous Space Needle!
4. If I am lucky, I _____ ride to the airport with my Uncle Jordan to pick her up.
5. Later tonight, I _____ going to make a Welcome Home card for her.
6. I'm pretty sure that I _____ have enough supplies on hand to make a big, colorful card.
7. A handmade card _____ brighten up Aunt Claire's night.
8. On the other hand, homemade cookies _____ bring a bigger smile to everyone's face!
9. If I _____ planning to make a card, I had better get started.
10. Do you think I _____ make cookies instead?

Publish

⁺Presentation

Publishing Strategy   Present my speech to the class.

Presentation Strategy   Use appropriate line breaks and margins to make the speech easier to read.

My speech is done and I can't wait to publish it. I decided to read it to my class, because I'm curious to see how they will react to my views. To make reading out loud from my paper easier, I will leave enough white space around the text and keep the lines at a good length—not too short and not too long. First I'll make sure it includes all the items on my final checklist.

My Final Checklist

Did I—
- ✔ use progressive tense verbs correctly?
- ✔ check spelling?
- ✔ use appropriate line breaks and margins?
- ✔ use neat handwriting or word-processing?

Apply

Make a checklist to check your speech. Then make a final copy to publish.

Stop Stealing Songs

by Luis

Last week, my friend and I were working on a history project together, and I borrowed his laptop for a minute to do some research. I work best with a little "study music," so he recommended one of the songs in his music folder. When I opened the folder, however, I was shocked. It contained almost 3,000 songs. He told me that he himself had downloaded them for free.

Here's the problem: These songs aren't really free—they are copyrighted material that has been shared illegally. I know that my views on this issue are unpopular, and that downloading music has been such a widespread practice that it has become a part of our modern culture. However, I think that if more people understand why this practice is wrong, they will stop. That's why I'm here today, asking each and every one of you to stop these illegal downloads.

Why do I feel so strongly about this issue? First of all, it violates copyright laws, which makes it illegal. Because my dad is a musician, I know that any song composed by an American before 1922 is in the public domain. That means that it belongs to everyone and can be shared or performed freely. Yet music composed after 1922 cannot be used without permission. And even with permission, royalties must be paid. So when you download songs on the Internet, you are violating the United States Copyright Act.

What are the consequences of breaking this law? Most people believe there are none. But tell that to the many people who are being prosecuted and punished. Many of these defendants, some of whom are teenagers just like us, are currently on trial. If convicted, they will have to pay hundreds of thousands of dollars in fines. Now you're probably thinking there's no way that the government can prosecute all file-sharers. But are you really willing to take that chance?

Even though people might be "getting away with" illegal file-sharing, isn't it really a broader issue? Many of us feel that it's somehow OK to break the law. Even worse, when we download illegal music, we teach this lack of respect to our younger brothers and sisters. And some kids might learn a more dangerous lesson: If it's OK to break one law, maybe it's OK to break others. When you look at it this way, illegal file-sharing could be a "gateway" to breaking other laws.

But the most important reason to stop illegal downloads concerns the songwriters. Music is composed by artists who own the rights to their songs. When a record label produces and sells an artist's music, the artist is paid royalty fees for each copy sold. This is how artists make money—it's their job.

When you download an artist's music without paying for it, you are stealing that person's livelihood.

As I mentioned before, my dad is a musician. Maybe that's why I feel so strongly about this issue. He knows that people find it hard to understand how anyone can actually "own" a piece of music. Once a song is played, it's out there on the public airwaves for everyone to hear, and it's true that no one can stop you from singing or playing a song unless, of course, you charge admission. But my dad recently gave me this analogy: Pirating music is the same as going into a sculptor's studio, deciding which piece of artwork you like, and walking out the door without paying for it. You wouldn't do that, would you? Then you shouldn't download music for free, either.

I hope I've made you think about what you're doing when you download "free" tunes. It's not like we have to give up music entirely. There are a lot of ways to build a great music library without spending tons of money. Start investigating these alternatives. Talk to your friends. And please, stop downloading copyrighted music for free.

Reflect

What do you think? Did Luis use all the traits of a good, convincing speech? Check his writing against the rubric. Don't forget to use the rubric to check your own speech, too.

What's a **Formal Proposal?**

It's a type of argument writing that is often used by researchers to convince committees to support their research. I want to enter my project in the school science fair. I'll write a proposal that will convince the teacher committee to approve my proposal and my science project.

What's in a **Formal Proposal?**

Proposal
A proposal is a formal offer to do or change something that requires permission and, sometimes, funds. For example, you may write a proposal to conduct a special research project or experiment, represent your school in another location, or conduct a fund raiser. Your audience could be one person, such as a teacher or a principal, or it could be a committee. Proposals are used in business, education, and many other fields.

Organization
Like an essay, a formal proposal has three parts: an introduction, body, and conclusion. The introduction presents the writer's proposal, or position, and states the writer's goal. The body provides the details of the project and sometimes includes a timeline. The conclusion summarizes the project. A proposal must be well organized and submitted on time.

Headings
Headings are the titles and subtitles used to organize the information in a formal proposal. They help the reader find the different parts in a proposal quickly. It's a good idea to use a word processor for writing proposals. Choose readable fonts, and use clear text formats and features.

Why write a Formal Proposal?

There are all kinds of reasons to write a proposal. I've listed some here, and I'll use these ideas to help me decide on a purpose for my own writing.

To Inform

A proposal can be a way to get the word out about what you want to accomplish. As you write out the facts of your project, you can explain exactly what you want to do and why it's important.

To Convince

When you write a proposal, you are trying to convince someone to help you make your project possible. Usually, you are asking for approval, funds, or some other kind of help. You want to make your case as clear as possible so that your reader will give you what you're asking for.

To Plan

Doing a project usually involves creating a process and keeping track of a lot of details. Drafting a proposal can help you think through your process and figure out exactly what you'll need to accomplish your project successfully.

Linking Argument Writing Traits to a Formal Proposal

In this chapter, you will write a formal proposal to convince your teacher that your science experiment is worth doing. Luis will guide you through the stages of the writing process: Prewrite, Draft, Revise, Edit, and Publish. In each stage, Luis will show you important writing strategies that are linked to the Argument Writing Traits below.

Argument Writing Traits

Ideas
- a clearly stated position or claim
- relevant supporting evidence that comes from reliable, credible sources
- alternate or opposing claims that are acknowledged and addressed with logical evidence

Organization
- a strong introduction that presents the writer's position, a body that supports the position, and a conclusion that sums up the argument and/or offers a call to action
- transitions that clarify the relationships among ideas

Voice
- a voice and tone that are appropriate for the purpose and audience

Word Choice
- language that is compelling

Sentence Fluency
- sentences that vary in length and structure

Conventions
- no or few errors in grammar, usage, mechanics, and spelling

Before you write, read Keisha Johnson's model proposal on the next three pages. Then use the formal proposal rubric on pages 338–339 to decide how well she did. (You might want to look back at What's a Formal Proposal? on page 332, too!)

Can Water Climb Walls?

by Keisha Johnson

Introduction

Proposal

Ms. Hahn's sixth grade class is studying how plants get food. I can help her students understand plants because our class is studying properties of water and I know all about water molecules. I can clearly demonstrate how capillary action carries nutrients up to leaves through the stems of plants.

Project goal

My demonstration of capillary action will be exciting to students as they watch the gravity-defying action. Colored water will climb up a paper towel and up the stem of a celery plant.

I will explain that water molecules tend to stick tightly to other water molecules (cohesion). At the same time, water molecules are attracted to other materials and they stick to those (adhesion), too. When water molecules stick to the walls of fibers in paper towels or tubes in plant stems, they pull other water molecules along upward in a chain reaction (capillary action).

Body

Project Description ← Heading

I will dip a strip of paper towel in colored water to show capillary action and explain how it works. Then I will put a stem of celery in the water to show capillary action in plants and talk about what will happen. At the end, I will show students the tubes of the celery stem.

Materials ← Heading

A glass half full of water colored dark red with food coloring; a strip of kitchen paper towel; a celery stalk with leaves

Procedure ← Heading

First I'll hold a strip of paper towel up in the glass barely touching the surface of the water. After about 30 seconds, I'll pull the strip out. I will explain how capillary action caused the water to move upward.

Then I'll put a celery stalk in the glass of water. I'll talk with the students about what they think will happen to the plant.

After the red water has been drawn into the leaves, I'll also show students the bottom of the stem, which will have red tubes.

Conclusion

Summary

The strip of paper towel will show that the water climbed up the towel. The leaves of the celery in the water will turn partly red, showing that capillary action has brought water to the leaves.

They might even create a multi-colored flower by splitting the stem of a white carnation or rose in half and setting each half in different-colored water.

My demonstration is easy enough to do at home. So students can repeat it for themselves or do their own further investigations. Most importantly, by watching capillary action take place, they will gain a clear understanding of how plants get their water and nutrients.

Rubric

Use this 6-point rubric to plan and score a formal proposal.

	6	5	4
Ideas	The proposal demonstrates a clear understanding of the topic. The project is summarized effectively.	The proposal is clear. The summary needs a few more details to be clear.	The proposal is not clear. The details in the summary may not all relate to the project.
Organization	The introduction presents the claim and the concluding section follows from and supports the argument presented. Transition words organize the information logically.	The introduction presents the claim and the concluding section follows from and supports the argument presented. Transition words organize most of the information logically.	The introduction and conclusion are fairly strong. More transition words are needed to organize the information in the body.
Voice	The writer's voice is convincing. The formal tone is ideal for the topic and audience.	The writer's voice is convincing. The tone is appropriate most of the time.	The writer's voice sounds convincing most of the time. The tone may be informal or inappropriate.
Word Choice	Precise words, phrases, and clauses create cohesion in the proposal.	Most of the words are precise and effective.	Too few words are precise. Several are overused.
Sentence Fluency	Sentences are direct and clear.	Most sentences are direct and clear.	A few sentences are too long and rambling.
Conventions	The writing has been edited with care. All words, including easily confused words, are used correctly.	Minor errors are present but do not interfere with meaning. All words are used correctly.	A few errors cause confusion. Words are used correctly.

✚ Presentation   The format and effective use of text features (boldface headings, bullets, numbering) make the information accessible.

3	2	1	
The project is not identified. The summary may be too short or incomplete.	The proposal is very weak. The summary is undeveloped or nonexistent.	A proposal is not presented.	**Ideas**
The introduction presents the claim. The conclusion is weak or incomplete. Transition words are needed.	The introduction and conclusion are weak or incomplete. Transition words are confusing or missing.	The writing is not organized as a proposal.	**Organization**
The writer's voice sounds unconvincing. The tone may be uninterested or uninformed.	The writer's voice is weak and unconvincing. The tone is not appropriate.	The voice is flat or absent. The writer does not reach out to the audience.	**Voice**
Word choice is limited to general words.	Several easily confused words (*accept/except*) are used incorrectly.	Many words are used incorrectly.	**Word Choice**
Many sentences are too long and rambling.	Sentences are hard to follow.	Sentences may be incomplete or incorrect.	**Sentence Fluency**
Many errors are repeated and cause confusion. Some words are used incorrectly.	Serious errors interfere with meaning. Many words are used incorrectly.	The writing has not been edited.	**Conventions**

See Appendix B for 4-, 5-, and 6-point argument rubrics.

Using the Rubric to Study the Model
Formal Proposal

Did you notice that the model on pages 335–337 points out some key elements of a formal proposal? As she wrote "Can Water Climb Walls?" Keisha Johnson used these elements to help her describe a science project. She also used the 6-point rubric on pages 338–339 to plan, draft, revise, and edit the writing. A rubric is a great tool to evaluate writing during the writing process.

Now let's use the same rubric to score the model. To do this, we'll focus on each trait separately, starting with Ideas. We'll use the top descriptor for each trait (column 6), along with examples from the model, to help us understand how the traits work together. How would you score Keisha on each trait?

 **Ideas**

- **The proposal demonstrates a clear understanding of the topic.**
- **The project is summarized effectively.**

After reading Keisha's proposal, I feel well informed about what she plans to do. She makes clear statements about what she wants to do and why, and she does a good job of describing all aspects of the project.

[from the writing model]

I will dip a strip of paper towel in colored water to show capillary action and explain how it works. Then I will put a stem of celery in the water to show capillary action in plants and talk about what will happen. At the end, I will show students the tubes of the celery stem.

Organization

- The introduction presents the claim and the concluding section follows from and supports the argument presented.
- Transition words organize the information logically.

Keisha's proposal is so well organized I had no trouble following it. Her introduction states her intentions, the middle gives the most important points of her project, and the end summarizes her goals. Look how her conclusion adds an interesting thought about the experiment. Notice how she uses *Most importantly* to remind the reader of her goal.

[from the writing model]

My demonstration is easy enough to do at home. So students can repeat it for themselves or do their own further investigations. Most importantly, by watching capillary action take place, they will gain a clear understanding of how plants get their water and nutrients.

Voice

- The writer's voice is convincing.
- The formal tone is ideal for the topic and audience.

I found Keisha's voice quite convincing. She keeps her tone formal, which is appropriate for a proposal that's intended for an audience of teachers. At the same time, she shows her enthusiasm for the demonstration.

[from the writing model]

My demonstration of capillary action will be exciting to students as they watch the gravity-defying action. Colored water will climb up a paper towel and up the stem of a celery plant.

Word Choice

- Precise words, phrases, and clauses create cohesion in the proposal.

Keisha correctly uses precise, specific words to explain the science concepts her demonstration will show. Instead of vague expressions such as *go along*, she uses specific phrases like *to stick tightly*. This helps me understand exactly what she means all the way through.

[from the writing model]

I will explain that water molecules tend to stick tightly to other water molecules (cohesion). At the same time, water molecules are attracted to other materials and they stick to those (adhesion), too.

Sentence Fluency

- Sentences are direct and clear.

Keisha's sentences go straight to the point. She never rambles, but always tells the reader exactly what she plans to do. Look how clearly she describes this step in her procedure section.

[from the writing model]

Then I'll put a celery stalk in the glass of water. I'll talk with the students about what they think will happen to the plant.

**Conventions**

- **The writing has been edited with care.**
- **All words, including easily confused words, are used correctly.**

I know it's really important to proofread everything that I have written. I also know that the words *sit* and *set* are easy to confuse. *Sit* is something you do when you're not on your feet, but *set* means "to place" or "to put" something. Keisha seems to have checked her writing for easily confused words.

[from the writing model]

They might even create a multi-colored flower by splitting the stem of a white carnation or rose in half and setting each half in different-colored water.

✛Presentation The format and effective use of text features (boldface headings, bullets, numbering) make the information accessible.

My Turn!

Now it's my turn to write a formal proposal. I'll use the rubric and good writing strategies to help me. Read on to see how I do it.

Prewrite

Focus on Ideas

The Rubric Says	The proposal demonstrates a clear understanding of the topic.
Writing Strategy	Decide on a topic. Make a list to plan a proposal.

I want to do a project for our school's science fair. A committee of teachers will approve projects before we exhibit them. So I need to write a proposal that clearly describes an experiment I want to do as my project. My teacher told me the deadline and gave me a copy of the fair's guidelines.

First I have to decide on my topic and what scientific principle I want to show. Then I'll jot down some details about the project.

There's a deadline for turning in science fair proposals, so I'll be careful to pace myself and not wait until the last minute to finish.

Topic: Why do boats float?
Scientific principle: density and volume
Project: —use clay to make a boat
—test clay boats to find one that floats
—measure density and volume of boat and water
—compare densities of boat and water

Apply

Choose a topic. Make a list to help you plan your proposal.

The Rubric Says The introduction presents the claim and the concluding section follows from and supports the argument presented.

Writing Strategy Use a Flow Chart to plan the proposal.

Flow Charts are great for organizing information that has to appear in a certain order and for showing how one part leads to the next. I'll use a Flow Chart to help me remember the different parts of a proposal and their order.

Introduction

Experiment will explain why boats float

Hypothesis: A boat floats when its volume includes enough air

Project Description

Measure mass and volume of water, clay block, and clay boat

Compute density of water, block, boat

Independent variable is shape of the boat

Dependent variable is whether boat floats

Materials

Modeling clay; graduated cylinder; balance with gram weights; containers to hold and catch water; displacement tank built from water jug and drinking straw

Procedure

Step 1: Find the mass and volume of water

Step 2: Find the mass and volume of the clay block

Step 3: Shape the clay block into a boat and test it in water

Step 4: When a boat floats, measure its mass and volume

Step 5: Compute the densities of water, clay block, boat that floats

Conclusion

It's the volume of a clay boat that makes it float

Air inside the boat makes the volume greater and the density less than the clay block

Boat has less density than water, so it floats

Reflect

Look at the Flow Chart. How will it help Luis to write his proposal?

Apply

Make a Flow Chart to organize the parts of your proposal.

Draft

Focus on Word Choice

The Rubric Says — Precise words, phrases, and clauses create cohesion in the proposal.

Writing Strategy — Use exact words.

Now I'll use my Flow Chart to help me write my proposal. The rubric says I should use precise, specific words. By using exact words, I'll help my readers understand my proposal. Vague words may be correct, but they won't help my proposal, because they won't convey a clear idea.

Right now I'm going to try to get all my ideas written down on paper. As I'm writing, I'll circle words that seem vague to me. Then I'll use a thesaurus or my science resources to replace them. As I draft my proposal, I'll look out for mistakes in grammar and spelling, but I won't worry too much about that now. I can go back and fix my mistakes later. Here's my draft.

[DRAFT]

Introduction

People who go swimming and lay spread out on top of the water will float. If they role themselves up into a ball, they will sink into the water. Even heavy ships can float. Most people are mystified by these "impossible" things. My idea will clear up the mystery and explain why such things really are possible. It will help people understand the important concept of bouyancy.

I will explain buoyancy by comparing the densities of a block of clay and the same block of clay formed into a "boat."

[precise word] → Density is the amount of mass an object has for each unit of its volume. The volume of a ship's hull is made up of its frame plus air that is inside of it.

People will be shocked and surprised when I point out that a boat floats because it has air in it, and air makes the boat less dense than water.

Project Description

First, I will measure the mass and volume of water, of a block of modeling clay, and of the block of clay when it is formed into a "boat" that floats. Then, I will figure out the density of each of these.

The independent variable is the shape of the clay. The dependent variable is whether the clay floats.

[precise words]

Reflect

Read the beginning of Luis's draft. Did he choose precise words in his revision?

Apply

Use your Flow Chart to write a draft of your formal proposal. Circle vague words you want to change to more precise words.

Revise

Focus on **Ideas**

The Rubric Says	The proposal demonstrates a clear understanding of the topic.
Writing Strategy	Provide accurate, complete information.

The purpose of my proposal is to present my science project and get it approved by the committee. Therefore I need to make sure all my information is accurate and complete. I read my draft again and realized that I need to include some helpful information about the size of the modeling clay in my Materials section. So I'll add it now.

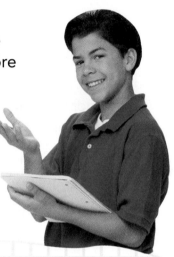

[DRAFT]

[clarified information]

Materials

about 2 cm x 8 cm x 2 cm   (100 mL)
Block of modeling clay; graduated cylinder; balance

with gram weights; 4 tofu containers; water;

Apply

Read your proposal. Make sure your Materials list is accurate and complete. Provide all necessary information.

The Rubric Says   The introduction presents the claim and the concluding section follows from and supports the argument presented. Transition words organize the information logically.

Writing Strategy   Use logical order to add and organize the information.

A proposal follows a logical order. The information in each part needs to be complete. The introduction presents my position and tells why the project is important. The middle part starts with a project description so the reader has the main idea of the project before reading the details. The details of the project come next. The conclusion summarizes the goals and expected results of the project. Each part must be complete in order to do its job.

I read through my proposal and found a place that could be strengthened. In the Project Description section I forgot to explain what I'll do with all the data I collect. I'll add that information and a transition word to guide the reader.

[DRAFT]

Project Description

[added transition word]

[added information]

First, I will measure the mass and volume of water, of a block of modeling clay, and of the block of clay when it is formed into a

→ Finally, I will record all the data in a data table and compare the densities, masses, and volumes.

"boat" that floats. Then, I will compute the density of each of these.

Reflect

How do Luis's changes improve this part?

Apply

Read your draft. Make sure the parts are in order and the transition words guide the reader.

Revise

Focus on Sentence Fluency

The Rubric Says   Sentences are direct and clear.

Writing Strategy   Break apart long, rambling sentences.

The purpose of a proposal is to give the reader information about a planned project. Clear, direct sentences will help the reader understand the information. Long, rambling sentences may confuse or completely lose the reader.

I read through my proposal again to see if it is clearly written and my sentences go straight to the point. I rewrote this part to break apart a sentence that just went on too long. The meaning is easier to understand now.

[DRAFT]

Then, I'll find the volume of the clay by placing it on top of the water in the displacement tank ~~and~~ ⊙ I'll ← **[broke up long sentence]** measure the volume of the water that comes out of the tank and record this as the volume of the block of clay.

Apply

Read your draft carefully. Revise any overly long or confusing sentences.

The Rubric Says	The writing has been edited with care. All words, including easily confused words, are used correctly.
Writing Strategy	Check the use of all words, especially words that can be easily confused.

Now it's time to proofread my proposal. I'll check for spelling, grammar, capitalization, and punctuation. The rubric reminds me to make sure that I check for words that can be easily confused. Even though I used spell-check and grammar-check software, the computer can't read my mind. If I use a word that's spelled correctly but wrong for the sentence, the software won't catch the problem.

I found two words that are spelled correctly but used incorrectly. I'll go ahead and fix them now.

[DRAFT]

[replaced incorrect words]

People who go swimming and ~~lay~~ lie spread out on top of the water will float. If they ~~role~~ roll themselves up into a ball, they will sink into the water.

Reflect

Is Luis's writing more accurate and effective now?

Apply

Edit your draft for spelling, punctuation, and capitalization. Also, make sure that you've used the correct words.

For more practice with using the right word use the exercises on the next two pages.

Using the Right Word

Know the Rule

People often confuse similar-sounding words or words that have similar spellings. For example, the words *accept* and *except* sound similar, but they have very different meanings. A computer spell-check program will not highlight the error for you. Instead, you have to carefully read your writing to catch this type of error.

Examples:

accept: to agree to   **affect:** to make something happen

except: not including   **effect:** something that happens as a result of something else

Practice the Rule

Choose the correct word to complete each sentence. Write the complete sentence on a separate sheet of paper.

1. I hope the committee will (accept/except) my project for the science fair.
2. The amount of water a plant gets will (affect/effect) its growth.
3. Ken tried three times, but then on his (forth/fourth) try, he got the ball through the hoop.
4. The cacti were in full bloom when I visited the (desert/dessert).
5. It is very cold today. I'll (adapt/adopt) to the cold by putting on a heavy coat.
6. Julia got all the answers correct on her test (accept/except) the one about water molecules.
7. A wire was (lose/loose), causing the lamp to flicker on and off.
8. Mixing vinegar and baking soda will produce a foaming (affect/effect) for the volcano model.
9. (Its/It's) too bad the cat is so miserable because (its/it's) paw has a thorn in it.
10. Please (set/sit) the plates on the table, and then we'll (set/sit) down to eat.

Using the Right Word

Know the Rule

Some words are confusing because they look similar or have similar meanings.

Examples:

cloths:	materials made by weaving fibers	**can:**	to be able to
clothes:	things worn over the body	**may:**	to ask for or receive permission
good:	of high quality	**between:**	in the middle of (when referring to two)
well:	in a satisfactory way	**among:**	in the middle of (when referring to more than two)

Practice the Rule

Number a sheet of paper 1–10. For each sentence, choose and write the word that belongs in the blank.

1. Rob wanted some soft, clean _____ to fill a bed for his dog. (cloths/clothes)

2. My brother said I _____ borrow his motor for my science project. (can/may)

3. At the science fair, I'll put my clay boat _____ the balance and the tank. (between/among)

4. Johan's proposal was written ____, so the committee approved his project. (good/well)

5. _____ hawks now live in the forest than before the forest fire. (Fewer/Less)

6. Kathy was so frightened by the lightning strike that she could hardly _____. (breath/breathe)

7. Please _____ your DVD about penguins with you when you come to my home. (bring/take)

8. What did you _____ (chose/choose) to study for your science project? I _____ lichens. (chose/choose)

9. Please _____ (lay/lie) the beach towel down on the sand so I can _____ on it. (lay/lie)

10. Luz, Pam, and Emily are going camping and will share the cost _____ them. (between/among)

Publish
✛Presentation

Publishing Strategy	Present the proposal to a teacher committee.
Presentation Strategy	Use clear formats and text features.

Now that I've finished editing my draft, I'll focus on publishing and presenting my proposal. I will present my proposal to a teacher committee soon, so it has to look professional. I'll use a word processor to prepare my final copy. My teacher reminded us to use clear fonts, formats, and features. Before I print out copies for the committee, I'll print one for me to make sure it's correct and includes all the items on my final checklist.

My Final Checklist

Did I—

✔ make sure all easily confused words are used correctly?

✔ check my spelling, capitalization, and punctuation?

✔ use a clear font and good margins to make the proposal easy to read?

✔ use formatting features, such as boldface headings, to make the organization easy to follow?

Apply

Make a checklist to check your proposal. Then make a final copy to publish.

Buoyancy: Why Do Boats Float?

by Luis

Introduction

People who go swimming and lie spread out on top of the water will float. If they roll themselves up into a ball, they will sink into the water. Even heavy ships can float. Most people are mystified by these "impossible" phenomena. My experiment will clear up the mystery and explain why such occurrences are possible. It will help people understand the important concept of buoyancy.

I will explain buoyancy by comparing the densities of a block of clay and the same block of clay formed into a "boat."

Density is the amount of mass an object has for each unit of its volume. The volume of a ship's hull is made up of its frame plus air that is inside of the hull.

I hypothesize that a boat floats when the volume of its hull includes enough air to make the ship's density less than the density of water.

Project Description

First, I will measure the mass and volume of water, of a block of modeling clay, and of the block of clay when it is formed into a "boat" that floats. Then, I will compute the density of each of these. Finally, I will record all the data in a data table and compare the densities, masses, and volumes.

The independent variable is the shape of the clay. The dependent variable is whether the clay floats.

Materials

Block of modeling clay about 2 cm x 8 cm x 2 cm; graduated cylinder (100 mL); balance with gram weights; 4 tofu containers; water; towel; displacement tank made from a 1-gal plastic distilled water jug and flex-elbowed clear plastic drinking straw

Procedure

1. First, I'll find the mass and volume of a sample of water using the graduated cylinder and the balance.
2. Next, I'll find the mass of the block of clay using the balance. Then, I'll find the volume of the clay by placing it on top of the water in the displacement tank. I'll measure the volume of the water that comes out of the tank and record this as the volume of the block of clay.
3. Now, I'll shape the clay into a boat that I think will float. I'll test the boat by placing it on top of water in a tofu container full of water. I'll keep reshaping the clay until I find a boat that floats.

4. I'll find the mass of the boat that floats. Then, I'll find the volume of the boat using the displacement tank and the graduated cylinder.

5. Finally, I'll compute the densities of the water, clay block, and clay boat.

Conclusion

I expect my data table will show that the mass of the clay block and the clay boat is the same, but their densities are different. What makes the density of the boat less is its volume, which is greater because air is added to the size of the boat. The density of the boat is less than the density of water, so it floats.

I think my experiment is an important one because it will demonstrate the powerful force of buoyancy, and it will answer the question many people have about why heavy objects can float.

Reflect

Does Luis's proposal use all the traits of a good formal proposal? Use the rubric to check your writing.

Argument
test writing

Read the Writing Prompt

When you take a writing test, you will be given a writing prompt. Most writing prompts have three parts:

Setup This part of the writing prompt gives you the background information you need to get ready to write.

Task This part of the writing prompt tells you exactly what you are supposed to write: an argument essay.

Scoring Guide This section tells how your writing will be scored. To do well on the test, you should include everything on the list.

Remember the rubrics you've used in writing class this year? When you take a writing test, you don't always have all of the information that's on a rubric. But a scoring guide is a lot like a rubric. It lists everything you need to think about to write a good paper. Like the rubrics you've used, many scoring guides are based on the six traits of writing:

Your school is looking for new ways to raise money to support social programs, such as afterschool sports and band. Some schools accept money from businesses in exchange for placing advertisements around their school facilities. The Super Soda Company has offered to buy your school an expensive scoreboard, provided they can place an advertisement for Super Soda on it. Do you think this is a good idea?

Write an argument essay to read to the school board. Decide whether you think the school should accept or reject this offer. Then give reasons to support your opinion.

Be sure your writing

- clearly states your claim and includes relevant evidence to support each reason.

- is well organized. You should make a claim, give a new reason in each paragraph, and then restate your claim in the conclusion.

- uses a voice and tone that are appropriate for the purpose and audience.

- has clear and compelling language.

- includes conditional sentences.

- contains correct grammar, punctuation, capitalization, and spelling.

Writing Traits
in the Scoring Guide

Look at the scoring guide in the writing prompt on page 359. Not every writing prompt will include all six writing traits, but this one does. The chart below can help you better understand the connection between the scoring guide and the writing traits in the rubrics you've been using. Before you turn in your test, make sure your work is neat and your name is on every page.

- Be sure your writing clearly states your claim and includes relevant evidence to support each reason.

- Be sure your writing is well organized. You should make a claim, give a new reason in each paragraph, and then restate your claim in the conclusion.

- Be sure your writing uses a voice and tone that are appropriate for the purpose and audience.

- Be sure your writing has clear and compelling language.

- Be sure your writing includes conditional sentences.

- Be sure your writing contains correct grammar, punctuation, capitalization, and spelling.

Look at Mika Peters' essay on the next page. Did she use the scoring guide?

Say "No, Thanks"

by Mika Peters

I know that Super Soda's offer of a new scoreboard for our school seems like a worthwhile offer, but I think the school board should politely say "no, thanks."

Many middle-school students tend to go along with the crowd. Because they want to do what other kids are doing, some students often have trouble making up their minds about what to wear, how to act, and what to eat. These kids sometimes purchase brand-name clothing to "fit in" with their peers. They buy the same brands of snacks and drinks that everyone else buys, instead of thinking for themselves.

Now, Super Soda has offered to give our school a new scoreboard for the gym. I'm sure the basketball fans would love it. But the scoreboard would probably display a large Super Soda advertisement so that no one would miss it.

You might ask yourself, what's wrong with that? Well, we kids see so many ads for products like Super Soda that we often don't even consider anything else when choosing a product. It's like we've all been brainwashed. When we go to a store or a vending machine, we usually pass up the healthy options and buy the junk food instead. That's because we reach for the product in the familiar package—the one with the same name that everyone else is buying.

I realize that some people are saying that the money the school could get from Super Soda would be enough to support special programs. I'm also aware that the school received over $20,000 last year from beverage sales in the Super Soda vending machines. I understand that the school wouldn't have to pay anything for our new scoreboard if we accept this offer. But wouldn't you agree that students' health is more important? If the scoreboard were free, that would be great. But in my opinion, the cost of the new scoreboard is way too high.

We students are never going to learn to make up our own minds or make smart choices if we keep allowing advertisers to brainwash us. That's why I'm taking a stand (and hoping you'll join me) by saying "no, thanks" to Super Soda's offer!

Using the Scoring Guide to Study the Model

Now we'll use the scoring guide to check Mika's writing test, "Say 'No, Thanks.'" Let's see how well her essay meets each of the six writing traits.

• **The writing clearly states your claim and includes relevant evidence that supports each reason.**

Mika clearly states her opinion regarding the school scoreboard issue. She believes the school should say "no, thanks" to Super Soda's offer. She includes several facts and examples to support her reasons.

When we go to a store or a vending machine, we usually pass up the healthy options and buy the junk food instead. That's because we reach for the product in the familiar package—the one with the same name that everyone else is buying.

• **The writing is well organized.**
• **The writing makes a claim, gives a new reason in each paragraph, and then restates the claim at the end.**

I like how Mika states her opinion early on and then provides lots of supporting details in the following paragraphs. She also restates her claim in her closing paragraph, just to send the message home.

We students are never going to learn to make up our own minds or make smart choices if we keep allowing advertisers to brainwash us. That's why I'm taking a stand (and hoping you'll join me) by saying "no, thanks" to Super Soda's offer!

Voice

• The voice and tone are appropriate for the purpose and audience.

Mika uses a voice that is casual and friendly, yet still informative and strong. She uses a tone that is appropriate for her audience, but not so casual that she loses credibility.

You might ask yourself, what's wrong with that? Well, we kids see so many ads for products like Super Soda that we often don't even consider anything else when choosing a product. It's like we've all been brainwashed.

Word Choice

• The writing is clear and compelling.

I like how Mika uses just the right words to explain her stance. Her words are precise and accurate. I also notice that she's careful to use neutral words when she addresses counterclaims. She treats opposing viewpoints fairly.

the school received over $20,000 last year from beverage sales in the Super Soda vending machines. I understand that the school wouldn't have to pay anything for our new scoreboard if we accept this offer. But wouldn't you agree that students' health is more important?

Using the Scoring Guide to Study the Model

- **The essay contains conditional sentences.**

Mika uses conditional sentences to present several convincing "what if" scenarios to her reader. The second and third sentences in this passage present the idea that "if" the school accepts Super Soda's offer, it will "probably" have a large advertisement on it.

Now, Super Soda has offered to give our school a new scoreboard for the gym. I'm sure the basketball fans would love it. But the scoreboard would probably display a large Super Soda advertisement so that no one would miss it.

- **The writing contains correct grammar, punctuation, capitalization, and spelling.**

It looks like Mika used correct grammar, spelling, capitalization, and punctuation. I know it's important to check for these kinds of mistakes, so I'll be sure to keep that in mind as I write. Don't forget to check for proper grammar and mechanics in your writing, too. This can be done at every step of the writing process.

Planning My Time

Before giving us a writing prompt, my teacher always tells us how much time we'll have to complete the test. Since I'm already familiar with each step of the writing process I can plan how much time I'll need for each one. Then I'll be sure to have enough time to complete the entire process. If the test takes an hour, here's how I'll organize my time. Planning your time will help you, too!

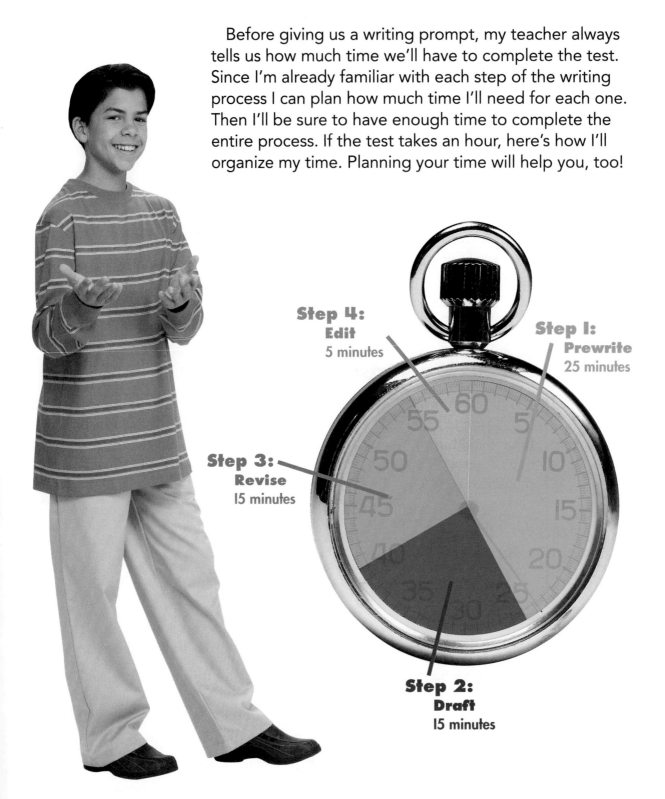

Step 4:
Edit
5 minutes

Step 1:
Prewrite
25 minutes

Step 3:
Revise
15 minutes

Step 2:
Draft
15 minutes

Prewrite

Focus on Ideas

Writing Strategy — **Study the writing prompt to find out what to do.**

When I take a writing test, I always study my writing prompt before I begin. It usually has three parts (the setup, task, and scoring guide), but they're not always labeled. You should look for (and label) these sections on your writing prompt, and you should circle key words that tell what kind of writing you will be doing and who your audience will be. I circled my topic in red below. I also used purple to circle what kind of writing I'll be doing (an argument essay) and who my audience will be (the people in my town).

My Writing Test Prompt

Setup — Your town owns some wooded land called the old Wingate property. Some people believe the land should be preserved for activities such as hiking and bird watching. Others think the town should sell the property to a real estate developer and use the money on schools and other municipal services.

Task — Write an argument essay for your townspeople, explaining whether you think the land should be sold or preserved. Explain your reasons.

Scoring Guide — Be sure your writing

- clearly states your claim and includes relevant evidence to support each reason.

- is well organized. You should make a claim, give a new reason in each paragraph, and then restate your claim in the conclusion.

- uses a voice and tone that are appropriate for the purpose and audience.

- has clear and compelling language.

- includes conditional sentences.

- contains correct grammar, punctuation, capitalization, and spelling.

Think about how the scoring guide relates to the six traits of good writing in the rubrics you've studied. Not all of the traits will be included in every scoring guide, but you'll still want to remember them all in order to write a good argument essay.

- **Be sure your writing clearly states your claim and includes relevant evidence to support each reason.**

I'll open my essay by stating my claim, and I'll include lots of facts and examples to support my reasons.

- **Be sure your writing is well organized. You should make a claim, give a new reason in each paragraph, and then restate your claim in the conclusion.**

I want my reader to understand my point of view and the reasons for it, so organization is important.

- **Be sure your writing uses a voice and tone that are appropriate for the purpose and audience.**

I'll be sure to use a voice that is appropriate for both my purpose and my audience.

- **Be sure your writing has clear and compelling language.**

Confusing or unclear words will weaken my purpose. I'll be sure to use strong, precise words.

- **Be sure your writing includes conditional sentences.**

I can be more convincing if I use conditional sentences that describe the "what ifs."

- **Be sure your writing contains correct grammar, punctuation, capitalization, and spelling.**

I know to check my grammar and mechanics whenever I write.

Prewrite

Focus on **Ideas**

Writing Strategy Respond to the task.

Writers always gather information before they begin writing, so that's what I'll do. Let's take another look at the task, since that's the part of the writing prompt that explains what I'm supposed to write. When you write for a test, you don't have much time, so you need to decide how you'll respond to the task before you start writing.

I'm supposed to write an argument essay about what the town should do with the old Wingate property. I already know I want the land to be saved, so I'll begin by jotting down the reasons why I feel this way.

Task —⎡ Write an argument essay for your townspeople, explaining
          ⎢ whether you think the land should be sold or preserved. Explain
          ⎣ your reasons.

Notes

✔ Open land costs the town less than developed land.

✔ Both people and animals benefit from open land.

✔ People need a place to get away.

✔ There's not much open land left in my town.

Apply

Be sure to think about how you're going to respond to the task before you start to write. Gather information by jotting down some notes.

Writing Strategy   Choose a graphic organizer.

I don't have a lot of time, so now I'll choose a graphic organizer. I already listed the reasons why I think the old Wingate property should be saved, so I think an Outline will help me organize facts and examples that support each of my reasons.

I'll state my claim at the top of the Outline, and I'll use Roman numerals for each of my reasons. Then, I'll use capital letters for supporting facts and examples.

Claim: The Wingate property should be preserved for the future of our town.

I. Open land costs the town less than developed land.
   A. If the land is used for homes, more tax money will be needed for schools.
   B. More homes require more services like fire and police protection.

II. Both people and animals benefit from open land.
   A. Animals would lose their habitats.
   B. Animals would come into people's yards and eat flowers and bushes.

III. People need a place to get away.
   A. We should get fresh air and sun outside, not inside a gym.
   B. Our moods are better when we find places with quiet space.
   C. I love to sit in a tree and read a book.

IV. There's not much open land left in our town.
   A. Only 20% of our town is undeveloped.
   B. We need to save open land while we can.

Reflect

How well do Luis's facts and examples support his reasons?

Apply

Choose a graphic organizer that will help you identify your main reasons and supporting details.

Prewrite

Focus on Organization

Writing Strategy   Check my graphic organizer against the scoring guide.

Without much time to revise during a test, prewriting is really important. Before I start to write, I'll check my Outline against the scoring guide in the writing prompt.

Claim: The Wingate property should be preserved for the future of our town.

I. Open land costs the town less than developed land.
   A. If the land is used for homes, more tax money will be needed for schools.
   B. More homes require more services like fire and police protection.

II. Both people and animals benefit from open land.
   A. Animals would lose their habitats.
   B. Animals would come into people's yards and eat flowers and bushes.

III. People need a place to get away.
   A. We should get fresh air and sun outside, not inside a gym.
   B. Our moods are better when we find places with quiet space.
   C. I love to sit in a tree and read a book.

IV. There's not much open land left in our town.
   A. Only 20% of our town is undeveloped.
   B. We need to save open land while we can.

Ideas

- Be sure your writing clearly states your claim and includes relevant evidence to support each reason.

I'll just turn my outline into an essay! I'll state my claim in my introduction, and I'll use the reason from each Roman numeral to make a separate supporting paragraph.

Organization

- Be sure your writing is well organized. You should make a claim, give a new reason in each paragraph, and then restate your claim in the conclusion.

After my introduction and supporting paragraphs, I'll restate my claim in my conclusion.

Voice

- Be sure your writing uses a voice and tone that are appropriate for the purpose and audience.

I'll use a formal voice and tone to connect with the audience.

Word Choice

- Be sure your writing has clear and compelling language.

I'll choose words that are precise, accurate, and fair.

Sentence Fluency

- Be sure your writing includes conditional sentences.

My outline already includes a few conditional sentences, but I'll be sure to use more of them as I write.

Conventions

- Be sure your writing contains correct grammar, punctuation, capitalization, and spelling.

I'll check for proper grammar and mechanics when I edit my essay.

Reflect

Can you think of anything that's missing from Luis's Outline?

Apply

Compare your graphic organizer with the scoring guide before you start to write. This way you'll know what to do when you begin drafting.

Draft

Focus on (Ideas)

Writing Strategy   Clearly state my claim and support it with facts and examples.

Well, it's time to start writing. The scoring guide says how important it is that I clearly state my claim for the reader. I think I'll state my claim in my opening paragraph. Then I'll provide supporting facts and details in the following paragraphs.

[DRAFT]

Preserve Our Future

by Luis

Soon voters in our town will be asked to determine the future of the old Wingate property. Some think it should become a housing development. But I say this land must be preserved!   **[clearly stated claim]**

Keeping the land as open space will cost taxpayers less than developing it. If the land is used for houses or apartments, the children who move there will need schools. The residents will require costly services like Fire and Police Protection, as well as trash collection. My aunt is a Firefighter, and she earns a pretty good living.

Also, both people and animals benefit from open land. If forced off their own land, wild animals would look for other places to live. They would come into our backyards and eat our plants and bushes.

Another important reason to keep Wingate as undeveloped and untouched land is that people need a place to vacation, relax, and unwind when they are feeling like they just need a break. In my opinion we are much healthier if we exercise outdoors, where we can get fresh air and sun, instead of paying to belong to a gym. Not to mention, looking at trees and grass is relaxing! It relieves stress and eases the mind.

Finally, there's not alot of open land left in our town. Over three fourths of our city's land is already developed. Our quality of life depends on our ability to walk around freely enjoy trees and flowers, and have room to get away from noise and crowds. We will begin saving what little open space we have left.

In conclusion, there are many good reasons to keep Wingate as open land. It's cheaper, and it's healthier for people, animals, and plants. Surely these facts outway any reasons <u>not</u> to keep Wingate for public use.

Reflect

What do you think? Did Luis make a strong case for preserving the old Wingate property?

Apply

Clearly state your claim so the reader will know why you're writing.

Revise

Writing Strategy   Use transition words.

The scoring guide says to keep my writing well organized. I know from past writing assignments that transition words help guide the reader through the main points in a logical order. I reread my essay to see if my ideas are easy to follow. I decided that I need to let the reader know right away that I have more than one reason against developing the land. Do you think my revision helps to organize my reasons?

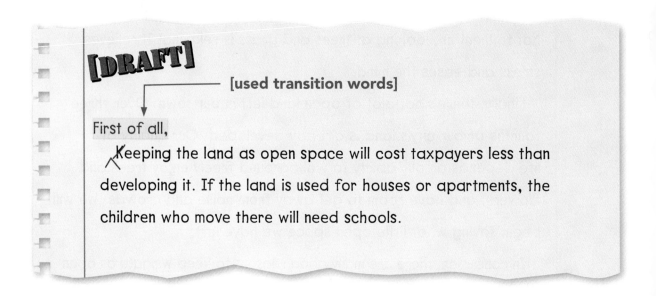

[DRAFT]

[used transition words]

First of all,

^Keeping the land as open space will cost taxpayers less than developing it. If the land is used for houses or apartments, the children who move there will need schools.

Apply

Read your essay to be sure your ideas are easy to follow. Use transition words to link your ideas.

Revise

Focus on **Voice**

Writing Strategy Use an appropriate voice and tone.

The scoring guide also reminds me to use an appropriate voice and tone to connect with my audience. I see a place where I can ask my reader a question. I think it will help to keep the reader engaged in my argument. I also want the reader to take me seriously, so I will keep my tone formal and polite. What do you think of my revision?

[DRAFT]

If forced off their own land, wild animals would look for other places

to live. They would come into our backyards and eat our plants and

bushes. I don't want that, do you? ◄── **[asked reader a question]**

Reflect

How does asking a question help to engage the audience in Luis's argument?

Apply

Read your essay. Be sure to ask a question that engages the reader.

Revise

Focus on Word Choice

Writing Strategy   Omit vague words.

The scoring guide reminds me to use precise words. As I read my essay again, I found one place where I used two words where one will do and, in the same sentence, used too many general words to describe a simple concept. It's easy to revise! All I have to do is use precise words. Do you agree with my changes?

[DRAFT]

Another important reason to keep Wingate as undeveloped
and untouched land is that people need a place to ~~vacation, relax,~~ get away
and unwind when they are feeling like they just need a break.

[deleted unnecessary words]   [used precise words]

Apply

Read your essay. Remove any unnecessary words. Replace general words with precise ones.

Focus on **Conventions**

Writing Strategy Check my grammar, punctuation, capitalization, and spelling.

I'm almost finished! The scoring guide says to use correct grammar, punctuation, capitalization, and spelling. I always leave plenty of time to check for errors in these important areas.

[**FINAL DRAFT**]

Preserve Our Future

by Luis

Soon voters in our town will be asked to determine the future of the old Wingate property. Some think it should become a housing development. But I say this land must be preserved!

First of all,
∧Keeping the land as open space will cost taxpayers less than developing it. If the land is used for houses or apartments, the children who move there will need schools. The residents will require costly services like ~~f~~Fire and ~~p~~Police ~~p~~Protection, as well as trash collection. ~~My aunt is a Firefighter, and she earns a pretty good living~~.

Apply

Check your grammar, punctuation, capitalization, and spelling every time you write for a test.

FINAL DRAFT

Shrubs and gardens are not the only things that could get damaged. Deer, rabbits, and coyotes carry diseases such as Lyme disease, rabies, and rabbit fever. People could get sick from the close contact.

Also, both people and animals benefit from open land. If forced off their own land, wild animals would look for other places to live. They would come into our backyards and eat our plants and bushes. I don't want that, do you?

Another important reason to keep Wingate as undeveloped ~~and untouched~~ land is that people need a place to ~~vacation, relax, and unwind when they are feeling like they just need a break~~ get away. In my opinion, we are much healthier if we exercise outdoors, where we can get fresh air and sun, instead of paying to belong to a gym. Not to mention, looking at trees and grass is relaxing! It relieves stress and eases the mind.

Finally, there's not ~~alot~~ a lot of open land left in our town. Over three fourths of our city's land is already developed. Our quality of life depends on our ability to walk around freely, enjoy trees and flowers, and have room to get away from noise and crowds. ~~We will~~ That's why we should begin saving what little open space we have left.

In conclusion, there are many good reasons to keep Wingate as open land. It's cheaper, and it's healthier for people, animals, and plants. Surely these facts ~~outway~~ outweigh any reasons _not_ to keep Wingate for public use.

Reflect

How did Luis do? Check his argument essay against the scoring guide. Remember to use your writing prompt's scoring guide to check your own writing anytime you take a test.

I'm finished! That wasn't so bad. The main thing to remember when you take a writing test is that you use the writing process. The process is a little different when you take a test, but if you keep in mind these important tips, you'll do OK.

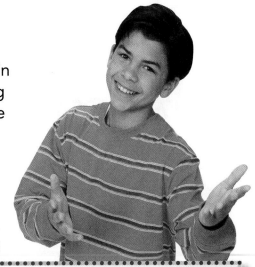

TEST TiPS

1. **Study the writing prompt before you start to write.** Most writing prompts have three parts: the setup, the task, and the scoring guide. The parts probably won't be labeled. You'll have to figure them out for yourself!

2. **Make sure you understand the task before you start to write.**
   - Read all three parts of the writing prompt carefully.
   - Circle key words in the task part of the writing prompt that tell what kind of writing you need to do. The task might also identify your audience.
   - Make sure you know how you'll be graded.
   - Say the assignment in your own words to yourself.

3. **Keep an eye on the clock.** Decide how much time you will spend on each part of the writing process and try to stick to your schedule. Don't spend so much time prewriting that you don't have enough time left to write.

4. **Reread your writing. Check it against the scoring guide at least twice.** Remember the rubrics you've used? A scoring guide on a writing test is like a rubric. It can help you keep what's important in mind.

5. **Plan, plan, plan!** You don't get much time to revise during a test, so planning is more important than ever.

6. **Write neatly.** Remember: If the people who score your test can't read your writing, it doesn't matter how good your essay is!

Descriptive writing describes something to the reader.

Hi, I'm Josh. I'm learning about descriptive writing in school, and I really think I'm going to have fun with it. I like sharing with my friends and family all the things that happen to me, and now I'll learn some strategies to turn those experiences into full-length pieces of descriptive writing.

IN THIS UNIT

- ☐ **Business Letter**
- ☐ **Scientific Observation**
- ☐ **Descriptive Vignette**
- SOCIAL STUDIES CONNECTION ▶ **Poem**
- ☐ **Writing for a Test**

Name: Josh
Home: Virginia
Hobbies: going to the movies,
playing baseball,
spending time at
the beach
Favorite Movie: *Star Wars*

What's a Business Letter?

It's a formal letter written to a person or a company. Knowing how to write a good business letter is an important skill that will help me communicate with people throughout the world beyond friends and family.

What's in a Business Letter?

Purpose
This is why I'm writing the letter in the first place. The purpose of my letter will help guide my writing. As I write, I'll keep my purpose and audience in mind.

Supporting Facts
I should think about my main idea or topic and back it up with well-chosen facts that support it. I'll build each paragraph around one supporting fact.

Tone
This is how I want my letter to sound. My tone has to suit my audience and my purpose, so I'll have to think about who will be reading the letter and why I'm writing it. This is a business letter, so I'll use a formal, respectful tone.

Clear Details
My letter should include exact details that describe my topic clearly. I also need to remember that all the details need to support my topic and clarify my purpose for writing.

Why write a Business Letter?

There are all kinds of reasons to write a business letter. I gave it some thought, and I came up with this list of ideas.

To Inform

Keeping people informed about a product or a service is a great reason to write a business letter. For example, I might want to present details about a school club or team, and ask a company to be our sponsor. Or I could let a business know I'd like some information about its products or store locations.

To Make a Request

A business letter is a good format to use when you want to convince a company to donate to a cause, make a new product, or take some other kind of action.

To Respond

If I buy a game that doesn't work or the school committee decides to cut music classes, I can respond by writing a letter. This way, I can describe my reaction in a calm, professional way.

Linking Descriptive Writing Traits to a Business Letter

In this chapter, you will write to someone to describe an issue. This type of descriptive writing is called a business letter. Josh will guide you through the stages of the writing process: Prewrite, Draft, Revise, Edit, and Publish. In each stage, Josh will show you important writing strategies that are linked to the Descriptive Writing Traits below.

Descriptive Writing Traits

Ideas
- a focused, complete topic
- relevant sensory details that support, describe, and develop the topic

Organization
- an introduction that previews a topic, a body that develops the topic, and a conclusion that follows and supports the description
- well-organized details that follow the order of the description, whether by time, location, or other order
- transitions that clarify relationships between ideas

Voice
- a voice and tone that are appropriate for the purpose and audience

Word Choice
- precise, descriptive language that creates a clear picture for the reader

Sentence Fluency
- sentences that vary in length and structure to make the writing flow

Conventions
- no or few errors in grammar, usage, mechanics, and spelling

Before you write, read Denny McCabe's business letter on the next three pages. Use the business letter rubric on pages 388–389 to decide how well he did. (You might look back at What's in a Business Letter? on page 382 too!)

1045 Stonegate Drive
Westmont, IL 60559
August 3, 2012

Mr. Ronald Richards, General Manager
Woodcreek Theaters
1 South Mall Drive
Clarendon Hills, IL 60514

Dear Mr. Richards:

Purpose

I am writing to tell you about the unpleasant experience that I had at your new theater complex this evening. I was expecting an exciting evening, especially after all the publicity about the twelve new screens with plush seating and state-of-the-art sound systems. It was at one of these screens—Theater 6, to be exact—that I arrived to see *Exploring Space*. My experience was disappointing, considering everything that happened tonight.

Supporting facts

Three problems made it impossible to enjoy the movie. The first relates to the lack of service in the lobby area. A large cinema complex should have more than one concession stand, and this one did. Two circular, glass-topped counters displayed a tempting array of candies, sodas, popcorn, and hot snacks such as nachos. Although the lobby was packed with movie-goers, only one counter was open because only two ushers were available to work. The lines were so long that people started pushing and shoving to get to the front. Some particularly impatient people even shouted out their orders before those in front of them could say what they wanted. After someone complained, the second concession stand was opened. This might have eased the problem, if the

Clear details

manager hadn't taken one of the ushers from the first counter to staff it. Now, two stands were functioning, but with only one staff member apiece. After waiting 15 minutes for popcorn, I left empty-handed, only to stand in another disgruntled, slow-moving crowd to get to my film on time.

Supporting fact

When I finally took my seat, I was immediately confronted with a second problem: the conditions inside Theater 6. For starters, the theater was freezing cold. Before the coming attractions even began, several people asked the manager to adjust the thermostat. She said she would take care of it, but the temperature never changed. Consequently, several people sitting around me got up and left about halfway through the movie. Other people opted to stay, fidgeting endlessly by shrugging on their coats and squirming in their seats, as if keeping in constant motion might keep them warm.

Supporting fact

Clear details

In addition, Theater 6 looked and felt as if it had never been cleaned. In my row, empty containers littered the floor, topped with a layer of discarded popcorn puffs stuck to a coating of spilled soda. This was a multi-sensory nightmare. Aside from the horrible sight of it, there was the sticky feel of jelly candies plastered to the back of my chair, and the sucking sound my sneakers made each time I lifted them off the floor. I assume that this problem stemmed from the same cause as the situation in the lobby: understaffing. Perhaps the lack of ushers made it impossible to keep up with between-show cleanings.

Supporting fact

The third problem was the presentation of the movie itself. First, there was the sound. Although we could barely hear our own movie, we could clearly hear the one in Theater 5. As soon as

Exploring Space began, people started asking for the volume to be adjusted. Even so, we couldn't really hear it until the film's final half hour. Then, the film suddenly stopped right at the high point of the movie! The technician got it started again pretty quickly, but it was too late. Along with everything else that had gone wrong, the interruption ruined any enjoyment I was getting out of the movie. At that point, I gave up and left.

Considering the events of this evening, I may not return to the new Woodcreek Theaters. I hope you consider this feedback because, without certain improvements, the new cinema complex might have an extremely short run.

← **Respectful tone**

Sincerely,

Denny McCabe

Denny McCabe

Rubric

Use this 6-point rubric to plan and score a business letter.

	6	5	4
Ideas	The letter focuses on one main idea or topic. Relevant, well-chosen facts and concrete details support the topic.	The letter focuses on one main idea or topic. Most facts and details support the topic.	The letter focuses on one main idea or topic. Some facts and details support the topic.
Organization	Each paragraph has a topic sentence and supporting details. Appropriate and varied transitions clarify relationships among ideas.	Each paragraph has a topic sentence and supporting details. Most transitions clarify relationships among ideas.	Most paragraphs have a topic sentence and supporting details. Most transitions clarify relationships among ideas.
Voice	The writer consistently uses a formal, respectful tone and second-person point of view.	The writer mostly uses a formal, respectful tone and second-person point of view.	The writer uses a somewhat formal, respectful tone and second-person point of view.
Word Choice	Precise language clarifies the message and strengthens the purpose for writing.	Precise language is used most of the time. Most of the writer's message is clear.	Some words are precise. Some of the writer's message is clear.
Sentence Fluency	A variety of concise sentences conveys the writer's message clearly.	Most sentences are varied and concise. Most convey the writer's message clearly.	Several sentences in a row share the same structure. Most of the writer's message is conveyed clearly.
Conventions	Correct subject-verb agreement makes the writing clear and easy for the reader to follow.	Errors in subject-verb agreement don't interfere with the reader's ability to understand the letter.	Minor errors in subject-verb agreement rarely interfere with the reader's ability to understand the letter.

✚ Presentation Correct business letter format gets the writer's message across.

3	2	1	
The letter focuses on one main idea or topic. Only a few details support the topic.	The main idea or topic may not be clear. Facts are not included. Details may not be related.	The main idea or topic is not clear. Facts and details are not included.	**Ideas**
One or more paragraphs lack topic sentences or are not in order. More transitions are needed.	Paragraphs are not in order or are very poorly formed. Transitions are confusing or missing.	The writing is not organized as a letter. Ideas are very hard or impossible to follow.	**Organization**
An appropriate tone is established in the beginning but fades. Point of view may be inconsistent.	The writer's tone may be inappropriate. The point of view may be inconsistent.	The voice is very weak or absent. A point of view is not established.	**Voice**
Some words are too general or ordinary. The writer's message is not conveyed clearly.	Many words are vague or dull. Some words may confuse the writer's message.	Few words are used correctly. No message is conveyed.	**Word Choice**
Many sentences share the same structure. Part of the writer's message may be repetitious.	Many sentences share the same structure and length. The writer's message may be confusing.	Sentences are incomplete or incorrect.	**Sentence Fluency**
Some errors in subject-verb agreement may affect the clarity of parts of the letter.	Many errors in subject-verb agreement make the letter confusing to the reader.	Subject-verb agreement is missing. The writing must be read word by word to understand it.	**Conventions**

See Appendix B for 4-, 5-, and 6-point descriptive rubrics.

Using the Rubric to Study the Model

Business Letter

Did you notice that the model on pages 385–387 points out some key elements of a business letter? As he wrote his business letter, Denny McCabe used these elements to help him describe an unpleasant experience at the movies. He also used the 6-point rubric on pages 388–389 to plan, draft, revise, and edit the writing. A rubric is a great tool to evaluate writing during the writing process.

Now let's use the same rubric to score the model. To do this, we'll focus on each trait separately, starting with Ideas. We'll use the top descriptor for each trait (column 6), along with examples from the model, to help us understand how the traits work together. How would you score Denny on each trait?

- **The letter focuses on one main idea or topic.**
- **Relevant, well-chosen facts and concrete details support the main topic.**

Denny's main idea is that his experience at the new theater complex was awful. He then describes each problem he encountered, using lots of relevant details. In this section, all the details are necessary to describe how understaffing led to a big mess.

[from the writing model]

Although the lobby was packed with movie-goers, only one counter was open because only two ushers were available to work. The lines were so long that people started pushing and shoving to get to the front. Some particularly impatient people even shouted out their orders before those in front of them could say what they wanted.

Organization

- Each paragraph has a topic sentence and supporting details.
- Appropriate and varied transitions clarify relationships among ideas.

Denny starts each paragraph with a strong topic sentence. In this example, the clear topic sentence states that there were *three problems*. Denny follows up later in the letter with the transitions *The first*, *a second*, and *The third*. These connect Denny's ideas and guide the reader.

[from the writing model]

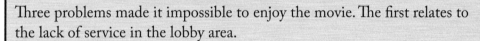

Three problems made it impossible to enjoy the movie. The first relates to the lack of service in the lobby area.

Voice

- The writer consistently uses a formal, respectful tone and second-person point of view.

Denny's tone is respectful and formal, despite his unpleasant experience at the cinema. He also uses the second-person pronoun *you* to directly address the reader, the cinema's general manager.

[from the writing model]

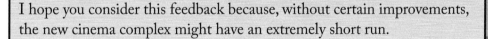

I hope you consider this feedback because, without certain improvements, the new cinema complex might have an extremely short run.

• **Precise language clarifies the message and strengthens the purpose for writing.**

Denny's words create an accurate picture of his movie night experience. It is almost like I was there! Words like *fidgeting*, *shrugging*, and *keeping in constant motion* help strengthen his purpose in a clear and powerful way. He uses each word correctly and is careful not to repeat words unnecessarily.

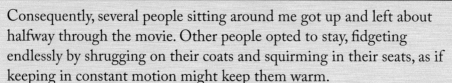

[from the writing model]

Consequently, several people sitting around me got up and left about halfway through the movie. Other people opted to stay, fidgeting endlessly by shrugging on their coats and squirming in their seats, as if keeping in constant motion might keep them warm.

• **A variety of concise sentences conveys the writer's message clearly.**

I enjoyed reading Denny's letter because his sentences held my interest. As I read, I noticed that the variety of sentences helped the writing flow smoothly. All the ideas are easy to follow and convey Denny's message clearly.

[from the writing model]

For starters, the theater was freezing cold. Before the coming attractions even began, several people asked the manager to adjust the thermostat. She said she would take care of it, but the temperature never changed.

Conventions

- **Correct subject-verb agreement makes the writing clear and easy for the reader to follow.**

Denny also does the little things well—like putting commas and periods in the right places, and checking his spelling. All his subjects and verbs agree, too. I don't see any errors in his writing, do you?

[from the writing model]

The third problem was the presentation of the movie itself. First, there was the sound. Although we could barely hear our own movie, we could clearly hear the one in Theater 5. As soon as *Exploring Space* began, people started asking for the volume to be adjusted.

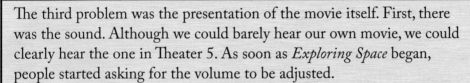

⊕Presentation Correct business letter format gets the writer's message across.

My Turn!

Now I'm going to write a business letter, but I'll focus on a positive experience. I'll use the 6-point rubric, along with good writing strategies, to help me write a detailed business letter. Read along to see how I do it.

Writing a Business Letter

Prewrite

Focus on **Ideas**

The Rubric Says   The letter focuses on one main idea or topic. Relevant, well-chosen facts and concrete details support the topic.

Writing Strategy   List the main idea or topic. Then list details that support it.

I enjoy going to the movies, too. So when I read Denny's letter, I understood how he felt. I also remembered an experience at the movie theater that could have been horrible if not for some quick thinking by the theater manager. I knew this would make a great topic for a business letter, so I jotted down the idea. Then I listed some supporting details.

Main Idea: To thank the manager of my local theater for how she handled a tough situation

Supporting Details:

- Biggest blockbuster of the summer; a lot of people; manager had us form different lines

- Temperature over 90°; many waited outside; manager handed out free water

- Film scheduled to start, and people still filing in; manager held up start time

- Not everyone got into the last show; manager gave free tickets to everyone in line and told them to come back the next day

Apply

Choose a topic for a business letter. Then write down your main idea and supporting details.

Prewrite

The Rubric Says   Each paragraph has a topic sentence and strong supporting details.

Writing Strategy   Make a Main-Idea Table to organize information.

Writer's Term

Main-Idea Table

A **Main-Idea Table** can help you structure a piece of writing by organizing your main idea and supporting details in a logical way. Write your main idea or topic at the top of the table. Then fill in the "legs" with supporting facts, details, and examples.

The rubric says that every paragraph should state a topic and provide supporting details. Creating a Main-Idea Table will help me structure well-written paragraphs. Each "leg" will list a topic and details. Since I'm going to write about how the manager solved problems, I'll use the labels *Problem* and *Solution*.

Main-Idea Table

Main Idea: I want to thank the manager of the York Street Theater for how she handled a tough situation.

Problem: When <u>Voyage to Mars</u> opened, the theater was swamped with people.

Solution: To let the crowd in faster, the manager had us form different lines.

Problem: The temperature was over 90°, and many people had to wait outside.

Solution: The manager had some employees walk down the lines and hand out free ice water.

Problem: When the film was scheduled to start, people were still filing into the theater.

Solution: The manager held up the start time until every seat was filled.

Problem: Not everyone in line got into the last show of the night.

Solution: The manager gave free tickets to everyone still in line and invited them back the next day.

Reflect

Do you think Josh included enough details to get started?

Apply

Use a Main-Idea Table to organize your main idea and supporting details.

Draft

Focus on **Ideas**

The Rubric Says   The letter focuses on one main idea or topic.

Writing Strategy   State the main idea clearly.

Now I'm ready to start writing my business letter. The rubric says I should focus on one main idea. I am sure the manager is a busy woman, so I will get right to the point. By clearly stating my purpose in the letter's opening, I not only show the manager that I value her time, but I also make it easier for her to understand my purpose. Then I will make sure that the body of my letter contains details that support the topic.

Right now, I'm just going to focus on getting my ideas down on paper. I'm going to write my letter in correct business letter format, including heading, inside address, greeting, body, closing, and signature. I'll do my best with spelling and grammar, but I know I can always go back and check for errors later. I'll also have a chance to look over my letter to make sure I've used all the format elements correctly. You can see most of my draft on the next page.

8301 Bell Avenue
Ivor, VA 23866
August 30, 2012 **[heading]**

Mrs. Paula Locascio, Manager
Main Street Theater
2 Main Street
Ivor, VA 23866 **[inside address]**

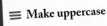

[DRAFT]

Dear Mrs. Locascio: ⟵ **[greeting]**

I am writing to thank you for the way you handled a really ⟵ **[main idea]**
tough situation on the night of August 5. As I'm sure you and your
staff recalls, that was the opening nite of the summer's biggest
blockbuster, <u>Voyage to Mars</u>. The theater was filled with people,
but thanks to your quick thinking, we didn't have to wait long.

[body] The high heat and humidity made us very uncomfortable. You acted
quickly to prevent what could have been an unbearable situation.
The heat was very annoying. Everyone standing—and wilting—
outside thought your idea of handing out free ice water was good!
You made the wait bearable.

Reflect

Did Josh state his purpose for writing in the first paragraph? What is it?

Apply

Write a draft using the notes from your Main-Idea Table. Remember to focus on one main idea or topic.

Revise

Focus on Organization

The Rubric Says Appropriate and varied transitions clarify relationships among ideas.

Writing Strategy Use transitions to guide the reader through the letter.

I've finished the draft. Now I'll use the rubric to revise my letter before sending it. It reminds me to use appropriate transitions to organize and clarify ideas. So I read my draft again and found a couple of places where I needed to add transitions to connect and clarify my ideas.

[DRAFT]

[added transition phrase]

[added transition word]

As we stood in long lines,
The high heat and humidity made us very uncomfortable. However, You acted

quickly to prevent what could have been an unbearable situation.

Writer's Term

Transitions are words or phrases that help the reader understand how the ideas are related. Sometimes they indicate time order (**before, during, as**). Other times they might indicate contrast (**but, on the other hand, however**).

Apply

Read your draft. Use transitions to connect and clarify your ideas.

The Rubric Says   The writer consistently uses a formal, respectful tone and second-person point of view.

Writing Strategy   Address the reader with a polite, formal tone.

After reading my business letter aloud, I realized that there were a few places where my tone could be more polite. It's important to state problems in a fair way and to be complimentary to the reader. The rubric says to use a formal and respectful tone. I will revise my writing to keep my tone polite. I am happy to see that I consistently used the second-person point of view.

[DRAFT]

[used formal tone]

~~The heat was very annoying.~~ Everyone standing—and wilting—outside

                         fantastic!

thought your idea of handing out free ice water was ~~good.~~ You made

    as comfortable as possible, and the crowd really appreciated it.

the wait ~~bearable.~~

Reflect

How do Josh's revisions improve the tone?

Apply

Read your letter aloud. Be sure your tone is appropriate and business-like. Also be sure to address the reader directly and politely.

Revise

Focus on Word Choice

The Rubric Says   Precise language clarifies the message and strengthens the purpose for writing.

Writing Strategy   Use exact words.

The rubric says that precise language will get my message across clearly. As I was reading my draft, I found a few vague words, such as *happy people*, that needed to be replaced. Using precise and specific language both clarifies my message and strengthens my purpose.

[DRAFT]

[used precise language]

those satisfied customers.

I'm happy to say that I count myself as one of ~~the happy people~~.

at your theater   the next blockbuster movie

You can be sure that I'll be back when ~~another good one~~ comes to

town.

Apply

Replace vague language with precise words and phrases to clarify your message and strengthen your purpose.

Edit

The Rubric Says Correct subject-verb agreement makes the writing clear and easy for the reader to follow.

Writing Strategy Make sure subjects and verbs agree.

Writer's Term

Subject-Verb Agreement

Every sentence has a **subject** and a **verb**. The subject is what the sentence is about. The verb tells what the subject does. The subject and verb must agree in number. If a subject is singular, the verb must be singular, too.

Now it's time to check my spelling, punctuation, and capitalization. The rubric also says to make sure that subjects and verbs agree. You can see some of my corrections below.

[DRAFT]

[corrected subject-verb agreement]

I am writing to thank you for the way you handled a really

tough situation on the night of August 5. As I'm sure you and your

→ recall

staff ~~recalls~~, that was the opening ~~nite~~ night of the summer's biggest

blockbuster, Voyage to Mars. The theater was filled with people,

but thanks to your quick thinking, we didn't have to wait long.

[corrected spelling error]

Reflect

Do Josh's edits make sense? Why is it important to edit one's writing?

Apply

Edit your draft for grammar and mechanics, making sure that all subjects and verbs agree.

For more practice with subject-verb agreement, use the exercises on the next two pages.

Subject-Verb Agreement

Know the Rule

Every **subject** and its **verb** must agree in number, but figuring out whether a subject is singular or plural can be tricky.

- A **collective noun,** such as *crowd, group,* or *team,* names more than one person or object acting together as a group. Collective nouns are almost always singular.
   Example: The **crowd forms** different lines.

- Most **indefinite pronouns,** including *everyone, nobody, nothing, something,* and *anything,* are singular, except for *many* and *several,* which are considered plural.
   Examples: Everyone has money for a ticket.
   Many have tickets already.

- A **compound subject** that includes the conjunction *and* is plural, but if the compound subject includes *or* or *nor,* the verb agrees with the last item in the subject.
   Examples: Sam and Jerry take people's tickets.
   Either popcorn or **nachos are** fine.

- Every verb must agree with its subject and not with the object of the preposition that comes before the verb.
   Example: My **favorite** of all movies **is playing** at this theater.

Practice the Rule

Rewrite the paragraph below on a separate sheet of paper, using the verb in parentheses that agrees in number with its underlined subject.

Whenever my <u>mother and I</u> (go/goes) to a grocery store, <u>we</u> always (look/looks) for your brand name. When <u>we</u> (see/sees) your products on the grocer's shelves, <u>it</u> (reassure/reassures) us that the store carries high-quality food. <u>Everyone</u> in my family (agree/agrees) that your <u>label</u> (mean/means) that we're getting excellent quality for a fair price. My <u>mother</u> (appreciate/appreciates) that your <u>company</u> (stand/stands) by your products. <u>She</u> (know/knows) she can return anything for a full refund. So far, my <u>family</u> (like/likes) everything you produce!

Subject-Verb Agreement, Special Cases

Know the Rule

The **subject** and its **verb** must agree. There are special rules for certain kinds of subjects. Titles of books, movies, stories, or songs are considered singular even if they end in -s.

> Example: **The Borrowers is** my little brother's favorite book.

- A **collective noun,** such as *collection*, *group*, *team*, or *family*, names more than one person or object acting together as one group. These nouns are almost always considered singular.

> Example: Katie's **team wins** every game.

- Most **indefinite pronouns**, including *everyone*, *nobody*, and *nothing* are considered singular.

> Example: **Everybody likes** pizza.

- A few indefinite pronouns, such as *all*, *many*, and *several*, are considered plural.

> Example: **Many like** spaghetti.

Practice the Rule

Rewrite the paragraph below on a separate sheet of paper, using the verb in parentheses that agrees with its subject.

I just got back from the movies, and let me say that *Outfield Angels* (is/are) a true inspiration. You see, my softball team (is/are) down on its luck this season. Most of the players (is/are) still optimistic, but some (is/are) really discouraged. Now that I've seen this movie, I know that if we work hard, things can only get better. I've even memorized my favorite line: "When a dream (live/lives) in your heart, nothing (gets/get) in your way." Tomorrow my sister's Girl Scout troop (is/are) going to see the movie. Next week my cousins' family (is/are) planning to see it. Most everyone in their family (play/plays) on a softball team. I hope the movie theater in their city (show/shows) the same preview I watched. It (feature/features) cast members of *Outfield Angels*. Anyone who's ever played baseball (need/needs) to hear what they have to say about hard work paying off!

Writing a Business Letter

Publish + Presentation

The Rubric Says Send the letter to the appropriate recipient.

Writing Strategy Use business letter format.

I've finally finished my business letter! The best way to publish a letter is to actually mail it. But before I do, I want to be sure I've included all the parts of a business letter: the heading, inside address, greeting, body, closing, and signature. I'll then read it one last time to make sure it includes all the items on my checklist.

My Final Checklist

Did I—

- ✔ proofread for spelling, grammar, and mechanics?
- ✔ make sure all the verbs agree with their subjects?
- ✔ check carefully for special cases in subject-verb agreement?
- ✔ include all the parts of a business letter?
- ✔ sign my full name beneath the closing?

Apply

Make a checklist to check your business letter. Then make a final copy of the letter to send.

8301 Bell Avenue
Ivor, VA 23866
August 30, 2012

Mrs. Paula Locascio, Manager
Main Street Theater
2 Main Street
Ivor, VA 23866

Dear Mrs. Locascio:

I am writing to thank you for the way you handled a really tough situation on the night of August 5. As I'm sure you and your staff recall, that was opening night of the summer's biggest blockbuster, *Voyage to Mars*. The theater was filled with people, but thanks to your quick thinking, we didn't have to wait long.

As we stood in long lines, the high heat and humidity made us very uncomfortable. However, you acted quickly to prevent what could have been an unbearable situation. Everyone standing—and wilting—outside thought your idea of handing out free ice water was fantastic! You made the wait as comfortable as possible, and the crowd really appreciated it.

Another problem you thoughtfully took care of was holding up the film's start time until all of the people in the theater were seated. Although you did your best to make the lines move quickly, not everyone was seated by 7:15. I was in this group, and I witnessed firsthand the anxiety that began to spread as people realized they might miss part of the movie. But by skipping the coming attractions and starting the film at 7:30, you allowed everyone to see the beginning.

The last thing you did was give free tickets to the people who were still outside when the last show of the night sold out. I know that theater managers are not obligated to satisfy everyone who shows up on a particular night. Considering this fact, I think your response was especially remarkable. By inviting those people back the next day and assuring them that they'd be the first ones allowed into the theater, you kept many customers.

I'm happy to say that I count myself as one of those satisfied customers. You can be sure that I'll be back at your theater when the next blockbuster movie comes to town. Please keep up the excellent work. I'm sure it will pay off in the long run!

Sincerely,

Josh Greene

Josh Greene

JOSH GREENE
8301 BELL AVE
IVOR VA 23866

MRS PAULA LOCASCIO
MAIN STREET THEATER
2 MAIN ST
IVOR VA 23866

Reflect

What do you think? Did Josh use all
the traits of a good business letter?
Check his letter against the rubric.
And don't forget to use the rubric to
check your own work, too!

What's a Scientific Observation?

It's writing that describes science experiments and summarizes what the observer has learned. When I write this kind of report, I like to make things as simple and clear as possible so that readers can follow my exact process.

What's in a Scientific Observation?

Voice
This is the style I use to present things to the reader. I'll narrate using the first-person *I*, but I'll remain objective and factual as I present my observation.

Organization
This is how I arrange my writing. I'll need to use clear labels to help readers follow my process and understand any conclusions.

Cause and Effect
A scientific observation describes test materials, experiments, and outcomes. After I explain the experiments, I'll note the causes and effects that were involved.

Conclusions
People perform experiments to test for certain results. My observation should end with the conclusions drawn from the experiments.

Why write a Scientific Observation?

There are many reasons to write a scientific observation. I write them all the time in science class, but here are some other purposes for this kind of writing.

To Describe

If I claim that one sneaker brand is better than another, I'll need evidence to explain why. If I run tests and write up what I observe, I can use this as proof of my claim.

To Inform

If I want to tell people about an experiment—like how my new backpack holds up under different kinds of weather—I can write an observation to inform readers of the results.

To Document

Science experiments involve a lot of elements: materials, procedures, results, tests, etc. I can write a scientific observation to organize and keep track of my information.

Linking Descriptive Writing Traits to a Scientific Observation

In this chapter, you will write to describe an experiment. This type of descriptive writing is called a scientific observation. Josh will guide you through the stages of the writing process: Prewrite, Draft, Revise, Edit, and Publish. In each stage, Josh will show you important writing strategies that are linked to the Descriptive Writing Traits below.

Descriptive Writing Traits

Ideas
- a focused, complete topic
- relevant sensory details that support, describe, and develop the topic

Organization
- an introduction that previews a topic, a body that develops the topic, and a conclusion that follows and supports the description
- well-organized details that follow the order of the description, whether by time, location, or other order
- transitions that clarify relationships between ideas

Voice
- a voice and tone that are appropriate for the purpose and audience

Word Choice
- precise, descriptive language that creates a clear picture for the reader

Sentence Fluency
- sentences that vary in length and structure to make the writing flow

Conventions
- no or few errors in grammar, usage, mechanics, and spelling

Before you write, read Hannah Prince's scientific observation on the next three pages. Then use the scientific observation rubric on pages 414–415 to decide how well she did.

Observing Solar Collectors

by Hannah Prince

Did you know that solar energy doesn't cost a penny? Well, when I heard that, I decided to conduct a series of experiments to find out how to improve the collection of solar energy. I predicted that the more insulation a collector was given the more heat it would collect.

Voice

MATERIALS

shoebox, larger box, masking tape, thermometer, timer, black construction paper, clear plastic wrap, packing peanuts

PROCEDURES

Organization

Experiment 1

First, I taped a thermometer inside one of the long sides of a shoebox. (See Diagram 1.) Then, I placed the uncovered shoebox outside and turned it so that the bottom of the box was directly in the sun and the thermometer bulb was in the shade. I left the box in that position for 15 minutes.

I recorded the temperature inside the box at the start of the experiment and again 15 minutes later. Here are my observations: The temperature inside the box at the start of the experiment was 72°F (22°C). The temperature inside the box after 15 minutes was 98°F (36.67°C).

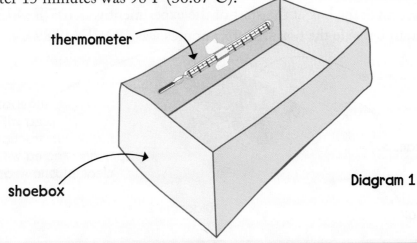

thermometer

shoebox

Diagram 1

Experiment 2

I did the experiment again, only this time I covered the inside of the shoebox with black construction paper. Then, I left the box for 15 minutes in the same position as before. (I did have to turn the box slightly to adjust for the movement of the sun.)

I again recorded the temperatures before and after the experiment. Here is what I observed: The temperature inside the box at the start of the experiment was 98°F (36.67°C). The temperature inside the box after 15 minutes was 98.5°F (36.94°C).

Experiment 3 ←——Organization

I did the experiment again. For this third time, however, I covered the top of the shoebox with clear plastic wrap. Then, I sealed the plastic wrap with masking tape so that no air could enter or leave the box. Next, I left the box for 15 minutes in the same position as before. (Again, I turned the box slightly to adjust for the movement of the sun.)

Once again, I recorded the temperatures and made these observations: The temperature inside the box at the start of the experiment was 98.5°F (36.94°C). The temperature inside the box after 15 minutes was 105°F (40.56°C).

Experiment 4

I did the experiment one last time. For this fourth time, I placed the shoebox inside another, larger box and then placed a layer of packing peanuts between the shoebox and the larger box. (See Diagram 2.) Next, I left the box for 15 minutes in the same position as before, again turning the box slightly to adjust for the movement of the sun.

Again, I recorded the temperatures and made these observations: The temperature inside the box at the start of the experiment was 105°F (40.56°C). The temperature inside the box after 15 minutes was 120+°F (48.89°C).

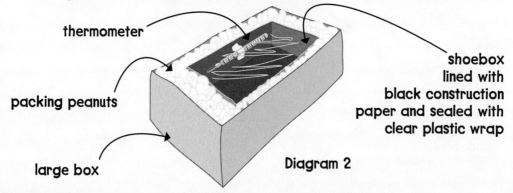

thermometer

packing peanuts

large box

shoebox lined with black construction paper and sealed with clear plastic wrap

Diagram 2

OBSERVATIONS

Each change that I made to my solar collector caused the inside Cause and effect of the shoebox to get hotter, resulting in a rise in temperature on the thermometer. When I placed the plain, uncovered shoebox in the sun, the Fahrenheit temperature increased 26°. When I covered the inside of the shoebox with black construction paper, the temperature increased another 0.5°. When I sealed the top of the box with plastic wrap, the temperature increased another 6.5°. When I placed the shoebox inside another box and put packing peanuts between them, the temperature increased another 15° before the thermometer topped out. Had my little thermometer gone beyond 120°F, I wonder how hot it would have gotten inside the shoebox! When I put my hand inside, the temperature change was pretty amazing. It felt almost twice as hot inside the shoebox as it felt outside that day.

CONCLUSIONS

Conclusions

I learned several things from my experiments: For one thing, I now understand the basics of collecting solar energy. For another, I learned that solar energy really is a clean, efficient, and cost-effective way to heat a space. I also learned that the best way to gather the most heat with a solar collector is to place it inside a larger, well-insulated space. (I drew this conclusion because the insulation in Experiment 4 sent the temperature in the shoebox sky-high.) I was able to prove that my prediction was correct by doing these experiments. Since solar energy can be so powerful, I guess it's no wonder that people in regions where there is a lot of winter sun have been harnessing the sun's energy for centuries.

Scientific Observation

Rubric

Use this 6-point rubric to plan and score a scientific observation.

	6	5	4
Ideas	The information is complete and accurate. The conclusion follows from and supports the information in the procedure and observations.	Most of the information is thorough and accurate. The conclusion is based on observations.	Some information is thorough. The conclusion is based on some observations.
Organization	Headings clearly and effectively organize the information. Transition words show cause-and-effect relationships.	Headings clearly and effectively organize the information. Most transition words show cause-and-effect relationships.	Some headings organize the information. Few transition words show cause-and-effect relationships.
Voice	The writer establishes and maintains a formal voice and an objective tone that are ideal for the purpose and audience.	The writer establishes a formal voice and objective tone throughout most of the writing.	The writer establishes a formal voice in the beginning. The writer's tone may be somewhat inconsistent.
Word Choice	The observation findings contain precise language and domain-specific vocabulary that explains the topic.	Most language is precise. Domain-specific vocabulary explains the topic.	Some language is not precise. Some domain-specific vocabulary explains the topic.
Sentence Fluency	The sentence structures enhance meaning. Repetition is used effectively.	The sentence structures support the meaning. Repeated words and phrases are used effectively.	Repetition is used, but it is not always effective. Sentences sound the same in places.
Conventions	Colons and hyphens and complete subjects and predicates are used correctly to make the writing clear for the reader.	Errors in the use of colons and hyphens and complete subjects and predicates rarely interfere with the reader's ability to understand the writing.	Errors in using colons and hyphens and complete subjects and predicates sometimes confuse the reader.

+ Presentation Useful visuals clarify the text at point of use.

3	2	1	
Information is limited and sometimes based on common knowledge rather than observations. The conclusion is unclear.	Information is sketchy or incomplete. The conclusion is unrelated to the observations.	The information is weak or inaccurate. A conclusion is not provided.	**Ideas**
Headings are needed to organize the information. Few transition words show cause-and-effect relationships.	Headings are needed to organize the information. Most transition words are confusing or not helpful.	Headings are not used to organize information. Transitions, if used, do not show cause-and-effect relationships.	**Organization**
The writer's voice and tone are inconsistent with the writer's purpose or audience.	The writer establishes an informal voice or inappropriate tone. The writer's purpose is not clear.	The writer's voice is very weak or absent. Tone is not established.	**Voice**
The language is too general in some places. Some domain-specific vocabulary is used.	Most of the language is vague or repetitious. Little domain-specific vocabulary is used.	Little or no precise language is used. Domain-specific language may be incorrectly used.	**Word Choice**
Too many sentences share the same structure. Some of the writing does not flow smoothly.	Too many sentences share the same structure or length. The writing is monotonous or choppy.	Many sentences are incomplete or incorrect. The writing is very hard to read.	**Sentence Fluency**
Several serious errors in using colons and hyphens and complete subjects and predicates confuse the reader.	Errors with colons and hyphens and complete subjects and predicates require rereading to make sense of the writing.	Many errors with colons and hyphens and complete subjects and predicates make reading difficult.	**Conventions**

See Appendix B for 4-, 5-, and 6-point descriptive rubrics.

Scientific Observation

Using the Rubric to Study the Model

Did you notice that the model on pages 411–413 points out some key elements of a scientific observation? As she wrote "Observing Solar Collectors," Hannah Prince used these elements to help her describe her observations of an experiment. She also used the 6-point rubric on pages 414–415 to plan, draft, revise, and edit the writing. A rubric is a great tool to evaluate writing during the writing process.

Now let's use the same rubric to score the model. To do this, we'll focus on each trait separately, starting with Ideas. We'll use the top descriptor for each trait (column 6), along with examples from the model, to help us understand how the traits work together. How would you score Hannah on each trait?

- **The information is complete and accurate.**
- **The conclusion follows from and supports the information in the procedure and observations.**

Hannah clearly and accurately describes her experiments and their results. All of her information is straightforward and easy to understand. Her conclusion is solidly based upon the results of her experiments.

[from the writing model]

CONCLUSIONS

I learned several things from my experiments: For one thing, I now understand the basics of collecting solar energy. For another, I learned that solar energy really is a clean, efficient, and cost-effective way to heat a space.

Organization

- Headings clearly and effectively organize the information.
- Transition words show cause-and-effect relationships.

Hannah uses headings to clearly organize her information. She also uses transition words such as *Each change, resulting*, and *When I*. These transition words helped me better understand the cause-and-effect relationships in her experiments.

[from the writing model]

OBSERVATIONS

Each change that I made to my solar collector caused the inside of the shoebox to get hotter, resulting in a rise in temperature on the thermometer. When I placed the plain, uncovered shoebox in the sun, the Fahrenheit temperature increased 26°.

Voice

- The writer establishes and maintains a formal voice and an objective tone that are ideal for the purpose and audience.

Hannah writes with a voice that fits her purpose and audience. She opens her scientific observation with a question that drew me in right away. She goes on to explain her experiments in a serious tone.

[from the writing model]

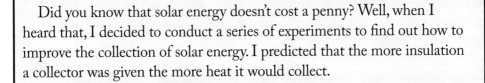

Did you know that solar energy doesn't cost a penny? Well, when I heard that, I decided to conduct a series of experiments to find out how to improve the collection of solar energy. I predicted that the more insulation a collector was given the more heat it would collect.

Word Choice

- **The observation findings contain precise language and domain-specific vocabulary that explains the topic.**

I like how Hannah uses scientific language throughout her report. Using precise language is important in a scientific observation! I also appreciate the temperature conversions she provides. We're learning Celsius in our class now, so I appreciated seeing them here. I checked them, and they're all accurate, too.

[from the writing model]

I again recorded the temperatures before and after the experiment. Here is what I observed: The temperature inside the box at the start of the experiment was 98°F (36.67°C). The temperature inside the box after 15 minutes was 98.5°F (36.94°C).

Sentence Fluency

- **The sentence structures enhance meaning.**
- **Repetition is used effectively.**

In an observation report, it's important to use concise sentences. Each sentence must be direct and clear. I also notice that Hannah repeats words like *again* and *temperature* to help me follow her observations. She uses the same sentence structures to describe the results of the experiments, so all of her ideas are easy to follow.

[from the writing model]

Once again, I recorded the temperatures and made these observations: The temperature inside the box at the start of the experiment was 98.5°F (36.94°C). The temperature inside the box after 15 minutes was 105°F (40.56°C).

Conventions

- Colons and hyphens and complete subjects and predicates are used correctly to make the writing clear for the reader.

In the passage below, Hannah uses a colon to separate the first two sentences, since the second one explains the first. She also uses a hyphen to connect *cost* and *effective*, which together, act as an adjective. Hannah uses complete subjects and predicates correctly.

[from the writing model]

I learned several things from my experiments: For one thing, I now understand the basics of collecting solar energy. For another, I learned that solar energy really is a clean, efficient, and cost-effective way to heat a space.

✛Presentation Useful visuals clarify the text at point of use.

My Turn!

I'm going to write a scientific observation that describes something I'm curious about. I'll follow the 6-point rubric and use good writing strategies. Read on to see how I do it!

Prewrite

Focus on **Ideas**

The Rubric Says The information is complete and accurate.

Writing Strategy Observe and take careful notes.

Recently, my teacher asked us to record and write a scientific observation. I'm a total baseball fanatic, so I decided to do some baseball experiments. I just read an article on how baseballs act under different conditions, so I decided to do a few of the experiments. I got my brother to help so I could focus on carefully observing and making accurate notes. I wrote down the questions I wanted to answer, and then continued from there.

My Notes

- **Question:** At what temperature (frozen, heated, or room temperature) will the rebound rate of a baseball be highest?
- **Prediction:** The warm baseball's rebound rate will be highest.
- **What I did:** Brian stood on a chair, held a tape measure 72 inches off the ground, and dropped a baseball straight down. I observed and recorded how high the ball bounced. I then divided that amount by 72 inches to get the rebound rate. We repeated the experiment three times with a cold baseball, a warm baseball, and a baseball at room temperature.
- **The Results:** The cold baseball had a rebound rate of 0.305. The warm baseball had a rebound rate of 0.236. The baseball at room temperature had a rebound rate of 0.292.
- **Conclusion:** My prediction was wrong. The cold baseball had the highest rebound rate, not the warm one.

Apply

Choose an experiment that interests you. Then run the experiment and describe what you see.

Prewrite

The Rubric Says   Transition words show cause-and-effect relationships.

Writing Strategy   Make Cause-and-Effect Links to organize the notes.

Writer's Term

Cause-and-Effect Links

When you write, use transition words such as **because, therefore,** and **as a result** to highlight the information in the **Cause-and-Effect Links** organizer.

There are two kinds of organization in a scientific observation. Sequence is important because I'll need to follow the proper order of steps in an experiment so that my results will be accurate. Cause and effect are important because each cause can result in a different outcome. To track these causes and effects, I'll use Cause-and-Effect Links.

Cause-and-Effect Links

 Cause: I refrigerated a baseball for eight hours. **Effect:** It rebounded 22 inches for a rebound rate of 0.305.

Cause: I wrapped a baseball in a heating pad for eight hours. **Effect:** It rebounded 17 inches for a rebound rate of 0.236.

 Cause: I left a baseball on the counter overnight. **Effect:** It rebounded 21 inches for a rebound rate of 0.292.

Reflect

How do you think Josh's Cause-and-Effect Links will help him?

Apply

Use Cause-and-Effect Links to organize your notes. Then use transition words in your draft to show cause-and-effect relationships.

Writing a Scientific Observation

Draft

The Rubric Says   Headings clearly and effectively organize the information.

Writing Strategy   Organize the information under the appropriate headings.

According to the rubric, I need to use appropriate headings to organize my information. I'll use the same four headings that Hannah used: *MATERIALS, PROCEDURES, OBSERVATIONS,* and *CONCLUSIONS.* I think these terms are pretty basic, so I don't expect my readers to have any trouble understanding my report. Here's what I'll put in each section.

- *MATERIALS:* I'll list all the equipment that I'm going to need for my experiments.
- *PROCEDURES:* I'll describe how I set up my experiments, and I'll include the subheadings *Experiment 1, Experiment 2,* and *Experiment 3.*
- *OBSERVATIONS:* I'll describe the causes and effects of the experiments.
- *CONCLUSIONS:* I'll explain what I learned from the experiments.

Now I'm ready to start writing my scientific observation. I'll do my best with spelling and grammar, but right now I just want to focus on getting everything down on paper. Later, I'll reread the whole thing and make corrections.

Observing the Rebound Ratings of a Baseball
by Josh

[headings]

I read in a book that in the 1950s, the Chicago White Sox used to keep their baseballs in a freezer before home games! That got me wondering: Does the temperature of a baseball noticeably affect its bounce? I decided to use my baseball to find out. (Note: The rebound rating is the ratio used to describe how well a ball bounces. To figure the rebound rating, take the length of the rebound and divide it by the length of the drop.) The book said that a baseball goes farther if the ball is warm. I predict that a ball that has been wrapped in a heating pad will bounce higher than the other balls tested.

MATERIALS

new baseball, heating pad, use of refrigerator, tape measure

PROCEDURES

Experiment 1

To begin the experiment, I unwrapped a new baseball and placed it in the refrigerator. I took the ball out of the refrigerator and had my brother Brian help me test the ball's rebound rating. Brian stood on a chair in our kitchen and held a tape measure 72 inches (6 feet) off the ground. (See Diagram 1.) He dropped the baseball.

When it bounced back up, I looked at the tape measure and saw that it had rebounded 22 inches. Rebound rating: 22 in. ÷ 72 in. = 0.305

— [headings]

[DRAFT]

Experiment 2

    I let the ball return to room temperature. I wrapped a heating pad around it and set the temperature on "low." Eight hours later, I took the ball out of the heating pad and had Brian help me test the ball's rebound rating. Brian had to stand on the same chair in the same spot in our kitchen. Again, he held a tape measure 72 inches (6 feet) off the ground. Then he dropped the baseball onto the hardwood floor. Again, I watched the ball carefully.

    When it bounced back up, I looked at the tape measure and saw that it had rebounded 17 inches. Rebound rating: 17 in. ÷ 72 in. = 0.236

Experiment 3

    I let the ball return to room temperature by letting it sit untouched on a counter. After school the next day, I had Brian help me test the ball's rebound rating. Brian stood on the same chair in the same spot in our kitchen. Again, he held a tape measure 72 inches (6 feet) off the ground. Then he dropped the baseball onto the hardwood floor. Again, I watched the ball carefully.

    When it bounced back up, I looked at the tape measure and saw that it had rebounded 21 inches. Rebound rating: 21 in. ÷ 72 in. = 0.292

[headings]

OBSERVATIONS

The baseball rebounded very differently under cold and hot conditions. Brian and I had a lot of fun changing the temperature of the baseball. A cold baseball feels rock hard, and a warmer baseball is a bit softer to the touch. When refrigerated, it rebounded to 22 inches (about a third of the height from which it was dropped). Warmed up it only rebounded to 17 inches (about a fourth of the height from which it was dropped). That was a difference of 5 inches. At room temperature, its rebound rating was closer to the rating of the cold ball, but it wasn't quite as high.

CONCLUSIONS

I learned that the temperature of a baseball really does affect its variations in rebound rating, a colder ball has a grater rebound. In a baseball game, a colder baseball would go farther than a warm one when hit off a bat. In a cool weather city would hit the ball farther than a team that plays in a warm weather city. I had predicted that the warmer ball would bounce higher. This is weird. How did I get these results? Brian and I had a lot of fun doing the experiments. I'll repeat my experiments next week to see if I get the same results.

Reflect

How do the headings help you as you read Josh's draft?

Apply

Make sure to use headings to organize your observations.

Revise

Focus on **Voice**

The Rubric Says	The writer establishes and maintains a formal voice and an objective tone that are ideal for the purpose and audience.
Writing Strategy	Use formal language but let personality and personal thoughts come through.

The rubric reminds me to consider my audience and purpose. My first sentence reveals some personal information to connect with the reader. I want my personality to shine through, but I also need to include scientific language to maintain a serious tone. After all, this is a scientific observation, so I need to sound believable. I will make revisions to keep my voice both engaging and formal.

[DRAFT]

I read in a book that in the 1950s, the Chicago White Sox used

to keep their baseballs in a freezer before home games! That got me

wondering: Does the temperature of a baseball noticeably affect its

rebound rating ~~bounce~~? I decided to ~~use my baseball~~ conduct some experiments to find out.

[improved voice]

Apply

Use a voice that is both engaging and formal to hold the interest of your reader.

The Rubric Says	The observation findings contain precise language and domain-specific vocabulary that explains the topic.
Writing Strategy	Use exact words to describe the observation. Define the words as necessary.

The rubric says to use precise language, and now that I am reading over my draft, I see a few places that need revision. Words like *ratio* and *rebound rating* are scientific and clear. I will make sure I use exact words to describe my observation to my audience. I want my readers to understand my findings.

[DRAFT]

I learned that the temperature of a baseball really does ~~affect its~~ **cause**
variations in rebound rating, a colder ball ~~has~~ **results in** a grater rebound. In a
baseball game, a colder baseball would go farther than a warm one
when hit off a bat.

[used exact words]

 **Reflect**

How do Josh's changes improve your understanding of his findings?

 Apply

Use precise language to describe your experiments and findings. Be sure to define any unfamiliar terms for the reader.

Revise

Focus on Sentence Fluency

The Rubric Says   The sentence structures enhance meaning. Repetition is used effectively.

Writing Strategy   Repeat sentence beginnings for better flow and to help connect related ideas.

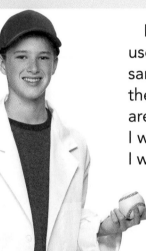

Now I need to revise my writing. The rubric says to use sentence structure to enhance meaning. If I use the same structure in two sentences, the reader will know that these sentences are related. In my *OBSERVATIONS* there are several pieces of information that are related. But as I was rereading this section, even I was a bit confused. I will repeat the beginnings of my sentences to link my ideas, but I will be careful to avoid unnecessary repetition. Too much repetition can be confusing or cause readers to lose their place as they read.

[DRAFT]

[repeated sentence beginnings to link ideas]

When refrigerated. it rebounded to 22 inches (about a third of the

When heated, however,

height from which it was dropped). ~~Warmed up~~ it only rebounded to 17

inches (about a fourth of the height from which it was dropped). That

When returned to

was a difference of 5 inches. ~~At~~ room temperature, its rebound rating

was closer to the rating of the cold ball, but it wasn't quite as high.

Apply

Use repetition to link your ideas.

Edit

The Rubric Says   Colons and hyphens and complete subjects and predicates are used correctly to make the writing clear for the reader.

Writing Strategy   Make sure colons and hyphens are used correctly and that all sentences have a complete subject and predicate.

✏️ Writer's Term

Colons and Hyphens

A **colon (:)** is used to separate two independent clauses when the second one explains the first. It can also be used to introduce a list at the end of a sentence. A **hyphen (-)** is used to separate words at the end of a line or to link two words that, when used together, act as an adjective.

The last thing to do is to check my observation for spelling, punctuation, and capitalization. I also need to be sure I use only complete sentences. I'll proofread carefully and correct any errors I find.

[DRAFT]

[correctly used a colon]

I learned that the temperature of a baseball really does ~~affect its~~ cause

variations in rebound rating: a colder ball ~~has a grater~~ results in greater rebound. As a result,

baseball game, a colder baseball would go farther than a warm one

So that must mean that a team that plays - when hit off a bat. In a cool weather city would hit the ball farther

than a team that plays in a warm weather city. I had predicted that

[used complete sentences] [correctly used hyphens]

Reflect

How do Josh's edits make his writing clearer?

Apply   **Conventions**

For more practice with colons, hyphens, and complete subjects and predicates, use the exercises on the next two pages.

Colons, Hyphens, and Ellipses

Know the Rule

A **colon** is used to separate two independent clauses when the second one explains the first.

> **Example:** I conducted an awesome experiment: I observed various items under a black light.

A **colon** can also be used to introduce a list at the end of a sentence.

> **Example:** Here is what I used: a white shirt, nail polish, and fluorescent paint.

A **hyphen** is used to separate words at the end of a line or to link two words that, when used together, form a compound adjective.

> **Examples: black-light** experiment; **greenish-yellow** tint

An **ellipsis** (. . .) is used to show where text from another source has been left out. If an ellipsis falls at the end of the sentence, place the ellipsis after the final period.

> **Example:** One of the chapters in a lengthy report that was first published in Boston in 1893, titled "Colorful First Colonies," lists plant-based pigments that were used to paint America's first homes in Virginia, Massachusetts, and New Hampshire.
> **Example:** One of the chapters in a lengthy report . . . "Colorful First Colonies," lists plant-based pigments that were used to paint America's first homes. . . .

Practice the Rule

Copy sentences 1–4 on a separate sheet of paper. Insert colons and hyphens where needed. Rewrite sentences 5–6, using ellipses to replace the unimportant text in italics.

1. I will conduct an experiment I will observe the rebound ratings of three balls.

2. I predict that two balls will have similar rebound ratings the tennis ball and the basketball.

3. A golf ball is a lightning fast ball.

4. British made golf balls are slightly smaller than American ones, so they probably have an even higher rebound rating.

5. It compares the effects of temperate weather conditions, *including sun, rain, sleet, snow,* on the materials used to make each ball.

6. The observer collected data for one year, *365 days,* using time-lapse photography, *thereby making a photographic record,* to record the changes that occurred.

Complete Subjects and Predicates

Know the Rule

The **complete subject** in a sentence is made up of a noun or pronoun and words that tell about it. The **complete predicate** in a sentence is made up of a verb and words that tell what the subject is, has, or does.

        [**complete subject**]   [**complete predicate**]

Example: Jake and I finished writing our final drafts late last night.

Practice the Rule

Copy the sentences below on a separate sheet of paper. Underline the complete subject. Circle the complete predicate. Then choose one sentence and replace the complete subject with a different complete subject of your choice. Choose a different sentence and replace the complete predicate with a different complete predicate of your choice.

1. I use a telescope to record the positions of the planets.
2. Some neighboring planets are visible without a telescope.
3. You can see Venus from the Northern Hemisphere on most clear nights.
4. I will study planetary motion for my next scientific observation.
5. My class and I visited the planetarium in Chicago last year.
6. A planetarium is a device that simulates the solar system.
7. Then my mom surprised me with a one-in-a-billion gift: a star named for me!
8. Stargazing is probably the world's oldest scientific observation.
9. All you need to get started is a curious mind and a pair of binoculars.
10. A guidebook of the night sky will be helpful, too.

Publish   + Presentation

Publishing Strategy   Include the observation in my science classroom.

Presentation Strategy   Add a diagram to help explain the information.

My scientific observation is done! Now I want to publish it. A lot of kids in my school like baseball, so I think I will hang my final copy on the school's science bulletin board. I even added a diagram to give a clear and accurate view of part of my experiment. A good diagram works with the written text to fully explain a scientific observation. I'll read through my draft again just to make sure it includes all of the items on my checklist.

My Final Checklist

Did I—

✔ use colons, hyphens, and ellipses correctly?

✔ use complete subjects and predicates to make complete, well-written sentences?

✔ include a diagram to illustrate part of my experiment?

✔ make sure my diagram works within the written text to explain my experiment clearly?

✔ proofread my writing for spelling and grammar mistakes?

Apply

Make a checklist to check your scientific observation. Then make a final copy to publish.

Observing the Rebound Ratings of a Baseball

by Josh

I read in a book that in the 1950s, the Chicago White Sox used to keep their baseballs in a freezer before home games! That got me wondering: Does the temperature of a baseball noticeably affect its rebound rating? I decided to conduct some experiments to find out. (Note: The rebound rating is the ratio used to describe how well a ball bounces. To figure the rebound rating, take the length of the rebound and divide it by the length of the drop.) The book said that a baseball goes farther if the ball is warm. I predict that a ball that has been wrapped in a heating pad will bounce higher than the other balls tested.

MATERIALS

new baseball, heating pad, use of refrigerator, tape measure

PROCEDURES

Experiment 1

To begin my experiment, I unwrapped a new baseball and placed it in the refrigerator. After eight hours, I took the ball out of the refrigerator and had my brother Brian help me test the ball's rebound rating. Brian stood on a chair in our kitchen and held a tape measure 72 inches (6 feet) off the ground. (See Diagram 1.) Then he dropped the baseball.

When it bounced back up, I looked at the tape measure and saw that it had rebounded 22 inches. Rebound rating: 22 in. $\div$ 72 in. $= 0.305$

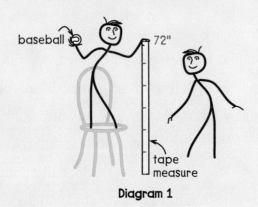

baseball

72"

tape
measure

Diagram 1

Experiment 2

I let the ball return to room temperature. The next day, I wrapped a
heating pad around it and set the temperature on "low." Eight hours later,
I took the ball out of the heating pad and had Brian help me test the ball's
rebound rating. Brian had to stand on the same chair in the same spot
in our kitchen. Again, he held a tape measure 72 inches (6 feet) off the
ground. Then he dropped the baseball onto the hardwood floor. Again,
I watched the ball carefully.

When it bounced back up, I looked at the tape measure and saw that
it had rebounded 17 inches. Rebound rating: 17 in. $\div$ 72 in. = 0.236

Experiment 3

I let the ball return to room temperature by letting it sit untouched on
a counter. After school the next day, I had Brian help me test the ball's
rebound rating. Brian stood on the same chair in the same spot in our
kitchen. Again, he held a tape measure 72 inches (6 feet) off the ground.
Then he dropped the baseball onto the hardwood floor. Again, I watched
the ball carefully.

When it bounced back up, I looked at the tape measure and saw that it had rebounded 21 inches. Rebound rating: 21 in. ÷ 72 in. = 0.292

OBSERVATIONS

The baseball rebounded very differently under cold and hot conditions. When refrigerated, it rebounded to 22 inches (about a third of the height from which it was dropped). When heated, however, it only rebounded to 17 inches (about a fourth of the height from which it was dropped). That was a difference of 5 inches. When returned to room temperature, its rebound rating was closer to the rating of the cold ball, but it wasn't quite as high.

CONCLUSIONS

I learned that the temperature of a baseball really does cause variations in rebound rating: A colder ball results in a greater rebound. As a result, in a baseball game, a colder baseball would go farther than a warm one when hit off a bat. So that must mean that a team that plays in a cool-weather city would hit the ball farther than a team that plays in a warm-weather city. I had predicted that the warmer ball would bounce higher. I'll repeat my experiments next week to see if I get the same results.

Reflect

What do you think? Did Josh use all the traits of a good scientific observation in his writing? Check it against the rubric. Don't forget to use the rubric to check your own report, too.

What's a Descriptive Vignette?

It's a short, descriptive sketch. The writer uses sensory details to describe a specific place, thing, or event. I think I'm going to like this kind of writing because I can challenge myself to bring description to life on the page!

What's in a Descriptive Vignette?

Organization
This is the structure of my description. I like to describe events from beginning to end, but sometimes I present things in order of importance or according to sensory details.

Narrator
The narrator is the person sharing the description. I do best when I describe something memorable, so I'll narrate an event that really stands out in my mind.

Sensory Details
Sensory details grab the reader's attention and bring the subject to life. Instead of *cold,* I'll write *nippy,* and I'll replace *nice scent* with *spicy aroma.* If I use details that appeal to all five senses, I'll create sharp, vivid images. Get the picture?

Figurative Language
This includes similes, metaphors, and personification. Similes and metaphors compare things, and personification brings an inanimate object to life. By including figurative language, I can help the reader see things in a new way.

Why write a Descriptive Vignette?

People write vignettes for many reasons. I'll list some here to help me decide on my purpose for writing one.

To Entertain

I like to read descriptions of awesome places and amazing events. Entertaining the reader is one reason to write a descriptive vignette.

To Reflect

Personal reflection is a good reason to describe a subject that has a strong effect on me. When I describe something, I realize what it really means to me.

To Inform

A thing can make such an impression on me that I can't wait to tell people about it. If I include a lot of details, I can really bring an event to life for my audience.

To Share

Have you ever felt the need to tell someone, "You've *got* to see this"? You might want to write so that you can share your description of a cool new gadget, a ball field, or your own science project.

Linking Descriptive Writing Traits
to a Descriptive Vignette

In this chapter, you will briefly describe a specific place, thing, or event. This type of descriptive writing is called a descriptive vignette. Josh will guide you through the stages of the writing process: Prewrite, Draft, Revise, Edit, and Publish. In each stage, Josh will show you important writing strategies that are linked to the Descriptive Writing Traits below.

Descriptive Writing Traits

- a focused, complete topic
- relevant sensory details that support, describe, and develop the topic

- an introduction that previews a topic, a body that develops the topic, and a conclusion that follows and supports the description
- well-organized details that follow the order of the description, whether by time, location, or other order
- transitions that clarify relationships between ideas

- a voice and tone that are appropriate for the purpose and audience

- precise, descriptive language that creates a clear picture for the reader

- sentences that vary in length and structure to make the writing flow

- no or few errors in grammar, usage, mechanics, and spelling

Before you write, read Gina Bedow's descriptive vignette on the next page. Then use the descriptive vignette rubric on pages 440–441 to decide how well she did.

The Concert

by Gina Bedow

narrator

Last night I went to the most deafening concert I've ever attended. My ears are still ringing from the music, and my throat is still sore from screaming above the crowd. I guess you could say that I experienced the concert with all five of my senses!

personification

The concert was outdoors, and there were food tents set up everywhere. The smoke from the barbecue ribs rose above the crowd. It curled a finger under Jackson's nose, beckoning him to eat. The pizza tent was next door, and Sharon couldn't resist the smell of fresh mozzarella. I chose corn on the cob. As I ate, butter dripped down my hand with each sweet, crunchy bite, and salt stung my lips like a thousand tiny bees.

simile

sensory details

personification

Hunger satisfied, we found a place to sit about halfway up a hill. The grass felt cool and stiff as we spread out our blanket. Stretching drowsily, the sun soon sank behind the hill. I felt a little chilly, so I untied my sweater from around my waist and slipped it over my head. Its gentle caress felt soft and warm, and I secretly thanked my mom for making me take it along.

organization

After a while, the concert began. When the band hit the stage, the crowd sprang to its feet. I saw two girls, arms locked, in a jerky kind of square dance. To their right, a boy stood playing an imaginary drum set. To his right, a group of people clapped in time with the music.

And then it started raining—hard. Within minutes, we were all drenched, and so was the ground. It was now a toboggan run of mud. I couldn't stand it anymore. I took off my shoes and socks, rolled up my jeans, and went flailing down the hill. There's nothing quite like the feel of cold, wet mud against the skin. By the time I finished, I looked like someone had turned me upside down and dipped me in a vat of chocolate.

metaphor

simile

The band tried to get everyone's attention by playing louder than the roar of the crowd. The bass was so loud that it rattled my bones. I plugged my ears with cotton, and it's a good thing I did! A few hours later, my ears were still ringing, and I practically had to shout to hear myself.

When I got home, my parents asked how the night had gone. I just laughed and shouted, "I'll tell you tomorrow, when I get my hearing back!"

Descriptive Vignette

Rubric

Use this 6-point rubric to plan and score a descriptive vignette.

	6	5	4
Ideas	Vivid sensory details support and develop the topic, bringing it to life.	The topic is well supported by sensory details that are interesting or unusual.	Some of the sensory details are interesting or unusual.
Organization	The organization guides the reader through the vignette. The introduction and ending grab the reader's attention.	The writing is well organized. The introduction and ending are satisfying.	Details are somewhat organized. The introduction and ending make sense.
Voice	The writer's voice and tone connect with the audience through first-person point of view, fresh insights, and personal feelings.	The writer connects with the audience through first-person point of view and personal feelings.	The writer connects with the audience through first-person point of view.
Word Choice	The action is captured in fresh, precise language that avoids vague or overused words.	Most of the action is captured in fresh, precise language that avoids vague or overused words.	Some of the action is captured in fresh, precise language. Some language may be cliché.
Sentence Fluency	Highly varied sentence structures are pleasing to the reader. Participial phrases make the writing flow.	Sentence structures are varied and easy to read. A few participial phrases are present.	There is some variety in sentence structures, and the writing is easy to read. Few participial phrases are used.
Conventions	Comparative and superlative forms and commas are used correctly to make the writing clear for the reader.	Errors in the use of comparative and superlative forms and commas rarely interfere with the reader's ability to understand the writing.	Errors in using comparative and superlative forms and commas sometimes confuse the reader.

✚ Presentation   The descriptive vignette is neat and legible.

3	2	1	
Details are very general and many lack sensory impact.	The topic is supported by few or no details.	The writing is unclear, and details are few or vague.	**Ideas**
Details are poorly organized. An introduction and ending are present, but one or both need work.	The writing is out of order. The introduction or ending may be missing.	The writing consists of a random list of thoughts. There is neither an introduction nor an ending.	**Organization**
The voice or tone may not fit the purpose. The writing lacks the writer's personal feelings.	Frequent shifts in point of view hide the writer's voice. An appropriate tone is not maintained.	The voice is very weak or absent. Tone is not established. The reader cannot determine the writer's purpose.	**Voice**
The language may be vague. Many words are overused.	Language is vague and unclear. The reader has to work to understand the meaning.	Too many vague or overused words distract from the meaning.	**Word Choice**
Sentence structures lack variety, and many begin the same way. Few or no participial phrases are used.	Sentence structures are limited and awkward to read. No participial phrases are used.	The writing has lots of sentence problems (incomplete, run-ons). It is difficult to read.	**Sentence Fluency**
Several serious errors in using comparative and superlative forms and commas confuse the reader.	Errors with comparative and superlative forms and commas require rereading to make sense of the writing.	Many errors with comparative and superlative forms and commas make reading difficult.	**Conventions**

See Appendix B for 4-, 5-, and 6-point descriptive rubrics.

Descriptive Vignette
Using the Rubric to Study the Model

Did you notice that the model on page 439 points out some key elements of a descriptive vignette? As she wrote "The Concert," Gina Bedow used these elements to help her describe an event in her life. She also used the 6-point rubric on pages 440–441 to plan, draft, revise, and edit the writing. A rubric is a great tool to evaluate writing during the writing process.

Now let's use the same rubric to score the model. To do this, we'll focus on each trait separately, starting with Ideas. We'll use the top descriptor for each trait (column 6), along with examples from the model, to help us understand how the traits work together. How would you score Gina on each trait?

 **Ideas**

- **Vivid sensory details support and develop the topic, bringing it to life.**

Gina is really good at painting mental pictures. She uses details that appeal to the reader's senses of sight, smell, taste, hearing, and touch. This passage contains one of my favorite descriptions. I could really visualize the different foods. I could almost smell them and taste them myself.

[from the writing model]

The smoke from the barbecue ribs rose above the crowd. It curled a finger under Jackson's nose, beckoning him to eat. The pizza tent was next door, and Sharon couldn't resist the smell of fresh mozzarella. I chose corn on the cob. As I ate, butter dripped down my hand with each sweet, crunchy bite, and salt stung my lips like a thousand tiny bees.

Organization

- The organization guides the reader through the vignette.
- The introduction and ending grab the reader's attention.

Gina organizes her vignette into paragraphs that focus on specific sensory details. She focuses on smell and taste in the first body paragraph, and she describes how things feel in the second body paragraph. In the next paragraph, Gina focuses on what she saw.

[from the writing model]

I saw two girls, arms locked, in a jerky kind of square dance. To their right, a boy stood playing an imaginary drum set. To his right, a group of people clapped in time with the music.

Voice

- The writer's voice and tone connect with the audience through first-person point of view, fresh insights, and personal feelings.

Gina writes her vignette using first-person point of view, which helps me easily connect with her experience. She shares her personal feelings and observations, which allows her personality to shine through. I find Gina's voice so engaging, I can't help but read on.

[from the writing model]

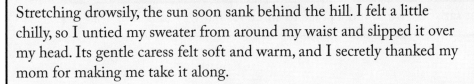

Stretching drowsily, the sun soon sank behind the hill. I felt a little chilly, so I untied my sweater from around my waist and slipped it over my head. Its gentle caress felt soft and warm, and I secretly thanked my mom for making me take it along.

Word Choice

- The action is captured in fresh, precise language that avoids vague or overused words.

I think Gina did a fantastic job with her use of language. It's just too easy to use cliché phrases or uncreative words, and Gina clearly worked hard to avoid that. Words like *drenched, toboggan*, and *flailing* all create a vivid and lasting image in my mind.

[from the writing model]

Within minutes, we were all drenched, and so was the ground. It was now a toboggan run of mud. I couldn't stand it anymore. I took off my shoes and socks, rolled up my jeans, and went flailing down the hill.

Sentence Fluency

- Highly varied sentence structures are pleasing to the reader.
- Participial phrases make the writing flow.

I remember what a participle is! It's a verb form that ends in *-ed* or *-ing,* and when it's included in a group of words or a phrase that acts as an adjective, it's called a participial phrase. In the passage below, Gina uses the participial phrase *Hunger satisfied* to describe the group of concert-goers.

[from the writing model]

Hunger satisfied, we found a place to sit about halfway up a hill.

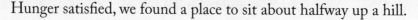

Conventions

- Comparative and superlative forms and commas are used correctly to make the writing clear for the reader.

Gina knows how to use the correct comparative and superlative forms of adjectives and adverbs. Notice her use of the superlative adjective form *most deafening* to explain that this was the loudest concert she has ever attended. Gina also knows how to correctly use commas to join two independent clauses into one sentence.

> **[from the writing model]**
>
> Last night I went to the most deafening concert I've ever attended. My ears are still ringing from the music, and my throat is still sore from screaming above the crowd.

Gina also uses the comparative adverb form *louder* to explain how loud the band played.

> **[from the writing model]**
>
> The band tried to get everyone's attention by playing louder than the roar of the crowd.

✚Presentation The descriptive vignette is neat and legible.

My Turn!

I'm going to write a descriptive vignette about something that's meaningful to me. I'll follow the rubric and use good writing strategies. Read on to see how I do it!

Writing a Descriptive Vignette

Prewrite

Focus on **Ideas**

The Rubric Says Vivid sensory details support and develop the topic, bringing it to life.

Writing Strategy Choose a personal experience. Jot down notes about what could be heard, smelled, tasted, and touched.

I live near the Atlantic Ocean, and I like to hang out at the beach. When I daydream about it, I can imagine what things sound, smell, taste, and feel like. So when my teacher said we were going to write descriptive vignettes, choosing my topic was easy for me. I closed my eyes to visualize my time at the beach. Then I jotted down the sensory details I remembered.

My Notes

- ✔ sun feels warm on my skin
- ✔ sunscreen smells like coconuts
- ✔ seagulls are calling overhead
- ✔ smell of salt is in the air
- ✔ ocean waves are crashing
- ✔ little kids are playing, talking, laughing, calling
- ✔ warm sand feels soft when my feet sink in
- ✔ water tastes salty on my lips
- ✔ salt dries my lips, hair, skin
- ✔ peanut butter and jelly sandwich tastes great (a tradition!)

Apply

Choose a memorable experience to describe. Gather information by noting sensory details.

Prewrite

The Rubric Says   The organization guides the reader through the vignette.

Writing Strategy   Make a Web to organize the details.

Writer's Term _____

Web

A **Web** organizes ideas around one topic. The topic goes in the center. Categories related to it, and details are attached to each category.

The rubric says my vignette needs to be organized. I think a Web will help me categorize my notes. Then I can use the Web categories as starting points for each of my paragraphs. I won't include the sense of sight because I want my readers to experience the beach through my other senses.

Web

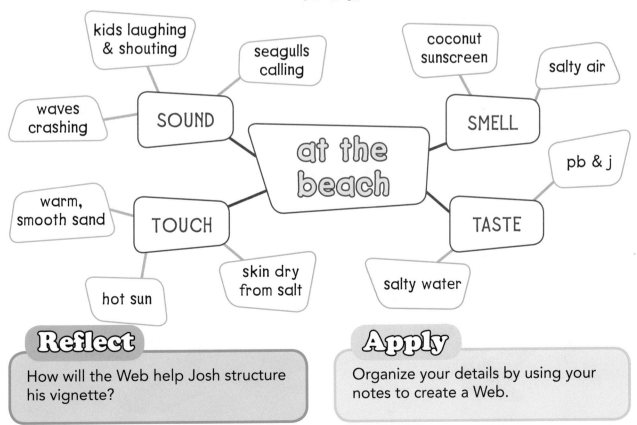

Reflect

How will the Web help Josh structure his vignette?

Apply

Organize your details by using your notes to create a Web.

Draft

Focus on **Voice**

The Rubric Says   The writer's voice and tone connect with the audience through first-person point of view, fresh insights, and personal feelings.

Writing Strategy   Speak directly to the audience and share personal experiences.

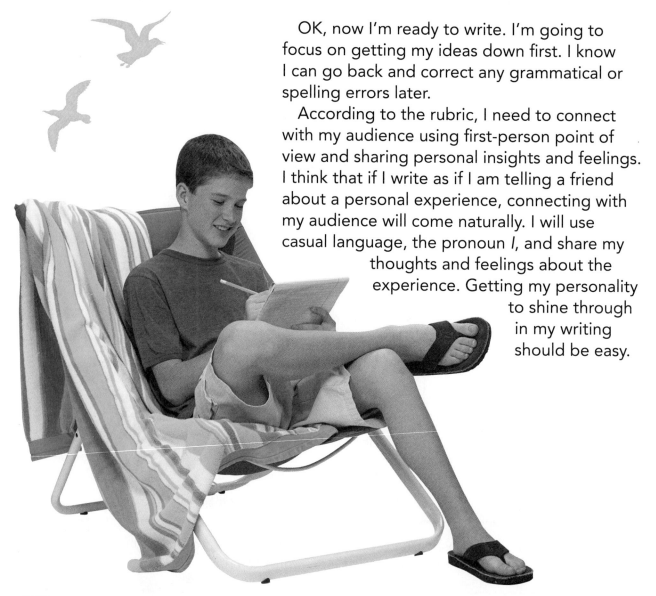

OK, now I'm ready to write. I'm going to focus on getting my ideas down first. I know I can go back and correct any grammatical or spelling errors later.

According to the rubric, I need to connect with my audience using first-person point of view and sharing personal insights and feelings. I think that if I write as if I am telling a friend about a personal experience, connecting with my audience will come naturally. I will use casual language, the pronoun *I*, and share my thoughts and feelings about the experience. Getting my personality to shine through in my writing should be easy.

[DRAFT]

[first-person point of view] **A Day at the Beach**

There is nothing I like better than a day at the beach, with all its sights, sounds, and sensations. Everything about it is so familiar. My favorite thing about the beach is the sound. If I close my eyes and consintrate, I can hear the water right now.

[fresh insights/ personal feelings] I also enjoy the sound of the seagulls circling overhead. I take pleasure in the children's voices, too. Some children talk quietly as they build sandcastles. Others giggle and squeal as they horse around in the water and are overcome by the waves. Some even call to their parents as they find "treasures" in the sand. Every new shell is a glistening piece of gold; every fossil is the more rare gem of all.

and then there are the feelings. The water is cooler and more refreshing than I remember as I immerse myself under its surface. When I emerge, I can feel its stinging saltiness as it dries on my lips. When I've had enough, I trudge slowly back to my blanket. Every time I step, my foot is swallowed by the sand and disappears into its softness.

Reflect

What do you think? How has Josh made it easy for you to connect with his descriptions?

Apply

Write a draft using first-person point of view. Share some personal insights about the event you are describing.

Revise

Focus on Ideas

The Rubric Says	Vivid sensory details support and develop the topic, bringing it to life.
Writing Strategy	Add rich, descriptive details.

Writer's Term

Figurative Language

Figurative language includes **similes, metaphors,** and **personification**. A simile is a comparison of two things, using **like** or **as: The girl sang like a bird**. A metaphor is also a comparison, but it says that one thing is another: **The sun is a fiery lion**. Personification is the technique of giving human qualities to an animal, object, or idea: **The dog smiled**.

After I finished writing my draft, I realized that I needed to include figurative language to help bring the topic to life. I then found a few spots where I could add some figurative language to liven things up.

[DRAFT]

[added a simile]

[added personification]

all its sights, sounds, and sensations. Everything about it is so
→ that it feels like my second home
familiar. My favorite thing about the beach is the sound. If I
It sings an endless song that swells and roars.
close my eyes and consintrate, I can hear the water right now.
Their squawking is a rhythmic lullaby.
I also enjoy the sound of the seagulls circling overhead. I take

[added a metaphor]

Apply

Use rich, descriptive details to enliven your writing.

Revise

The Rubric Says   The action is captured in fresh, precise language that avoids vague or overused words.

Writing Strategy   Replace clichés, vague words, and overused words with precise words.

Writer's Term

Clichés, Vague Words, and Overused Words

A **cliché** is an expression such as **white as snow** that is used so often that it becomes stale. **Vague words** don't present a precise picture. For example, **James looked** is not as specific as **James stared intently**. **Overused words** have been used so often that they become repetitive and boring. Instead of constantly writing **Rob said,** try using **Rob replied** or **Rob stated**.

I read my draft to a classmate. She liked it, but she noticed that I used some vague words. She also spotted two clichés near the end. The rubric says to replace this kind of language with precise words, so that's what I did.

[DRAFT]

[replaced cliché with precise words]

cramped with hunger

I'm ~~so hungry I can eat a horse~~, so I pull out my traditional

peanut butter and jelly

beach snack, a sandwich.

[added precise words]

Reflect

How have Josh's new word choices improved his writing?

Apply

Replace vague and overused language with precise words.

Revise

The Rubric Says   Highly varied sentence structures are pleasing to the reader. Participial phrases make the writing flow.

Writing Strategy   Use participial phrases to create sentence variety.

✏️ **Writer's Term** _____

Participial Phrases

A **participial phrase** is a group of words that includes a participle, or a verb form that ends in **-ed** or **-ing**. A participle acts as an adjective in a participial phrase by modifying the subject of a sentence.

I need to continue to revise. The rubric says to use participial phrases so that my sentences don't all sound the same. I looked over my draft to see if there were any repetitive sentence patterns, and, sure enough, there were. To vary my writing, I changed the beginning of one of the sentences.

[DRAFT]   [formed participial phrases] ⌐

The water is cooler and more refreshing than I remember as

Emerging from the water, ◄

I immerse myself under its surface. ~~When I emerge,~~ I can feel its

stinging saltiness as it dries on my lips. When I've had enough, I

trudge slowly back to my blanket.

Apply

Use participial phrases to add variety to your writing.

Edit

The Rubric Says Comparative and superlative forms and commas are used correctly to make the writing clear for the reader.

Writing Strategy Make sure adjectives, adverbs, and commas are used correctly.

Writer's Term_____

Comparative and Superlative Forms
The **comparative form** of an adjective or adverb compares two people, places, things, or actions. The **superlative form** compares three or more people, places, things, or actions.

Now it's time to check for errors in spelling, punctuation, and capitalization. The rubric also says to make sure that comparative and superlative forms, as well as commas, are used correctly.

[DRAFT]

call to their parents as they find "treasures" in the sand. Every

~~gorgeous,~~

new shell is a glistening piece of gold; every fossil is the ~~more rare~~ rarest

gem of all.
[correct use of a comma]

[correct superlative form]

Reflect

How have Josh's edits strengthened his descriptive vignette?

Apply Conventions

Edit for errors in grammar and mechanics. Be sure to use comparative and superlative forms, as well as commas, correctly.

For more practice with comparative and superlative forms, and commas, use the exercises on the next two pages.

Comparative and Superlative Forms

Know the Rule

The **comparative form** of an adjective or adverb compares two people, places, things, or actions.
- Add an *-er* ending to short adjectives and adverbs.
  Examples: loud, loud**er**; small, small**er**
- Use the word *more* or *less* before long adjectives and adverbs (of three or more syllables) to create the comparative form.
  Examples: wonderful, **more** wonderful, **less** wonderful

The **superlative form** compares three or more people, places, things, or actions.
- Add an *-est* ending to short adjectives and adverbs.
  Examples: loud, loud**est**; small, small**est**
- Use the word *most* or *least* before long adjectives and adverbs.
  Examples: wonderful, **most** wonderful, **least** wonderful

Practice the Rule

Number a sheet of paper 1–10. Read the sentences carefully. Write the word or phrase in parentheses that correctly completes each sentence. Then write whether the form is **Comparative** or **Superlative**.

1. The (more memorable/most memorable) teacher I've ever known was my swim instructor.
2. I swim (more skillfully/most skillfully) than my brother.
3. When I swam (slower/slowest) than he did, he used to tease me.
4. I think the Mediterranean beaches have the (more beautiful/most beautiful) sand.
5. Though the butterfly is (harder/more hard) than the breaststroke, I still want to learn it.
6. My dad was the (better/best) butterfly swimmer in his high school.
7. He won a total of 44 swim meets by his senior year, the (more/most) any athlete had ever won.
8. Compared to my brother, Dad is (more patient/most patient) with me.
9. When he's at our practices, my brother plays (fewer/fewest) tricks on me.
10. My dad makes sure that the rules are (fairer/more fair) than the ones my brother makes!

Using Commas

Know the Rule

A **comma** is used to separate items in a series. The last comma in a series goes before the conjunction (*and, or*).

> **Example:** The dentist carefully inspected Joshua's tongue, gums, and teeth.

A comma is also used to separate pairs of related adjectives (*teeming, bustling city*). To decide whether to put a comma between adjectives, read the sentence with the word *and* inserted between the adjectives. If the word *and* sounds natural, use a comma.

> **Example:** I sat at the fountain all afternoon, sketching its towering marble columns and cascading, crystalline waterfalls.

Practice the Rule

Write the following sentences, and place commas where they are needed.

1. I need to remember to pick up some eggs milk whole wheat bread and apples from the store on the way home.

2. The huge dog looked like a giant next to the delicate fluttering hummingbird.

3. I wanted to purchase that enormous purple octopus at the gift shop, but I did not come with enough money.

4. Mother told Toshi she could have scrambled eggs fresh fruit low-fat yogurt or cereal for breakfast.

5. We sat for hours beneath the ancient flowering tree and talked of our plans for the summer.

6. Jenny planted seventeen breathtaking varieties of daffodils on a cool damp day last fall.

7. When we go camping in August, we always take along bedrolls sweat suits hats and gloves!

8. Our school supply list included markers pens notebooks in bold colors and a three-ring binder.

9. Music class is our favorite class because our teacher is fun imaginative and always excited about new songs.

10. Many people say that few composers can top Bach Beethoven or Mozart!

Publish   +Presentation

Publishing Strategy Post my vignette on the class bulletin board or website.

Presentation Strategy Use neat handwriting or a computer.

My descriptive vignette is finished! I need to decide how I will publish it. I may submit my writing to a magazine that publishes student writing. Before I publish, I'll read my draft one last time to make sure all my changes are easy to read. Then I'll use a computer to type my final copy. I'll also use a writing checklist to make sure I've covered everything.

My Final Checklist

Did I—

✔ use superlative and comparative forms correctly throughout my vignette?

✔ use commas correctly to punctuate series and groups of related adjectives?

✔ use neat handwriting or a limited number of clear fonts?

✔ proofread for any errors in spelling, grammar, or punctuation?

Apply

Make a checklist to check your descriptive vignette. Then make a final copy to publish.

A Day at the Beach

by Josh

There is nothing I like better than a day at the beach, with all its sights, sounds, and sensations. Everything about it is so familiar that it feels like my second home. My favorite thing about the beach is the sound. If I close my eyes and concentrate, I can hear the water right now. It sings an endless song that swells and roars. I also enjoy the sound of the seagulls circling overhead. Their squawking is a rhythmic lullaby. I take pleasure in the children's voices, too. Some children talk quietly as they build sandcastles. Others giggle and squeal as they frolic in the water and are overcome by the waves. Some even call to their parents as they find "treasures" in the sand. Every new shell is a gorgeous, glistening piece of gold; every fossil is the rarest gem of all.

And then there are the feelings. The water is cooler and more refreshing than I remember as I immerse myself under its surface. Emerging from the water, I can feel its stinging saltiness as it dries on my lips. When I've had enough, I trudge slowly back to my blanket. Every time I step, my foot is swallowed by the sand and disappears into its softness.

The sun beams down at me like a loving friend. It warms my skin and hair and dries me again. As I dry, the saltwater parches my skin. It feels as tight on my body as shrink-wrap.

I'm cramped with hunger, so I pull out my traditional beach snack, a peanut butter and jelly sandwich. It is a savory blend of sweet, nutty, and salty flavors. Sticking to the roof of my mouth, the peanut butter prompts me to wash it down with some water.

Startled from my daydream, I realize that I'm not at the beach at all. I am holding my pen, writing, and dreaming about the beach.

Reflect

Did Josh use all the traits of a good vignette in his writing? Check it against the rubric. Don't forget to use the rubric to check your own work, too.

What's a Poem?

It's a piece of writing that expresses emotions, thoughts, or ideas. A poem can be a creative way to share knowledge about just about anything—a person, an event, an object, or a feeling.

What's in a Poem?

Lines
Words in a poem are arranged in lines. A line can be one word, a phrase, or a full sentence. Lines are separated into groups called verses or stanzas. The words, lines, and verses of a poem flow together rhythmically, sometimes rhyming.

Figurative Language
A poem uses figurative language, or figures of speech. These include metaphors, similes, and personification. Figurative language creates vivid images in the mind of the reader. I can use figurative language to make my poem say exactly what I want with very few words.

Imagery and Symbols
The pictures you create in your mind when you listen to a poem are called imagery. A good poet uses precise words and figures of speech to create imagery for readers. Poets also use symbols—concrete objects or people that stand for larger ideas. For example, a dove is often used as a symbol for peace.

Why write a Poem?

There are many reasons to write a poem. A poem is a creative way to share my thoughts and ideas.

To Describe

I can write a poem to describe just about anything—a place, an event, a time, a person, an object, or a feeling or emotion. I can use a poem to describe something in a new way.

To Reflect

A poem is a good way to write a personal reflection. For example, I can write about what an event in history means to me or how it has affected my community.

To Inform

I can write a poem to help people understand an event, a place, or a person better. I can include details that give them information they didn't have before. For example, I could write a poem about a woman who fought in the Revolutionary War to help people understand how passionately people felt about independence.

Linking Descriptive Writing Traits to a Poem

In this chapter, you will write a poem about a social studies topic such as an historical event. Josh will guide you through the stages of the writing process: Prewrite, Draft, Revise, Edit, and Publish. In each stage, Josh will show you important writing strategies that are linked to the Descriptive Writing Traits below.

Descriptive Writing Traits

Ideas
- a focused, complete topic
- relevant sensory details that support, describe, and develop the topic

Organization
- an introduction that previews a topic, a body that develops the topic, and a conclusion that follows and supports the description
- well-organized details that follow the order of the description, whether by time, location, or other order
- transitions that clarify relationships between ideas

Voice
- a voice and tone that are appropriate for the purpose and audience

Word Choice
- precise, descriptive language that creates a clear picture for the reader

Sentence Fluency
- sentences that vary in length and structure to make the writing flow

Conventions
- no or few errors in grammar, usage, mechanics, and spelling

Before you write, read Ian Davidson's poem on the next page. Then use the poem rubric on pages 462–463 to decide how well he did. (You might want to look back at What's in a Poem? on page 458, too!)

The Ballad of Deborah Sampson, Revolutionary War Soldier

by Ian Davidson

Line

The drums pound, the horns sound,
The men march off to war.
And what about the womenfolk,
Left home to mind the store?

Imagery

Stanza

We yearn for independence too,
We're colonists—that's right!
And one among us, brave as an eagle,
Is off to join the fight.

Her name is Deborah Sampson,
And she's put off female dress.
She wears a soldier's boots and gun,
She's fighting with the best.

Figurative language

A lonely life it is for her,
Her secret she must hide.
Her fellow soldiers must not learn
A woman fights by their side.

Someday when freedom lights this land,
When war's been fought and won,
She'll put away her manly clothes,
She'll set aside her gun.

Demure in flowered dress and bonnet,
She'll live a life of peace.
She'll spin and weave and work and teach,
But memories will not cease.

Symbol

Freed from tyranny we'll recall
Her courage under fire.
A glowing torch of freedom,
For a nation she'll inspire.

Poem

Rubric

Use this 6-point rubric to plan and score a poem.

	6	5	4
Ideas	The subject of the poem is focused and complete. Vivid details support and develop the subject.	The subject of the poem is focused. Most of the details support and develop the subject.	The subject of the poem is somewhat focused. Some of the details support and develop the subject.
Organization	The lines and stanzas, if used, are organized logically. The ideas are easy to follow.	The lines and stanzas, if used, are organized. Most of the ideas are easy to follow.	One line may be out of order, making ideas hard to follow.
Voice	The voice and tone suit the writer's purpose and audience perfectly.	The voice and tone suit the writer's purpose and audience most of the time.	The voice and tone suit the writer's purpose some of the time.
Word Choice	Precise words describe the subject effectively. Figurative language enhances imagery.	Most words are precise. Most figurative language is effective.	Some words are precise. Some figurative language may be ineffective.
Sentence Fluency	The words and lines establish an appropriate cadence and rhythm.	Rhythm and flow are maintained most of the time. One or two lines may need improvement.	Rhythm and flow are maintained some of the time. Several lines need improvement.
Conventions	The writing has been carefully edited. Apostrophes are used correctly.	Minor errors are present but do not interfere with meaning. Apostrophes are used correctly.	A few errors cause confusion. Apostrophes may be used incorrectly.

✛ Presentation The poem is legible and placed attractively on the page.

3	2	1	
The subject of the poem is not focused. Too few details support and develop the subject.	The subject of the poem is not focused. The details do not support or develop the subject.	Details are not written as a poem. Details may be merely listed or unrelated to one subject.	**Ideas**
Many lines may be out of order, making ideas hard to follow.	The lines seem to run together. The ideas are hard to follow.	The writing is not organized into lines.	**Organization**
The voice or tone may be inconsistent. A connection with the audience is not maintained.	The voice or tone may not be appropriate for the purpose or audience.	The voice is absent. The audience does not know the writer's purpose.	**Voice**
Many words are too general. Figurative language is not effective.	Words are general or vague. Figurative language is not used.	Words are vague or used incorrectly. Figurative language is not used.	**Word Choice**
The rhythm is inconsistent. Some line breaks interrupt the flow.	Rhythm is not established. The lines do not flow.	The lines do not make a poem.	**Sentence Fluency**
Many errors are repeated and cause confusion. Some apostrophes are used incorrectly.	Serious errors interfere with meaning. Many apostrophes are used incorrectly.	The writing has not been edited.	**Conventions**

See Appendix B for 4-, 5-, and 6-point descriptive rubrics.

Using the Poem Rubric to Study the Model

Did you notice that the model on page 461 points out some key elements of a poem? As he wrote "The Ballad of Deborah Sampson, Revolutionary War Soldier," Ian Davidson used these elements to help him describe an event in American history. He also used the 6-point rubric on pages 462–463 to plan, draft, revise, and edit the writing. A rubric is a great tool to evaluate writing during the writing process.

Now let's use the same rubric to score the model. To do this, we'll focus on each trait separately, starting with Ideas. We'll use the top descriptor for each trait (column 6) along with examples from the model, to help us understand how the traits work together. How would you score Ian on each trait?

 **Ideas**

- **The subject of the poem is focused and complete.**
- **Vivid details support and develop the subject.**

Ian chose an intriguing subject for his poem, a woman who dressed as a man to serve as a soldier in the Revolutionary War. He uses vivid details to describe what Deborah Sampson had to do in order to fight. These details express his admiration.

[from the writing model]

She wears a soldier's boots and gun,
She's fighting with the best.

Organization

- The lines and stanzas, if used, are organized logically.
- The ideas are easy to follow.

Ian's poem has seven stanzas, each with four lines. Each stanza focuses on a specific idea, and together they tell Deborah Sampson's story in chronological order. The poem swept me along from the introduction of Deborah as a soldier to the last stanza about how she continues to be a symbol of courage long after the war is over.

[from the writing model]

Freed from tyranny we'll recall
Her courage under fire.
A glowing torch of freedom,
A nation she'll inspire.

Voice

- The voice and tone suit the writer's purpose and audience perfectly.

Ian's voice and tone match his purpose. He places himself in the position of women in colonial times who cared as much as the men about independence from Britain. In the second stanza the tone conveys the mood of the time and really comes through to the reader!

[from the writing model]

We yearn for independence too,
We're colonists—that's right!
And one among us, brave as an eagle,
Is off to join the fight.

Poem

Word Choice

- Precise words describe the subject effectively.
- Figurative language enhances imagery.

Ian does a great job using precise words to convey the feelings of the colonists. In the last stanza, he uses a powerful symbol to describe what Deborah's actions mean to the nation. He also uses the specific word *tyranny* to describe exactly what he means.

[from the writing model]

Freed from tyranny we'll recall
Her courage under fire.
A glowing torch of freedom,
A nation she'll inspire.

Sentence Fluency

- The words and lines establish an appropriate cadence and rhythm.

It's always important in a poem that the words, lines, and stanzas flow together well. I like the way Ian's poem sounds when I read it aloud. It has a consistent rhythm throughout. Not all poems have to rhyme, but he chose to rhyme the last word of the second and fourth line in each stanza.

[from the writing model]

The drums pound, the horns sound,
The men march off to war.
And what about the womenfolk,
Left home to mind the store?

Conventions

- The writing has been carefully edited.
- Apostrophes are used correctly.

Ian knows how to use apostrophes correctly. Look how he uses apostrophes to form contractions in the fifth stanza.

[from the writing model]

Someday when freedom lights this land,
When war's been fought and won,
She'll put away her manly clothes,
She'll set aside her gun.

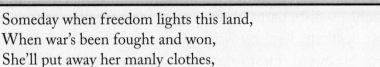

Presentation The poem is legible and placed attractively on the page.

My Turn!

Now it's my turn to write a poem. I'll use the rubric and good writing strategies to help me. Follow along to see how I do it.

Prewrite

The Rubric Says   Vivid details support and develop the subject.

Writing Strategy   Choose a topic. Make a list of details.

My teacher wants us to share something we have learned about in social studies, by writing a poem. I could write about a person or an event. First I need to choose a topic. Then I need to think about how I want to describe the event or person. Will I write as if I'm observing the event? Will I take the point of view of a participant? I've been reading about the Industrial Revolution in America and how children were affected. This would make a great topic for a poem! I think the poem will be most effective if I pretend I'm an adult who worked in factories when I was a kid. I jotted down some ideas.

Notes

✔ Industrial Revolution—people began working in factories
✔ children worked long hours
✔ children did not go to school
✔ worked in textile factories making cloth
✔ started work before sunrise, ended after dark
✔ hot in summer, cold in winter
✔ no breaks, ate lunch while working
✔ lots of dust in the air
✔ respiratory diseases
✔ laws made to protect children

Apply

Choose an event or a person from history. Collect details about the subject for your poem.

Prewrite

The Rubric Says   The lines and stanzas, if used, are organized logically. The ideas are easy to follow.

Writing Strategy   Use a Web to plan the poem.

Writer's Term

Web

A **Web** organizes ideas around one topic. The topic goes in the center. Categories related to the topic are attached to it, and details are attached to each category.

The rubric says I should organize the lines and stanzas in my poem logically. I'll start with completing a graphic organizer, like a Web, to help me organize my notes. The categories can be stanzas in my poem.

Web

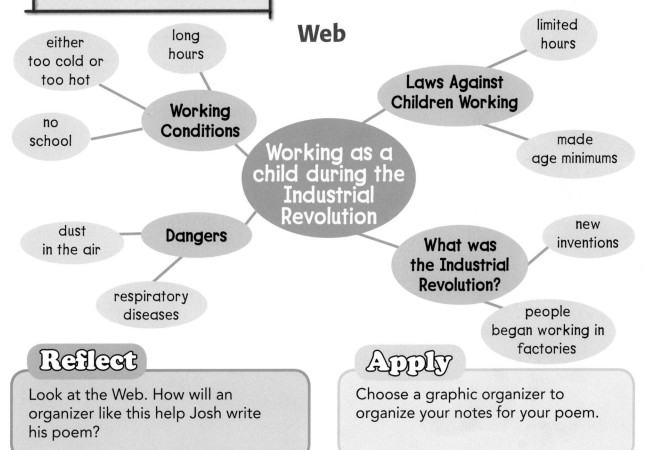

Reflect

Look at the Web. How will an organizer like this help Josh write his poem?

Apply

Choose a graphic organizer to organize your notes for your poem.

Draft

The Rubric Says Precise words describe the subject effectively. Figurative language enhances imagery.

Writing Strategy Use precise words and figurative language.

> ✏ **Writer's Term**___
>
> **Metaphor and Simile**
> **Metaphors and similes** are comparisons between two things or ideas. A poet uses metaphors and similes to create images in the reader's mind. A simile uses the words **like** or **as**; a metaphor does not.

The words I write are always important. But they are especially important in poetry because there are so few of them. Every word really counts!

According to the rubric, I should use figurative language to create imagery. I can use similes and metaphors to help the reader understand and "see" my subject.

To get started, I'll work on getting my ideas down in a draft. I'll look out for grammar and spelling, but I know I can fix my mistakes later. Here's my draft.

[DRAFT]

Factory Life

The steam engine opened the way.

Then the cotton gin came to stay.

With the telegraph

We were on a new path

The Industrial Revolution would

have its day.

The workers got up before the sun,

And labored past when day was

done.

School there was not,

Children were rarely taught.

So they worked for fear they'd

have none.

[precise words]

At the time I was just a young boy,

striving hard in a factory's employ.

We made fine cloth of white,

worked late into the night,

were paid little and had no joy.

The air trapped dirt and debris.

It was air you could touch and see.

Cold in winter,

Hot in summer,

We thought we would never

breathe free.

[figurative language]

Finally the country made laws,

Wed no longer work without pause.

We had set hours, things were not

quite as bad,

We'd escaped from the factorys

claws!

Reflect

How does the figurative language help you form a clear picture of the conditions in the factory?

Apply

Write a draft of a poem using ideas from your graphic organizer. Use precise words and figurative language to create imagery for your reader.

Writing a Poem

Revise

The Rubric Says   Vivid details support and develop the subject.

Writing Strategy   Use details that bring the subject to life.

After I finished writing my draft, I remembered that I should include vivid details. Vivid details will help the readers imagine what the poem describes. The details have to be very good ones. No ordinary details for my poem! I looked back at my draft to find details that I could make more creative and engaging. In this stanza, I found a place where I could use a more striking detail to express how little children were paid to work.

[DRAFT]

At the time I was just a young boy,

striving hard in a factory's employ.

We made fine cloth of white,   [added vivid detail]

worked late into the night,

were paid less than the price of a toy.

~~were paid little and had no joy~~

Apply

Read your draft. Add vivid details to bring your subject to life for the reader.

Revise

The Rubric Says   The lines and stanzas, if used, are organized logically. The ideas are easy to follow.

Writing Strategy   Check the order of the lines and stanzas.

I read my draft again to check the order of the lines and stanzas. I want the reader to be able to follow all my ideas. I think my poem does a pretty good job of describing the working conditions in the factory. Reading closely, however, I noticed two stanzas that are not in logical order. I'll switch them around so my ideas are easier to follow and make better sense.

[DRAFT]

[placed stanzas in logical order]

The workers got up before the sun,

And labored past when day was done.

School there was not,

Children were rarely taught.

So they worked for fear they'd have none.

At the time I was just a young boy,

striving hard in a factory's employ.

We made fine cloth of white,

worked late into the night,

were paid less than the price of a toy.

~~were paid little and had no joy.~~

Reflect

Do Josh's revisions make the ideas easier to follow?

Apply

Read your draft for the order of ideas. Arrange the lines and stanzas so your poem makes the most sense.

Writing a Poem

Revise

Focus on  **Sentence Fluency**

The Rubric Says The words and lines establish an appropriate cadence and rhythm.

Writing Strategy Place line breaks where they make sense.

The rubric reminds me that the words and lines in my poem should establish a rhythm. In poetry, the lines and where they break are very important. They should make the poem flow rhythmically. To decide if my line breaks are placed correctly, I read my poem aloud. I found one line that didn't fit with the rhythm or the rhyme scheme I'm using. I'll add a line break and change a few words to fit my rhyme scheme.

[DRAFT]

[improved rhyme scheme]

Finally the country made laws,

[added line break]

Wed no longer work without pause.

~~Set hours we had,~~

We had set hours,

Things were not quite as bad,

We'd escaped from the factorys claws!

Apply

Read your poem aloud. Change the order of words, if necessary, to improve rhythm and flow.

Edit

The Rubric Says   The writing has been carefully edited. Apostrophes are used correctly.

Writing Strategy   Check the use of apostrophes in contractions and possessive nouns.

Writer's Term

Apostrophes

An **apostrophe** is used to replace letters in a contraction. An apostrophe is also used to form possessive nouns, such as **Susan's hat**.

Now is the time to check for spelling, grammar, and punctuation errors. The rubric also says to check apostrophes in contractions and possessive nouns. I checked my draft and found a couple places where I had forgotten to use an apostrophe.

[DRAFT]

Finally the country made laws,   **[added apostrophe to contraction]**

We'd no longer work without pause.

~~Set hours we had,~~
We had set hours,

things were not quite as bad,

We'd escaped from the factory's claws!   **[added apostrophe to form possessive]**

Reflect

Look at Josh's edits. Has he used apostrophes correctly?

Apply   **Conventions**

Edit carefully for errors in grammar, mechanics, and spelling. Be sure to use apostrophes correctly.

For additional practice with apostrophes and possessive nouns, use the exercises on the next two pages.

Apostrophes

Know the Rule

Use an **apostrophe** to replace letters omitted from a contraction. A **contraction** is two words that have been shortened and combined (*do not = don't*). Also use a contraction to show possession. To form the **possessive** of a singular noun, add an apostrophe and *s* (*Mike's cleats*). For plural nouns that end in *s*, add an apostrophe (*sisters'* bedrooms). For plural nouns that do not end in *s*, add an apostrophe and *s* (*children's shoes*).

Practice the Rule

Number a sheet of paper 1–10. Read each sentence and write the correct form of the word on your paper.

1. Clara knows she (wouldn't/would'nt) have much time to eat lunch.
2. (Claras/Clara's) machine moved very quickly, and she had to pay attention.
3. She had been told that she (couldn't/could'nt) have any breaks.
4. Her (mother's/mothers) brother ran the factory.
5. Clara worked hard to make money for her family because they (didn't/did'nt) have much.
6. One day when she was sick, her (father's/fathers') nephew went to work for her.
7. The (boss's/bosses) sons also worked at the factory.
8. They (weren't/wer'ent) forced to work as hard as the other children.
9. By the end of the day, the (workers's/workers') bodies were tired.
10. Clara thought, "(Theyr'e/They're) exhausted, just like me."

Possessive Nouns

Know the Rule

A **possessive noun** shows ownership or close relationship. Be sure to use the correct form of possessive nouns in your sentences. A possessive noun can be singular or plural.

> **Example:** The child's uncle fought in the war. (singular)
> **Example:** The boys' friends worked on their farm. (plural)

Practice the Rule

Number a sheet of paper 1–10. Write each possessive noun and whether it is **singular** or **plural**.

1. The colonists' ideas about how to face Britain were very different.
2. Many felt the large country's power was too much to challenge.
3. Others felt Britain's King should not be allowed to control them.
4. The stamp tax's effects on the colonists were severe.
5. The tax collectors' efforts were often met by angry colonists.
6. The citizens' homes were required to house soldiers.
7. As people began to protest, the homeland's troops increased in number.
8. The colonists' anger was expressed through organized actions.
9. His Majesty's Intolerable Acts soon followed.
10. The Patriots' ranks began to swell.

Publish ✛Presentation

Publishing Strategy   Present the poem in a multimedia presentation.

Presentation Strategy   Display information clearly.

My poem is finished! Now I'd like to publish it. I think I'll create a multimedia presentation around my poem. Photographs, music, and video clips will help people to learn more about my topic. For example, pictures of what the conditions were like in a factory during the Industrial Revolution will really authenticate my poem. I will need to research what photographs are available for me to use. Once I find some pictures, I will add the lines of my poem to my visual display. I'll need to make sure my poem is written or typed legibly and placed neatly on the page or slide so that my audience can read it easily.

My Final Checklist

Did I—

✔ check spelling, grammar, and punctuation?

✔ make sure I used apostrophes correctly?

✔ choose photos, music, or video clips that enhance the meaning of my poem?

✔ make sure my poem is legible and well placed for easy reading?

Apply

Make a checklist to check your poem and multimedia presentation. Then create and publish an attractive final copy.

Factory Life

by Josh

The steam engine opened the way.
Then the cotton gin came to stay.
With the telegraph
We were on a new path
The Industrial Revolution would have its day.

At the time I was just a young boy,
striving hard in a factory's employ.
We made fine cloth of white,
worked late into the night,
were paid less than the price of a toy.

We arose with no sign of the sun,
And labored past when day was done.
School there was not,
We were rarely taught.
So we worked for fear we'd have none.

The air trapped dirt and debris.
A haze you could touch and see.
Freezing in winter,
Stifling in summer,
We thought we would never breathe free.

Finally the country made laws,
We'd no longer work without pause.
Set hours we had,
Things were not quite as bad,
We'd escaped from the factory's claws!

Reflect

Did Josh use all the traits of a good poem in his writing? You can check his poem against the rubric. Use the rubric to check your own poem too.

Descriptive test writing

Read the Writing Prompt

You will be given a writing prompt when you take a test. Most writing prompts have three parts:

Setup This is the introduction to the writing prompt. It gives you some background information so that you can begin to think about your topic.

Task This part of the writing prompt tells you what you're supposed to write: a descriptive vignette.

Scoring Guide This section tells how your writing will be scored. To do well on the test, you should include everything on the list.

Remember the rubrics you've been using? When you take a writing test, you won't always have all of the information that's on a rubric. But don't worry. The scoring guide is just like a rubric. It tells you everything you need to think about in order to do well on a written test. Like the rubrics you're used to seeing, most scoring guides are based upon the six traits of writing:

Writing MODEL Prompt

Think about a memorable personal experience. What is it about this event that stands out in your mind?

Write a descriptive vignette that describes a memorable personal experience.

Be sure your writing

- has a focused, complete topic that is supported and enhanced by relevant sensory details.

- has well-organized paragraphs that follow a sequence that unfolds naturally and logically.

- has an appropriate voice and tone for the purpose and audience.

- uses precise, descriptive language that creates an accurate picture for the reader.

- has sentences that vary in length and structure to make the writing flow.

- contains no or few errors in grammar, usage, mechanics, and spelling.

Writing Traits
in the Scoring Guide

Look at the scoring guide in the writing prompt on page 481. Not every writing prompt will include all six writing traits, but this one does. The chart below can help you better understand the connection between the scoring guide and the writing traits in the rubrics you've been using.

- Be sure you have a focused, complete topic that is supported and enhanced by relevant sensory details.

- Be sure you write well-organized paragraphs that follow a sequence that unfolds naturally and logically.

- Be sure your voice and tone are appropriate for your purpose and audience.

- Be sure you use precise, descriptive language that creates an accurate picture for the reader.

- Be sure your sentences vary in length and structure to make the writing flow.

- Be sure your writing contains no or few errors in grammar, usage, mechanics, and spelling.

Amy Lee's descriptive vignette is on the next page. Did she follow the scoring guide?

Summer at the Park

by Amy Lee

It was the second week of summer vacation, but the weather had been chilly and wet. Today, however, the clouds were nowhere to be seen. The sun's rays shone through my bedroom window and woke me from my slumber. It finally felt as though summer had arrived.

My sister, my mom, and I decided to start the season with a picnic at the park. When we arrived, we discovered we were not the only ones lured by the warm weather. Kids were riding their bikes along the winding paths while mothers pushed babies and toddlers along in strollers. The picnic tables were taken, so we laid out our big, comfy blanket on the grass.

I sat for a few minutes and watched the young children running through the fountains, splashing and laughing. Then, I kicked off my flip-flops and moved them from the blanket to the grass. Although the sun was warm, the grass was still cool and damp.

I got out my book of poems, which I had checked out from the library. As soon as school had ended, I went straight to the library to load up on reading material. Amber, on the other hand, put on her headphones so she could listen to music. It was time to settle in, so I rolled over on my stomach and started to read.

"Amy," my mother said, "wake up. It's lunchtime."

Without realizing it, I had fallen asleep, lulled by the warmth of the sun and the sounds of children playing. I stretched my body from head to toe and sat back up. Mom had packed sweet, juicy honey chicken and a thermos of tangy, homemade lemonade. For dessert, she brought fresh, sweet purple plums. "The first of the season," she told us.

After lunch, Amber and I ran down to the fountains. Water squirted up and drenched us, and we laughed and squealed, just like the other kids.

It didn't take long for us to dry off in the sun. By now even the grass was dry. Eventually we packed up our bags and headed back to the car. Even though I was sad the day was over, I was happy that summer had finally come!

Using the Scoring Guide to Study the Model

Now let's use the scoring guide to check Amy's writing test, "Summer at the Park." How well does her vignette meet each of the six writing traits?

Ideas

- The vignette has a focused, complete topic that is supported and enhanced by relevant sensory details.

Amy focuses on one special event. She uses plenty of sensory details to help the reader visualize her day at the park. Her description of the picnic lunch really makes my mouth water!

> Mom had packed sweet, juicy honey chicken and a thermos of tangy, homemade lemonade. For dessert, she brought fresh, sweet purple plums. "The first of the season," she told us.

Organization

- The vignette has well-organized paragraphs that follow a sequence that unfolds naturally and logically.

Amy's description is very well organized. The paragraphs are in the right order, and she describes the action as it happened. The vignette is easy and enjoyable to follow.

> My sister, my mom, and I decided to start the season with a picnic at the park. When we arrived, we discovered we were not the only ones lured by the warm weather. Kids were riding their bikes along the winding paths while mothers pushed babies and toddlers along in strollers. The picnic tables were taken, so we laid out our big, comfy blanket on the grass.

Voice

- **The voice and tone are appropriate for the purpose and audience.**

Since this is a vignette about an upbeat, informal event, Amy uses a friendly voice and tone to speak directly to the reader. They help set the mood for the description. Her personality comes through, so it was easy for me to connect with the writer who is obviously a student like me. I prefer books to music, too!

I got out my book of poems, which I had checked out from the library. As soon as school had ended, I went straight to the library to load up on reading material. Amber, on the other hand, put on her headphones so she could listen to music.

Word Choice

- **The vignette has precise, descriptive language that creates an accurate picture for the reader.**

Amy uses exact words in her description to describe her day. In the passage below, she doesn't just say the kids were playing; she says they were *splashing and laughing*. She could have said she took off her sandals, but instead, she says, *I kicked off my flip-flops.*

I sat for a few minutes and watched the young children running through the fountains, splashing and laughing. Then, I kicked off my flip-flops and moved them from the blanket to the grass. Although the sun was warm, the grass was still cool and damp.

Using the Scoring Guide to Study the Model

• The vignette has sentences that vary in length and structure to make the writing flow.

I noticed right away that Amy uses sentences of different structures and lengths. I also noticed that she begins some sentences with transition words and others with clauses. The mixture of sentences adds interest and makes the writing flow smoothly from beginning to end.

It didn't take long for us to dry off in the sun. By now even the grass was dry. Eventually we packed up our bags and headed back to the car. Even though I was sad the day was over, I was happy that summer had finally come!

• The vignette contains no or few errors in grammar, usage, mechanics, and spelling.

It looks like Amy used correct grammar, spelling, capitalization, and punctuation. I know it's important to check for these kinds of mistakes, and I'll be sure to keep that in mind as I write. But you should check for proper grammar and mechanics in your writing, too. Don't forget that this can be done at every step of the writing process!

Planning My Time

Before handing out a writing prompt, our teacher always tells us how much time we'll have to finish a test. Since I already know the steps of the writing process, I like to think about how much total time I'll need for each step. If the test takes an hour, here's one way that I can plan my time. When taking a writing test, you should plan your time, too. Believe me, it helps!

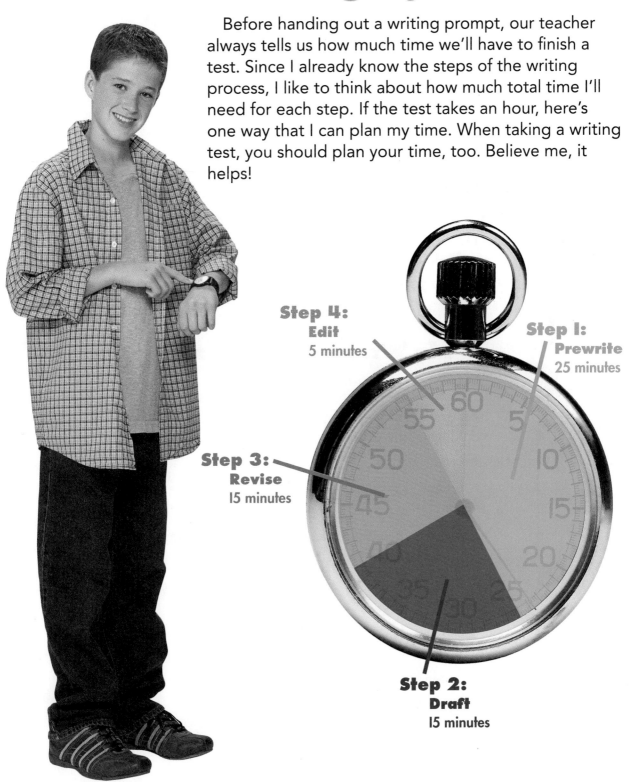

Step 4:
Edit
5 minutes

Step 1:
Prewrite
25 minutes

Step 3:
Revise
15 minutes

Step 2:
Draft
15 minutes

Prewrite

Focus on **Ideas**

Writing Strategy   Study the writing prompt to find out what to do.

After my teacher gives me a writing prompt, I study it to make sure I know exactly what I should do. A writing prompt usually has three parts, even though they aren't always labeled. When you study the writing prompt, you should first find the setup, the task, and the scoring guide. Then you can label them like I did below. Circle key words in the setup and the task that tell what kind of writing you need to do and who your audience will be.

My Writing Test Prompt

Setup — Think about the (seasons of the year.)

Task — Write (a descriptive vignette) about a specific activity that you like to do during one of the four seasons.

Scoring Guide — Be sure your writing

- has a focused, complete topic that is supported and enhanced by relevant sensory details.

- has well-organized paragraphs that follow a sequence that unfolds naturally and logically.

- has an appropriate voice and tone for the purpose and audience.

- uses precise, descriptive language that creates an accurate picture for the reader.

- has sentences that vary in length and structure to make the writing flow.

- contains no or few errors in grammar, usage, mechanics, and spelling.

Now it's time to think about how the scoring guide relates to the six writing traits in the rubrics you've studied. Not all of the traits will be included in every scoring guide, but you'll still want to remember them all in order to write a good vignette.

Ideas

- Be sure you have a focused, complete topic that is supported and enhanced by relevant sensory details.

To keep my topic focused, I'll choose an event I can describe in a short time. To make my description come alive, I'll use plenty of sensory details.

Organization

- Be sure you write well-organized paragraphs that follow a sequence that unfolds naturally and logically.

I'll choose an order for my description and stay with it throughout my vignette. That way readers will be able to follow the story easily.

Voice

- Be sure your voice and tone are appropriate for the purpose and audience.

Since this is a descriptive vignette, I'll be sure to use a tone that's less formal and more upbeat.

Word Choice

- Be sure you use precise, descriptive language that creates an accurate picture for the reader.

As I write, I'll try to avoid using vague, dull words. Precise words create vivid images in the reader's mind.

Sentence Fluency

- Be sure your sentences vary in length and structure to make the writing flow.

I'll make sure I use different types of sentences and vary their length to keep my writing from being too dull or choppy.

Conventions

- Be sure your writing contains no or few errors in grammar, usage, mechanics, and spelling.

I'll be sure to think about using proper grammar and mechanics as I write!

Prewrite

Focus on **Ideas**

Writing Strategy Respond to the task.

I know that good writers gather information before they start to write. I'll begin by rereading the task, since that's the part of the writing prompt that tells what I'm supposed to do. But I have to remember that time is limited! That's why it's a good idea to think about how I'm going to respond before I start writing.

My task is to write a descriptive vignette, a short, descriptive sketch, about one of the seasons. Since I wrote about summer once before, I think I'll write about a winter experience this time. Last year, my friends and I made our own outdoor hockey rink, so I think I'll write about that. I'll jot down some notes right now.

Task — Write a descriptive vignette about a specific activity that you like to do during one of the four seasons.

Notes

✔ Built a hockey rink; had to wait for it to freeze

✔ Found out it froze

✔ Wore warm clothes; different than inside hockey

✔ Had to skate around to warm up

✔ Played a game of hockey

✔ Can't wait to play again

Apply

Before you write, think about how you'll respond to the task in the writing prompt. Then write some notes to help you gather information.

Prewrite

Writing Strategy Choose a graphic organizer.

The clock is ticking, so I have to begin organizing my ideas right away. First, I'll choose a graphic organizer. I remember plenty of sensory details about the time we built our rink. But I think I'll use a Story Map to help me remember the order of events.

Title: "Winter on Ice"

Setting

Where Outdoor hockey rink, behind Austin's barn   **When** Last winter

Major Character Me (Josh)

Minor Character(s) Austin, Colin

Theme Wintertime is fun.

Plot

Event 1	Event 2	Event 3	Event 4
My friends and I built an outdoor hockey rink.	I found out the rink was frozen, and I "suited up."	We warmed up by skating around the rink.	We played a game of hockey.

Outcome We hoped the weather would stay cold, and we couldn't wait to play again.

Reflect

In what ways will a graphic organizer help Josh write?

Apply

Choose a graphic organizer that will help you sequence ideas and events before you write.

Prewrite

Focus on **Organization**

Writing Strategy   Check the graphic organizer against the scoring guide.

There's not much time to revise when you write for a test. That's why prewriting is really important! Before I start to write my draft, I'm going to check my Story Map against the scoring guide in the writing prompt.

Title: "Winter on Ice"
Setting

Where Outdoor hockey rink, behind Austin's barn   **When** Last winter

Major Character Me (Josh)

Minor Character(s) Austin, Colin

Theme Wintertime is fun.

Plot

Event 1	Event 2	Event 3	Event 4
My friends and I built an outdoor hockey rink.	I found out the rink was frozen, and I "suited up."	We warmed up by skating around the rink.	We played a game of hockey.

Outcome We hoped the weather would stay cold, and we couldn't wait to play again.

Ideas

- Be sure you have a focused, complete topic that is supported and enhanced by relevant sensory details.

Like I said, I remember that day really well. As I write, I'll include all the sensory details I can remember.

Organization

- Be sure you write well-organized paragraphs that follow a sequence that unfolds naturally and logically.

My Story Map makes it pretty clear that I should organize my paragraphs in chronological order.

Voice

- Be sure your voice and tone are appropriate for the purpose and audience.

The theme from my Story Map will remind me to use a fun, upbeat tone.

Word Choice

- Be sure you use precise, descriptive language that creates an accurate picture for the reader.

My Story Map only shows the main events, but I don't think it will be hard to avoid dull words when I write. This is an exciting memory!

Sentence Fluency

- Be sure your sentences vary in length and structure to make the writing flow.

As I write, I'll try to use clauses to create a more interesting mix of sentence types.

Conventions

- Be sure your writing contains no or few errors in grammar, usage, mechanics, and spelling.

When I edit my draft, I'll check for proper grammar and mechanics.

Reflect

After checking the Story Map against the scoring guide, do you see anything that Josh forgot to include?

Apply

Before you write, you'll want to reread the writing prompt to be sure you're on track with what needs to be done.

Draft

Focus on **Ideas**

Writing Strategy   Use sensory details throughout.

I have to remember that I'm writing a descriptive vignette. That means the reader should be able to visualize my story. The more sensory details I include, the easier this will be for my reader. Playing outdoor hockey in the winter is something I really enjoy doing, so including details to describe it will be easy.

Now, how should I begin my story? The first event listed on my Story Map is the building of our outdoor hockey rink. I think I'll begin there.

Winter on Ice

by Josh

I remember it like it was yesterday. My friends and I actually built our own outdoor hockey rink!

We set up our rink in a field behind Austin's barn. We laid four 2x4s in a big rectangle on the ground, and we flooded it with water. Since it was already wintertime, all we had to do was weight for the water to freeze. Austin called to say it was time—the rink had frozen.

I immediately went to my closet to pull out my warmest clothes. I stopped when I saw my hockey shorts and jersey. I always wear my team uniform. But today, we would be playing outside! And we wear the most mismatched clothing ever! We wear long pants and sweats, sweatshirts and turtlenecks, knit hats and helmets, and plenty of pads. So I "suited up" in my warmest gear, and I rubbed my toes to warm them before putting on my skates.

Soon we were all on the rink. Although there was snow on the ground, it wasn't snowing at the moment. Other than the action on the ice, everything around us seemed so still. We all skated back and forth across the rink, just to keep warm.

Then Colin dropped the puck. Game on! he shouted. Soon, we were shouting to each other and passing the puck back and forth across the rink. We were sweating through our clothes, and steam was rising from our bodies. The game didn't even matter anymore: We were playing hockey on our very own rink!

After nearly two hours, we were wet and tired. We sat down in the snow banks and realized it was long past time to get a drink. We grabbed our thermoses and started to sip on hot coco, cider, and tea. As we sat there, I realized we weren't only drinking in the frothy liquid, we were also drinking in the sights and sounds of a frozen winter day.

Reflect

How did Josh's sensory details grab your attention?

Apply

Include sensory details throughout your vignette to vividly describe the event.

Revise

Focus on Organization

Writing Strategy   Use transition words to organize events.

Now that my draft is written, I can go back and read it to see what needs to be revised. The scoring guide says my writing should be well organized. I know that transition words, such as *a week later*, *today*, and *after two hours*, all help guide the reader through a story. I found a paragraph that could use some transition words. I will make the revision now.

[added transition words]

We set up our rink in a field behind Austin's barn. We laid four

2x4s in a big rectangle on the ground, and we flooded it with

water. Since it was already wintertime, all we had to do was

About a week later,

weight for the water to freeze. Austin called to say it was

time—the rink had frozen.

Use transition words to organize the events in your descriptive vignette.

Revise

Writing Strategy   Connect with the reader.

The scoring guide says my voice and tone should be appropriate for my audience and purpose. Since I'm describing an experience shared by my friends and me, I'm using an informal tone and first-person point of view. After reading my draft again, I found a place where I can address the reader in a more friendly, relaxed way that might improve the overall tone of my story. What do you think of my revision?

[DRAFT]

[addressed the reader]

I immediately went to my closet to pull out my warmest clothes.

I'll let you in on a secret!

I stopped when I saw my hockey shorts and jersey. I always wear

my team uniform.

Reflect

How does Josh's revision improve the tone of his vignette?

Apply

Use first-person point of view to express a personal experience. Use a friendly and informal tone in your writing to help the reader connect with your story.

Revise

Focus on **Word Choice**

Writing Strategy   Replace vague words with precise words.

I reread my paper once again to see if there was anywhere that needed to be clearer. The scoring guide says I should replace vague words with precise words. I think some of my explanations in the final paragraph are a little dull, so I'll replace them with precise words.

[DRAFT]

[used precise words]

soaked and worn out   plopped

After nearly two hours, we were ~~wet and tired~~. We ~~sat~~ down in

the snow banks and realized it was long past time to ~~get a drink~~.
quench our thirst

Apply

The words that you choose to use in your story make a big difference. Replace dull words with precise words to make your writing lively and original.

Edit

Writing Strategy Check the grammar, punctuation, capitalization, and spelling.

Now there's just one last step. The scoring guide says to check my grammar and mechanics, so I'll read my draft one last time to make sure there aren't any mistakes. If there are, I'll just correct them on the page, so that my teacher can see that I tried my best. I've got five minutes left, so I better get started.

Winter on Ice

by Josh

I remember it like it was yesterday. My friends and I actually built our own outdoor hockey rink!

We set up our rink in a field behind Austin's barn. We laid four 2x4s in a big rectangle on the ground, and we flooded it with water. Since it was already wintertime, all we had to do was ~~weight~~ wait for the water to freeze. About a week later, Austin called to say it was time—the rink had frozen.

I immediately went to my closet to pull out my warmest clothes. I stopped when I saw my hockey shorts and jersey. I'll let you in on a secret! When I play indoors, I always wear my team uniform. But today, we would be playing outside! And when Colin and Austin and I play hockey outside, we wear the most mismatched clothing ever! We wear long pants and

Check your grammar, punctuation, capitalization, and spelling every time you write for a test.

[FINAL DRAFT]

sweats, sweatshirts and turtlenecks, knit hats and helmets, and plenty of pads. So I "suited up" in my warmest gear, and I rubbed my toes to warm them before putting on my skates.

Soon, we were all on the rink*, shushing along and scraping through the ice*. Although there was snow on the ground, it wasn't snowing at the moment. Other than the action on the ice, everything around us seemed so still. We all skated back and forth across the rink, just to keep warm.

Then, Colin dropped the puck. "Game on!" he shouted. Soon, we were shouting to each other and passing the puck back and forth across the rink. We were sweating through our clothes, and steam was rising from our bodies. The game didn't even matter anymore: We were playing hockey on our very own rink!

After nearly two hours, we were ~~wet and tired~~ *soaked and worn out*. We ~~sat~~ *plopped* down in the snow banks and realized it was long past time to ~~get a drink~~ *quench our thirst*. We grabbed our thermoses and started to sip on hot ~~coco~~ *cocoa*, cider, and tea. As we sat there, I realized we weren't only drinking in the frothy liquid, we were also drinking in the sights and sounds of a frozen winter day.

Reflect

What do you think? Is Josh ready to turn in his test? Why or why not? Remember to use your writing prompt's scoring guide to check your writing when you take a test.

I'm done! I never knew taking a test could be so easy! I guess when you use the scoring guide, it really helps out. But also remember to keep in mind these important tips when you write for a test.

TEST TIPS

1. **Study the writing prompt before you start to write.** Most writing prompts have three parts: the setup, the task, and the scoring guide. The parts probably won't be labeled. You'll have to figure them out for yourself!

2. **Make sure you understand the task before you start to write.**

   - Read all three parts of the writing prompt carefully.
   - Circle key words in the task part of the writing prompt that tell what kind of writing you need to do. The task might also identify your audience.
   - Make sure you know how you'll be graded.
   - Say the assignment in your own words to yourself.

3. **Keep an eye on the clock.** Decide how much time you will spend on each part of the writing process and try to stick to your schedule. Don't spend so much time prewriting that you don't have enough time left to write.

4. **Reread your writing. Compare it to the scoring guide at least twice.** Remember the rubrics you've used? A scoring guide on a writing test is like a rubric. It can help you keep what's important in mind.

5. **Plan, plan, plan!** You don't get much time to revise during a test, so planning is more important than ever.

6. **Write neatly.** Remember: If the people who score your test can't read your writing, it doesn't matter how good your essay is!

Appendix A
Grammar Practice

Predicate Nouns

Know the Rule

A **predicate noun** follows a linking verb and tells more about who or what the subject is.

Example:

Anime is an abbreviated **term** for Japanese animation.

Practice the Rule

Number a sheet of paper from 1–10. Write each sentence. Underline the linking verb. Circle each predicate noun.

1. Japanese comic books are the inspiration for some animated films.
2. Japanese video games are resources for animators.
3. One major appeal of anime is the beautiful artwork.
4. Fans point out that anime is a medium for both teens and adults.
5. Two distinctive features of anime characters are large eyes and unusual hair colors.
6. Anime conventions are popular places for fans to meet.
7. Many anime fans are avid collectors of anime merchandise.
8. Anime figures are small statues depicting anime characters.
9. The Japanese were the biggest fans of anime until it gained popularity in the West.
10. One result of anime's popularity is a renewed interest in Japanese culture.

Verbals: Participles and Participial Phrases

Know the Rule

A **verbal** is a word that is formed from a verb but that plays another role in a sentence. One type of verbal is a **participle**. A participle may be a present participle (*observing*) or a past participle (*observed*). A **participial phrase** is made up of a participle and other words that complete its meaning. A participial phrase can act as an adjective. In the following example, *Possessing powerful jaws* is a participial phrase that describes the turtles. *Possessing* is the participle.

Example:

Possessing powerful jaws, loggerhead turtles can crush crabs and other hard-shelled animals.

Practice the Rule

Number a sheet of paper from 1–10. After each number, write the participial phrase in the sentence. Circle the participle.

1. Named for its large head, the loggerhead turtle is a fascinating sea creature.
2. Born on land, loggerheads face many challenges early in life.
3. Using her hind flippers, a female loggerhead digs a hole in the sand to lay her eggs.
4. Leaving the eggs behind, she heads back to the sea.
5. The eggs, lying in their holes, sometimes fall prey to raccoons and other animals.
6. The hatchlings, emerging from the eggs, face new dangers.
7. Climbing out of their sand holes, they begin a perilous journey to the sea.
8. Measuring about two inches long, the hatchlings have to find their way to the ocean.
9. Threatened by fishing nets and other hazards, adult loggerheads face dangers of their own.
10. Laws protecting the turtles from harm are in place but must be enforced.

Verbals: Infinitives and Infinitive Phrases

Know the Rule

An **infinitive** is a phrase made up of the word *to* followed by the present form of a verb (*to climb*). Infinitives may act as adjectives, adverbs, or nouns. An **infinitive phrase** is made up of an infinitive and any other words that complete its meaning.

Example:
I walk by a knitting shop every day and often stop **to look in the window**.

Practice the Rule

Number a sheet of paper from 1–10. For each sentence, write the infinitive phrase and circle the infinitive.

1. I asked my mother to teach me about knitting.
2. She was surprised to hear that request from me.
3. I explained that it didn't seem difficult for a beginner to make scarves.
4. It would be nice to give my friends homemade gifts.
5. Mom asked if I was sure I wanted to work with wool in the heat of the summer.
6. I said that it just might take longer than I think to produce a bunch of scarves.
7. The good news is that I know I will be able to match each person's taste perfectly.
8. Mom got some wool and needles to show me the basics.
9. It wasn't difficult to learn the stitches.
10. I decided it was wise to begin the process early!

Parallel Structure

Know the Rule

A sentence may contain more than one participial phrase or infinitive phrase. Using more than one verbal of the same type to express similar ideas is using **parallel structure**. Using more than one verbal of different types to express similar ideas (*I like to run and listening to music*) is considered poor style and can confuse the reader. In your writing, use parallel structure when expressing two or more similar ideas.

> **Example:**
> **To discover** interesting facts about bugs and **creating** drawings of them are passions of Jaime's. (incorrect)
> **Discovering** interesting facts about bugs and **creating** drawings of them are passions of Jaime's. (correct)

Practice the Rule

Number a sheet of paper from 1–4. Write the correct form of the underlined verbs so that all phrases are parallel in structure.

1. When <u>to show</u> his drawings and telling about the bugs, Jaime is happy.

2. Observing living bugs and <u>to create</u> realistic drawings of them is a special skill.

3. Jaime, having an artistic talent and <u>to find</u> science fascinating, has discovered a career that combines the two fields.

4. <u>To become</u> a scientific illustrator and making detailed drawings of animal and plant life seem perfect.

Number a sheet of paper from 5–8. Write the correct form of the underlined verbs so that all infinitive phrases are parallel in structure.

5. Ayana's aunt gave her a beautiful scarab ring, so Ayana decided to research scarabs and <u>locating</u> pictures of them.

6. She was disappointed to learn that scarabs are dung beetles and <u>seeing</u> photos of dull-looking creatures.

7. She kept looking, though, and soon she was excited <u>discovering</u> tropical scarabs and to see bright, radiant colors.

8. Ayana planned <u>treating</u> her ring with respect and to take good care of it.

Passive and Active Voice

Know the Rule

In sentences written in **active voice,** the subject performs the action. Most sentences are written in active voice because it is generally clear and direct.

Example:
More people **use** computers now than ever before.

In sentences written in **passive voice,** the subject is acted upon, or receives the action. Passive voice is often used in scientific writing. It is also used when the writer wants to emphasize the action or what is acted upon, rather than the doer of the action.

Example:
Computers **are used** by more people now than ever before.

Practice the Rule

Number a sheet of paper from 1–8. Write each sentence. Circle the simple subject; underline the simple predicate. Be sure to include helping verbs. Write **A** if the verb is in the active voice. Write **P** if it is in the passive voice.

1. I volunteered to teach basic computer skills at the senior center.
2. Through my lessons, people were introduced to the Internet.
3. Some people had never used e-mail before.
4. They were amazed by the whole process of e-mail.
5. The mouse baffled a few of my students.
6. Typing on the computer was easy for those people who had used typewriters.
7. A broadband connection was installed by a technician.
8. My students were so excited to receive their first e-mails!

Independent and Dependent Clauses

Know the Rule

An **independent clause** is a group of words with a subject and a predicate that makes sense by itself. An independent clause is a complete sentence. A **dependent clause** has a subject and a predicate, but it does not express a complete thought by itself. It needs—or is dependent on—an independent clause. Often a dependent clause begins with a subordinating conjunction, such as *when, since, now that, because, while, if,* and *as.*

> **Example:**
> The number of hedgehogs in Britain is declining, **even though they are popular animals**. (The clause in dark print is a dependent clause.)

Practice the Rule

Number a sheet of paper from 1–10. Copy the sentences onto your paper. Draw one line under each dependent clause and two lines under each independent clause. Circle the subordinating conjunction that begins the dependent clause.

1. Drivers are a major cause of their decline, since there are so many cars on the road.
2. Hedgehogs come out at night, when they are difficult to see.
3. Because forests and bushes are being cut down, hedgehogs have fewer places to live.
4. Now that people are aware of the problem, they are working to save the animals.
5. Hedgehogs stay at rescue centers while they heal.
6. When a hedgehog is healthy again, it is returned to the wild.
7. Hedgehogs are useful in gardens because they eat insect pests.
8. Since hedgehogs are small and shy, they are not harmful to humans.
9. When a hedgehog is threatened by another animal, it rolls into a ball.
10. Since the hedgehog has sharp spines, predators are discouraged.

Compound and Complex Sentences

Know the Rule

A **compound sentence** is made up of two closely related independent clauses. The clauses can be joined by a comma and a coordinating conjunction (*and*, *but*, or *or*) or by a semicolon (;).

Example:
According to surveys, most shoppers still shop in brick-and-mortar stores; "brick and mortar" means a traditional store with an actual building.

A sentence made up of an independent clause and one or more dependent clauses is a **complex sentence**.

Example:
When they shop online, people are unable to touch the merchandise.

Practice the Rule

Number a sheet of paper from 1–10. After each number, write **compound** if the sentence is a compound sentence or **complex** if it is a complex sentence.

1. People like shopping in stores; it is a social experience.
2. Although shopping online is not a social experience, it is fast and convenient.
3. Some families live far from brick-and-mortar stores, and for them the ability to shop online is a real advantage.
4. When people see empty stores in malls, they assume that online shopping is taking business away from the stores.
5. If the economy is bad, stores may go out of business.
6. Online shoppers find returns difficult; they have to repackage them and mail them back.
7. Some retailers have an online store only, but others also have brick-and-mortar stores.
8. If people think that real stores will disappear, they should visit a mall.
9. Friends gather at malls, and they shop or eat together.
10. Because people are naturally social, technology will never replace the shopping experience.

More Compound-Complex Sentences

Know the Rule

Compound sentences, made up of two closely related independent clauses, and **complex sentences**, made up of an independent clause and a dependent clause, can be combined to make a **compound-complex** sentence. Use a variety of sentences in your writing to make it flow.

Example:

As he was waiting for his job interview, he encountered a good friend who was also interviewing for the job; perhaps there would be a job for each of them.

Practice the Rule

Number a sheet of paper from 1–8. Identify each sentence as either **compound, complex,** or **compound-complex**.

1. It was eight o'clock at night, and Deon was finally finishing up his work, when his boss walked into the office with a pile of papers.

2. As Deon looked at the papers glumly, his boss surprised him by offering Deon a promotion.

3. As she continued doing boring work, Kaylee hoped her job would get more interesting, or she would have to look for another job.

4. When she answered her cell phone, her friend Nicole told her about a great job that Kaylee should apply for immediately.

5. Although Kaylee didn't think she did well in her interview, she was offered the job, and so she took Nicole out to dinner.

6. Evan studied economics in college, and he found a great job at a university in Chicago.

7. At first he didn't know whether he would like the job, but after a while he decided it was a good fit for him.

8. After applying for several jobs, Nicole chose a job as a teacher, even though she wanted to go into publishing.

Adjective Clauses

Know the Rule

An **adjective clause** is a dependent clause that describes a noun or a pronoun. An adjective clause always follows the word it describes and begins with a relative pronoun such as *who, whom, whose, which,* or *that.*

Example:
Dr. Maya Angelou, **who was born in Missouri in 1928**, faced the racial discrimination of the times.

Practice the Rule

Number a sheet of paper from 1–10. Write the adjective clause in each sentence. Then write the noun it describes.

1. Dr. Maya Angelou, who is a poet and strong civil rights activist, is celebrated throughout the world.

2. Her career, which was considerably varied, included being the first female cable car conductor.

3. As a single mother, who was raising her son alone, she worked any job she could find.

4. However, it was her artistic talents that led to fame.

5. By the 1950s, Angelou, whose talents were praised everywhere, had found her passion.

6. It was her international travels that led her to writing.

7. She worked with Dr. Martin Luther King, whose assassination devastated her.

8. Not long after this event, she wrote *I Know Why the Caged Bird Sings*, which received worldwide acclaim.

9. For President Clinton's inauguration, she composed a poem that was broadcast around the world.

10. She has written more than thirty titles, which have all been best sellers.

Adverb Clauses

Know the Rule

An **adverb clause** is a dependent clause that tells about a verb, an adjective, or an adverb. Adverb clauses tell where, when, why, or how much. They often begin with a subordinating conjunction such as *than, although, after, because, if, as, so that, while, when,* or *whenever.* Put a comma after the clause when it begins the sentence.

Example:
We carried our empty bottles to the store **because we wanted to recycle them. Because the store was closed,** we brought the bottles home.

Practice the Rule

Number a sheet of paper from 1–10. After each number, write the adverb clause in the sentence.

1. I save bottles and cans so that I can recycle them.
2. If I take them back to the store, I receive a refund.
3. Whenever I see cans lying on the sidewalk, I pick them up.
4. Bottles and cans are reused after they are recycled.
5. Companies use much less energy when they make products from recycled materials.
6. Whenever people recycle goods, they help to create jobs.
7. Because recycling has become more common, new jobs have been created.
8. If it is recycled, glass can be used indefinitely.
9. Many people donate books and clothing to charities so that the items can be reused.
10. We keep newspapers and magazines because we know we can recycle them.

Conventions: Grammar, Usage & Mechanics

Noun Clauses

Know the Rule

When a dependent clause acts as a noun, it is called a **noun clause**. It begins with a relative pronoun, such as *who, which, how, what,* or *that.*

- A noun clause can be the subject of a verb.
    Example:
    That you have ten pairs of jeans amazes me.

- A noun clause can be the object of a verb.
    Example:
    I believe **that you love clothes**.

Practice the Rule

Number a sheet of paper from 1–10. After each number, write the noun clause in the sentence. Tell whether the clause is the **subject** or **object** of the verb.

1. I think that there is an ATM in the supermarket.
2. That I have overdrawn my account shocks me.
3. Who spent all the money is a mystery.
4. Now I realize what must be done.
5. I know which store I should go to.
6. I wonder what nice things I'll find on sale there.
7. That you are still spending money surprises me.
8. You should learn how you can budget your money.
9. I understand that I handle my money poorly.
10. I need to learn how I can improve my spending habits.

Appendix A: Grammar Practice 513

Verbals: Gerunds and Gerund Phrases

Know the Rule

A **gerund** is a verbal that acts as a noun. All gerunds are verb forms that end in *-ing*. A **gerund phrase** is made up of a gerund and the other words that complete its meaning. Gerund phrases add information to sentences.

> **Example:**
> **Stepping on a cat's tail** is not recommended.

Practice the Rule

Number a sheet of paper from 1–10. After each number, write the gerund phrase and circle the gerund.

1. Playing with your cat gives both of you exercise.
2. Stroking a soft, fluffy cat relaxes many people.
3. Cats decide if they can fit in a space by testing the width with their whiskers.
4. Sleeping up to sixteen hours a day is normal for a cat.
5. Grooming itself uses up another chunk of a cat's day.
6. Talking to your cat adds to its sense of security.
7. Having a lifespan of fifteen years is average for an indoor cat.
8. One way a cat shows it is happy is by kneading with its paws.
9. Owning pets helps people live longer, have less stress, and suffer fewer heart attacks.
10. An indoor cat can enjoy safe outdoor time by learning to walk on a leash.

Concrete and Abstract Nouns

Know the Rule

A **concrete noun** names something recognized by your senses—sight, hearing, smell, touch, and taste (*apple, dog, thunder*). An **abstract noun** names something that is not recognized by your senses, such as an idea, a quality, or an emotion (*love, fear, happiness*).

Practice the Rule

Number a sheet of paper from 1–10. After each number, write the noun(s) in the sentence. Underline abstract nouns once and concrete nouns twice.

1. Leshawn didn't think he had any acting talent.
2. It took a lot of courage for him to audition.
3. When he got the lead role, he thought he was headed for failure.
4. He was amazed by his success and filled with relief.
5. Leshawn's favorite part was when the curtain rose.
6. Applause filled the auditorium.
7. Leshawn was excited as he stepped onstage for the first time.
8. The play was a huge success.
9. Leshawn's friends shared in his happiness.
10. Leshawn now knows the thrill of being on the stage.

Singular and Plural Nouns

Know the Rule

A **singular noun** names one person, place, thing, or idea. A **plural noun** names more than one.

Most nouns add -s or -es to form the plural. The spelling of some nouns changes when -es is added to form the plural (*story, stories; shelf, shelves*). A few nouns do not add -s or -es to form the plural; instead, they change spelling (*mouse, mice*). A few other nouns have the same form in the singular and plural (*sheep, sheep*).

Practice the Rule

Number a sheet of paper from 1–10. After each number, write the nouns in the sentence. Underline singular nouns once and plural nouns twice.

1. The giant saguaro cactuses are native to Arizona.
2. The largest cactuses are more than fifty feet tall.
3. Saguaros can live for two centuries.
4. The cactuses are sometimes called the condos of the desert.
5. They provide homes and shelter for many animals.
6. Woodpeckers make nesting holes in the cactuses.
7. A saguaro doesn't bloom until it has lived about fifty years.
8. The flowers come out only at night and are pollinated by bats, hummingbirds, and other birds.
9. When it is very dry in the desert, animals such as deer and rabbits nibble at the cactus for moisture.
10. Pack rats, desert foxes, and other animals may seek shelter in the shade of the cactus.

Possessive Pronouns

Know the Rule

Possessive pronouns show ownership or a close relationship.
- The possessive pronouns *her, his, its, their, my, our,* and *your* can replace possessive nouns.

    Example:
    Daniel's action figures are pretty cool. **His** action figures are pretty cool.

- The possessive pronouns *hers, his, theirs, mine, ours,* and *yours* can replace a noun that is a possession.

    Example:
    Daniel's collection is bigger than my collection. Daniel's collection is bigger than **mine**.

- The possessive pronoun *his* can replace both a possessive noun and the noun that is a possession.

    Example:
    Those action figures are Daniel's. Those action figures are **his**.

Practice the Rule

Number a sheet of paper from 1–10. After each number, write the possessive pronoun in the sentence. There may be more than one.

1. My oldest sister, Katelyn, is selling many of her dolls at an online auction.
2. Her photos show all of the dolls' features, even their faults.
3. Katelyn wants her buyers to be happy with their purchases.
4. My brother, Daniel, noticed her success and decided to sell his action figures.
5. One of his rare figures brought a very good price.
6. They are saving their money for things they prefer now that they are older.
7. "Why don't you sell your old train set?" Daniel asked my father.
8. "No way," replied Dad. "It's mine, and it isn't going anywhere."
9. "We're glad these collections of ours are no longer taking up room," my brother responded.
10. I wanted to sell my old teddy bear, but my sister pointed out that it is missing its eyes and some of its fur.

Relative and Interrogative Pronouns

Know the Rule

When the pronouns *who, whom, whose, which,* and *that* are used to introduce an adjective clause, they are called **relative pronouns**. A relative pronoun always follows the noun described by the adjective clause it begins.

Example:
The little gadget **that** is called a cell phone has become very popular.

When the pronouns *who, whom, whose, which,* and *what* are used to begin a question, they are called **interrogative pronouns**.

Examples:
Whose cell phone is this?

Practice the Rule

Number a sheet of paper from 1–10. After each number, write the relative or interrogative pronoun in the sentence. Identify each relative pronoun by writing **R** next to it and each interrogative pronoun by writing **I**.

1. Who invented the cell phone?
2. It was Martin Cooper whose pioneering work led to the first cell phone.
3. The police car radio, which was invented in the 1940s, was the inspiration for the cell phone.
4. Cooper, who made the first actual cell phone in 1973, applied new technology to the car phone to make it portable.
5. What were the first cell phones like?
6. Cell phones that were made available to the public in 1984 were very large and expensive.
7. The first cell phone, which weighed two pounds, cost $3,995.00.
8. Early buyers, whose coat pockets could hardly hold such a phone, used it as their car phone.
9. The first cell phone started a revolution in design and function that continues today.
10. Cell phones, which now do so much, are definitely not just for talking anymore.

Demonstrative Pronouns and Adjectives

Know the Rule

This, these, that, and *those* are **demonstratives**. **Demonstrative adjectives** describe nouns and tell which one.

> **Example:**
> **This** photograph shows a camel with two humps.

Demonstrative pronouns take the place of nouns. *This* and *these* refer to a thing or things close by. *That* and *those* refer to a thing or things farther away.

> **Example:**
> **Those** are camels with one hump instead of two.

Practice the Rule

Number a sheet of paper from 1–10. Copy the sentences on your paper. Circle each demonstrative pronoun. Underline each demonstrative adjective.

1. These camels have saddles.
2. This camel is the calmest and easiest to ride.
3. Those have especially bad tempers.
4. Notice that this camel is kneeling down, ready for a rider to climb on.
5. Riding these is different from riding horses.
6. Like all camels, this one will sway from side to side.
7. Those saddles have no stirrups, so riders must grip with their knees.
8. Once a rider gets used to that motion, the ride is quite enjoyable.
9. These camels' ancestors were ridden thousands of years ago.
10. Those early camels carried both freight and riders, much like camels do today.

Action Verbs and Linking Verbs

Know the Rule

An **action verb** shows action. It usually tells what the subject of a sentence or clause is doing, will do, or did. An action verb may include one or more helping verbs in addition to the main verb.

Example:
I **read** about poison frogs.

A **linking verb** connects the subject of a sentence to a word(s) that describes or renames the subject. Linking verbs are often forms of *to be*, such as *am, is, was, were, been*, and *will be*. The verbs *become, seem, appear*, and *look* can also be used as linking verbs. A linking verb may include one or more helping verbs in addition to the main verb.

Example:
Poison dart frogs **are** dangerous.

Practice the Rule

Number a sheet of paper from 1–10. Write each verb from the sentences. Label it as an **action** verb or a **linking** verb.

1. Poison dart frogs live in the rain forests of Central and South America.

2. These frogs are some of the most beautiful rain forest creatures.

3. The frogs seem harmless at first sight.

4. Yet their bright colors warn of their poisonous nature.

5. The golden dart frog is the most dangerous of all.

6. Its poison can kill 10,000 rats or seven or more humans.

7. Some Amerindian tribes make poison darts from the frogs' poison.

8. A female frog lays about seven eggs.

9. The male frog tends the eggs until they hatch.

10. Then he carries the tadpoles on his back to a pond.

Emphatic Present and Past Tense

Know the Rule

To give force or emphasis to a verb, use the **emphatic forms** of the verb. The emphatic form is often used to answer a question.

- The **present emphatic** is made by adding the auxiliary *do* or *does* to the present tense of the verb.
  Example:
  I **do feed** the dog every day.

- To form the **past emphatic**, add *did* to the present tense.
  Example:
  I **did walk** the dog this afternoon.

Practice the Rule

Number a sheet of paper from 1–10. After each number, write an answer to the question. Use the emphatic form of the verb.

1. Do you realize that a dog needs lots of care?

2. Does a dog require care and attention?

3. Did you take care of a dog before?

4. Do you want your own dog?

5. Do you think Kya wants you to adopt a puppy?

6. Did you pick out the puppy you want?

7. Does the puppy want to go home with you?

8. Did she explain how to care for the puppy?

9. Are you sure you have time to care for a puppy?

10. Do you believe you and the puppy are meant to be together?

 **Grammar, Usage & Mechanics**

Transitive and Intransitive Verbs

Know the Rule

A **transitive verb** is an action verb that transfers its action to a direct object.
> **Example:**
> Rafael **planted** a garden.

An **intransitive verb** does not have a direct object. An intransitive verb shows action that the subject does alone. Many verbs can be either transitive or intransitive, depending on whether there is a direct object. One way to tell whether a verb is transitive or intransitive is to ask *What?* or *Whom?* after it. If those questions can't be answered, the verb is intransitive.
> **Example:**
> Even in the city, the garden **thrives**.

Practice the Rule

Number a sheet of paper from 1–10. After each number, write **intransitive** if the underlined verb is intransitive or **transitive** if it is transitive.

1. Vegetables <u>grow</u> in that part of the garden.
2. Rafael <u>waters</u> the garden every day.
3. Some worms <u>ate</u> the tomatoes.
4. Rafael <u>complained</u> about the worms.
5. Those marigolds <u>keep</u> some pests away.
6. Rafael <u>gardens</u> after school.
7. He <u>pulls</u> the weeds.
8. He <u>plans</u> his garden in the winter.
9. Those flowers <u>make</u> the garden even more colorful.
10. Next year, he will <u>grow</u> herbs, too.

Adverbs

Know the Rule

Adverbs modify verbs, adjectives, or other adverbs. They tell how, when, where, or to what extent (how much). Many adverbs end in *-ly* (*carefully*). Other common adverbs are *fast, very, often, again, sometimes, soon, only, too, later, first, then, there, far,* and *now.*

Practice the Rule

Number a sheet of paper from 1–10. After each number, write the adverb in the sentence and the word it modifies.

1. Many people react fearfully to bats.
2. Bats are very useful to humans.
3. They use their sharp, curved claws to hold firmly to their roosts.
4. They sleep peacefully during the day.
5. At night, they fly swiftly into the dark to hunt for insects.
6. They benefit humans because they often eat mosquitoes and other annoying insects.
7. Austin, Texas, has an impressively large number of bats that live under the Congress Bridge.
8. Crowds gather nightly to watch as 1.5 million bats shoot out into the darkness.
9. Bats find insects by using their exceptionally sensitive ears.
10. The bats emit extremely high-frequency sounds that bounce off surrounding objects and tell bats where the objects are.

Prepositions

Know the Rule

A **preposition** shows a relationship between the noun or pronoun that follows the preposition (the **object of the preposition**) and another word or group of words in the sentence. The preposition, its object, and the word(s) between them make a **prepositional phrase**. Prepositional phrases add information to sentences.

Examples:
Gabríel García Márquez has written novels **about a town named Macondo**.
Unusual events take place **in Macondo**.

Practice the Rule

Number a sheet of paper from 1–10. After each number, write the prepositional phrase(s) in the sentence and circle the preposition(s).

1. Author Gabríel García Márquez is best known for his book *One Hundred Years of Solitude* (*Cien Años de Soledad*).

2. The novel tells the story of a fictional town named Macondo.

3. Life in Macondo is wonderful and strange, since unreal events happen every day.

4. Although the book is about Macondo, it touches upon things that we all experience in life.

5. García Márquez sees magic in everyday life, and through his books readers may find the magic in their own lives.

6. The author was born in Colombia and started his career as a journalist.

7. He worked in Europe, Cuba, and Latin America, among other locations.

8. Although his books have fantastical elements, they tell about important topics, such as poverty.

9. García Márquez was awarded the Nobel Prize for Literature in 1982.

10. *One Hundred Years of Solitude* is still the most popular of all his novels.

Correlative Conjunctions

Know the Rule

Correlative conjunctions always appear in pairs. They connect words or groups of words and provide more emphasis than coordinating conjunctions. Some common correlative conjunctions are *both… and, either… or, neither… nor, not only… but (also)*, and *whether… or*.

Example:
Both the eating utensils we use **and** the way we use them are the result of centuries of experimentation.

Practice the Rule

Number a sheet of paper from 1–10. After each number, write the correlative conjunction pair in the sentence.

1. In ancient times, people used either carved stones or shells as spoons.

2. By the fifth century, a knife served as both a weapon and an eating utensil.

3. During the Middle Ages, people used neither a knife nor a spoon because most of them ate with their hands.

4. Forks had been invented by the sixteenth century, but were considered both amusing and pretentious.

5. By the seventeenth century, though, forks were used not only to hold food steady as a knife cut it, but also to carry the food to one's mouth.

6. The ends of knives became blunted, either for comfort or to keep them from being used as weapons.

7. During the Victorian era, all kinds of utensils appeared, whether they were necessary or not.

8. In the eighteenth century, neither forks nor sharp knives were exported to America.

9. Americans had to use spoons both to steady food while cutting and, switching the spoon to the other hand, to scoop up the food.

10. Whether by habit or desire, Americans still switch the utensil, now a fork, from one hand to the other after cutting.

Negatives

Know the Rule

A **negative** is a word that means "no" or "not." The words *no, not, nothing, none, never, nowhere,* and *nobody* are negatives. The negative word *not* is found in contractions such as *don't* and *wasn't.* Use only one negative in a sentence to express a negative idea. Use the contraction *doesn't* with singular subjects, including *he, she,* and *it.* Use the contraction *don't* with plural subjects, including *we* and *they.* Also use *don't* with *I* and *you.* Avoid the use of *ain't.*

Examples:
Many quilts **don't** contain **no** messages, but some special ones do. (incorrect)
Many quilts **don't** contain messages, but some special ones do. (correct)

Practice the Rule

Number a sheet of paper from 1–10. Write the negative word that completes each sentence correctly.

1. Before and during the American Civil War, slaves _____ allowed to learn reading or writing.

2. Writing _____ the only way for clever people to send messages.

3. Code words and phrases were created that could be understood by _____ except those who were taught the code.

4. Some say that quilts were used to give directions to the Underground Railroad, though others say they _____.

5. Those quilts _____ on beds but were hung over railings to air, where everybody could see them.

6. A quilt _____ have to be just a decorative covering for a bed.

7. Quilts held memories for pioneers because they _____ made out of new fabric, but rather from pieces of worn clothing.

8. Through the years, quilts _____ always been the most popular form of art, but there have always been quilters.

9. Modern quilts _____ without memories, since they often recognize events in our country or call attention to problems.

10. Who _____ heard of the AIDS quilt, a huge quilt that was made as a memorial to the lives of people who died from the disease?

Compound Words

Know the Rule

A **compound word** is formed when two or more words are joined to form a new word that has its own meaning. There are three types of compound words.

- **Closed compounds** are written as single words (*goldfish*, *newspaper*).
- **Hyphenated compounds** are separated by hyphens (*mother-in-law*, *editor-in-chief*).
- **Open compounds** are written as separate words (*high school*, *post office*).

Practice the Rule

Number a sheet of paper from 1–10. After each number, write the compound word(s) in the sentence. Then write which kind of compound word it is.

1. Ali's mother and stepfather decided to move.
2. This upset Ali because she loved her high school.
3. Ali did not want to be uprooted from the only home she had lived in since she was born.
4. Ali's mother had been offered the position of vice president in her company if she moved.
5. The company was a start-up that was doing very well.
6. This was a big decision, but everyone knew that everything would work out somehow.
7. Before long Ali and her family were sitting in the waiting room of a real estate agent.
8. The Lamberts chose a house with lots of sunlight and a garden filled with wildflowers.
9. Ali was excited to have her own bedroom.
10. To celebrate the decision, the Lamberts went for ice cream.

Verb Moods

Know the Rule

The **indicative mood** is very common. It is used to express facts or information.
Example:
Mike always crosses the street in a crosswalk.

The **imperative mood** is also quite common. Use it to give orders or make requests.
Example:
Be careful crossing the street.

The **conditional mood** expresses the likeliness of an event happening. The word *if* is used with a verb that conveys whether something is very likely or not very likely to happen.
Examples:
If you run out into the street, you will get hit by a car. (The situation hasn't happened yet, but it is very likely.)
If you ran out into the street, you would need an ambulance. (The situation hasn't happened yet, but the situation is not very likely.)

The **subjunctive mood** is not very common. One of its uses is in a dependent clause attached to an independent clause that uses an adjective, such as *essential* or *important*, to express urgency. The third-person form of the verb drops the *–s*.
Example:
It is important that David take care when crossing the street.

Practice the Rule

Number a sheet of paper from 1–8. Write the name of the mood that is expressed in each sentence.

1. The London Eye opened in 2000.
2. It looks like a giant Ferris wheel.
3. The London Eye is the fourth tallest structure in London.
4. If you ride to the top, you will be able to see 25 miles.
5. It is necessary that a visitor purchase tickets in advance.
6. The lines can get very long during school vacation times.
7. If you got there too late, you would never get to ride on the London Eye.
8. Be sure to visit the London Eye when you go to London.

Abbreviations

Know the Rule

An **abbreviation** is a shortened form of a word. **Titles of respect** are usually abbreviated. So are words in **addresses**, such as Street (*St.*), Avenue (*Ave.*), and Boulevard (*Blvd.*). The names of **days**, the names of most **months**, and certain words in the names of **businesses** are often abbreviated in informal notes. These abbreviations begin with a capital letter and end with a period. An **initial** can replace a person's or a place's name. The initial is written as a capital letter followed by a period.

Practice the Rule

Number a sheet of paper from 1–10. Write the correct abbreviations for the underlined words. Remember to add periods where necessary.

1. <u>President</u> Ulysses S. Grant served in office from 1869 to 1877.
2. <u>Doctor</u> Susanne Weinberg is a surgeon.
3. She is a member of the American Medical <u>Association</u>.
4. I much prefer the month of <u>August</u> to the month of <u>February</u>.
5. Robert <u>Edward</u> Lee commanded the Confederate Army during the Civil War.
6. <u>Friday</u>, or maybe <u>Saturday</u>, has to be the best day of the week.
7. <u>Professor</u> Elise Berwick is my neighbor.
8. We live on Forest <u>Boulevard</u>, just west of Strathmore <u>Road</u>.
9. Harold J. Freeman <u>Senior</u> is Harry's father.
10. I didn't know you lived in <u>Saint</u> Louis, <u>Mister</u> Mendez.

Acronyms

Know the Rule

An **acronym** is formed from the first letters of two or more words and pronounced as a single word. Some acronyms, such *NASA* (*National Aeronautics and Space Administration*) are written in capital letters. Others, such as *scuba* (*self-contained underwater breathing apparatus*), are written as regular lowercase words.

An **initialism** is a type of acronym in which each letter is pronounced separately (*DJ*). In formal writing, write out all the words the first time they appear.

Practice the Rule

Number a sheet of paper from 1–12. Next to each number, write the words from which the acronym is formed. Check a dictionary or look online for each acronym or initialism to see if your response is correct.

1. PIN
2. IQ
3. IM
4. LOL
5. URL
6. EU
7. DVD
8. FAQ
9. ATM
10. FYI
11. radar
12. ASAP

Parentheses

Know the Rule

Parentheses are used to set off explanations and information that are useful but not necessary. This kind of information is called nonessential or nonrestrictive.
   Example:
   The phoenix **(a bird)** is on the flag of San Francisco.

Practice the Rule

Number a sheet of paper from 1–10. After each number, write the word(s) or phrase(s) that should be in parentheses in that sentence.

1. There are many legends about the phoenix pronounced **fee** • nix.

2. It is said that the phoenix visits one place a cool well every morning.

3. There it sings a song that is so beautiful, even the golden star the sun stops to listen.

4. The phoenix has a colorful plumage feathers that is predominately a golden red and purple.

5. If the phoenix is injured, it can heal itself and lives for five centuries 500 years or longer.

6. At the end of its life, legend says that it builds a nest of aromatic spices spices that smell sweet.

7. Once in the nest, it sets the nest and itself on fire, until only ashes are left that is not the end of the story.

8. Not long after, the phoenix rises from the ashes and begins its life anew again, but in a different way.

9. Because of this, the phoenix is associated connected with rebirth being born again.

10. The phoenix is also connected with comfort because of its powers of healing and regeneration growing whole again.

Semicolons

Know the Rule

A **semicolon** can be used instead of a comma and a conjunction to separate the independent clauses in a compound sentence. It can also be used before a conjunctive adverb that joins the clauses. A conjunctive adverb is followed by a comma.

Examples:
My friends were ready to leave, **but** I was not. (comma and conjunction)
My friends were ready to leave; I was not. (semicolon)
My friends were ready to leave; **however,** I was not. (semicolon and conjunctive adverb)

Practice the Rule

Number a sheet of paper from 1–10. Copy the sentences onto your paper. Use a semicolon to separate the clauses.

1. Jenna and Ana wanted to go to the mall I didn't.

2. I think hanging out there is a waste of time however, they don't.

3. I suggested going to a movie nevertheless, they preferred the mall.

4. Ana said she was meeting someone there she wouldn't say who.

5. I texted my friend Emily to see if she wanted to go for a run indeed, she did.

6. We talked as we ran it was really fun.

7. Afterwards, we watched an old movie it was kind of cool.

8. I talked to Jenna later that night Ana's friend never showed up.

9. They were bored waiting around consequently, they went to a movie.

10. It was a really good movie I'll get Emily to see it with me.

Conventions # Conventions Grammar, Usage & Mechanics

More Practice

Predicate Nouns

Number a sheet of paper from 1–8. Write each sentence. Underline the subject and the predicate noun. Circle the linking verb.

1. The play is a mystery.
2. Antonio and Kate are the lead actors.
3. I'm glad our drama teacher is the narrator.
4. Mr. McGuire will be the costumer.
5. When the police examine the evidence, Kate will be a suspect.
6. Antonio remains her ally.
7. As the play goes on, Antonio and Kate become a team.
8. The end is quite a surprise.

Participial Phrases

Number a sheet of paper from 1–5. After each number, write the participial phrase in the sentence. Circle the participle.

1. Hearing an unusual noise, the rabbit froze.
2. Twitching his nose, he smelled a fox.
3. He stood like a statue, filled with fear.
4. The rabbit raced in the other direction, terrified by the close call.
5. Hopping quickly across the field, he reached his burrow.

Infinitive Phrases

Number a sheet of paper from 1–5. For each sentence, write the infinitive phrase.

1. Raul decided to build his own computer.
2. He couldn't afford to buy the powerful computer he wanted.
3. He knew he needed to find some instructions and tips.
4. To locate the information on the Internet was too time consuming.
5. He went to the library to look for help and found exactly what he needed.

More Practice

Parallel Structure

Number a sheet of paper from 1–5. Write each sentence, correcting the verb in parentheses so that it has a parallel structure.

1. I enjoy telling stories at the library and (watch) the children's expressions.
2. Locating folktales to learn and (tell) to the children is fun.
3. When I find a tale I think they will like, I learn it by saying the words out loud and (practice) where I will pause.
4. I can tell that the children are enjoying it and (hope) for more.
5. By watching a real storyteller, I learned to read at a good pace and (use) lots of expression.

Active and Passive Voice

Number a sheet of paper from 1–5. Write whether each sentence is **active** or **passive.**

1. Adopting good eating habits makes sense.
2. Recommendations for daily servings of fruits and vegetables have been made by experts.
3. Common sense tells us to avoid eating too much fried food.
4. Instead of drinking soda, drink plain water.
5. Your eating habits will be determined by you and you alone.

Independent and Dependent Clauses

Number a sheet of paper from 1–5. Copy the sentences onto your paper. Draw one line under each dependent clause and two lines under each independent clause. Circle the subordinate conjunction that begins the dependent clause.

1. It was a beautiful day at the start of our hike, although that soon changed.
2. As the sun disappeared behind the clouds, a strong wind began to blow.
3. When the rain started, we couldn't find any shelter.
4. When Jaden saw a hole in the rock wall above, we headed for it as quickly as possible.
5. It was a cave large enough to protect us, unless something big and scary lived in it.

More Practice

Compound and Complex Sentences

Number a sheet of paper from 1–5. After each number, write **compound** if the sentence is a compound sentence, or **complex** if it is a complex sentence.

1. Our next-door neighbor was evicted because the bank foreclosed on his loan.
2. All his furniture was out on the sidewalk; it was really sad.
3. He was an elderly man, and he had always been very nice to us.
4. Because I knew he had no relatives, I asked my parents if we could help him.
5. We stored his furniture in the basement, and we let him use the spare room.

Adjective Clauses

Number a sheet of paper from 1–5. Write the adjective clause in each sentence. Then write the noun it describes.

1. Elena, who grew up in Mexico, is in charge of our Cinco de Mayo celebration.
2. Cinco de Mayo, which means the fifth of May, is a holiday celebrating a Mexican victory many years ago.
3. I'm glad it's a celebration that inspires people like Elena to throw a big party.
4. Elena, whose party skills are well known, decorated the gym with tissue paper flowers and streamers in the colors of the Mexican flag.
5. She and our DJ chose Mexican music that was modern, lively, and perfect for a party.

Adverb Clauses

Number a sheet of paper from 1–5. After each number, write the adverb clause in the sentence.

1. When my cousin was training for the Coast Guard, he had the opportunity to sail around the world on a large, old-fashioned sailing ship.
2. We received beautiful postcards from amazing places while he was gone.
3. After they set anchor in a port, they had several days to explore the city.
4. When he returned, my cousin showed us the pictures he'd taken on his trip.
5. I think my life would be complete if I had the chance to take such a trip.

More Practice

Noun Clauses

Number a sheet of paper from 1–5. After each number, write the noun clause in the sentence.

1. I don't think that I would like to live in the city.
2. How I would manage with all the people, I just don't know.
3. I wouldn't know which bus I should take to get to school.
4. That the city offers many things to do doesn't change my mind.
5. I just know that I like where I am living now.

Gerunds and Gerund Phrases

Number a sheet of paper from 1–5. After each number, write the gerund phrase.

1. Living on an island is not for everyone.
2. Growing up on one makes me feel lucky, though.
3. Living in a small town is very similar to island life.
4. One of the hardest things is waiting for a boat to bring your mail and groceries.
5. Hearing a foghorn always reminds me of the island.

Concrete and Abstract Nouns

Number a sheet of paper from 1–5. After each number, write the noun(s) in the sentence. Underline abstract nouns once and concrete nouns twice.

1. Riding my bike on the path along the river always brings me peace.
2. For some reason sadness just disappears.
3. It isn't long before joy takes its place.
4. When I am back in my home, some tiredness does set in.
5. I know that I will sleep soundly through the night.

More Practice

Singular and Plural Nouns

Number a sheet of paper from 1–5. After each number, write the noun(s) in the sentence. Underline singular nouns once and plural nouns twice.

1. Technology has changed daily life.
2. Computers are used in just about every office.
3. No one uses a typewriter any longer.
4. Cell phones make it very easy to make phone calls.
5. Besides phone calls, cell phones can take pictures and connect to the Internet.

Possessive Pronouns

Number a sheet of paper from 1–5. After each number, write the possessive pronoun(s) in the sentence.

1. "Your cat has been eating the bird seed in my feeder," said a note from our neighbor.
2. My brother and I went next door to explain that, if a cat was doing that, it wasn't ours.
3. We decided to keep watch on her yard.
4. Sure enough, we saw a squirrel enjoying its fill of bird seed.
5. My brother took pictures with his cell phone, and when we showed them to our neighbor, she apologized for her mistake.

Relative and Interrogative Pronouns

Number a sheet of paper from 1–5. After each number, write the relative or interrogative pronoun in the sentence. Write **R** next to each relative pronoun and **I** next to each interrogative pronoun.

1. Who left all these books on the stairs?
2. Sarah, who had just been to the library, admitted the books were hers.
3. The books, which were for her term paper, would give her most of the information she needed.
4. Internet sites that covered the topics would give her additional information.
5. The paper, which was due in two days, would cause some sleepless nights.

More Practice

Demonstrative Pronouns and Adjectives

Number a sheet of paper from 1–5. Copy these sentences onto your paper. Underline each demonstrative pronoun. Circle each demonstrative adjective.

1. These are pictures of a new species of frog.
2. This frog is amazing because of how its color changes.
3. Look at those mountains in the pictures.
4. They are in Papua, New Guinea, where that frog was discovered.
5. It lives in that forest on the mountaintop.

Action Verbs and Linking Verbs

Number a sheet of paper from 1–5. Copy the sentences onto your paper. Underline each action verb once and each linking verb twice.

1. That coffee tastes strong.
2. It appears to be a day old.
3. I tasted one of those cookies.
4. Suddenly my dog appeared in the kitchen.
5. I tossed a piece of cookie to him.

Emphatic Present and Past Tense

Number a sheet of paper from 1–5. After each number, write the emphatic verb in the sentence. If there is no emphatic verb, write **none**.

1. Yes, I do want to go skiing.
2. My dad won't let me go with you, though.
3. He is afraid because I have never skied before.
4. You did tell me that your father would teach me how.
5. He and my mother would rather be there with me when I learn.

More Practice

Transitive and Intransitive Verbs

Number a sheet of paper from 1–5. After each number, write the verb in the sentence. Write **I** if the verb is intransitive; write **T** if it is transitive.

1. That plant thrives in the south window.
2. Those cactuses just arrived.
3. You should place them in a south window.
4. The cactus blooms in the spring.
5. I will water the philodendron.

Adverbs

Number a sheet of paper from 1–5. After each number, write the adverb(s) in the sentence and the word it modifies.

1. I wish school did not start as early as it does.
2. Getting up at 6:30 A.M. is very hard for me.
3. At least my school is located nearby.
4. If my mom drives me, I can get there easily and quickly.
5. Only once did I arrive late for school.

Prepositions

Number a sheet of paper from 1–5. After each number, write the prepositional phrase or phrases in the sentence.

1. My horse always greets me by trotting to the fence.
2. She knows that I will have an apple for her.
3. When we head out for a ride, her foal always goes along.
4. The little one always stays near her mother.
5. On the way to our home, I let the horses stop and take a drink of water.

More Practice

Correlative Conjunctions

Number a sheet of paper from 1–5. After each number, write the correlative conjunction pair in the sentence.

1. Oral history is not only a way to learn about the past, but sometimes it is the only way to hear some stories.

2. Some older people who remember past events have either not learned to write or don't think their stories are important enough to write about.

3. Whether they think their stories are important or not, the stories are interesting to historians.

4. Almost all people have lived through major events in our country's history and remember both the events and how they felt at the time.

5. Neither history books nor old newspapers can capture what everyday life was like for people.

Negatives

Number a sheet of paper from 1–5. Write the word(s) that correctly completes each sentence.

1. Hasan tells his parents that he doesn't want to go to (any/no) college.

2. There's not (nothing/a thing) that is more important to him than music.

3. There isn't (anywhere/nowhere) he can learn as much as he can with his band.

4. Nobody else in the band wants to go to college (either/neither).

5. It will be a problem, though, if the band (doesn't have/has) no success.

Compound Words

Number a sheet of paper from 1–5. After each number, write the compound word(s) in the sentence.

1. Isabella was so absent-minded that she put her T-shirt on inside out and wore different colored socks.

2. It was bad enough that she thought it was the weekend and not a school day.

3. At noontime she realized she had left her lunch on the countertop at home.

4. Isabella decided she was overburdened with homework and after-school activities.

5. She needed to organize her day-to-day routines.

More Practice

Verb Moods

Number a sheet of paper from 1–5. Write the name of the mood (**indicative, imperative, subjunctive, conditional**) that is expressed in each sentence.

1. If I could play the guitar, I would be a famous rock star.
2. It is necessary that a person practice hard in order to become a musician.
3. Even when a person is very good at an instrument, practice is important.
4. Some people practice for many hours every day.
5. Play a song for me, please.

Abbreviations

Number a sheet of paper from 1–8. Write the complete word(s) for which each underlined abbreviation stands.

1. His whole name is Joshua Samuel Winters <u>Jr</u>.
2. Have you ever been to the Twin Cities, Minneapolis and <u>St.</u> Paul?
3. <u>Gen.</u> Dwight D. Eisenhower became <u>Pres.</u> Dwight D. Eisenhower.
4. <u>Prof.</u> Manolo lives next door to us.
5. You moved to Beecher <u>Blvd.</u> in <u>Sept.</u>, didn't you?
6. That bookcase is 5 <u>in.</u> too long for the space.
7. My aunt works in the Crystal Harbor <u>Bldg</u>.
8. I received a letter from my friend in <u>HI</u>.

Parentheses

Number a sheet of paper from 1–5. Each sentence below has a section that should be set off by parentheses. Rewrite the sentences, placing parentheses where they are needed.

1. Isle Royale a national park is an island in Lake Superior.
2. It is a real wilderness, home to moose and wolves mosquitoes and black flies, too.
3. The only way to get to Isle Royale is by boat Park Forest or commercial.
4. People who go there to hike must bring in everything they need tents, food, water, first aid.
5. There are campsites shelters, tent sites, and group sites along the trails.

More Practice

Semicolons

Number a sheet of paper from 1–5. Write the sentences, using a semicolon to separate the clauses.

1. I could see the bus in the distance I could never make it.

2. I keep thinking I will go to bed earlier however, I don't.

3. Now I would have to wait for my mother to drive me on her way to work she wasn't close to being ready yet.

4. I called Sher to see if she had left yet indeed she had.

5. There was nothing to do but to be late again I was in trouble.

Transitions

Certain words and phrases can help make the meaning of your writing clearer. Below are lists of words and phrases that you can use to help readers understand more completely what you are trying to say.

Time Order

about	first	today	later
after	second	tomorrow	finally
at	to begin	until	then
before	yesterday	next	as soon as
during	meanwhile	soon	in the end

Cause and Effect

and so	as a result	because	besides
consequently	once	since	so
therefore			

Compare and Contrast

Compare:	also	as	both
	in the same way	like	likewise
	one way	similarly	
Contrast:	although	but	even though
	however	still	on the other hand
	otherwise	yet	

Words and phrases that can show location:

above	across	around	behind
below	beneath	beside	between
down	in back of	in front of	inside
near	next to	on top of	outside
over	under		

Words and phrases that can conclude or summarize:

finally	in conclusion	in the end	lastly
therefore	to conclude		

Prepositions

This is a list of common prepositions. Becoming familiar with the list will help you recognize prepositions when you see them and use prepositions effectively in your own writing.

A
aboard
about
above
across
after
against
along
amid
among
around
as
at

B
before
behind
below
beneath
beside
besides
between
beyond
but (meaning
 except)
by

C
concerning

D
despite
down
during

E
except
excepting
excluding

F
following
for
from

I
in
inside
into

L
like

M
minus

N
near

O
of
off
on
onto
opposite
outside
over

P
past
per
plus

R
regarding
round (meaning
 around)

S
save (meaning
 except for)
since

T
than
through
to
toward
towards

U
under
underneath
unlike
until
up
upon

V
versus
via

W
with
within
without

Appendix B
Rubrics

Narrative Writing Rubric

	4	3	2	1
Ideas	An engaging topic, experience, or series of events is supported by relevant details. Memorable descriptions develop the narrative. Carefully selected ideas completely satisfy the reader.	Most of the details are relevant and supportive. Descriptions are adequate. The ideas selected by the author frequently meet the needs of the reader.	The narrative is not supported by enough relevant details. Descriptions are inadequate. The ideas selected by the author sometimes meet the needs of the reader.	The topic is not clear. Details are unrelated to the topic.
Organization	The narrative has an engaging beginning and an ending that leaves the reader thinking or feeling. Events are logically and creatively sequenced. A variety of effective transition words, phrases, and clauses signifies shifts in the setting and plot.	The beginning and the conclusion are functional, but one may be stronger than the other. The sequence of events is logical, but may have a flaw or two. More or better transitions may be needed to guide the reader.	The beginning does not get the reader's attention, or the ending does not satisfy. Some events are out of order. Transitions are needed.	The writing is not organized into a beginning, middle, and ending.
Voice	The voice, mood, and tone are perfect for the purpose and audience. Dialogue, if used, is realistic and fits all the characters.	The voice, mood, and tone are appropriate in places, but inconsistent. Dialogue, if used, usually fits the characters.	The voice sounds disinterested. Mood and tone are weak. Dialogue, if used, is unrealistic or does not fit the characters.	Voice, mood, and tone are not established.
Word Choice	Clear and precise nouns and verbs consistently capture the imagery and action of the story. Descriptive language clearly conveys the experiences and events. Modifiers are strong.	Some nouns and verbs are strong, but others are weak. Descriptive language conveys most of the imagery, experiences, and events. Modifiers are satisfactory.	Many nouns and verbs do not capture the imagery or action of the story. The descriptive language is overly dependent on modifiers, and many of these are weak.	Words are overused, very weak, or incorrect. Descriptive language is not used.
Sentence Fluency	A variety of sentence structures and sentence beginnings makes the narrative flow smoothly. To read this paper aloud with inflection and feeling is effortless.	A few sentences share the same structures, lengths, or beginnings. The writing flows reasonably well. It is possible to read this writing aloud with inflection and feeling.	Many sentences have the same structures, lengths, or beginnings. The flow is robotic or rambling. It is difficult to read this writing aloud with inflection and feeling.	Sentences are incorrectly written or incomplete. The writing is difficult to follow.
Conventions	The narrative has been carefully edited. Grammar, usage, and mechanics are correct.	The narrative contains some minor errors that may distract the reader, but meaning remains clear.	The narrative contains many errors. Line-by-line editing in specific places is needed.	The writing has not been edited. Serious errors affect or alter the meaning.

Informative/Explanatory Writing Rubric

	4	3	2	1
Ideas	The topic is introduced clearly. It is developed and supported with relevant facts and concrete details. If included, quotations are relevant, accurate, and insightful. Carefully selected ideas completely answer the reader's main questions.	The topic is introduced adequately. Some facts, details, and quotations (if included) support the topic adequately. The reader's main questions are frequently answered.	The topic is introduced. Facts, details, and quotations (if included) do not develop and support the topic effectively. A few of the reader's questions are answered.	The topic is not clear. The topic is not supported by facts and details. The author did not think about what questions the reader might have.
Organization	The ideas, concepts, and information are organized into a strong introduction, body, and conclusion. Varied, appropriate, and unique transitions connect and clarify relationships among ideas.	The ideas, concepts, and information are organized into an introduction, body, and conclusion. More or better transitions may be needed.	An introduction, body, and conclusion are present. Some transitions may be inappropriate or incorrect.	The text is not organized into an introduction, body, and conclusion. It is hard or impossible to follow the ideas.
Voice	The writer's voice is appropriate for the purpose and audience. The tone is informative, respectful, and consistent.	The writer's voice is mostly appropriate for the purpose and audience. The tone is mostly informative and respectful, but may be too informal in some places.	The writer's voice is not very appropriate for the purpose or audience. The tone is inconsistent.	The writer's voice is very weak or absent. The tone is not established.
Word Choice	The language is exact and concise. Domain-specific vocabulary is used correctly and explained, as needed. Nouns and verbs are clear and precise, supported by a few carefully selected modifiers.	Some of the language is exact, but some is too general or vague. Some domain-specific vocabulary is used but not explained. Some nouns and verbs are weak, requiring too much help from modifiers. Modifiers are satisfactory.	Some language is confusing. Domain-specific vocabulary may be used incorrectly. Nouns and verbs lack clarity and precision. Too many or too few modifiers are used, and many of these are weak.	Many words are repeated or used incorrectly. Domain-specific vocabulary is not used.
Sentence Fluency	The sentences vary greatly in length and structure, adding style and interest. Almost all sentences begin differently. The text flows smoothly and is effortlessly read aloud with inflection.	Sentence length and structure vary somewhat, with some sentences adding style or interest. Some sentence beginnings are repeated. Parts of the text flow smoothly. The paper can be read aloud with inflection.	In many places, the writing does not flow smoothly because sentences are the same length or begin the same way. The paper is difficult to read aloud with inflection.	Sentences are incomplete or incorrect. The text does not flow smoothly.
Conventions	The text has been carefully edited. Grammar, usage, and mechanics are correct.	The text contains some minor errors that may distract the reader, but meaning remains clear.	Many errors are repeated. Line-by-line editing in specific places is needed. The errors interfere with meaning in some places.	The text has not been edited. Serious errors affect or alter the meaning.

	4	3	2	1
Ideas	The writer's claim is stated clearly. Counterclaims are anticipated and addressed very well. Accurate reasons and evidence from credible sources support the claim.	The writer's claim is stated adequately. The author may fail to anticipate or address one or more common counterclaims. One or two reasons or pieces of evidence may not be from credible sources.	A claim is stated. Counterclaims are not anticipated or are not addressed well. There is little accurate support for the writer's claim.	The writer does not state a claim. Reasons and evidence are not provided.
Organization	The argument is organized logically, including a strong introduction. A compelling conclusion restates the thesis and includes a call to action. Clear and unique transitions clarify the relationships between the claim, reasons, supporting evidence, and counterclaims.	The argument is organized logically, including an introduction. The conclusion may not restate the thesis or may not include a call to action. More or better transitions may be needed to clarify the relationships between the claim, reasons, supporting evidence, and counterclaims.	The argument is not organized logically. The introduction or conclusion is missing (or problematic). Transitions are not appropriate or effective. Counterclaims are not addressed.	The writing is not organized as an argument. The introduction and conclusion are missing. Transitions are not used. Counterclaims are not addressed.
Voice	The voice strongly supports the writer's purpose and consistently connects with the audience. A respectful, confident tone is maintained.	The voice mostly supports the writer's purpose. The tone is mostly respectful and confident, but may be too informal in some places.	The voice is fairly weak or passive throughout the piece and fails to connect with the audience. The tone is inconsistent.	The voice is flat or absent.
Word Choice	Compelling language conveys the writer's ideas and engages the reader. Nouns and verbs are clear and precise, supported by a few carefully selected modifiers.	Some of the language is compelling, but some is vague or ineffective. Some nouns and verbs are strong, but others are weak, requiring too much help from modifiers. Modifiers are satisfactory.	Much of the language is vague or ineffective. Nouns and verbs lack clarity or precision. Too many or too few modifiers are used, and many of these are weak.	The language is not compelling. Words are weak, negative, or used incorrectly.
Sentence Fluency	The sentences vary greatly in length and structure, adding style and interest. Almost all sentences begin differently. The text flows smoothly and is effortlessly read aloud with inflection.	Sentence length and structure vary somewhat, with some sentences adding style or interest. Some sentence beginnings are repeated. Parts of the text flow smoothly. The paper can be read aloud with inflection.	In many places, the writing does not flow smoothly because sentences are the same length or begin the same way. The paper is difficult to read aloud with inflection.	Sentences are incomplete or incorrect. Sentence beginnings are repeated over and over again. The text does not flow smoothly.
Conventions	The writing has been carefully edited. Grammar, usage, and mechanics are correct.	The writing contains some minor errors that may distract the reader, but meaning remains clear.	Many errors are repeated. Line-by-line editing in specific places is needed. The errors interfere with meaning in some places.	The writing has not been edited. Serious errors affect or alter the meaning.

Descriptive Writing Rubric

	4	3	2	1
Ideas	The topic is focused and exactly the right size. Sensory details clearly develop, describe, and reveal the subject. Carefully chosen ideas help the reader to completely experience what is being described.	The topic may need to be more carefully focused. Some sensory details reveal the subject. The author's ideas sometimes help the reader experience what is being described.	The topic is not well focused. Too few sensory details reveal the subject. The ideas fail to consistently help the reader experience what is being described.	The topic is unfocused or unclear. Details are random or missing. The ideas do not support the reader's experience of the topic.
Organization	The description is organized logically and creatively, including an engaging introduction and a thoughtfully crafted conclusion. Varied and appropriate transitions clarify relationships between ideas.	The description is organized logically, including a functional introduction and conclusion. More or better transitions may be needed to clarify relationships between ideas.	The description is not well organized. The introduction or the conclusion is weak or missing. Transitions are weak or confusing. Some of the ideas are hard to follow.	The writing is not organized. The introduction and the conclusion are missing. Transitions are not used.
Voice	An authentic, clear voice conveys the writer's purpose and connects with the reader. The mood is perfect, and the tone conveys respect for the subject and the audience.	The voice connects with the reader in some places. The tone is appropriate but inconsistent. An appropriate mood is somewhat established.	The voice may convey purpose but does not connect with the reader. The mood and tone may not be appropriate.	The voice is weak or absent. Mood and tone are not established.
Word Choice	Precise, descriptive words (including nouns, verbs, and modifiers) bring the subject to life. Figurative language and comparisons create a clear, coherent picture.	Some words are precise and descriptive, but others are not. Some nouns and verbs may rely too heavily on modifiers for clarity. Figurative language and/or comparisons sometimes create a clear picture.	Nouns and verbs lack precision and clarity. Too many or too few modifiers are used, and many of these are weak. Figurative language and/or comparisons do not create a clear picture.	Words are basic and very limited. Figurative language and comparisons are not used.
Sentence Fluency	A variety of sentences and/or lines adds interest and energy to the description. The writing flows very smoothly. Reading this aloud with inflection and feeling is effortless.	Some sentences and/or lines are varied and interesting. The writing flows smoothly some of the time. It can be read aloud with inflection and feeling.	Many sentences and/or lines are not varied or interesting. Most of the writing does not flow smoothly. It is difficult to read aloud with inflection or feeling.	Sentences and/or lines are incomplete or incorrect. The writing does not flow.
Conventions	The description has been carefully edited. Grammar, usage, and mechanics are correct.	The description contains some minor errors that may distract the reader, but meaning remains clear.	Many errors are repeated. Line-by-line editing in specific places is needed. Errors interfere with meaning in places.	The writing has not been edited. Serious errors affect or alter the meaning.

	5	4	3	2	1
Ideas	An engaging topic, experience, or series of events is supported by relevant details. Memorable descriptions develop the narrative. Carefully selected ideas completely satisfy the reader.	Most of the details are relevant and supportive. Most descriptions are memorable. Carefully selected ideas satisfy most of the reader's needs.	Some of the details may be unrelated or marginally supportive, but descriptions are adequate. The ideas selected by the author frequently meet the needs of the reader.	The narrative is not supported by enough relevant details. Descriptions are inadequate. The ideas selected by the author sometimes meet the needs of the reader.	The topic is not clear. Details are unrelated to the topic.
Organization	The narrative has an engaging beginning and an ending that leaves the reader thinking or feeling. Events are logically and creatively sequenced. A variety of effective transition words, phrases, and clauses signifies shifts in the setting and plot.	The narrative has an interesting beginning and satisfying ending. Events are logically sequenced. Most transitions are effective, especially as they signify shifts in the setting and plot.	The beginning and the conclusion are functional, but one may be stronger than the other. The sequence of events is logical, but may have a flaw or two. More or better transitions may be needed to guide the reader.	The beginning does not get the reader's attention, or the ending does not satisfy. Some events are out of order. Transitions are needed.	The writing is not organized into a beginning, middle, and ending.
Voice	The voice, mood, and tone are perfect for the purpose and audience. Dialogue, if used, is realistic and fits all the characters.	The voice, mood, and tone are appropriate. Dialogue, if used, is realistic and usually fits the characters well.	The voice, mood, and tone are appropriate in places, but inconsistent. Dialogue, if used, sometimes fits the characters.	The voice, mood, and tone do not fit the characters.	Voice, mood, and tone are not established.
Word Choice	Clear and precise nouns and verbs consistently capture the imagery and action of the story. Descriptive language clearly conveys the experiences and events. Modifiers are strong.	Most of the nouns and verbs are clear, capturing the imagery and action of the story. Descriptive language conveys the experiences and events well. The majority of the modifiers are strong.	Some nouns and verbs are strong, but others are weak. Descriptive language conveys most of the imagery, experiences, and events. Modifiers are satisfactory.	Many nouns and verbs do not capture the imagery or action of the story. The descriptive language is overly dependent on modifiers, and many of these are weak.	Words are overused, very weak, or incorrect. Descriptive language is not used.
Sentence Fluency	A variety of sentence structures and sentence beginnings makes the narrative flow smoothly. To read this paper aloud with inflection and feeling is effortless.	Most sentence structures and sentence beginnings are varied and flow well. Most of the sentences are well crafted. It is easy to read this writing aloud with inflection and feeling.	A few sentences share the same structures, lengths, or beginnings. The writing flows reasonably well. It is possible to read this writing aloud with inflection and feeling.	Many sentences have the same structures, lengths, or beginnings. The flow is robotic or rambling. It is difficult to read this writing aloud with inflection and feeling.	Sentences are incorrectly written or incomplete. The writing is difficult to read.
Conventions	The narrative has been carefully edited. Grammar, usage, and mechanics are correct.	The narrative contains one or two minor errors that are easily corrected.	The narrative contains some minor errors that may distract the reader, but meaning remains clear.	The narrative contains many errors. Line-by-line editing in specific places is needed.	The writing has not been edited. Serious errors affect or alter the meaning.

Informative/Explanatory Writing Rubric

	5	4	3	2	1
Ideas	The topic is introduced clearly. It is developed and supported with relevant facts and concrete details. If included, quotations are relevant, accurate, and insightful. Carefully selected ideas completely answer the reader's main questions.	The topic is introduced well. Almost all the facts and details support the topic well. If included, quotations are relevant and accurate. Almost all of the reader's main questions are answered.	The topic is introduced adequately. Some facts, details, and quotations (if included) support the topic adequately. The reader's main questions are frequently answered.	The topic is introduced. Facts, details, and quotations (if included) do not develop and support the topic effectively. A few of the reader's questions are answered.	The topic is not clear. The topic is not supported by facts and details. The author did not think about what questions the reader might have.
Organization	The ideas, concepts, and information are organized into a strong introduction, body, and conclusion. Varied, appropriate, and unique transitions connect and clarify relationships among ideas.	The ideas, concepts, and information are organized into an introduction, body, and conclusion. Most transitions are appropriate and helpful.	The ideas, concepts, and information are organized into an introduction, body, and conclusion. More or better transitions may be needed.	An introduction, body, and conclusion are present. Some transitions may be inappropriate or incorrect.	The text is not organized into an introduction, body, and conclusion. It is hard or impossible to follow the ideas.
Voice	The writer's voice is appropriate for the purpose and audience. The tone is informative, respectful, and consistent.	The writer's voice is appropriate for the purpose and audience most of the time. The tone is almost always informative and respectful.	The writer's voice is mostly appropriate for the purpose and audience. The tone is mostly informative and respectful, but may be too informal in some places.	The writer's voice is not very appropriate for the purpose or audience. The tone is inconsistent.	The writer's voice is very weak or absent. The tone is not established.
Word Choice	The language is exact and concise. Domain-specific vocabulary is used correctly and explained, as needed. Nouns and verbs are clear and precise, supported by a few carefully selected modifiers.	Most of the language is exact and concise. Domain-specific vocabulary is used correctly and usually explained, as needed. Most nouns and verbs are clear and precise. Most modifiers are carefully selected.	Some of the language is exact, but some is too general or vague. Some domain-specific vocabulary is used but not always explained. Some nouns and verbs are weak, requiring too much help from modifiers. Modifiers are satisfactory.	Some language is confusing. Domain-specific vocabulary may be used incorrectly. Nouns and verbs lack clarity and precision. Too many or too few modifiers are used, and many of these are weak.	Many words are repeated or used incorrectly. Domain-specific vocabulary is not used.
Sentence Fluency	The sentences vary greatly in length and structure, adding style and interest. Almost all sentences begin differently. The text flows smoothly and is effortlessly read aloud with inflection.	Most of the sentences vary in their beginnings, lengths, and structures. Several add style or interest. Most of the text flows smoothly and is easy to read aloud with inflection.	Sentence length and structure vary somewhat, with some sentences adding style or interest. Some sentence beginnings are repeated. Parts of the text flow smoothly. The paper can be read aloud with inflection.	In many places, the writing does not flow smoothly because sentences are the same length or begin the same way. The paper is difficult to read aloud with inflection.	Sentences are incomplete or incorrect. The text does not flow smoothly.
Conventions	The text has been carefully edited. Grammar, usage, and mechanics are correct.	The text contains one or two minor errors, but the meaning remains clear.	The text contains some minor errors that may distract the reader, but meaning remains clear.	Many errors are repeated. Line-by-line editing in specific places is needed. The errors interfere with meaning in some places.	The text has not been edited. Serious errors affect or alter the meaning.

Argument Writing Rubric

	5	4	3	2	1
Ideas	The writer's claim is stated clearly. Counterclaims are anticipated and addressed very well. Accurate reasons and evidence from credible sources support the claim.	The writer's claim is stated clearly. Counterclaims are anticipated and addressed well. Most of the reasons and evidence are accurate and from credible sources.	The writer's claim is stated adequately. The author may fail to anticipate or address one or more counterclaims. One or two reasons or pieces of evidence may not be from the writer's claim.	A claim is stated. Counterclaims are not anticipated or are not addressed well. There is little accurate support for the writer's claim.	The writer does not state a claim. Reasons and evidence are not provided.
Organization	The argument is organized logically, including a strong introduction. A compelling conclusion restates the thesis and includes a call to action. Clear and unique transitions clarify the relationships between the claim, reasons, supporting evidence, and counterclaims.	The argument is organized logically, including a good introduction. The conclusion restates the thesis and may include a call to action. Most transitions clarify the relationships between the claim, reasons, supporting evidence, and counterclaims.	The argument is organized logically, including an introduction. The conclusion may not restate the thesis or include a call to action. More or better transitions may be needed to clarify the relationships between the claim, reasons, supporting evidence, and counterclaims.	The argument is not organized logically. The introduction or conclusion is missing (or problematic). Transitions are not appropriate or missing. Counterclaims are not addressed effectively.	The writing is not organized as an argument. The introduction and conclusion are missing. Transitions are not used. Counterclaims are not addressed.
Voice	The voice strongly supports the writer's purpose and consistently connects with the audience. A respectful, confident tone is maintained.	The voice supports the writer's purpose and almost always connects with the audience. A respectful, confident tone is maintained.	The voice mostly supports the writer's purpose. The tone is mostly respectful and confident, but may be too informal in some places.	The voice is fairly weak or passive throughout the piece and fails to connect with the audience. The tone is inconsistent.	The voice is flat or absent.
Word Choice	Compelling language conveys the writer's ideas and engages the reader. Nouns and verbs are clear and precise, supported by a few carefully selected modifiers.	Most of the language is compelling. Nouns and verbs are mostly clear and precise. Most modifiers are carefully selected.	Some of the language is compelling, but some is vague or ineffective. Some nouns and verbs are strong, but others are weak, requiring too many or too few modifiers. Modifiers are satisfactory.	Much of the language is vague or ineffective. Nouns and verbs lack clarity or precision. Too many or too few modifiers are used, and many of these are weak.	The language is not compelling. Words are weak, negative, or used incorrectly.
Sentence Fluency	The sentences vary greatly in length and structure, adding style and interest. Almost all sentences begin differently. The text flows smoothly and is effortlessly read aloud with inflection.	Most of the sentences vary in their beginnings, lengths, and structures. Several add style or interest. Most of the text flows smoothly and is easy to read aloud with inflection.	Sentence length and structure vary somewhat, with some sentences adding style or interest. Some sentence beginnings are repeated. Parts of the text flow smoothly. The paper can be read aloud with inflection.	In many places, the writing does not flow smoothly because sentences are the same length or begin the same way. The paper is difficult to read aloud with inflection.	Sentences are incomplete or incorrect. Sentence beginnings are repeated over and over again. The text does not flow smoothly.
Conventions	The writing has been carefully edited. Grammar, usage, and mechanics are correct.	The writing contains one or two minor errors, but the meaning remains clear.	The writing contains some minor errors that may distract the reader, but meaning remains clear.	Many errors are repeated. Line-by-line editing in specific places is needed. The errors interfere with meaning in some places.	The writing has not been edited. Serious errors affect or alter the meaning.

Descriptive Writing Rubric

	5	4	3	2	1
Ideas	The topic is focused and exactly the right size. Sensory details clearly develop, describe, and reveal the subject. Carefully chosen ideas help the reader to completely experience what is being described.	The topic is focused and the right size. Many sensory details develop, describe, and reveal the subject. The ideas selected usually enable the reader to experience what is being described.	The topic may need to be more carefully focused. Some sensory details reveal the subject. The author's ideas sometimes help the reader experience what is being described.	The topic is not well focused. Too few sensory details reveal the subject. The ideas fail to consistently help the reader experience what is being described.	The topic is unfocused or unclear. Details are random or missing. The ideas do not support the reader's experience of the topic.
Organization	The description is organized logically and creatively, including an engaging introduction and a thoughtfully crafted conclusion. Varied and appropriate transitions clarify relationships between ideas.	The description is organized logically, including a strong introduction and a strong conclusion. Most of the transitions clarify relationships between ideas.	The description is organized logically, including a functional introduction and conclusion. More or better transitions may be needed to clarify relationships between ideas.	The description is not well organized. The introduction or the conclusion is weak or missing. Transitions are weak or confusing. Some of the ideas are hard to follow.	The writing is not organized. The introduction and the conclusion are missing. Transitions are not used.
Voice	An authentic, clear voice conveys the writer's purpose and connects with the reader. The mood is perfect, and the tone conveys respect for the subject and the audience.	The voice is clear and connects with the reader most of the time. The mood is appropriate, and the tone conveys respect for the subject and audience most of the time.	The voice connects with the reader in some places. The tone is appropriate but inconsistent. An appropriate mood is somewhat established.	The voice may convey purpose but does not connect with the reader. The mood and tone may not be appropriate.	The voice is weak or absent. Mood and tone are not established.
Word Choice	Precise, descriptive words (including nouns, verbs, and modifiers) bring the subject to life. Figurative language and comparisons create a clear, coherent picture.	Most words (including nouns, verbs, and modifiers) are precise and descriptive. Figurative language and comparisons create a clear, coherent picture most of the time.	Some words are precise and descriptive, but others are not. Some nouns and verbs may rely too heavily on modifiers for clarity. Figurative language and/or comparisons sometimes create a clear picture.	Nouns and verbs lack precision and clarity. Too many or too few modifiers are used, and many of these are weak. Figurative language and/or comparisons do not create a clear picture.	Words are basic and very limited. Figurative language and comparisons are not used.
Sentence Fluency	A variety of sentences and/or lines adds interest and energy to the description. The writing flows very smoothly. Reading this aloud with inflection and feeling is effortless.	Most sentences and/or lines are varied and interesting. The writing flows smoothly most of the time. It is easy to read aloud with inflection and feeling.	Some sentences and/or lines are varied and interesting. The writing flows smoothly some of the time. It can be read aloud with inflection and feeling.	Many sentences and/or lines are not varied or interesting. Most of the writing does not flow smoothly. It is difficult to read aloud with inflection or feeling.	Sentences and/or lines are incomplete or incorrect. The writing does not flow.
Conventions	The description has been carefully edited. Grammar, usage, and mechanics are correct.	The description contains one or two minor errors that are easily corrected. Meaning is clear.	The description contains some minor errors that may distract the reader, but meaning remains clear.	Many errors are repeated. Line-by-line editing in specific places is needed. Errors interfere with meaning in places.	The writing has not been edited. Serious errors affect or alter the meaning.

Narrative Writing Rubric

	6	5	4	3	2	1
Ideas	An engaging topic, experience, or series of events is supported by relevant details. Memorable descriptions develop the narrative. Carefully selected ideas completely satisfy the reader.	Most of the details are relevant and supportive. Most descriptions are memorable. Carefully selected ideas satisfy most of the reader's needs.	Some of the details may be unrelated or marginally supportive, but descriptions are adequate. The ideas selected by the author frequently meet the needs of the reader.	The narrative is not supported by enough relevant details. Descriptions are inadequate. The ideas selected by the author sometimes meet the needs of the reader.	The topic may not be clear. Many details are unrelated. The author did not consider the needs of the reader.	The topic is not clear. Details are unrelated to the topic.
Organization	The narrative has an engaging beginning and an ending that leaves the reader thinking or feeling. Events are logically and creatively sequenced. A variety of effective transition words, phrases, and clauses signifies shifts in the setting and plot.	The narrative has an interesting beginning and satisfying ending. Events are logically sequenced. Most transitions are effective, especially as they signify shifts in the setting and plot.	The beginning and the conclusion are functional, but one may be stronger than the other. The sequence of events is logical, but may have a flaw or two. More or better transitions may be needed to guide the reader.	The beginning does not get the reader's attention, or the ending does not satisfy. Some events are out of order. Transitions are needed.	The beginning and ending are weak. The sequence of events is seriously flawed. Transitions are not used.	The writing is not organized into a beginning, middle, and ending.
Voice	The voice, mood, and tone are perfect for the purpose and audience. Dialogue, if used, is realistic and fits all the characters.	The voice, mood, and tone are appropriate. Dialogue, if used, is realistic and usually fits the characters well.	The voice, mood, and tone are appropriate in places, but inconsistent. Dialogue, if used, sometimes fits the characters.	The voice sounds disinterested. Mood and tone are weak. Dialogue, if used, is unrealistic or does not fit the characters.	The voice, mood, and tone are inappropriate for the audience. Dialogue, if used, is unrealistic.	Voice, mood, and tone are not established.
Word Choice	Clear and precise nouns and verbs consistently capture the imagery and action of the story. Descriptive language clearly conveys the experiences and events. Modifiers are strong.	Most of the nouns and verbs are clear, capturing the imagery and action of the story. Descriptive language conveys the experiences and events well. The majority of the modifiers are strong.	Some nouns and verbs are strong, but others are weak. Descriptive language conveys most of the imagery, experiences, and events. Modifiers are satisfactory.	Many nouns and verbs do not capture the imagery or action of the story. Descriptive language is overly dependent on modifiers, and many of these are weak.	Words are not powerful or precise. Descriptive language is not used.	Words are overused, very weak, or incorrect.
Sentence Fluency	A variety of sentence structures and sentence beginnings makes the narrative flow smoothly. To read this paper aloud with inflection and feeling is effortless.	Most sentence structures and sentence beginnings are varied and flow well. Most of the sentences are well crafted. It is easy to read this writing aloud with inflection and feeling.	A few sentences share the same structures, lengths, or beginnings. The writing flows reasonably well. It is possible to read this writing aloud with inflection and feeling.	Many sentences have the same structures, lengths, or beginnings. The flow is robotic or rambling. It is difficult to read this writing aloud with inflection and feeling.	Sentences have little variation. The narrative does not flow well.	Sentences are incorrectly written or incomplete. The writing is difficult to follow.
Conventions	The narrative has been carefully edited. Grammar, usage, and mechanics are correct.	The narrative contains one or two minor errors that are easily corrected.	The narrative contains some minor errors that may distract the reader, but meaning remains clear.	The narrative contains many errors. Line-by-line editing in specific places is needed.	Serious errors affect or alter the meaning.	The writing has not been edited.

Informative/Explanatory Writing Rubric

	6	5	4	3	2	1
Ideas	The topic is introduced clearly. It is developed and supported with relevant facts and concrete details. If included, quotations are relevant, accurate, and insightful. Carefully selected ideas completely answer the reader's main questions.	The topic is introduced well. Almost all the facts and details support the topic well. If included, quotations are relevant and accurate. Almost all of the reader's main questions are answered.	The topic is introduced adequately. Some facts, details, and quotations (if included) support the topic adequately. The reader's main questions are frequently answered.	The topic is introduced. Facts, details, and quotations (if included) do not develop and support the topic effectively. A few of the reader's questions are answered.	The topic is not introduced, or more than one topic is introduced. Details are not relevant. Facts are not included. The author did not think about what questions the reader might have.	The topic is not clear. The topic is not supported by facts and details.
Organization	The ideas, concepts, and information are organized into a strong introduction, body, and conclusion. Varied and unique transitions connect and clarify relationships among ideas.	The ideas, concepts, and information are organized into an introduction, body, and conclusion. Most transitions are appropriate and helpful.	The ideas, concepts, and information are organized into an introduction, body, and conclusion. More or better transitions may be needed.	An introduction, body, and conclusion are present. Some transitions may be inappropriate or incorrect.	The text is not well organized. The introduction and conclusion are weak or missing. Transitions are not used.	The text is not organized into an introduction, body, and conclusion. It is difficult to follow the ideas.
Voice	The writer's voice is appropriate for the purpose and audience. The tone is informative, respectful, and consistent.	The writer's voice is appropriate for the purpose and audience most of the time. The tone is almost always informative and respectful.	The writer's voice is mostly appropriate for the purpose and audience. The tone is mostly informative and respectful, but may be too informal in some places.	The writer's voice is not very appropriate for the purpose or audience. The tone is inconsistent.	The writer's voice is not appropriate. The tone is too informal.	The writer's voice is very weak or absent. The tone is not established.
Word Choice	The language is exact and concise. Domain-specific vocabulary is used correctly and explained, as needed. Nouns and verbs are clear and precise, supported by a few carefully selected modifiers.	Most of the language is exact and concise. Domain-specific vocabulary is used correctly and usually explained, as needed. Most nouns and verbs are clear and precise. Most modifiers are carefully selected.	Some of the language is exact, but some is too general or vague. Some domain-specific vocabulary is used but not explained. Some nouns and verbs are weak, requiring too much help from modifiers. Modifiers are satisfactory.	Some language is confusing. Domain-specific vocabulary may be used incorrectly. Nouns and verbs lack clarity and precision. Too many or too few modifiers are used, and many of these are weak.	The language is very basic and limited. Domain-specific vocabulary is used incorrectly. Nouns and verbs are vague, unclear, or confusing. Modifiers may be missing.	Many words are repeated or used incorrectly. Domain-specific vocabulary is not used.
Sentence Fluency	The sentences vary greatly in length and structure, adding style and interest. The text flows smoothly and is effortlessly read aloud with inflection.	Most of the sentences vary in their beginnings, lengths, and structures. Several add style or interest. Most of the text flows smoothly and is easy to read aloud with inflection.	Sentence length and structure vary somewhat, with some sentences adding style or interest. Some sentence beginnings are repeated. Parts of the text flow smoothly. The paper can be read aloud with inflection.	In many places, the writing does not flow smoothly because sentences are the same length or begin the same way. The paper is difficult to read aloud with inflection.	Most sentences are the same length and structure. Sentence beginnings are repeated over and over again. The flow is too robotic or rambling.	Sentences are incomplete or incorrect. The text does not flow smoothly.
Conventions	The text has been carefully edited. Grammar, usage, and mechanics are correct.	The text contains one or two minor errors, but the meaning remains clear.	The text contains some minor errors that may distract the reader, but meaning remains clear.	Many errors are repeated. Line-by-line editing in specific places is needed. The errors interfere with meaning in some places.	Serious errors affect or alter the meaning.	The text has not been edited.

Argument Writing Rubric

	6	5	4	3	2	1
Ideas	The writer's claim is stated clearly. Counterclaims are anticipated and addressed very well. Accurate reasons and evidence from credible sources support the claim.	The writer's claim is stated clearly. Counterclaims are anticipated and addressed well. Most of the claims and evidence are accurate and from credible sources.	The writer's claim is stated adequately. The author may fail to anticipate or address one or more common counterclaims. One or two reasons or little accurate support for the writer's claim.	A claim is stated. Counterclaims are not stated clearly. Counterclaims are not addressed well. Reasons and evidence are unrelated or inaccurate.	The writer's claim is not stated clearly. Counterclaims are not stated clearly. Reasons and evidence are not provided.	The writer does not state a claim. Reasons and evidence are not provided.
Organization	The argument is organized logically, including a strong introduction. A compelling conclusion restates the thesis and includes a call to action. Clear and unique transitions clarify the relationships between the claim, reasons, supporting evidence, and counterclaims.	The argument is organized logically, including a good introduction. The conclusion restates the thesis and may include a call to action. Most transitions clarify the relationships between the claim, reasons, supporting evidence, and counterclaims.	The argument is organized logically, including an introduction. The conclusion may not restate the thesis or may not include a call to action. More or better transitions may be needed to clarify the relationships between the claim, reasons, supporting evidence, and counterclaims.	The argument is not organized logically. The introduction or conclusion is missing (or problematic). Transitions are missing. Counterclaims are not used.	The argument is not organized logically. The introduction and conclusion are missing. Transitions are not used. Counterclaims are not addressed.	The writing is not organized as an argument.
Voice	The voice strongly supports the writer's purpose and consistently connects with the audience. A respectful, confident tone is maintained.	The voice supports the writer's purpose and almost always connects with the audience. A respectful, confident tone is maintained.	The voice mostly supports the writer's purpose. The tone is mostly respectful and confident, but may be too informal in some places.	The voice is fairly weak or passive throughout the piece and fails to connect with the audience. The tone is inconsistent.	The voice is weak or inappropriate for the purpose and audience. A respectful, confident tone is not established.	The voice is flat or absent.
Word Choice	Compelling language conveys the writer's ideas and engages the reader. Nouns and verbs are clear and precise, supported by a few carefully selected modifiers.	Most of the language is compelling. Nouns and verbs are mostly clear and precise. Most modifiers are carefully selected.	Some of the language is compelling, but some is vague or ineffective. Some nouns and verbs are strong, but others are weak, requiring too much help from modifiers. Modifiers are satisfactory.	Much of the language is vague or ineffective. Nouns and verbs lack clarity or precision. Too many or too few modifiers are used, and many of these are weak.	The language is not compelling. Many words are very basic. Nouns and verbs are vague, unclear, or confusing. Modifiers may be missing.	Words are weak, negative, or used incorrectly.
Sentence Fluency	The sentences vary greatly in length and structure, adding style and interest. Almost all sentences begin differently. The text flows smoothly and is effortlessly read aloud with inflection.	The sentences vary in their beginnings, lengths, and structures. Several add style or interest. Most of the text flows smoothly and is easy to read aloud with inflection.	Sentence length and structure vary somewhat, with some sentences adding style or interest. Some sentence beginnings are repeated. Parts of the text flow smoothly. The paper can be read aloud with inflection.	In many places, the writing does not flow smoothly because sentences are the same length or begin the same way. The paper is difficult to read aloud with inflection.	Most sentences are the same length and structure. Sentence beginnings are repeated over and over again. The flow is too robotic or rambling.	Sentences are incomplete or incorrect. The text does not flow smoothly.
Conventions	The writing has been carefully edited. Grammar, usage, and mechanics are correct.	The writing contains one or two minor errors, but the meaning remains clear.	The writing contains some minor errors that may distract the reader, but meaning remains clear.	Many errors are repeated. Line-by-line editing in specific places is needed. The errors interfere with meaning in some places.	Serious errors affect or alter the meaning.	The writing has not been edited.

Descriptive Writing Rubric

	6	5	4	3	2	1
Ideas	The topic is focused and exactly the right size. Sensory details clearly develop, describe, and reveal the subject. Carefully chosen ideas help the reader to completely experience what is being described.	The topic is focused and the right size. Many sensory details develop, describe, and reveal the subject. The ideas selected usually enable the reader to experience what is being described.	The topic may need to be more carefully focused. Some sensory details reveal the subject. The author's ideas sometimes help the reader experience what is being described.	The topic is not well focused. Too few sensory details reveal the subject. The ideas fail to consistently help the reader experience what is being described.	The topic is not focused. Details are scarce, or may relate to more than one subject. The ideas do not support the reader's experience of the topic.	The topic is unfocused or unclear. Details are random or missing.
Organization	The description is organized logically and creatively, including an engaging introduction and a thoughtfully crafted conclusion. Varied and appropriate transitions clarify relationships between ideas.	The description is organized logically, including a strong introduction and a strong conclusion. Most of the transitions clarify relationships between ideas.	The description is organized logically, including a functional introduction and conclusion. More or better transitions may be needed to clarify relationships between ideas.	The description is not well organized. The introduction or the conclusion is weak or confusing. Transitions are weak or confusing. Some of the ideas are hard to follow.	The description is not organized. The introduction and the conclusion are missing. Transitions are incorrect or missing. The ideas are hard to follow.	The writing is not organized. Transitions are not used.
Voice	An authentic, clear voice conveys the writer's purpose and connects with the reader. The mood is perfect, and the tone conveys respect for the subject and the audience.	The voice is clear and connects with the reader most of the time. The mood is appropriate, and the tone conveys respect for the subject and audience most of the time.	The voice connects with the reader in some places. The tone is appropriate but inconsistent. An appropriate mood is somewhat established.	The voice may convey purpose but does not connect with the reader. The mood and tone may not be appropriate.	The voice does not convey purpose or connect with the reader. The mood and tone are inappropriate.	The voice is weak or absent. Mood and tone are not established.
Word Choice	Precise, descriptive words (including nouns, verbs, and modifiers) bring the subject to life. Figurative language and comparisons create a clear, coherent picture.	Most words (including nouns, verbs, and modifiers) are precise and descriptive. Figurative language and comparisons create a clear, coherent picture most of the time.	Some words are precise and descriptive, but others are not. Some nouns and verbs may rely too heavily on modifiers for clarity. Figurative language and/or comparisons sometimes create a clear picture.	Nouns and verbs lack precision and clarity. Too many or too few modifiers are used, and many of these are weak. Figurative language and/or comparisons do not create a clear picture.	Words are vague or confusing. Figurative language or comparisons are incomplete or missing.	Words are basic and very limited. Figurative language and comparisons are not used.
Sentence Fluency	A variety of sentences and/or lines adds interest and energy to the description. The writing flows very smoothly. Reading this aloud with inflection and feeling is effortless.	Most sentences and/or lines are varied and interesting. The writing flows smoothly most of the time. It is easy to read aloud with inflection and feeling.	Some sentences and/or lines are varied and interesting. The writing flows smoothly some of the time. It can be read aloud with inflection and feeling.	Many sentences and/or lines are not varied or interesting. Most of the writing does not flow smoothly. It is difficult to read aloud with inflection or feeling.	Sentences and/or lines are very basic, limited, or repetitive. The writing is predictable and dull.	Sentences and/or lines are incomplete or incorrect. The writing does not flow.
Conventions	The description has been carefully edited. Grammar, usage, and mechanics are correct.	The description contains one or two minor errors that are easily corrected. Meaning is clear.	The description contains some minor errors that may distract the reader, but meaning remains clear.	Many errors are repeated. Line-by-line editing in specific places is needed. Errors interfere with meaning in places.	Serious errors affect or alter the meaning.	The writing has not been edited.

Index